D0462175

.chool
2510 Elliott Ave.
Seattle, WA 98121
theseattleschool.edu

WITHDRAWN

The Christian Faith

DATE DUE

The Seattle School

10029435

FORTRESS TEXTS IN
MODERN THEOLOGY

BOARD OF CONSULTANTS

B. A. Gerrish, Chair
University of Chicago Divinity School

John Clayton
University of Lancaster, England

Marilyn C. Massey
Marymount Manhattan College

James O. Duke
Pacific School of Religion

Robert P. Scharlemann
University of Virginia

IN THE SERIES

FORTRESS TEXTS IN MODERN THEOLOGY

The Christian Faith

Ernst Troeltsch

**Based on lectures delivered
at the University of Heidelberg in 1912 and 1913**

**With a foreword by Marta Troeltsch
Edited by Gertrud von le Fort
Translated by Garrett E. Paul**

Fortress Press   **Minneapolis**

THE CHRISTIAN FAITH

Copyright © 1991 Augsburg Fortress.

First English-language edition published in 1991 by Fortress Press, Minneapolis. Original German edition published in 1925 under the title *Glaubenslehre,* edited by Gertrud von le Fort, by Duncker and Humblot, Berlin. Reprinted by Scienta Verlag, Aalen, 1986.

All rights reserved. Except for brief quotations in critical articles or reviews, no part of this book may be reproduced in any manner without prior written permission from the publisher. Write to: Permissions, Augsburg Fortress, 426 S. Fifth St., Box 1209, Minneapolis, MN 55440.

Cover Design: Jim Churchville

Library of Congress Cataloging-in-Publication Data

Troeltsch, Ernst, 1865–1923.
    [Glaubenslehre. English]
    The Christian faith = Glaubenslehre : based on lectures delivered
at the University of Heidelberg in 1912 and 1913 / by Ernst
Troeltsch ; with a foreword by Marta Troeltsch ; edited by Gertrud
von le Fort ; translated by Garrett E. Paul.
        p. cm.—(Fortress texts in modern theology)
    Translation of: Glaubenslehre.
    Includes bibliographical references and index.
    ISBN 0-8006-3209-5
    1. Theology, Doctrinal.   I. Le Fort, Gertrud, Freiin von,
1876–1971.   II. Title.   III. Title: Glaubenslehre.   IV. Series.
BT75.T76413   1991
230'.044—dc20   90–19370
                                                                         CIP

The paper used in this publication meets the minimum requirements of American National Standard for Information Sciences—Permanence of Paper for Printed Library Materials, ANSI Z329.48–1984.   ∞™

Manufactured in the U.S.A.   AF 1–3209
95   94   93   92   91   1   2   3   4   5   6   7   8   9   10

Contents

Preface to the Translation

Translation is an art whose difficulty can be appreciated only by those who have tried it. I have striven for a rendering that is accurate and readable without departing from the style of the original more than necessary. The lectures have been translated in a more conversational style than the dictation. But whenever the goals of accuracy and readability have conflicted, accuracy has won out. As with any translation, the original should be consulted whenever possible, particularly for important or difficult passages.

Some specific observations are in order. Gertrud von le Fort's edition of Troeltsch's lectures separated the dictation, which was printed in italics, from the lectures. I have followed her practice, except for the use of italics. She added a very small number of annotations, which in this edition are clearly identified as hers. All other annotations are my own.

Troeltsch called his theology *Glaubenslehre*, a word for which there is no English equivalent. It combines the words *Glauben*, which can mean "faith" or "belief," and *Lehre*, which can mean "teaching," "instruction," or "doctrine." The lack of an English equivalent is unfortunate, for Troeltsch identified *Glaubenslehre* as a unique theological method, very different from what is ordinarily called "dogmatics" or "theology." Hence I usually left the word untranslated, only rarely rendering it as "theology" and never as "dogmatics." This also posed some problems for the English title of the book. "The Christian Faith" was chosen as the title because Friedrich Schleier-

ix

macher, whom Troeltsch explicitly identified as his model, published his own *Glaubenslehre* under the title "The Christian Faith."

Troeltsch made several biblical allusions that he did not identify. If I recognized a reference that was identical or nearly identical to a passage in Luther's Bible, I simply identified it (Ps. 18:3); but if it was an inexact quotation or a paraphrase, my citation is preceded by "see" (See Ps. 18:3).

Decisions concerning capitalization were sometimes difficult, since German and English practices differ. I have capitalized or left uncapitalized some words, like "spirit," "church," and "word," according to the context. "Spirit," for example, is used when Troeltsch is referring to the Holy Spirit or the divine Spirit, while "spirit" is used in other contexts. The reader should remember, however, that nouns in German are *always* capitalized, and that the choice to use "Spirit" or "spirit" merely reflects the translator's judgment.

The German text employs the device of showing emphasis by enlarging the spaces between the letters of important words. But since entire phrases or even sentences are thus emphasized, it was not possible to italicize all the corresponding words in the translation without producing a text with an ungainly appearance. Hence I have usually italicized one or two key words from the emphasized phrase or sentence.

Words and phrases in parentheses belong to the original text. Those within brackets are my own additions.

Throughout the entire text of the lectures, a period followed by a dash (.—) appears at the end of a paragraph from time to time. This punctuation is not explained; it may indicate the end of a day's lecture. This punctuation is simply reproduced in the translation.

I have striven for a translation that is as nonsexist as possible, particularly in the case of the German *Mensch*, which is rendered as "human," "human being," or "human person." The English "man" is generally reserved for the German *Mann*. *Er* and *ihm* are translated either as "they" and "them," or as "he" and "him," depending on the context.

It is now my happy duty to thank several persons who have played important roles in making this translation possible. I am grateful to Professor Brian A. Gerrish of Chicago for having introduced me to Troeltsch and for guiding my doctoral studies; to Professor James Luther Adams of Harvard for sharing with me his boundless enthusiasm for Troeltsch; to Davis Perkins for his help in initiating this project at Fortress Press, and to Michael West, Renée Fall, and Timothy Staveteig of Fortress for seeing it through to publication. Professor Adams read the manuscript at various stages of completion and offered numerous helpful suggestions; Dr. Mark Chapman of the University of Sheffield also offered helpful suggestions, as did my colleague Dr. Jack Clark of Gustavus Adolphus College. I also profited greatly from Professor Clark's careful reading of the Introduction, for which our colleague Dr. William Dean also offered helpful advice. Donna Landmark, a senior at Gustavus Adolphus College, helped prepare the index. Of course, responsibility for all mistakes and infelicities must remain mine alone. I also wish to thank Gustavus Adolphus College for a year's academic leave to complete the translation. Thanks are also due to my parents, Eleanor and Gilbert Paul, for their continuing personal and spiritual support, and to my wife Betsy and our sons Christoph and Hans, who cheerfully assisted me in countless important ways during the many hours consumed by this project, especially now as we all await the arrival of a new baby. Without the help of all these persons and many others, this book would never have been finished.

—Garrett E. Paul
St. Peter, Minnesota

Introduction to the English Edition

Garrett E. Paul

Who was Ernst Troeltsch, and why is interest in his thought greater today than at any time since his death nearly seventy years ago? Or perhaps even greater than during his lifetime? Why is interest also now more widespread, as demonstrated by the formation of an international association of Troeltsch scholars, with members in eastern and western Europe, North America, and Japan? Who is this early twentieth century thinker who seems so relevant now, even as the world of the late twentieth century is fast disappearing?

These questions are both simple and difficult to answer. Simple, because Troeltsch, at the beginning of this century, was keenly aware of many trends that have become apparent to most observers only at its end: the collapse of Eurocentrism; the recognition of the relativity of all historical events and knowledge (including scientific knowledge); an awareness that Christianity is relative to its Western, largely European history and environment; the emergence of a profound global pluralism; the growing impact of the social sciences on our view of the world and ourselves; and dramatic changes in the role of religious institutions and thought in society.

But it can also be very difficult to explain Troeltsch's significance. His thought was never a finished system, but rather a fabric of syntheses that he himself began to unravel no sooner than they were completed. He had numerous programs and projects, but he lived to complete almost none of them. A study of Troeltsch, therefore,

leaves us with many suggestions and intuitions but few finished products. And the subsequent theological generation repudiated him
altogether.

Moreover, Troeltsch was a profoundly interdisciplinary thinker
who made significant and enduring contributions not only to theology (his official academic appointment for most of his career), but
also to philosophy,[1] history of Christianity, sociology of religion,[2]
philosophy of history,[3] and ethics.[4] His thought does not fit neatly
into any one of these various disciplines. Indeed, appreciation for
Troeltsch was greater outside of theological circles. He was also active
in politics, serving as the University of Heidelberg's representative to
the Baden state parliament. After World War I, he helped organize
the German Democratic Party and was elected to the Prussian state
parliament, serving as Undersecretary of State for Ecclesiastical
Affairs and Public Worship in the Prussian cabinet during the crucial
beginnings of the Weimar Republic.[5] He was also a respected political journalist, whose newspaper columns chronicled the painful
struggles of the young republic.[6] He was even mentioned as a candi-
date for president.[7] All this took place before he reached his fifty-

1. Including an important book on Kant, Ernst Troeltsch, *Das Historische in Kants
Religionsphilosophie* (The role of history in Kant's philosophy of religion).

2. Ernst Troeltsch, *The Social Teachings of the Christian Churches*, originally published 1911, is perhaps still the standard history of Christian social ethics from Jesus to
the Enlightenment, and it is also a classic in the sociology of religion. It shaped H.
Richard Niebuhr's influential *Christ and Culture* (New York: Harper & Row, 1951, and
continuously in print since that time). Niebuhr himself said of his book, "In one sense
[it] undertakes to do no more than to supplement and in part to correct [Troeltsch's]
work on *The Social Teachings*" (p. xii). Even today it is difficult to pick up any general
text in the sociology of religion that does not have a significant and appreciative, even
if critical, reference, to Troeltsch's typology of church, sect, and mystic; in this field,
too, he is a figure with whom one must reckon. Troeltsch was a friend and close
associate of Max Weber for several years; they shared a house in Heidelberg and
traveled together to the United States in 1904.

3. Troeltsch's monumental and only half-finished *Der Historismus und seine Probleme* (The problems of historicism) continues to play a significant role in this field.

4. Including Troeltsch, *Social Teachings;* idem, "Atheistische Ethik" (Atheistic ethics), pp. 525–51, and "Grundprobleme der Ethik" (Basic problems of ethics), pp. 552–
672, in *Gesammelte Schriften* II.

5. See Hartmut Ruddies, "Soziale Demokratie und freier Protestantismus," in
Hartmut Ruddies and Friedrich Wilhelm Graf, eds., *Troeltsch-Studien*, vol. 3, *Protestantismus und Neuzeit;* and Shinichi Sato, "Das Problem des Religionsunterrichts
am Anfang der Weimarer Republik, dargestellt am Beispiel von Ernst Troeltsch,"
Mitteilungen der Ernst-Troeltsch-Gesellschaft 4 (1989):45–69.

6. Many of these columns have been collected in *Spektator-briefe* (Spectator letters), ed. Hans Baron.

7. See Wilhelm Pauck, *Harnack and Troeltsch: Two Historical Theologians*, p. 83.

ninth birthday. He died in 1923, with the future of Germany, the
republic, religion, and Western culture all very unclear.

Born in 1865, Troeltsch was the son of a Bavarian physician. Medicine, natural science, history, law, philology, metaphysics, and religion
all attracted his interest, but he eventually decided on theology
because "it appeared to him to raise metaphysical problems and at
the same time get one involved in intense historical questions."[8] Initial studies at Erlangen were followed by studies at Göttingen. After
a brief vicarate, he obtained an appointment at Göttingen, where he
worked closely with several biblical historical scholars, including
Wilhelm Bousset, William Wrede, and Johannes Weiss. This "little
Göttingen faculty" helped give birth to the so-called *religionsgeschichtliche Schule* ("history of religions school"), which sought to
include Christianity in the history of all religions. Troeltsch came to
be known as the school's theologian.[9] He later moved to Heidelberg,
where he became professor of dogmatics in 1892 and later also taught
courses in philosophy. In 1915, the year after the outbreak of World
War I, he accepted an appointment to the philosophical faculty in
Berlin, the city where he died eight years later in the midst of a flurry
of scholarly and political activity.

Proper assessment of Troeltsch's significance and impact has been
made even more difficult by the received interpretation of his work.
Karl Barth and a host of other theologians viewed his work as both
the epitome and the ultimate collapse of nineteenth-century liberal
theology. In particular, Barth interpreted Troeltsch's move from the
theological faculty at Heidelberg to the philosophical faculty at Berlin in 1915 as the end of an era in theology, an open admission that
liberal theology had failed, having become nothing more than a philosophy of culture.[10] Whatever theological influence Troeltsch did
continue to have was strongest in the United States, where it was
mediated by such figures as Wilhelm Pauck, Reinhold Niebuhr, H.
Richard Niebuhr, Paul Tillich, Roland Bainton, and James Luther
Adams.

8. Ibid., p. 52.
9. See Troeltsch, "The Dogmatics of the *'Religionsgeschichtliche Schule.'* "
10. Karl Barth, "Evangelical Theology in the Nineteenth Century," in *The Humanity of God,* p. 14. The situation was more complex than Barth was willing to realize.
Troeltsch had been interested in joining the theological faculty at Berlin, but conser-
vatives on that faculty, including Reinhold Seeberg, blocked it. The invitation from the
philosophical faculty was then arranged. A thorough account is in Toshimasa Yasukata,
Ernst Troeltsch: Systematic Theologian of Radical Historicality, pp. 121–26.

But for the last twenty years there have been signs that this long neglect is coming to an end. Indeed, it seems that a Troeltsch revival is now in progress.[11] Articles, dissertations, and translations in English, Italian, French, and Japanese have appeared with increasing frequency. The appearance of this translation of his *Glaubenslehre* may serve to illustrate the change. Long thought not to be worth reading or translating,[12] these lectures now appear in English, ready to become part of the contemporary conversation. The man once thought to be the last theologian of the nineteenth century may yet turn out to be the first theologian of the twentieth—or even the twenty-first.

MAJOR THEMES IN TROELTSCH'S
RELIGIOUS THOUGHT

When Troeltsch, near the end of his life, was invited to write an article describing his thought, he did not write a systematic account of his ideas; instead, he submitted an autobiographical essay, "My Books," in which he described how he had come to the place he was, and where he hoped to go. His approach was appropriate, for Troeltsch was ever a thinker on a pilgrimage, and his thought was more like a flowing river than a stable edifice. It is impossible to give a systematic account of Troeltsch's thought, for it was open and dynamic, not static and closed. Instead, we will recount some of the major themes of his religious thought, in roughly chronological order.[13]

A Historical Approach

Troeltsch took a historical approach to the study of religion and theology from the beginning of his scholarly career until it ended in the midst of a massive investigation of history and the historical

11. See James Luther Adams, "Why the Troeltsch Revival?"
12. Barth called it "a blind alley" (*Humanity of God*, p. 41), and Benjamin A. Reist claimed without qualification that it would be pointless to reconstruct Troeltsch's theology on the basis of his *Glaubenslehre*. See Reist, *Towards a Theology of Involvement*, pp. 191–92. Barth did have some occasional good words for Troeltsch, however, recognizing the latter's piety and brilliance (*Humanity of God*, p. 29; see also n. 47 below).
13. See Hans-Georg Drescher, "Ernst Troeltsch's Intellectual Development," in John Powell Clayton, ed., *Ernst Troeltsch and the Future of Theology*, pp. 3–32; Robert Morgan, "Introduction: Ernst Troeltsch on Theology and Religion," in *Ernst Troeltsch: Writings on Theology and Religion*, ed. and trans. Robert Morgan and Michael Pye, pp. 1–51; and Pauck, *Harnack and Troeltsch*, pp. 58–91.

method. He was convinced that there was no reason to exclude
Christianity from the history of religion as a whole. The Bible, Jesus,
and the church were all part of history, to be studied by the historical
method. They were not supernatural entities, somehow exempt from
historical investigation. This meant that almost all of late nineteenth-
century theology was on shaky ground. "Everything is tottering!" he
exclaimed in 1896 after a lecture by Julius Kaftan, initiating an
exchange that ended with Troeltsch slamming the door behind him
as he left the room.[14] Everything is tottering—because modern historiography had indisputably demonstrated that Christianity was
influenced by a host of non-Christian and non-Jewish factors, that
Jesus was relative to his origins and history, and that Christianity
could not, on historical grounds, be proven final or absolute.
Troeltsch stated this conclusion in *The Absoluteness of Christianity*—
somewhat tentatively in the first edition of 1902, and more clearly in
the second edition of 1912. The same conclusion was applied to Jesus
in "The Significance of the Historical Existence of Jesus for Faith"[15]
in 1911. Not that we could now dispense with the historical Jesus,
who remains indispensable to the religion of the present, for "we
possess these religions of the present only in association with the
present and revered person of Christ."[16] Troeltsch continued to apply
these insights with ever greater consistency throughout his subsequent career.

A Synthesis of Empiricism
and Rationalism[17]

Troeltsch's interest in history and historical relativity was also
expressed in a long-standing interest in philosophy and metaphysics,
particularly the philosophy of history[18] and the philosophy of religion.[19] Having rejected the notion of supernatural absolutes that
stand completely above history and are yet manifested in history, he

14. Walther Köhler, *Ernst Troeltsch*, p. 1.
15. In *Ernst Troeltsch*, ed. and trans. Morgan and Pye, pp. 182–207.
16. Ibid., p. 206.
17. See Garrett E. Paul, "*Religionswissenschaft:* The Development of Ernst
Troeltsch's Philosophy of Religion, 1895–1914," pp. 78–123.
18. See Ernst Troeltsch, "Geschichte und Metaphysik" (History and metaphysics);
idem, "Die Moderne Geschichtsphilosophie" (Modern philosophy of history), in
Gesammelte Schriften II, pp. 673–728, and, of course, idem, *Der Historismus*.
19. See Ernst Troeltsch, *Psychologie und Erkenntnistheorie in der Religionswissenschaft* (Psychology and epistemology in the science of religion); idem, "The Essence of
Religion and of the Science of Religion," in *Ernst Troeltsch*, ed. and trans. Morgan and
Pye, pp. 82–123; idem, *Das Historische in Kants Religionsphilosophie;* idem, "Reli-

increasingly turned his attention to the question of how the absolute could be present in the midst of history with all its relativities and yet remain absolute. His fascination with empirical historiography, as well as his reading of William James's *The Varieties of Religious Experience,*[20] led him to reject all rationalistic attempts to impose a transcendent, rational order on history and experience. Unhistorical rationalism was no better than unhistorical supernaturalism. At the same time, following Kant, Troeltsch believed that history and experience were impossible without some kind of transcendental, a priori rational order. Hence there *was* a rational aspect to all history and experience, and it could be detected through analysis of empirical investigation. James had erred by limiting himself to simple empiricism and rejecting any search for a rational order. But even James was unable to observe his self-imposed restraints, and reintroduced rational and teleological categories in the concluding chapter of *The Varieties of Religious Experience.*[21] But rationalistic Hegelians, like his friend Wilhelm Bousset, sought to impose a rationalistic order on history from the outside, taking the historically conditioned ideas of God, the world, and the soul to be universal absolutes of consciousness.[22] Troeltsch insisted that rationality is immanent in all experience, including religion and history, and that it can be discovered through careful study and analysis of experience. Religion and history are therefore *both* rational and empirical, universal and particular, absolute and relative. Religious experience was irrational and

---

gionsphilosophie" (The philosophy of religion), in *Die Philosophie im Beginn des zwanzigsten Jahrhunderts, Festschrift für Kuno Fischer,* ed. Wilhelm Windelband, pp. 104–62; and idem, "Zur Frage des religiösen Apriori" (On the question of the religious a priori), in *Gesammelte Schriften* II, pp. 754–68.

20. See Troeltsch's review of *The Varieties of Religious Experience* by William James; and Troeltsch's extended discussions of James in *Psychologie und Erkenntnistheorie,* pp. 14–22, and in his "Empiricism and Platonism in the Philosophy of Religion." Discussion of Troeltsch's views on James has unfortunately focused on the last-named article, which, while the longest, is probably the least illuminating. Indeed, the position taken there seems to be remarkably inconsistent with the general trend of his thought. See Henry Samuel Levinson, *The Religious Investigations of William James,* pp. 277–80; and Roger A. Johnson, "Idealism, Empiricism, and 'Other Religions': Troeltsch's Reading of William James."

21. See Troeltsch, *Psychologie und Erkenntnistheorie,* p. 19. Both Levinson and Johnson seem to miss the full force of Troeltsch's objection.

22. See Troeltsch, "Logos und Mythos in der Religionsphilosophie" (Logos and mythos in theology and the philosophy of religion), in *Gesammelte Schriften* II, pp. 805–36, esp. 816–17. See also Paul, *"Religionswissenschaft,"* pp. 217–38.

mystical as well as rational.[23] Troeltsch continued to struggle with the relationship of irrationality to rationality for the rest of his life, and his *Glaubenslehre* reflects this.[24]

Christianity as a Social Phenomenon: Church, Sect, and Mystic

While living in Heidelberg, Troeltsch formed a close friendship with the sociologist Max Weber (1864–1930). Their friendship had a marked impact on Troeltsch and on the disciplines of the history of Christianity and the sociology of religion. Weber alerted Troeltsch to the importance of the Marxist doctrine of infrastructures and super-structures,[25] which caused Troeltsch to look at the history of religion, and Christianity in particular, in a new way—as conditioned by its social environment. Troeltsch had already called attention to the historical relativity of Christian texts and ideas; now he addressed their social and institutional relativity as well. The result of his application of these insights to the history of Christianity—to Christian institutions and social teachings in particular—was the nearly one thousand pages of *The Social Teachings*. He thus helped to give birth to the sociological study of Christianity that thrives today, particularly in biblical and early Christian studies.[26] In this book Troeltsch explicated the typology of church, sect, and mystic that remains influential today.[27] Each of these three types of Christianity, he said, exists in a particular form of social organization, which, in turn, corresponds to a particular ethic. The church, into which one is born (like the medieval Catholic church), has an ethic of compromise and conservation; the sect, which one must leave society in order to join (like the Anabaptists), has an ethic of rigor, perfection, and transformation; while the mystic is primarily an individual, subjectively religious person, who is not linked to any particular form of social organization (or, if linked to one, does not find it very important). All three types,

23. "The harmony of the apriori-rational-universal with the factual-irrational-particular is the secret of reality and the fundamental problem of all knowledge," Troeltsch, *Psychologie und Erkenntnistheorie*, p. 49.
24. See below, pp. xxv–xxvi.
25. See "My Books," in Ernst Troeltsch, *Religion in History* (Minneapolis: Fortress Press, 1991).
26. To name but a few recent examples: Norman K. Gottwald, *The Tribes of Yahweh: A Sociology of the Religion of Liberated Israel, 1250–1050 B.C.E.;* Wayne A. Meeks, *The First Urban Christians: The Social World of the Apostle Paul;* Richard A. Horsley, *Sociology and the Jesus Movement;* and Bengt Holmberg, *Sociology and the New Testament.*
27. See Troeltsch, *The Social Teachings*, I:331–43; II:729–41, and esp. 993–99.

according to Troeltsch, are authentically Christian, and all three have their strengths as well as their weaknesses. But the mystical type—in Troeltsch's view, the fastest growing—was also the most socially and ethically impotent.

Not only did Troeltsch see mysticism increasing in Western society, he also appeared to be deeply attracted to it in his own thought and life. By mysticism, Troeltsch did not mean miraculous visions, signs, or supernatural experiences. He referred instead to a personal and subjective form of religion that was more inner than outer, more individual than institutional, more experiential than scriptural. For the mystic, membership in church or sect was of no significance; it was the free, inward, personal experience that really mattered. Yet Troeltsch was no simplistic individualist. He knew that religion would die without symbol, cult, myth, and institution, and he knew that without institutions, religion would grow socially and ethically impotent. But he still saw and personally felt the strong appeal of subjective religion.[28] His frequent references in the *Glaubenslehre* to "free," "inward," "internal," and "personal" religion, as well as his positive references to mystics such as Sebastian Franck and Meister Eckhart,[29] serve to illustrate this. Indeed, one may say that the *Glaubenslehre* is fairly dominated by this type of religiosity.

Troeltsch ended his history of the social teachings with the eighteenth century, saying that "the old theories no longer suffice" in the modern world, and that "new theories must be constructed, composed of old and new elements."[30]

In the following academic year (1912–13), Troeltsch delivered the lectures here translated, which Gertrud von le Fort edited and published after his death. They clearly reflect both his continued commitment to the Christian faith and his growing awareness of its social and historical relativity. It was also the last time that Troeltsch was to lecture on the topic.

A Contemporary Cultural Synthesis

In the next year, a shot fired in the Balkans finally ignited the powder keg that was Europe, and World War I broke out. It began an era of convulsive change for Europe, and for Germany in particu-

---

28. This inner tension in Troeltsch's thought is admirably developed in Yasukata, *Ernst Troeltsch*, pp. 61–66.
29. See below, pp. 49 and 185, respectively.
30. Troeltsch, *Social Teachings*, I:25.

lar, where even at this writing, the dismantling of the Berlin wall is only now bringing one chapter in that story to an end. The Russian Revolution, the German Revolution, and then the struggles that raged about the young Weimar Republic demanded ever greater attention. Troeltsch felt the demands of the new historical situation keenly. In 1915, culminating negotiations that had been going on for some time, he accepted an appointment to the philosophical faculty at Berlin. His attention was now turned primarily to the philosophy of culture, particularly the philosophy of history. But more than anything else, the growing crisis of Germany and Europe dominated Troeltsch's attention during his Berlin years.

Troeltsch believed that the crisis was historical in nature, and hence required a philosophy of history that could clarify the origins of the crisis and the options it presented. He began work on a two-volume philosophy of history, *Der Historismus und seine Probleme*, of which only the first volume—"The logical problem of the philosophy of history," nearly eight hundred pages long—was completed. The book, published in 1922, opened with a section on "The contemporary crisis of history": not a crisis of the discipline of history, but of *history itself*. It was a crisis of the very flow of events. Troeltsch held that our knowledge of the values bequeathed to us by history—values of religion, philosophy, culture, art, and the like—is unstable; and not only our knowledge of these values, but *the values themselves* are in flux.[31] The cultural and historical synthesis that had sustained European-North American culture was dissolving, and there was nothing to take its place. We need, he said, to construct a new, contemporary *cultural synthesis*.[32] Nor do we construct this synthesis in a peaceful, idyllic situation! Rather,

> in the midst of the storm of building a new world, where every ancient word must be tested for practical workability or unworkability, where what appeared to be solemn and earnest—and often truly was—is now nothing more than mere cliche or scraps of paper. The earth quakes under our feet, and the various possibilities for the future dance circles around us, especially where the World War has meant a complete revolution, in Germany and in Russia.[33]

We no longer know where we are going, nor even where we have been.

31. Troeltsch, *Der Historismus*, p. 5.
32. Ibid., p. ix.
33. Ibid., p. 6.

Troeltsch did not live to complete his version of the synthesis, and one of the darkest of those various possibilities that danced round him—National Socialism—soon triumphed, if only for a time. All he could do was sketch the directions in which his constructive philosophy of history, which was to take the form of a "universal history of European culture," might go.[34] This was *not* a Eurocentric vision, as though Europe somehow stood at the center of all world history; it was simply an admission that "for us" there could be no universal world history, that "for us" European culture, in the context of its interactions with other cultures, was what we had to work with in our task of building a contemporary cultural synthesis.

Troeltsch's concerns for building such a synthesis found political expression as well. He had been active in politics prior to the war, representing the University of Heidelberg in the Baden state parliament, but, as the war wore on and opposition to the Kaiser grew, Troeltsch became much more active. He partipated in the founding of the German Democratic Party (DDP), a liberal-intellectual party somewhat to the right of the Social Democrats, and he ran for election to the first Prussian state parliament in the infant Weimar Republic. He won, securing an appointment to the Ministry of Education and Public Worship, where he served as Undersecretary of State for Ecclesiastical Affairs during the crucial period when relations between the churches and the state were being redefined. Here too Troeltsch saw the need for a new synthesis and was practically involved in the struggle, much frustrated and saddened by the adversities and ignominies the new republic had to suffer.[35]

Troeltsch's career was cut off by his death in 1923 at the age of fifty-eight, before he could begin the second volume of *Der Historismus.* He had repeatedly expressed the wish that he could return to the study of religion,[36] but he did not live to fulfill it.

---

34. Ibid., p. 710. Some clues to the form Troeltsch's constructive synthesis might have taken are to be found in chap. 4 of *Der Historismus* (pp. 694–772), and also in the essays contained in *Christian Thought: Its History and Application,* ed. Friedrich von Hügel, esp. pp. 37–129.

35. The best account of Troeltsch's political writing is the chapter entitled "An Intellectual in Politics," in Robert Rubanowice, *Crisis in Consciousness: The Thought of Ernst Troeltsch,* pp. 99–130.

36. Troeltsch, "My Books," in *Religion in History;* see also idem, *Der Historismus,* p. viii.

THE FORM AND METHOD
OF TROELTSCH'S *GLAUBENSLEHRE*:
HISTORY AND SUBJECTIVITY IN THEOLOGY[37]

The Background of the Lectures

Ernst Troeltsch's *Glaubenslehre* is based on his seminar in dogmatic theology for 1912 and 1913.[38] Gertrud von le Fort, a student in that seminar, took verbatim notes of Troeltsch's dictation and careful (although not stenographic) notes of the lectures that followed the dictation. She was unable to capture everything Troeltsch said, but, since he "constantly reiterated his concepts with a variety of formulations . . . , it was always possible to take at least one . . . and write it down in essence" (p. 5). Von le Fort circulated these notes privately for several years and also showed them to Troeltsch, who expressed satisfaction with them. A scholarly consensus as to their reliability has now emerged.[39]

---

37. There is a growing body of literature in English on Troeltsch's theology, and the *Glaubenslehre* in particular. B. A. Gerrish, "Ernst Troeltsch and the Possibility of a Historical Theology," in Clayton, ed., *Ernst Troeltsch and the Future of Theology,* pp. 100–135, is an excellent and elegant introduction. Walter E. Wyman, Jr., in *The Concept of Glaubenslehre: Ernst Troeltsch and the Theological Heritage of Schleiermacher,* provides a careful study of the *Glaubenslehre*'s method and content, but underestimates the importance of the irrational and mystical quality of religion in Troeltsch's interpretation. The best overall discussion of Troeltsch as a theologian in English is Yasukata's *Ernst Troeltsch.* Sarah Coakley, *Christ Without Absolutes,* is particularly insightful and incisive on the question of Troeltsch's relativism, and represents the cutting edge of English-language Troeltsch scholarship. A helpful account that relates Troeltsch's *Glaubenslehre* to his other theological writings is Mark Chapman, " 'Theology as Vocation'—Ernst Troeltsch as Philosophical Theologian" (Ph.D. diss., Oxford University, 1988), pp. 355–91. Also worth consulting is Claude Welch's discussion of Troeltsch in *Protestant Thought in the Nineteenth Century,* vol. 2, *1870–1914,* pp. 266–301. See also Paul, *"Religionswissenschaft,"* pp. 157–90.

38. The date given in the German edition is 1911–12. Wyman, however, has shown that the date must have been 1912–13 (see Wyman, *Concept of Glaubenslehre,* p. 208 n. 37). In personal correspondence, Dr. Mark Chapman of the University of Sheffield has pointed out that, according to the Heidelberg University catalogs, the lectures were given over two semesters: Summer 1912 and Winter 1912–13.

39. Reist, who was largely critical of Troeltsch, disputed the reliability of the text, primarily because Troeltsch did not publish it himself (*Towards a Theology of Involvement,* p. 155). Yet Troeltsch indicates that he takes the task of the *Glaubenslehre* very seriously—indeed passionately. The dictations are accurate, and the lecture notes closely match the dictations. For a thorough discussion and affirmation of the overall reliability of Gertrud von le Fort's work, see Wyman, *Concept of Glaubenslehre,* pp. xiii–xviii. Also see Gerrish, "Historical Theology," in Clayton, ed., *Ernst Troeltsch,* pp. 113–14. My own experience in translating the document bears out Wyman's judgment: the dictation clearly manifests Troeltsch's characteristic language, style, and sentence structure; and the text of the lecture notes, while not as complex and finely nuanced as the dictation, also clearly reflect his thought and language.

It is also noteworthy that the lectures, which constitute the larger
share of the volume, are more conversational in character than most
academic theology, then or now. Troeltsch takes an idea, plays with
it, reflects on it, develops it, illustrates it with examples, and generally thinks out loud in front of his students. As a result, the
Glaubenslehre is much more like a theology in process, not a finished
product. This is particularly appropriate for a scholar who emphasized the dynamic, historical, and incomplete character of all religious
thought—indeed of all thought. Troeltsch speaks not from some lofty
Mt. Olympus of finished dogma, but from the perspective of one
immersed in a continuing intellectual, personal, and social struggle. It
is this conversational character that makes his *Glaubenslehre* so
engaging.

Glaubenslehre:
A Theology of Consciousness

Troeltsch, following Schleiermacher, chose to refer to his theology
as *Glaubenslehre*, rejecting the term "dogmatics." The whole idea of
dogma—timeless, nonhistorical facts about God, Jesus, the Church,
and so on—had been completely undermined by research into the
history of Christianity and religion in general. The Bible, the creeds,
and even Jesus had all been historicized and relativized. Without
dogma, theology could no longer be called dogmatics: "We are no
longer in the business of fixing permanent dogmas from an inspired
Bible. Instead, we formulate teachings [*Lehren*] which express the
essence of Christian piety" (p. 16). Hence the term *Glaubenslehre,*
which can be translated variously as "doctrine of faith," "faith-teach-
ing," "teaching of faith," or "teaching-faith."[40] For the English title,
however, I have chosen "The Christian Faith," the title under which
Schleiermacher's *Glaubenslehre* was published, for, as Troeltsch
himself said, "No other contemporary theologian stays as close to
Schleiermacher's method and approach, nor feels himself in such inner agreement with him" (p. 113).

What, then, does a theology without dogmas look like? Its theological statements are not statements of objective facts about God
and salvation; instead, they "express the preconditions and contents

40. Tillich, however, in his own lectures on systematic theology—delivered the very
year after the publication of Troeltsch's *Glaubenslehre*—rejected the term *Glaubenslehre* and revived the term "dogmatics," because "dogmatics" carries with it the
connotation of *Angriff* ("attack" or "assault"). Paul Tillich, *Dogmatik: Marburger
Vorlesung von 1925*, p. 1. Tillich acknowledges Troeltsch's contribution as having been
to "clear the table," p. 2.

of the Christian consciousness of faith, that is, a living, practical-theoretical orientation to God, the world, and humanity" (pp. 111–12). "We have a theology of consciousness instead of a theology of facts" (p. 115). A "theology of facts" wishes that reason "might be able to do what the eyes cannot—make everything as precise and compact as possible." But for a theology of consciousness, these matters "can never be known apart from subjective experience" (ibid.).

Subjectivity, Historicity, and Intersubjectivity in Theology

Troeltsch, then, emphasizes the subjective and even personal character of all theology. But this does not mean that he capitulated to a simplistic subjectivism or solipsism. His theology is a highly sophisticated combination of personal experience and social history, of subjectivity, historicity, and intersubjectivity.

First, let us consider the subjectivity. The words "subjective," "personal," "personality," "inner," and so forth, appear with great frequency:

> Redemption is to be portrayed as the *present experience of union with God* which occurs ever anew in the inner experience of each Christian. (pp. 261–62)

> There is much that is intensely personal in our attempt to grasp God on the basis of these sparks in our soul. (p. 114)

> The other-worldly can signify nothing other than . . . an ever deeper inner growth in a divine world of spirit. (p. 38)

> It comes not from the desk, but from life. (p. 67)

Religion is primarily a matter of experience and subjectivity, not dogma and fact.

Yet Troeltsch's subjectivism is finely honed, nuanced, and delimited. While these things "can never be known apart from subjective experience," it is nevertheless "not a frivolous subjectivity, but something that takes shape within us, overwhelming us with an irresistible inner sovereignty" (p. 65). Subjectivity "does not mean a matter of arbitrary taste, but a subjectivity which is saturated with God" (p. 115). In other words, there is something more to authentic subjectivity than the mere subject alone.

Troeltsch's concern for that which is more than merely subjective is especially apparent in his critique of simplistic appeals to *autonomy*. "The modern concept of autonomy does not mean that everything must be self-produced. That would quickly put an end to all mathematics!" Autonomy does not *produce* faith, but rather makes it "a part of one's own life" (p. 80). Genuine faith "lift[s] the individual subject above its own limitations and brings it into full and living contact with the divine life for the first time" (p. 75).

This brings us to Troeltsch's emphasis on the indispensable role played by *history* and *community*. History is one of the trans-subjective elements in religion and theology. The autonomous subject never—not even in the case of Jesus—spontaneously produces faith of itself. It needs the stimulus and impetus of history and community. Any attempt to sever the ties that bind would result in the destruction of genuine religion and "an utterly individual, personal, and emaciated mysticism" (p. 75). History and community must, to be sure, be subjectively appropriated and even transformed, but to sever all connection with history would destroy autonomy as well.

Another way in which Troeltsch makes the same point is to say that history is always more than history: "Wafting over history is the fragrance of supra-history, inextricable from the unity of the divine life" (p. 81). That is, history, which appears to be merely external to the subject, also includes overtones of that which is internal to the subject—the divine life.

The theologian's task of formulating and interpreting the Christian faith—a task that belongs not just to the theologian, but also to the community—is not accomplished simply by making the observation that it involves both the subjective and historical, the subjective and the trans-subjective. To realize that they are interwoven does not finish the task, but only identifies the conditions under which it must be undertaken. What Troeltsch says of the concept of God applies to the whole of the theological task: "We must now have the courage to risk it on the basis of our decision" (p. 116). There is no purely objective criterion on which a decision can based, no purely suprahistorical idea, nor any unsurpassable idea from the past. Truth is neither static nor ahistorical. "What we have is a truth that is *becoming*, always in the process of approximating, something that can never fully empty itself into human life." "We . . . have a truth which is now always just taking form" (p. 85). Or, as B. A. Gerrish puts it, "The theologian is summoned, in the end, not just to *write* history, but to *make* history."[41]

But this decision does *not* consist in the mere assertion of one's own autonomy and subjectivity; authentic decision lifts one *above* mere autonomy. Nothing is purely supra-historical, but everything

41. Gerrish, "Ernst Troeltsch," in Clayton, ed., *Ernst Troeltsch,* p. 125.

historical is *more* than historical. This *more* is "a truth . . . that can never fully empty itself into human life" (p. 82). It does empty itself into human life—perhaps, indeed, into all life—not *fully*, but *really*: "The light that no one sees, the light from which a few sparks fall upon our souls," that is, God (p. 114).

Hence Troeltsch's theology, while not a theology of purportedly objective facts, is not merely subjective either. Neither does it simply glory in the great multiplicity and diversity of interpretations without seeking *some* order, like those varieties of postmodernism which are less *post*-modern than they are *hyper*-modern.[42] Indeed, Troeltsch considers it an important task of theology to prune faith's "disorderly and excessive growth . . . back to a practical religious foundation" (p. 44). "Left to itself, faith has a propensity to excrescence, dissipation, and indifference," which is why theology must "regulate faith and give order to the wild and luxuriant growth of its images" (p. 51). Hence history, community, and reason all have important roles to play in ordering and even enabling subjectivity, without ever crushing it. Troeltsch's theology is certainly not objective and authoritarian, but neither is it merely subjective and autonomous; it is *intersubjective* or dialogical (although these are not his terms), similar in some ways to the thought of his American admirer, H. Richard Niebuhr.[43]

Faith and History

Troeltsch's name has long been linked with the problem known to twentieth-century theology as "faith and history." This is the question of how history can serve as the basis for faith or even have any relevance to faith. Indeed, Troeltsch gave this problem its most succinct and cogent formulation. The issues are closely related to those we have just considered. The problem may be stated thus: History is relative, not absolute. We cannot even be sure of the facts of history, for all historical judgments are merely probabilistic. For example, we cannot be utterly certain of how and why the crucifixion took place,

42. David Ray Griffin makes a similar point when he distinguishes between "deconstructive" or "eliminative" postmodernism (exemplified by Jacques Derrida) and his own "constructive" or "revisionary" postmodernism. The former, he contends, "simply carr[ies] the premises of modernity through to their logical conclusions," and hence can be called "ultramodernism." See Griffin, "Introduction to Series," in Griffin et al., eds., *Varieties of Postmodern Theology,* pp. xii–xiii; see also his essay "Postmodern Theology and A/theology: A Response to Mark C. Taylor," in ibid., pp. 29–61.
43. See H. Richard Niebuhr, *The Responsible Self,* pp. 69–89. Gerrish, in his insightful discussion of intersubjectivity in Troeltsch's theology, suggests that Troeltsch would have benefited greatly had he developed this intersubjectivity more explicitly ("Historical Theology," in Clayton, ed., *Ernst Troeltsch,* pp. 127–28.)

or even that there was a crucifixion, for we have only "biased sources."

Troeltsch repeatedly considers the problem throughout his writings, and he gives prominent place to the topic in his *Glaubenslehre*.[44] He begins with the empirical observation that, in Christianity, faith and history are inseparable. He then identifies, and responds to, six modern objections to making faith dependent on history in any way.[45]

It is true, Troeltsch admits, that we will have to understand the relationship between faith and history differently. We cannot simply lift our faith whole from the Bible or even Jesus, for they are both historically relative and bound to their time; nor can we be absolutely certain of the details of Jesus' life and teaching. But we cannot separate faith from history. Autonomy does not mean that religion can be self-produced; the religious past is part of the religious present, and the same holds true for the religious future. While we are unable to be certain of every detail of Jesus' life, there can be no doubt that "we can still know the person of Jesus with great clarity" (p. 84). Finally, if religion were to become separated from history, nothing would be left but a "general mystical sensitivity" that would be "ethically impotent" (p. 79).

Hence we have both the need and the resources to bind our contemporary religious life to history. But the reverse holds true as well: the religious significance of the past, in some ways, depends on both present and future appropriations of it. "History is everywhere bound up and intermingled with what lies behind it" (p. 81).

The Organization of the Glaubenslehre

The interplay between the trans-subjective and the subjective, and between the historical-communal and the autonomous-mystical, is reflected in the structure of Troeltsch's *Glaubenslehre*. The main body of the book (after the lengthy prolegomenon) is divided into two parts: "the historical-religious and the contemporary-religious elements of faith" (p. 64). The historical elements are relatively less subjective and more communal, while the contemporary components are relatively more subjective and internal. Christian theology takes "the historic power, context, and direction" of Christianity, including

44. §6, pp. 73–84. The discussion here should be compared with "Glaube und Geschichte" (Faith and History), in *Religion in Geschichte und Gegenwart*, 1st ed.; and "What does 'Essence of Christianity' Mean?" and "The Significance of the Historical Existence of Jesus for Faith," both in *Ernst Troeltsch*, ed. and trans. Morgan and Pye, pp. 124–207.

45. The objections are based on *(a)* autonomy, *(b)* the relativity of the sources, *(c)* the uncertainty of historical judgments, *(d)* the historical relativity of Christianity, *(e)* the history of religions, and *(f)* the relativist attitude of the present (p. 74).

the present, and makes them "part of the contemporary world" (p. 64). Part One, then, deals with the religious significance of Christ, including his background in the religion of Israel and his impact on the subsequent history of Christianity, while Part Two expounds the Christian concepts of God, the world, the soul, redemption, religious community, and the consummation as *contemporary* experiences, concepts which, while rooted in history, are nevertheless "relatively independent" of history (p. 69). Parts One and Two reflect the two poles of Troeltsch's method: relatively less subjective history, and relatively more subjective contemporary interpretation, combined through intersubjective interpretation.

THE CONTENT OF THE GLAUBENSLEHRE

The Christian Principle

Troeltsch could define theology as the exposition of the Christian principle, a "summary formula" or "synopsis" for the "entire religious disposition of Christianity," a "central formula that will express the unifying root and driving force behind the whole" (p. 63). The task of defining the principle is another fine example of the interweaving of the historical and the subjective, of the past, present, and future. The principle is a historical reality, by no means subject to mere whim or personal desire. Yet it cannot be formulated without making a decision about what is more important or less important in Christianity, and, perhaps even more important, a decision about where Christianity is going in the future.[46] For Troeltsch, the Christian principle, at this time in history, is a "monotheistic religion of personality . . . anchoring individual souls in God and uniting souls together through God" (p. 66).

Part One: The Religious Significance of Jesus Christ

Part One of Troeltsch's *Glaubenslehre,* which follows the methodological prolegomenon, is devoted to the "historical-religious" elements of theology, centering about "Jesus Christ as the Object of Faith."[47] This "Jesus Christ" is not identical to what is sometimes

---

46. See also Troeltsch, "What Does 'Essence of Christianity' Mean?" in *Ernst Troeltsch,* ed. and trans. Morgan and Pye, pp. 163–70.

47. It is interesting that when Barth defends his decision to locate his Christology *prior* to the doctrine of sin, he appeals to Troeltsch, among others, for having set the precedent! This did not, however, change Barth's opinion concerning the ultimate futility of Troeltsch's theology. See Karl Barth, *Church Dogmatics,* vol. IV, no. 1, p. 391; and also Eberhard Jüngel, *Karl Barth, A Theological Legacy,* p. 116.

called the "historical Jesus," although he is surely rooted in history. Jesus Christ as an object of faith includes "the religious significance" of both the history of Israel (§7) and the history of Christianity (§9), as well as of the person of Jesus (§9). Troeltsch emphasizes the "personality" of Jesus, which includes the entirety of the social and psychological impact that Jesus' personality made, and continues to make, on the Christian community. It is the "historical personality" of Jesus that reveals the Christian life-world, that makes the redemptive self-surrender of the Christian soul to God possible, and gathers and concentrates the community around that personality (p. 89). The impact of Jesus is mediated socially, psychologically, and historically, not metaphysically or supernaturally. But, like all history, it is not *merely* historical; it is supra-historical as well.

Part Two: Redemption as a Present Experience of God

The second part of the *Glaubenslehre* is by far the longest, and it could have been even longer. Due to time limitations, Troeltsch lectured in full on only three of the six chapters in Part II, although he did lecture briefly on the fourth chapter in the closing days of the semester. For the last two chapters, we have only his dictation, some of which comes from earlier semesters.

Part Two develops the "contemporary-religious" statements that are anchored in history but remain relatively independent of history. They are divided into six concepts, but there is a great deal of overlapping. They are God, the world, the soul (including sin), redemption, religious community (the church), and the consummation (eschatology). Among these, the concept of God does seem to occupy a prominent and central location, for all the other concepts must relate to it, and it takes the most space by far—more than one-fourth of the entire book, and over one-third of Part Two alone. But the amount of space devoted to the soul and to redemption is also striking. Troeltsch states that each of these concepts "includes within itself the whole of this faith: the religious and ethical idea of redemption and personality. Only the exemplification changes" (p. 111).

God

Troeltsch devotes a great deal of space and energy to the concept of God. It is unquestionably central to his religious thought in a way that those who have not studied the *Glaubenslehre* may not expect. The richness and nuance of Troeltsch's discussion defies summary. God is a mysteriously experienced reality, "immediately present to us, concealed in our most deeply hidden feelings" (p. 112). Nevertheless, "we can describe . . . not God himself, but [only] our thoughts about God" (p. 119). Troeltsch's approach to God is not that of a speculative metaphysics or a deductive biblicism, but *descriptive:* describing "the Christian disposition and the religious concepts or beliefs contained in it."

Troeltsch's favorite word to describe the concept of God is "personalistic," and he freely admits that there is a degree of anthropomorphism in such an approach (pp. 123–24). But it is an essential weapon in his arsenal against what he considered the chief rival to the Christian concept of God in his day—monistic pantheism.[48] Yet while Troeltsch does insist on the concept of the personality of God, he certainly refrains from speaking of God as some kind of a superman. It is not that God *is* a personality, but rather that God is person-like (p. 127).

God is also distinct from the world. Troeltsch cheerfully describes his position as dualist: not necessarily the dualism of body and soul or flesh and spirit (although his anthropology is confusing on this point), but rather simply in the sense of making a distinction between God and world, between what is and what ought to be, between what is and what will be.

The chief attributes Troeltsch ascribes to God are will, essence, holiness, and love. The concept of will calls attention to the divine creativity and irrationality. As Troeltsch summarizes the Hebrew prophets and their vision of Yahweh: "Whatever he commands comes to pass. God formed everything purely by himself. He is the will that can make something exist. . . . The God of Israel is not limited by the given" (p. 126). God simply *is,* for no reason other than God's own self. But this will is not simply arbitrary. It contains an eternal essence within it, a goal, an enduring unity and integrity. Furthermore, this same essence is immanent in the human soul, a presence that is the result of the soul's free, inward surrender to the will of God (p. 121). God as will alone would be utterly extrinsic to the soul. It is the essence that makes God intrinsic as well.

Just as Troeltsch conceives God in terms of absolute will and absolute essence, so too in terms of absolute *holiness:* that is, the divine will is "eternally directed toward, and . . . personally embodies, the *good*" (p. 152). Troeltsch characteristically rejects any notion of the holiness of God and the moral law as completely external to the

---

48. Discussion of this topic is scattered throughout the *Glaubenslehre*. A lengthy refutation of monism is found on pp. 142–47, but also see pp. 127 and 136.

self: "The moral law is revealed in our inner life" (p. 160). Yet this inner life must be expressed in outward moral striving.

God's holiness is understood in Christianity as being expressed in a holy love that not only demands the good but also enables the good by communicating God's own self to the soul. This is the "ultimate secret of creation and the world's existence: the loving act of God whereby his essence is reproduced and multiplied in innumerable realms of spirit, and in these very realms reclaims itself" (p. 175). Hence there is no need for a vicarious atonement; God is already self-communicated to the soul that surrenders to his love.

The love of God raises an old and very difficult issue that Troeltsch addresses at length: "how this divine love relates to the immeasurable physical and moral misery of the real world," that is, *theodicy* (p. 177). He emphasizes the unacceptability of the various orthodox solutions to the problem. While he does not propose a comprehensive solution, he does assert that God participates in the suffering of creation: "God's own self-submission to the concomitant suffering of nature . . . [and to the] spiritual and moral errors" of the creation (p. 178). God's participation in suffering and error is such that the process of redemption can even be said to include "God's own self-redemption" (ibid.). In this context, Troeltsch grants a certain relative truth to the pantheism he so vigorously disputes elsewhere: "The upward struggle of the finite spirit is a moment in the life of God himself" (p. 193).

The World

Here Troeltsch expounds the concept of the world as the creation of God, in the service of divine goals, manifesting the inner life of God in individual events. He is careful to yield to science the task of describing the age of the earth, the origin of humankind, and the fate of the earth. "We renounce all attempts to arrange a shotgun wedding between Moses and Darwin by counting each of the biblical days of creation as millions of years!" Christianity is "a religious stance toward the world, viewing it as a whole that is willed by God" (p. 197). This does not mean that science can be ignored; the modern scientific world picture must be taken into account. Nor can science dictate to faith: throughout the *Glaubenslehre,* Troeltsch repeatedly criticizes those who would draw simplistic religious conclusions—usually monistic ones—from modern science.[49]

49. See, e.g., pp. 211–13.

The world is both strongly differentiated from God—the concept of divine transcendence—and closely related to God—divine immanence. The world expresses the divine will, or providence, but not directly in each individual event. The world is *generally* directed toward "the goal of the soul's salvation" (p. 210), but Troeltsch at least considers extending this goal to include nature as a whole, even the lichens clinging to boulders high in unseen Alpine valleys (pp. 149, 213). Finally, the individual soul is also aware of "an immediate relation to God's ruling goodness" in the individual moment, or a sense of miracle (p. 217).

The Soul

Troeltsch is at his most dualist when he considers this topic. He is also at his most passionate: "For our age, . . . the *soul* is the central question of life. 'Save your soul' is the authentic cry of our day" (p. 239). The soul is "supra-empirical," (p. 232) although unquestionably dependent on its "bodily substrate" (p. 235). In a remarkably brief treatment of the image of God, he asserts that if we are to affirm the image of God, we must affirm life after death (p. 240). A rather lengthy discussion of sin emphasizes its character as mistrust, refusal of God, or simply a relative good that refuses to share in the struggle (pp. 250–51). Finally, all this is taken to imply a vision of history as the story of the spirit's "struggle with the flesh" (p. 255), although this struggle can no longer be thought to issue in a continuous progress toward some ideal historical civilization.

Redemption

Although its position in the *Glaubenslehre* and the abbreviated character of Troeltsch's lecture at the end of the semester might suggest otherwise, it could be argued that the doctrine of redemption is the most important in his *Glaubenslehre,* or that it is at least equal in importance to his doctrine of God. Redemption is the goal of both Christianity and the soul, insofar as the goal can be described. God's goal, and even the world's goal, are not restricted to this redemptive elevation of the soul, but must surely include it.

Redemption is the "present experience of union with God which occurs ever anew in the inner experience of each Christian." It is both an action by God and an interaction between God and the soul (pp. 261–62), a redemption from world-weariness [*Weltleid*], from the consciousness of guilt, and from ethical and religious impotence. It is a present experience, but also "proceeds from Jesus and the Christian community." This recapitulates yet again Troeltsch's insistence on the

interpenetration of the historical and the subjective (p. 263). Perhaps
surprisingly, he rejects the idea of the soul's cooperation with the
Holy Spirit in regeneration, endorsing instead the doctrine that
regeneration is the work of the Holy Spirit alone; and with this, he
acknowledges, the foundation has been laid for a doctrine of predestination, not as a metaphysical determinism, but as a corollary of the
doctrine of grace[50] (pp. 272–73).

Religious Community

There was not sufficient time for Troeltsch to lecture on this and
the following section of the *Glaubenslehre,* so that all we have is his
dictation, some of which comes from earlier semesters.[51] He emphasizes the great importance of community to all religion, Christianity
in particular. The Kingdom of God, or the church, is both an immanent, human community, and a transcendent state of affairs effected
by God (p. 292). The community is necessary, in opposition to "the
churchlessness and religious individualism of the present" (p. 294).
Reference is also made to the Word, which is tied to the Bible but is
not identical with it; Law and Gospel, a distinction of little importance to Troeltsch; and the sacraments, whose cultic significance is
described but not greatly emphasized.

The Consummation

This is the most fragmentary section, consisting only of a few
pages of dictation, although another brief discussion of the topic
occurs at the conclusion of the lectures on the concept of redemption
(pp. 287–89). The essence of the consummation is a "complete separation from nature" and a "complete unification with God" (p. 302)
or "return to God" (p. 303). Yet Troeltsch can also speak in the
admittedly pantheistic terms of a "submergence" [*Untergang*] into
God (p. 288). This is "only one of God's final goals," and we can say
nothing of those who will not attain it, nor of what other divine goals
there may be. But "all who acknowledge this should set their lives on
this goal" (p. 304).

---

50. Predestination is discussed several times in the *Glaubenslehre.* Troeltsch rejects
any *double* predestination, but does affirm a single predestination of sorts: the higher
life seems to be an impossibility for some persons, and our experience of God as
absolute *will* suggests particularity in the divine love. See pp. 176–77, 187–88, and
213–14.
51. See von le Fort's comments in her "Prefatory Remarks," p. 6.

THE PROSPECTS FOR TROELTSCH'S
GLAUBENSLEHRE

We began by suggesting that Troeltsch, far from being the last theologian of the nineteenth century, may actually have been the first theologian of the twenty-first. And many of what we have seen to be Troeltsch's chief concerns do have a distinctly contemporary ring: his interest in plurality and subjectivity puts him very close to issues that are central to contemporary discussions in philosophy and theology; his concern for community and historicity relates him to the communitarian movement in moral philosophy and social science; and his interest in the social sciences places him at what is in many ways the cutting edge of religious research. Even his remarks about "those curious persons who think that ancient Germanic polytheism can be revived in earnest" and whose rallying cry is "Back to Wotan!"[52] are reminiscent of contemporary neo-pagan and New Age movements.

We can identify several characteristics of Troeltsch's *Glaubenslehre* that qualify it to be an important participant in present-day theological conversation. Many of these are linked to Troeltsch's sensitivity to plurality: (1) he champions a nondogmatic approach to theology; (2) he values a limited plurality of interpretations and viewpoints in theology; (3) he understands theology as a process of interpretation and reinterpretation within a historical framework; (4) he takes non-Christian religions seriously in a theological sense, going so far as to include discussions of Buddhist, Hindu, Islamic, and Jewish understandings of God, will, eschatology, and so on; and (5) he likewise takes science and its impact on contemporary theological formulations seriously.

Other aspects of Troeltsch's relevance are related to his deep appreciation of the importance of subjectivity as well as its limits: (6) his sensitivity to the need for subjective, individual religious experience—what he called "mysticism," and what today might be called "spirituality"—is very much in line with changes that have taken place in the socialization of European and North American religion since his time; (7) and yet he is able to combine this sensitivity to mysticism and spirituality with a healthy skepticism of the religious subjectivism and solipsism that infects our age even more than his. Likewise, (8) he does not capitulate to an easy relativism, but insists on the strenuous task of formulating, and even creating, an appropri-

52. See. pp. 132–33.

ate statement of the Christian principle for our time; and (9) his emphasis on the *bond* between the mystical and historical, and on the need for both subjectivity *and* intersubjectivity, leads to a creative interplay between the historical and our contemporary appropriation of it.

Still other advantages of Troeltsch's *Glaubenslehre* are tied to (10) his sociological and historical sophistication, which enabled him to recognize that religious concepts cannot be understood apart from their social and historical location; (11) an emphasis on the historical, social, and psychological dimensions of religion, which made him far more open to empirical religious research than most theologians, who (even today) often seem to have little interest in what is going on in the religious life of the society beyond the walls of the academy or the denomination; and (12) his awareness of the need for *institutions* in religion, which provides another important counterbalance to the religious subjectivism already discussed.

This is not to say that there are not serious difficulties in Troeltsch's theology. Several problems arise from his handling of the conflict between monism and personalism: (1) his inability to reconcile his personalism with his pantheistic leanings, for which he harshly criticizes Schleiermacher but seems unable to avoid himself; (2) his concept of the soul as an immaterial, ideal reality, which seems unable to avoid landing squarely in what today would be thought an indefensible mind-body dualism; and (3) a somewhat negative attitude toward the physical world as something to be gotten beyond.[53]

Another problem concerns (4) Troeltsch's treatment of evil: despite the fact that he cannot be accused of holding to any simplistic idea of progress, we may still question whether his understanding of sin and evil is adequate to embrace the experience of the twentieth century. To this must be added the matter of (5) his too-polemical approach to non-Christian religions and modern Western science, treating them more as rivals and opponents than as potential resources; (6) a failure to take "primitive" religions seriously at all; and (7) occasional remarks that suggest some anti-Jewish sentiment.[54]

Finally, we must call attention to some problems with excessive individualism, which are surprising, given his emphasis on the social character of religion: (8) his excessively individualistic approach to theology, wherein formulating the Christian principle seems to be a

53. See, e.g., pp. 279 and 284.
54. Such as, e.g., his desire to portray Jesus as un-Jewish in some respects (pp. 91, 158).

task for the solitary university professor;[55] and (9) a one-sided preference for mysticism. All these weaknesses could be discussed at length, but the last criticism, expressed most recently and effectively by Toshimasa Yasukata, particularly requires elaboration.

A one-sided emphasis on mysticism is clearly contrary to Troeltsch's own intention, for it undermines his desire to maintain a balance between the subjective and the communal. He shows that it is necessary that Christianity express itself in a social form if it is to have any continuing vitality. Without a community, Christianity will be sociologically impotent, indeed even unable to reproduce itself. Yet, particularly in the *Glaubenslehre,* Troeltsch repeatedly seems to favor mysticism over both the church and the sect, despite the fact that Troeltsch knew that mysticism is the least organized and organizable form of religion. As Yasukata states, the problem is that mysticism is "derivative and parasitic in character [and] sociologically impotent." Troeltsch seems to have been stuck in a dilemma, an internal contradiction that he failed to recognize, one which Yasukata judges to have been "fatal to his entire scientific endeavor."[56] But the dilemma is not limited to Troeltsch. It is probably the distinguishing characteristic of liberal Protestantism in contemporary Europe and North America, and it affects much of the rest of contemporary Christianity as well. What Troeltsch saw in his time is even more true today: Mysticism is the secret (but not so secret anymore!) religion of the educated classes. He did not adequately consider the impact that this has had and will continue to have on religious community. As religion becomes an ever more individual and subjective matter, identification with a community, tradition, and history will be greatly weakened. Recent studies indicate that this is precisely what is happening in the United States, with more and more persons "shopping around" for a church that meets their "spiritual needs," often worshiping with three or four different congregations without making a commitment to any.[57] Their individual religious lives may or may not be enriched by this variety, but will their "mysticism" provide any

55. This point is made particularly well by Gerrish, "Historical Theology," in Clayton, ed., *Ernst Troeltsch,* pp. 127–28. See also Wyman, *Concept of Glaubenslehre,* p. 107, and S. W. Sykes, "Ernst Troeltsch and Christianity's Essence," in Clayton, ed., *Ernst Troeltsch,* pp. 170–71.

56. Yasukata, *Ernst Troeltsch,* p. 65.

57. See the discussion of the privatization of religion in Robert Bellah et al., *Habits of the Heart,* pp. 219–49. See also Wade Clark Roof and William McKinney, *American Mainline Religion: Its Changing Shape and Future;* and Robert Wuthnow, *The Restructuring of American Religion.*

support or renewal for those congregations? Will these persons have
any sense of community? How many congregations will be left for
the next generation to "shop around" in? By any empirical measure—membership, giving, impact on society—liberal Protestantism
is headed for a crisis that demands that this problem be confronted.
This provides ironic evidence for Troeltsch's contemporary relevance.
He saw the problem quite clearly almost one hundred years ago, but
he was not able to solve it, either.[58]

While Troeltsch clearly envisioned many of the changes that were
beginning in his own time and have continued throughout the entire
century, there are of course significant changes that he did not anticipate. Among these must be numbered the growth in the importance
of the Third World, where the majority of the Christians of the twenty-first century will live; the growing disparity between rich and poor
nations; the growing attention given to gender and sexuality in human
experience; and the threat of nuclear or ecological holocaust. It may
be that the last-named development has caused the bureau of eschatology to reopen.[59] But while Troeltsch could not foresee all these
developments, he did recognize the possibility that the ascendancy of
European-North American civilization could come to an end, and
even that the entire human race could someday just as well climb
back up into the trees from which we came down (p. 258). One thing
he did not fully appreciate, however, was the possibility that Christianity might someday be equally at home in non-European and non-
North American cultures.

Despite these difficulties and limitations, and despite the changes
that have swept over the world since these lectures were given in
1912–13, Troeltsch's *Glaubenslehre* is well suited to enter the contemporary theological discussion. He remains a thinker who is eminently relevant to the present situation. His rich engagement with, as

58. Another way of stating the same problem is this: Troeltsch envisioned theology
as a critical exposition of the consciousness of the contemporary Christian community.
He knew that this was not an easy task, and that there were different versions of just
what that consciousness was, but he did not question whether there was such a community in the first place. Today, the extraordinarily malleable character of contemporary religious opinion and behavior, and the growing permeability of the boundaries
that define religious communities, make the assumption that there is one Christian
community questionable. Hence, how can Troeltsch speak of one Christian principle
rather than many? Yet to allow everyone to have their own unique Christian principle
would render it neither a principle nor Christian, and indeed would make it impossible
to evaluate—just the sort of radical religious autonomy Troeltsch rejects, and which
would be unsustainable in any case.
59. "The bureau of eschatology is generally closed these days" (p. 38).

well as his contributions to, the social sciences, his historical sophistication, his willingness to discuss scientific and non-Christian religious perspectives, his awareness of the mystical character of much contemporary religiosity, and his understanding of the need for community in authentic religion all make his *Glaubenslehre* a rich resource for contemporary religious reflection.

BIBLIOGRAPHY

This list includes only materials cited in the introduction. For a complete bibliography of Ernst Troeltsch's works, consult Friedrich Wilhelm Graf and Hartmut Ruddies, *Ernst Troeltsch Bibliographie* (Tübingen: J.C.B. Mohr, 1982). For secondary works on Troeltsch, see John Powell Clayton, ed., *Ernst Troeltsch and the Future of Theology*, pp. 200ff., and Friedrich Wilhelm Graf, "Bibliographical Essay," in Ninian Smart, et al., eds., *Nineteenth-Century Religious Thought in the West*, vol. 3 (Cambridge: Cambridge University Press, 1985).

Works by Ernst Troeltsch

Christian Thought: Its History and Application. Edited by Friedrich von Hügel. London: University of London Press, 1923.
"The Dogmatics of the '*Religionsgeschichtliche Schule.*'" *American Journal of Theology* 17 (1913):1–21.
"Empiricism and Platonism in the Philosophy of Religion." *Harvard Theological Review* 5 (1912):401–22.
Ernst Troeltsch: Writings on Theology and Religion. Edited and translated by Robert Morgan and Michael Pye. Atlanta: John Knox Press, 1977.
Gesammelte Schriften. Vol. II, *Zur religiösen Lage, Religionsphilosophie, und Ethik.* Tübingen: J.C.B. Mohr, 1922.
"Geschichte und Metaphysik." *Zeitschrift für Theologie und Kirche* 8 (1898):1–69.
"Glaube und Geschichte." *Religion in Geschichte und Gegenwart.* 1st ed. Tübingen: J.C.B. Mohr, 1910–1913.
Das Historische in Kants Religionsphilosophie. Berlin: Reuther & Richard, 1904.
Der Historismus und seine Probleme. Tübingen: J.C.B. Mohr, 1922.
Psychologie und Erkenntnistheorie in der Religionswissenschaft. Tübingen: J.C.B. Mohr, 1905.
Religion in History. Translated by James Luther Adams and Walter Bense. Minneapolis: Fortress Press, 1991.
"Religionsphilosophie." In *Die Philosophie im Beginn des zwanzigsten Jahrhunderts, Festschrift für Kuno Fischer,* edited by Wilhelm Windelband. 2d ed. Heidelberg: Carl Winters, 1904.

The Social Teachings of the Christian Churches. Translated by Olive Wyon. New York: Harper & Row, 1960.

Spektator-briefe. Edited by Hans Baron. Tübingen: J.C.B. Mohr, 1925.

Review of *The Varieties of Religious Experience,* by William James. *Deutsche Literaturzeitung* 25 (1904):3021–27.

Other Works Cited

Adams, James Luther. "Why the Troeltsch Revival?" *Unitarian Universalist Christian* 29 (1974):4–15.

Barth, Karl. *Church Dogmatics.* Vol. IV, No. 1. Translated by G.W. Bromiley. Edinburgh: T. & T. Clark, 1956.

———. *The Humanity of God.* Translated by John Newton Thomas. Atlanta: John Knox Press, 1960.

Bellah, Robert, et al. *Habits of the Heart.* Berkeley: University of California Press, 1985.

Clayton, John Powell, ed. *Ernst Troeltsch and the Future of Theology.* Cambridge: Cambridge University Press, 1976.

Coakley, Sarah. *Christ Without Absolutes.* Oxford: Clarendon Press, 1988.

Gottwald, Norman K. *The Tribes of Yahweh: A Sociology of the Religion of Liberated Israel, 1250–1050 B.C.E.* Maryknoll, N.Y.: Orbis Books, 1979.

Griffin, David Ray, et al., eds. *Varieties of Postmodern Theology.* Albany: SUNY Press, 1989.

Horsley, Richard A. *Sociology and the Jesus Movement.* New York: Crossroad, 1989.

Holmberg, Bengt. *Sociology and the New Testament.* Minneapolis: Fortress Press, 1990.

Johnson, Roger A. "Idealism, Empiricism, and 'Other Religions': Troeltsch's Reading of William James." *Harvard Theological Review* 80 (1987): 449–76.

Jüngel, Eberhard. *Karl Barth, A Theological Legacy.* Translated by Garrett E. Paul. Philadelphia: Westminster Press, 1986.

Köhler, Walther. *Ernst Troeltsch.* Tübingen: J.C.B. Mohr, 1941.

Levinson, Henry Samuel. *The Religious Investigations of William James.* Chapel Hill, N.C.: University of North Carolina Press, 1981.

Meeks, Wayne A. *The First Urban Christians: The Social World of the Apostle Paul.* New Haven: Yale University Press, 1983.

Niebuhr, H. Richard. *Christ and Culture.* New York: Harper & Row, 1951.

———. *The Responsible Self.* New York: Harper & Row, 1963.

Pauck, Wilhelm. *Harnack and Troeltsch: Two Historical Theologians.* New York: Oxford University Press, 1968.

Paul, Garrett E. "*Religionswissenschaft:* The Development of Ernst Troeltsch's Philosophy of Religion, 1895–1914." Ph.D. diss., University of Chicago, 1980.

Reist, Benjamin A. *Towards a Theology of Involvement.* Philadelphia: Westminster Press, 1966.

Roof, Wade Clark, and William McKinney. *American Mainline Religion: Its Changing Shape and Future*. New Brunswick, N.J.: Rutgers University Press, 1987.

Rubanowice, Robert. *Crisis in Consciousness: The Thought of Ernst Troeltsch*. Tallahassee: University Presses of Florida, 1982.

Ruddies, Hartmut, and Friedrich Wilhelm Graf, eds. *Troeltsch-Studien*, Vol. 3, *Protestantismus und Neuzeit*. Gütersloh: Gerd Mohn, 1984.

Tillich, Paul. *Dogmatik: Marburger Vorlesung von 1925*. Edited by Werner Schüssler. Düsseldorf: Patmos-Verlag, 1986.

Welch, Claude. *Protestant Thought in the Nineteenth Century*. Vol. 2, *1870–1914*. New Haven: Yale University Press, 1985.

Wuthnow, Robert. *The Restructuring of American Religion*. Princeton: Princeton University Press, 1988.

Wyman, Walter E., Jr. *The Concept of Glaubenslehre: Ernst Troeltsch and the Theological Heritage of Schleiermacher*. Chico, Calif.: Scholars Press, 1983.

Yasukata, Toshimasa. *Ernst Troeltsch: Systematic Theologian of Radical Historicality*. Atlanta: Scholars Press, 1986.

Glaubenslehre

Von

ERNST TROELTSCH

Nach Heidelberger Vorlesungen
aus den Jahren 1911 und 1912

Mit einem Vorwort von

MARTA TROELTSCH

1925

Verlag von Duncker & Humblot
München und Leipzig

Foreword

Marta Troeltsch

Ernst Troeltsch's scholarly career has come to an end, and his completed work now lies open before the whole scholarly world. What has been published since his death have been either prepared manuscripts, such as the lectures he wrote for the trip he planned to England,[1] or collections of previously published materials, such as the *Spektatorbriefe* ["Spectator letters"],[2] the various essays and addresses on cultural and philosophical matters that were published under the title *Deutscher Geist und Westeuropa* ["The German Spirit and Western Europe"],[3] and, finally, the fourth volume of his collected works.[4] This last-named volume, a collection of essays on the history of ideas [*Geistesgeschichte*], is, sad to say, the closest he ever came to completing his material philosophy of history.[5]

1. Ernst Troeltsch, *Christian Thought: Its History and Application,* ed. Friedrich von Hügel (London: University of London Press, 1923).
2. Ernst Troeltsch, *Spektator-briefe. Aufsätze über die Deutsche Revolution und die Weltpolitik*, ed. Hans Baron (Tübingen: J.C.B. Mohr, 1925).
3. Ernst Troeltsch, *Deutscher Geist und Westeuropa,* ed. Hans Baron (Tübingen: J.C.B. Mohr, 1925).
4. Ernst Troeltsch, *Gesammelte Schriften*, vol. IV, *Aufsätze zur Geistesgeschichte und Religionssoziologie* (Tübingen: J.C.B. Mohr, 1924).
5. Ernst Troeltsch, *Der Historismus und seine Probleme* (The problems of historicism) (Tübingen: J.C.B. Mohr, 1922) was intended as the first of a two-volume study of the philosophy of history. The first volume was devoted to the problems faced by contemporary philosophy of history, while the second volume, which never appeared, was to contain Troeltsch's own constructive material philosophy of history.

3

But the lectures here recorded for posterity are something entirely different: a written account of his spoken word. It is a solitary blossom of Troeltsch's creative work, coming down to us from a time now long gone: a seminar from the Heidelberg years. It is a series of lectures, with all the advantages and disadvantages of that format. Hence it is not a comprehensive scholarly treatise, but primarily a human document. Its strength lies in its character as a spontaneous, living confession. A proper appreciation of the book is possible only if this is kept in mind.

I do not need to make any further concessions concerning the format of this book. Troeltsch's unique personality and style clearly come alive in these lectures. Here we see not the learned author who often tried to compress the entire breadth and depth of his knowledge into highly convoluted sentences, but the born talker who could give forceful expression to the most earnest problems, the "last things," in ways that would nowadays be thought to lie outside the narrow confines of the theological world.

This is precisely what his friends and students have both wanted and needed. Here, for one more time, we can clearly see his far-reaching vision, his daring openness, and, most of all, his profound, reverent piety. No one can truly understand Ernst Troeltsch without understanding these, his basic religious convictions. Therefore I have consented to the requests of his friends and students—who have a claim on these lectures—to have them published, despite my own reservations about bringing them out after they have been shelved for so long, and when their author never had the opportunity to review them for publication. I know myself to be one with his friends in the wish that the Heidelberg theologian be not altogether forgotten in the Berlin philosopher of culture.

This edition includes both the written dictations given to the students at the beginning of each session and the free, spontaneous lectures which followed. Each supplements the other. If anyone merits recognition for this book, it is Baroness Gertrud von le Fort. Her notes, which served as the basis for this book, are a true record of the lectures such as could be kept only by a listener who fully shared in the speaker's conceptual world. In the following pages, we hear Ernst Troeltsch speaking to us once again, even though the echo of his voice has now long since faded away.

Charlottenburg, Easter 1925

Prefatory Remarks

Gertrud von le Fort

In this edition of Ernst Troeltsch's lectures on *Glaubenslehre,* the dictation given at the beginning of each session is printed in italics to distinguish it from the spoken word.[1]

The account of the latter is not a stenographic record, but it is still a mostly literal account. Because the late master constantly reiterated his concepts with a variety of formulations drawn from the great wealth of his creative thought, it was always possible to take at least one of these formulations and to write it down in essence. All of his characteristic expressions and illustrations were actually recorded during the seminar; only the linking adverbs were later inserted. The completed manuscript was personally inspected by the late master, and he expressed satisfaction with it.

For the sake of accuracy, no additions were made to the spoken lecture, despite the inadequacy of the notes, except for the brief synopsis of the chapter on "The Christian Concept of Redemption."[2] As the end of the semester drew near, the notes completely broke off here at several points. The sentences and passages that are interpolated into this chapter, particularly in the second half, are drawn from my transcripts of other lectures by Ernst Troeltsch, especially his lectures on "Practical Christian Ethics," so that even here only

---

1. **This convention is not followed in this translation.**

2. The original has "The Christian Concept of the Soul," but it appears that it is actually the synopsis of the lectures on the concept of redemption that is meant. See below, p. 279.

actual transcriptions of the master's own expressions are used. His words are never supplemented or elaborated by anyone else's.

The lectures conclude with the concept of redemption. Ernst Troeltsch never again dictated or lectured on the two following chapters, which were to complete the system. Only fragmentary sketches of these chapters were found in the deceased master's estate, and they clearly date from a much earlier time. This explains the abrupt denial of the doctrine of the *apokatastasis* [universalism] in contradiction to other parts of the *Glaubenslehre*. To compensate in part for this denial, two sentences from a paragraph which Ernst Troeltsch sketched (but never dictated) for the chapter on "The Christian Concept of the Soul" were used in the paragraphs on "The Universality and Particularity of Grace."

INTRODUCTION AND
PRIOR QUESTIONS

§1. The Concept of *Glaubenslehre* and the Task of the Dogmatic System in Relation to the Principles of the Philosophy of Religion

DICTATION

1. The short introductions of former times started either with a brief discussion of a presupposed universal, rational belief in God, or else with a brief natural theology; in either case, the introduction quickly moved on to affirm the exclusive, supernatural revelation of the Bible. Only then did the real work of dogmatics begin: the systematic organization and scholastic formalization of Bible verses. But since the reorganization of modern theology that began with the work of Schleiermacher,[1] those short introductions have been replaced by a more comprehensive treatment of the principal results of the philosophy of religion. Instead of constructing a natural theology, we now conduct a general investigation into the phenomena and essence of religion; and where an exclusive, supernatural authority was once claimed, we now assess the place of Christianity in the history of religions with reference to a philosophy of history. Hence the Bible is now viewed as a human document, an artifact of Christian history.

This led, in turn, to the development of a new, *independent* component of *Glaubenslehre*, concerned with the essence of religion, the historical stages of the development of religion, and the place of Christianity in the history of religions. Today this task has largely separated from dogmatics and grown into an independent discipline in its own right, sometimes called fundamental theology, the doctrine of religious certainty, or the philosophy of religion. Its results may be summarized as follows: Religion is a unique, essentially independent component of human consciousness. Apart from religion, human consciousness would either succumb to an overwhelming sense of resignation, or else completely wither away. Within this unique domain of human life, a genuine interpenetration of the human spirit and the divine spirit occurs. This presence of God in the human soul has been expressed in the most different forms, depending on the situation, over the course of the development of the human race. Generally speaking, these expressions have ascended through a num-

---

1. Friedrich Schleiermacher (1768–1834), professor of dogmatics at Berlin, exercised great influence on Protestant theology throughout the nineteenth century. His influence extended to Catholic thought in this century and still continues today. He is usually regarded as the father of modern theology.

ber of stages, manifesting a tendency toward higher ethical and spiritual development. In all these forms, we can see the various revelations and self-disclosures of God as they correspond to the particular conditions of the time.

In this perspective, Christianity appears as the definitive and comprehensive breakthrough to a universal, ethical, and purely spiritual religion of redemption that cultivates the values of personality. Insofar as it embraces the most profound and comprehensive, and yet the most inner and personal, communion with God in Christ—a communion that powerfully triumphs over sorrow and sin—Christianity is the highest revelation. And as such it also embraces the highest developments of antiquity.

2. This establishes the important first principles of the independence of religious knowledge and the central place of Christianity. This brings us to the concept of Christianity as a whole, to the general idea of the Christian faith in God, or the concept of the Christian *principle*.[2] "Principle" is simply a summary term for the many diverse religious and ethical ideas and powers of Christianity, signifying a highly diverse and yet individual formation that retains the capacity for continued historical development. This concept of the Christian principle replaces the old concept of biblical authority, while retaining the unity of the spiritual-religious life power that the biblical records express. It now becomes our task to explicate the religious content of this life, comprehended as a unity, in (1) specific concepts of faith, and (2) precepts for living. The former is the task of *Glaubenslehre,* the latter the task of ethics. This brings us to task of the dogmatic system.

3. No discussion of the Christian principle can limit itself solely to a consideration of its original biblical form; we must also consider its impact and subsequent development over the course of the history of Christianity. The Christian principle has passed through the following *stages of development:* early Christianity, Catholicism, old Protestantism, and neo-Protestantism. A contemporary Protestant *Glaubenslehre* will presuppose that the present spiritual and social situation of the Christian life-world has arrived at the stage of neo-Protestantism. Hence theology can no longer simply lift its doctrines from the Bible; it must freely develop them from contemporary Christian life. But since that life is most closely bound to the Bible

2. When Troeltsch uses the word *Prinzip* ("principle"), it carries a far richer meaning than it does in English, where it is usually thought of as an abstraction from concrete reality. What Troeltsch has in mind, however, is no mere abstraction, but an eminently concrete, historical, empirical reality.

and early Christianity, the Bible will continue to exert its proper influence on the form taken by a *Glaubenslehre*.
4. Moreover, theology's significance and its role in the church have also been significantly transformed in the light of a new and different conception of the church. The modern Protestant view of the *church* sees Christianity as a living unity and redemptive power that proceeds from Jesus; but in the broadest sense the church is seen simply as the continued working of the spirit of Christ in general. On the other hand, the various ecclesiastical organizations—churches in the narrower sense—are only the particular and fluctuating forms that serve to propagate this spirit of Christ and to cultivate it in culture. Of course, the particular form that the spirit of Christianity has taken within the various church institutions is, on the whole, basic and binding. But the modern development of the Protestant churches, under the influence of just the sort of fundamental theology we have described here, has tended toward a much looser and less binding organization. Hence our task is only to give an account of the common Christian life of Protestantism, as it corresponds to its own scientific and religious convictions.

This means that theology has now become a somewhat confessional matter, an expression of diverse and individual versions of the living substance of Protestant religiosity. A *Glaubenslehre* will retain nothing of the legislative character of a universally authoritative rule book of religious belief. It will therefore manifest all sorts of individual differences, and it can never be more than a guide to developing one's own insight into the religious beliefs that should undergird practice.

5. The dogmatic system, therefore, should take the form of a consistent, coherent exposition of Protestant Christian beliefs, with reference to all other human knowledge, in such a way as to serve as the center of a *normative, comprehensive worldview*. The need for a systematic expression of the Christian faith is rooted in the systematic nature of human thought, which strives to connect, organize, and unify its diverse contents, never resting until it has achieved a relatively unified perspective (insofar as this is logically possible). This means that a scientific theology must continually take account of, and accommodate itself to, the life of the spirit in general. Hence the dogmatic system is not merely a logical and theoretical exposition of religious faith; it must also concern itself with practical religious meaning. This means that theology, as it constructs a system of beliefs, must seek an inner transformation of the religious life analogous to the transformation of the scientific world-picture. A *Glaubenslehre* is

therefore itself a participant in the never-ending process of religious production. It is a formation of religious faith, corresponding to a particular set of circumstances. However, to be sure, the system itself can come only after the more important task of making adjustments and forming opinions, a process the system can only abstractly summarize.

6. Turning to the development of the system itself, the first question we must consider is that of our *sources*, i.e., identifying those specific manifestations of the Christian principle that can be elevated into a form that corresponds to the present. This question is dealt with under §2. But since, for us, this principle is not merely a historical force but also a revelation of the divine life, we come next to the question of its objective divine content and subjective human manifestation, i.e., the problem of the *essence of revelation* and of faith. This is considered under §3. This practical, living reality is the raw material from which the Christian principle must be scientifically elaborated throughout all theology. Such an elaboration presupposes scientific and philosophical sophistication, which raises the question of the relationship of religious knowledge to philosophical knowledge, i.e., the *relationship of theology and philosophy,* the subject of §4. Only then will we be able to describe the conceptual divisions of the *Glaubenslehre* itself, i.e., the *classification* of the dogmatic material, which will be taken up in §5.

LECTURE

The dogmatics of bygone days was on quite familiar terms with two presuppositions that are no longer with us today. The first was the presupposition of a universal, rational knowledge of God. Its disappearance coincided with the disappearance of a universal normative philosophy—a story that belongs to the history of philosophy. The second was the presupposition of the inspiration of the Bible. The Bible used to yield a supernatural knowledge of God that could be unproblematically tacked on to that prior rational knowledge. According to this thesis, the Bible is in fact not a book at all; those who recorded it were simply God's instruments. It was really written by the Holy Spirit. All this was proven from the Bible's own witness to itself. The considerable age of the Bible also was used to support this view: it seemed to be a miracle that this immutable text could have survived the centuries. The inner criterion of all this was the conversions that the Scriptures produced: no one could read the Bible with open eyes and fail to be moved to faith and to receive miraculous power. This line of reasoning, however, came up against the difficulty that other books seemed capable of producing the same effects. This problem was solved by appeal to the example of the hymnal: the hymnal, like the Bible, did produce spiritual effects, but the hymnal's effects were merely natural, while the Bible's were supernatural.

Given this sort of theological-scientific apparatus, dogmas that were otherwise difficult to defend naturally became quite simple to prove. If the Bible was the chief miracle, all that remained was to provide a synopsis of all the truths it contained. There was a plethora of Bible verses to work with. Hence the task of dogmatics was to organize the depositions that the Holy Spirit had scattered throughout the text, to extract a unified content, and to harmonize the various passages and lacunae that did not fit—for the Holy Spirit's intentions could never be anything but consistent and unified. Beyond this, it was necessary to attend to such dogmas as were difficult to find in the Bible, like the only infrequently mentioned Trinity. It had to be shown that all these dogmas were intended by the Scriptures, and that all the doctrines of Nicaea and Chalcedon were nothing more than the logical consequence of the Scriptures. Since this style of dogmatics had not yet become indolent, all such dogmas had to be formulated according to a specific method. It depended not on the whim of the old masters bound in leather volumes, but was universally observed in all quarters.

Such dogmatics—in the sense of a formalization of the Bible—are rarely encountered today. They are still to be found in America, however, and it is noteworthy that America now constitutes the best market for the older European textbooks of dogmatics. Here, however, this dogmatics has been weakened by a series of assaults, the first of which was pietism. Pietism is essentially identical with modern biblicistic dogmatics. Both have given up on the idea of a general starting point, i.e., the natural knowledge of God (which had become little more than a showpiece anyway). According to the pietist view, the natural man receives nothing of the Spirit of God[3] and is deeply sunk in sin and darkness; at best he has no more than a longing for God, a longing that will nevertheless come to naught. Hence there is no need for philosophy. For both the biblicist and the pietist, the Bible is of course much the same thing that it is for the orthodox, except that there are now fewer proofs of its inspiration. Issues of grammar and natural science are not given great weight, since they

---

3. 1 Cor. 2:14.

can be attributed to human weaknesses and not the Holy Spirit; belief is produced primarily by intensity of feeling. But this approach encounters serious practical difficulties, for it is not easy to tell where inspiration leaves off and where it picks up again. The older theory was cruder, but at least it was more consistent.

Biblicist dogmatics continues to make concessions, but it does so as though it did not. Its biblical criticism busies itself with harmless matters, the faithful hear nothing about it, and things stay just the same as they were in the old days. Of course there is a genuine spirituality and warmth in these circles, certainly deeper than one finds in orthodoxy, but even this spirituality and warmth have their dark side; anyone who does not share their experience is immediately branded as obdurate and hard-hearted. But as soon as the armor of the seventeenth century is cast on the junk heap, human language has already become freer. In fact, these people stand closer to the Bible than they do to Chalcedonian dogmatism. Kähler's ingenious and, in its own way, modern dogmatics may serve as an example.[4]

Schleiermacher rejected both the old Protestant and pietist dogmatics alike. He does, to be sure, have a universal starting point, but it is not the Aristotelian knowledge of God; instead, he begins with the observable religiosity of the human race as a whole. Since religion is to be found everywhere among human beings, then it must be part of being human. Hence Schleiermacher raises the more general issue of religion and the religious consciousness as such. This is the topic of his *Speeches*.[5] Schleiermacher locates the essence of religion in the basic human disposition toward the divine, and in the presence of the divine in the human. On the human side, this presence takes the form of a feeling of absolute dependence, which is also simultaneously a feeling of a divine, sustaining power. But at this point, all that Schleiermacher had managed to conclude was that everyone, from the worst pagan to a Plato, possessed a more or less true religious consciousness; he still had no answer to the question of how a higher consciousness was to be distinguished from a lower one. How could one get from here to the positive, i.e., actual, forms of religions? Is the babel of their differences irrelevant, so that all we need

4. Martin Kähler (1835–1912), *Die Wissenschaft der christlichen Lehre* (The science of Christian doctrine) (Erlangen: A. Deichert, 1885, 3d ed. 1905); and idem, *Dogmatische Zeitfragen* (Dogmatic questions of our time), 2 vols.(Leipzig: A. Deichert, 1898).
5. Friedrich Schleiermacher, *On Religion: Speeches to Its Cultured Despisers*, trans. Richard Crouter (New York: Cambridge University Press, 1988). This highly influential book first appeared in 1799; revised editions appeared in 1806, 1821, and 1831.

do is identify their common basis and separate it from the historical husks? This question divides many. For our part, we lay the greatest emphasis on drawing the distinction: there is a world of difference between the God-consciousness of a wild native of Tierra del Fuego and that of a Christian who acknowledges the command to "Love your neighbor." The holier the divine essence becomes for us, and the more directly that it confronts the human personality, the more important it becomes to make this distinction. This was Schleiermacher's second task: to determine the characteristic features of religion and to ascertain the various stages of religious value and truth. He understood religious life, like life in general, in terms of a development through ascending stages. This series moves in the direction of an ever more pronounced ethics and interiority through the following stages: (1) polydemonic paganism, (2) the era of the great polytheisms bound to powerful nations and empires, wherein the gods already bore spriftual values, and (3) the era of the purely monotheistic-spiritual-ethical religions. The last stage includes two large groups: the religions that grew out of Judaism, and the redemption religions of Buddhism. It is the distinction between the personal and impersonal religions of redemption that becomes important here, and it is on this basis that Schleiermacher affirms Christianity as the highest religion. What we have, then, is not the inspiration of the Bible, but something much broader: the whole of Christianity, comprehended as a unity. Schleiermacher called it a "teleological or ethical religion,"[6] but we prefer to call it a "personalistic religion of redemption." The Bible now becomes simply a moment, albeit one of the most important: It is the literary artifact of the origins. Its significance arises from the fact that it contains the earliest historical documents.[7]

The present will always continue to measure its values against the Bible, but the Bible will never again be taken as inspired. It will also no longer serve as the insuperable limit to Christianity. Instead, it will lead and fructify the development of Christianity, a development that will go beyond the Bible. In reality, not one of the great Christian confessions is wholly, without exception, in agreement with the Bible. For example, the eschatological expectation and the demand

6. See Friedrich Schleiermacher, *The Christian Faith* (1830), trans. H. R. Mackintosh and J. S. Stewart (Edinburgh: T. & T. Clark, 1928), p. 52.
7. See ibid., p. 594.

to refrain from participation in government and society have fallen by the wayside, like much else; for the Bible was not written by the finger of God, even though it often enough is the highest expression for the highest things.

This inner transformation of theology effected a corresponding change in terminology. Where earlier eras had favored the word "dogmatics," Schleiermacher substituted the term *Glaubenslehre,* for we are no longer in the business of fixing permanent laws drawn from the dogmas of an inspired Bible. Instead, we formulate teachings [*Lehren*] which express the essence of Christian piety.

Since Schleiermacher, most theologies have been hodgepodges of various kinds.

One of the more recent of these hodgepodges is the school of Albrecht Ritschl, from which Wilhelm Herrmann comes.[8] It consciously blends biblicistic-authoritarian dogmatics with modern historical theology and philosophy of religion. It embraces Schleiermacher's starting point, except in such a weakened form that it is rendered largely ineffective. The essence of religion is construed such that one must immediately turn to a strict revelation. Religion in general is viewed as nothing more than a desire to unite with a higher power that rules over life; religion is a mere postulate, not a possession. Apart from Christianity, all knowledge is illusion: apart from Christianity there can be no certainty, only a despair to which one must finally succumb. Apart from Christianity there is a tendency to religion, but no revelation.

Somebody has said, "On these terms, I would be an atheist," for not only is revelation supposed to be found only in Christianity, but this same claim is supposed to prove the truth of Christianity as well. For the Ritschlians, anyone who does not share the experience cannot be helped; the experience is prior to everything. The situation is almost as bad for anyone who is tormented by historical doubts concerning the person of Jesus; for it is not scholarship that counts, but personal-mystical experience. But as for any soul on non-Christian

8. Albrecht Ritschl (1822–1889) was one of the most influential theologians of the latter half of the nineteenth century. See his *The Christian Doctrine of Justification and Reconciliation* (1881), trans. H. R. Mackintosh and A. B. Macaulay (Clifton, N.J.: Reference Book Publishers, 1966). Wilhelm Herrmann (1846–1922) was closely identified with Ritschlianism. He was highly critical of Troeltsch, who had made no secret of his opposition to the Ritschlian school. Herrmann also exercised a major influence on the young Karl Barth. See Herrmann, *The Communion of the Christian with God* (1886), trans. Robert T. Voelkel (Philadelphia: Fortress Press, 1971).

soil who feels this desire for God, as soon as they become acquainted with the Bible, humble themselves, and learn to mistrust their own power, they will be redeemed by divine might. The Ritschlian system is therefore really an attenuated philosophy of religion and biblicism; it is no longer really centered in the Bible, but in a christocentric theology.[9] The Old Testament points to Christ and his personality, but Christ himself is no abstract dogma; he is a human individual that we acknowledge in personal experience. Dogmatics is then the unfolding of an interpretation of the world which proceeds from this experience. Ritschl was concerned with the authoritative teaching of Jesus, while Herrmann is more mystical. But neither of them sees the relevance of any scientific knowledge concerning the soul or the world, for that would be purely external knowledge. All that counts is the light of knowledge in Christ.

This is the point at which the Ritschlian school is most vulnerable. The idea that all non-Christian piety is no more than a postulate is simply impossible: all true piety is an experience of God. There have been attempts to mitigate this difficulty by speaking of an "unconscious Christianity." But something about which one need not know anything hardly seems to be indispensable. It is also impossible to claim that the image of Christ carries everything within it. Ritschl is concerned not with the exalted Christ, but with the historical Jesus. Yet we see him only through the mist of two millennia. Jesus can therefore no longer serve as the authority for everything. What does belong to Jesus is what has come from him: a spirit that has brought forth infinitely much that was not there before. But claims of the sort made by the Ritschlian school have been the starting point for all polemics, Protestant and Catholic alike—polemics that have always brought violence, difficulty, and intolerance in their wake.

And so we return to Schleiermacher's approach, according to which the highest living religious power is to be found in Christianity. This, however, immediately sets that great complex we call Christianity before us. How can we get a clearer, sharper picture of Christianity? Christianity is rich in majesty, but also in mediocrity and even caricature. If we look at Christianity, we see the great confessions of the Catholic and Protestant churches, the sects, and, finally, the vaguely religious attitudes—indifferent to institutions—characteristic

---

9. One cannot help but observe the remarkable similarity between Troeltsch's description of Ritschl's and Herrmann's theology and what was soon to emerge as the "new" theology of Karl Barth.

of the modern world. This brings us back to Harnack's quest for the *essence* of Christianity.[10]

Catholicism rejects the question out of hand: You ask only because you don't know! We have infallibility, the living power, so we don't need to formulate it. We know what Christianity is, because we have the Bible, the tradition, the councils, and the pope to interpret them. No further clarification is necessary. Lutheran orthodoxy also finds the question quite simple: The Bible is the Lutheran pope. On the other hand, the pietists say, The essence of Christianity is the Bible plus the personal experience of salvation, for the Bible is no dead book, but witnesses to itself in inner experience. One side turns to the pope and the church, the other to the Bible, but both sides turn to a clearly circumscribed object. But if we follow Schleiermacher, we turn to the totality of Christianity. All that then remains is to identify the essential, basic elements within the whole, and to isolate and exclude the misshapen, accidental, and changeable. Schleiermacher did this in his famous definition: "The essence of Christianity is redemptive, moral monotheism."[11] Hegel found the essence of Christianity in the redemptive perception of the eternal God.[12] For Harnack, it is the forgiveness of sins and the works of the Kingdom of God that it makes possible.[13] But in our *Glaubenslehre,* we will seek to determine the essence of Christianity on the basis of the totality of its historical development.

This approach to determining the essence of Christianity presupposes a knowledge of church history and symbolics. First of all there is the Bible, the literary artifact of the earliest times, which brought Judaism into contact with the entire spiritual vista of late antiquity. This was followed by the age of missions, which was still characterized by a remnant of the earlier messianic hope and by the fervent eschatological expectation that pervades the entire New Testament. But these no longer characterize our situation. The Christianity of

10. See Adolph Harnack, *What Is Christianity?* (1900; the German title, *Wesen des Christentums,* means "Essence of Christianity"), trans. Thomas Bailey Saunders, Fortress Texts in Modern Theology (Philadelphia: Fortress Press, 1986). Also see Troeltsch's lengthy review of Harnack's book, "What does 'Essence of Christianity' mean?" (1903) in *Ernst Troeltsch: Writings on Theology and Religion,* ed. and trans. Robert Morgan and Michael Pye (Atlanta: John Knox Press, 1982), pp. 124–79.

11. Cf. Schleiermacher, *The Christian Faith,* p. 52: "Christianity is a monotheistic faith, belonging to the teleological type of religion."

12. See G.W.F. Hegel (1770–1831), *Phenomenology of Spirit* (1807), trans. A. V. Miller (Oxford: Clarendon Press, 1977); and idem, *Lectures on the Philosophy of Religion* (1832), trans. E. B. Speirs and J. Burdon Sanderson (New York: Humanities Press, 1968).

13. See Harnack, *What Is Christianity?* pp. 57–74.

those times was largely identified with the lower classes of the urban centers of the ancient world. There was no contact with art, science, or philosophy, and the people lived in the full glow of immediate perception. Once this is understood, it becomes clear that it is impossible simply to lift the essence of Christianity from the Bible; only a few world-rejecting sects can ever be capable of doing that. But this insight also frees us from a great many difficulties. We can understand the Bible from its fruits, which even frees us, to a certain extent, from the difficulties that biblical criticism otherwise poses. And we are freed from the obligation to pretend that two millennia of history never happened!

The earliest era and the age of missions was succeeded by Catholicism. This development was neither a lapse nor a perversion, but a step that needed to be taken. Catholicism accepted the challenge of winning the world instead of simply withdrawing and waiting. With the waning of the eschatological hope, Catholicism conceived a plan to encompass and unite the entire human race. That is its greatness! It sought to combine morality, science, and culture with Christian religious and ethical convictions. Catholicism originated the concept of the Christian state. But alongside this it also made use of much that was pagan: the concept of the priesthood, the sacrificial mass, and the twofold ethic. But for our purposes, these are inconsequential; it is the other things that constitute Catholicism's enduring greatness.

To Protestantism fell the task of internalizing religious belief. Much of Catholicism was retained; only the Anabaptists went completely back to the New Testament. But what is the character of Protestantism today? Protestantism has itself undergone development. We shall here presuppose a Protestantism that has grown out of the older Protestantism and made a sharp break with it. Our *Glaubenslehre* is based on the conviction that the authentic, living development of Christianity is now to be found in neo-Protestantism. A theoretical knowledge of this new Protestantism comes, first of all, from its practical, lived reality. Like Schleiermacher, we too build on the contemporary consciousness of the community. A theology of consciousness does not seek the definitive exposition of all Christianity; it only seeks to comprehend contemporary Christianity. But this is no easy task; it is to be undertaken only by one who has the courage and willingness to take a personal stand. Anyone who attempts it will incur a degree of personal risk and responsibility. His *Glaubenslehre* can yield only its own proof, for there is nothing more than the feeling that *here* is the great and powerful flow that takes the present and bears it toward the future. Strictly scientific inquiry leaves off at this point, while personal influence and practical decision are everything. Even Schleiermacher held that *Glaubenslehre* is a matter of decision, although he found it much easier to remain in agreement with the rest of his culture than we do. In his day, the community still had one unified standpoint, but our present world is far more differentiated.

This brings us to the concept of the *church*, something which has undergone a quite remarkable transformation. The dogmatics of the Catholic era were thoroughly determined by the doctrine of the church as the great appointed institution of human salvation. The Protestantism which subsequently emerged thought of itself not as another church, but as the true church. Since its doctrine was based purely on Scripture, the laity were required to submit to it. Censorship followed, and no other form of belief was tolerated. From the universities and their theologians down to the dance teacher, there was one and only one belief—the true belief—throughout the land. It was at least no longer necessary to put unbelievers to death, but they were driven into exile; and it could and did happen that some would be driven from one land to the next and the next and would never find a home, simply because no one anywhere would accept them as orthodox. Today we no longer find ecclesiastically uniform countries, a state of affairs that would have been inconceivable in earlier times. It was formerly thought that the Word of God required uniformity; but today it is only the pietistic groups that strive, somewhat more freely, for the same sort of uniformity, while still submitting their theology to the individual confirmation of personal experience.

This altered conception of the church inexorably leads us to the conclusion that there is no longer any uniform, authoritative truth, but that all partake of it. Nobody believes that Catholicism is the Antichrist any more. A union of the two Protestant churches has taken place.[14] Today even the theologians themselves often display a reserved attitude toward the confessions. Even the Salvation Army

14. The union to which Troeltsch refers took place between the Lutheran and Reformed churches in Prussia in 1817 at the behest of King Friedrich Wilhelm III. It was named the Evangelical Church of the Union (EKU). Schleiermacher's *The Christian Faith,* first issued in 1821–22, endorsed the union, asserting that there was no reason for Lutheran and Reformed to remain divided: "The separation of the two has lacked sufficient grounds" (p. 107). The union nevertheless stirred up much opposition and resentment, particularly among Lutherans. (The North American offshoot of the EKU was the German Evangelical Synod, which produced Reinhold Niebuhr and H. Richard Niebuhr.)

now enjoys official recognition and rights. After the three great confessions have consigned each other to the devil for so many centuries, finally nobody believes that any of them has a monopoly on the truth. This development logically leads to the separation of church and state, something which is already a reality in some places. What really concern people are the fruits of the moral life, while everything else is tolerated.

Another result of this development is the increasing impact that not only tolerance, but also relativism and subjectivism have had on the churches themselves. The confessional differences within Protestantism have now largely disappeared. The most diverse viewpoints can now be found in one and the same congregation. Not long ago a pastor described a succession of his vicars to me: one was a rationalist who preached intellectual and scholarly sermons; another was obsessed with belief in miracles, answer to prayer and the like; and yet another was a former Catholic who had not been able to divest himself altogether of his former beliefs. The congregation took in all of this rather like a short course on the varieties of religious belief; they were greatly interested, and not troubled in the least. Similarly kaleidoscopic preaching can be found every day. The personal devotion and warmth of the pastor increasingly counts for more than the preaching. Hence what we need today is not dogmatically defined doctrine, but an elusive, shared ethical and religious spirit saturated with piety. The pastor is now under much greater pressure to give evidence of regeneration.[15] He no longer simply conveys the Word through which God miraculously works with no regard for his own relationship to it; his personality must now be engaged. It is of the essence of this new dogmatics to see that uniformity is a thing of the past; every significant point in the new dogmatics is touched by this insight. Each person has the right to go their own way. Hence this decidedly new form of *Glaubenslehre* implies the independence of religious communities.

These developments lead some people to insist that the restoration of a unified church is of the greatest importance. The decisive and divisive question is: Shall we give up the people's church [*Volkskirche*] so that we may cling to a firm and unchanging dogmatics, or shall we preserve the people's church and allow dogmatics

15. If it were not for the (relative) anachronism involved, this sentence could have been translated somewhat more literally: "The pastor is now under much greater pressure to show that he is born again." While the term "born again" was not the shibboleth in Troeltsch's world that it is in contemporary popular American religion, it is the literal translation of *wiedergeboren*.

to develop freely? One side recoils at the idea of independent communities, while the other admits that it involves dangers but argues that it is impossible to turn back the clock; life itself has already decided against conformity. Conformity could be achieved, at most, only among the clergy; even Catholicism has not been able to achieve it among the laity. Now even a Haeckel[16] is no longer thrown out of the territorial church. It is only when a pastor holds a divergent opinion that conformity is thought to be under attack. There may have been some justification for this as long as there was still some official uniformity; but why, when this is no longer the case, should the actual nature of the church be concealed?

Most people thoughtlessly presume that here, like everywhere else, order is probably a good thing, even though they know that life itself does not conform. But as long as we have a people's church, we can do no other than make allowances for the existing voices. We cannot insist on a single mind after the fashion of an army; otherwise we will have a church in name only. And even if the whole business is turned over to the professors of theology, who are charged with such matters, the results will be the same; for they, by virtue of their participation in the world of academic freedom, are exposed to the same ideas that constantly bombard the church in the press and in modern life in general. The only way out of this dilemma is a broad-minded church leadership that can respond to all exigencies. A pastor in the neighborhood of Baden has introduced a strongly catholicized form of worship in his parish; and there is nothing wrong with that as long as the people are edified by it. Jatho has had a powerful personal impact—in the name of God! His influence could never have been as harmful as his forcible removal.[17] The worst possible thing would be for the people to believe that their pastors were saying not what they believed, but what they had been told to say. That would be a grave illness for the church. Any other danger pales by comparison. This can be illustrated by Bremen, the ecclesiastical paradise of Germany,

16. The controversial biologist Ernst Haeckel (1834–1919) vigorously promoted Darwinian opinions in Germany, advocated a monistic naturalism, and harshly criticized the church, belief in creation, and traditional religion in general. He was a founder of the *Monistenbund* (Society of Monists).

17. Karl Jatho (1851–1913) was a controversial pastor in Cologne. The liberal opinions he expressed from the pulpit began to elicit opposition in 1905, and he was ultimately dismissed in 1911. His dismissal provoked a great deal of opposition in liberal Protestant circles. See Troeltsch's 1911 essay about the issues raised by the Jatho case, "Gewissensfreiheit" (Freedom of conscience), in *Gesammelte Schriften*, vol. II, *Zur religiösen Lage, Religionsphilosophie, und Ethik* (Tübingen: J.C.B. Mohr, 1922), pp. 134–145. See also Shinichi Sato, "Ernst Troeltsch und der Fall Jatho im Jahre 1911," in *Mitteilungen der Ernst-Troeltsch-Gesellschaft* 4 (1989): 6–21.

where every conceivable opinion was and is possible: the congregation of a Kalthoff, who denied the historicity of Jesus, has since dissolved.[18] What is sensational ultimately becomes boring.

Freedom is not as dangerous as many believe, but conflict certainly is. And behind that conflict stands politics. There is also the concomitant danger that people will no longer realize that ecclesiastical office can still be a wonderful thing. Congregations are not as fractious and quarrelsome as they are often thought to be; it is only in the seriously disturbed, faceless proletarian congregations that things are truly hopeless, and that is just where patience must be exercised at any price. Tolerance and restraint are necessary for academics as well, although not so as ultimately to untie the knot (as Schleiermacher put it), thereby removing all distinction between Christianity and barbarism, between unbelief and culture.—[19]

On the other hand, one might even question whether theology is even necessary anymore, whether it might not be better if everyone did it for themselves. But if we wish to represent so great a complex of ideas, we must do so in such a way that a unified presentation of them is possible. In the interest of truth, it is necessary that an at least partially closed system stand behind the proclamation. Theology is concerned not with scientific but with specifically religious propositions, not with the impact of science but of personality. Science gives us only the systematic and logical principles that guide our inquiry. But a *Glaubenslehre* must be formulated like a worldview, and that means that it must work out an adjustment to the entire spiritual and social environment, including science. This adjustment must be worked out even when theology takes a sharply polemical turn; sometimes theology must adjust to the spirit of the times [*Zeitgeist*] by breaking with it. Even a theology that acknowledges the *Zeitgeist* need not accept everything that comes with it. It is not a question of always scrambling to imitate the most recent fashion, but rather of dealing with the entire spiritual structure of the last few centuries. It is not possible, within the horizon of theology, to take account of the entirety of modern developments; but it is absolutely necessary to come to terms with them.

This important function of theology is often cheerfully omitted. Some people talk as though the difference between faith and knowl-

18. Albert Kalthoff, a cofounder of the *Monistenbund,* denied the historicity of Jesus.

19. The dash (—) following the last period in this paragraph occurs unexplained in the original, here and at a few other places in the lectures. They may signify an omission in the notes, or the end of the day's lecture.

edge confers license to disregard all knowledge. Of course the Bible does not settle cosmological questions for us. But many a *Glaubenslehre* makes the serious mistake of overlooking these issues. In places where these are not burning issues, as in a few rural parishes, it is naturally unnecessary to raise them; but, on the whole, these problems are familiar to everybody and cannot be ignored. The word "apologetics" has a bad ring to it, for it can be used to cover all kinds of fatuous and lazy artifices. Orthodox dogmatics, for example, will bring forth all sorts of specious proofs that the earth is the center of the universe, such as the earth being the only place where human beings can live. Mars would be the only other possibility, but it is too small: "Our Fatherland must be the bigger one."

It is disagreeable always to have to be on the defensive; adjustment is better. Here too Schleiermacher sets a good example. We must have the courage and determination to discharge a lot of ballast. The adjustment will have to come by a process of rejection and refinement.

§2. The Sources of the System

DICTATION

1. *Glaubenslehre* is the dogmatic exposition of the Protestant Christian principle. The principle itself is primarily derived from the consciousness of the contemporary Christian community. But contemporary Christianity simultaneously includes within itself the history of Christianity and its classic developments, which function as the source and norm of contemporary Christianity; hence this contemporary consciousness is historically conditioned through and through. Thus it is necessary to identify the various layers upon which this contemporary consciousness is built. The Bible and the history of Christianity attain their full significance here, because our consciousness is built upon: *(a)* the foundational certainties and impulses that flow from the *Bible,* in particular from the picture of Christ that it contains; *(b)* the great *historical developments* that followed, among which the Reformation occupies an essential place; and finally *(c)* the contemporary forms that *religious experience* takes under present-day conditions.

2. In accordance with the principle that the foundational and productive religious personalities of every religion are authoritative for reproductive religiosity, and in accordance with the particular implications of this principle for Christianity, the authentic and classic

source of all Christian beliefs is the *personality* and *proclamation of Jesus.* Jesus' proclamation is not, however, to be understood as a set of unassailable dogmatic propositions; it should rather be viewed as setting forth a personal religious-moral life and religious-moral spirit. This religious-moral spirit signifies a new and unique ideal of humanity, inaugurating a new, internally redemptive relationship to God. The impact of Jesus' personality continues to persist alongside all dogmatic and cultic christologies; indeed, the importance of Jesus' personality has been enhanced.

This development is the result of the modern historical-critical approach to the Bible and also of the growing emphasis on religious feeling that is part of pietism's legacy. Nevertheless, Jesus' personality is to be viewed not in isolation, but rather *(a)* as the consummation of the prophets, interpreted in terms of their faith in God and their ethics, and *(b)* as the object of the apostolic faith, which first elevated Jesus from Judaism and simple messianism to the level of world significance as the universal redeemer of the human race, and also drew forth the implications of his ethics in opposition to the Jewish Law. Insofar as the Bible sets forth this picture of Jesus—in the Old Testament as the presupposition of his influence, and in the apostolic writings as the documents of the earliest and original faith in Christ—it is the chief stimulus and decisive criterion for all Christian belief. No more extensive explanation of the Bible's meaning and impact is required.

3. The Gospel of Jesus cannot, however, be the sole source and norm of belief; rather, it is the original and seminal form of the Christian life or the Christian principle that grew out of it and subsequently emerged into the broader world of antiquity. This seminal form was laid aside in its subsequent development, and Christianity went on to become a universal, comprehensive principle of life.

Just which personalities in these subsequent developments one emphasizes will vary with personal choice, interpretation, and knowledge; but we must certainly highlight Augustine, the great saints, the mystics, and above all the Reformers as the renewers and developers of the basic strengths of Christianity. The Reformation in particular signified a momentous internalization and moral elevation for Christianity, both of which remain basic to our contemporary Christianity. If we need a comprehensive word to cover all these subsequent developments, the Catholic term *tradition* suggests itself. This tradition, however, is no legislative authority, but something to be freely worked through. That is what distinguishes the Protestant understanding of tradition from the Catholic view. The idea of tradition has now returned to the foreground of contemporary thinking as the result of the modern concept of development; the Reformers lacked this understanding of tradition, thinking that they worked exclusively with the Bible.

4. In addition to the essential role played by historical development in Christianity's ecclesiastical forms, the modern period has brought with it a host of powerful *nonecclesiastical* influences on the Christian religious consciousness; and they too must be counted among our sources. The modern era has not only produced negative attacks on religion, but has also brought about new and positive religious developments that have largely blended with Christian piety, even though they developed on their own, quite apart from Christianity. But they have achieved depth and strength only when merged with Christianity.

These new developments and influences are the following: *(a)* the new understanding of the *value of history,* which means that history can now be understood only as deposit, stimulus, and prototype, and not as a redemptive, cosmic intervention by God into the world— which, in turn, means that redemption is reinterpreted as the acquisition of a higher spiritual life; *(b)* the new *world-picture,* which has spelled the end for both anthropocentrism and the anthropocentric conception of God alike, but which has also goaded piety to a greater level of seriousness and a more elevated majesty; *(c)* the new meaning of *belief in miracles,* which no longer involves detailed, specifically Christian proofs that particular events had a direct divine cause, but now refers rather to an awareness of the presence and influence of God in every evidence of the divine life as a whole; *(d)* the rejection of an absolute *contradiction* between the Christian world and the non-Christian world, which is replaced by the relative contrast of higher and lower stages of religious development, which, in turn, implies a more tolerant and comprehensive religious feeling and a more flexible understanding of the Christian life-world; *(e)* the end of the *concept of the church* as an exclusive, supernatural, authoritative instrument of salvation that possesses unchanging, dogmatic, and universal truths, which has been dismissed in favor of a free and flexible spiritual community, while the organized church institutions now serve as a more or less effective means of propagating this community; *(f)* the dissolution of *sacramentalism* (belief in the efficacy of clerical miracle-working through certain visible means and institutions), which implies the complete transformation of religion into disposition and faith as well as a highly different understanding of the so-called sacraments; *(g)* the displacement of the negative emphasis on *sin* and *conversion* by the impulse to free religious activity; *(h)* the reinterpretation of all *dogmatic and ethical rules* in terms of free and inner attitudes, individually and differently expressed, implying the displacement of all eudaemonistic and external eschatology by the concept of inner development; *(i)* the struggle to combine the purely religious Christian ethic of personality and love with the practical tasks that modern life and modern human activity set before us; *(j)* the influence of the *concept of development* on Christian dualism and pessimism, which has introduced the task of progress and higher development into the concept of redemption. These concepts are all positive forces that have left none of contemporary dogmatics untouched, and we must make explicit reference to them. The extent and character of their influence can be determined only later, in the detailed theological exposition.

5. We come finally to the observation that Jesus and the Bible, the history of Christianity and the Reformation, and modern religious life and thought all can have a genuine religious impact on life *only* if they are personally and subjectively appropriated. All these influences must be blended and unified in personal religious experience. This brings us to the concept of *contemporary religious experience,* or what the older dogmatics called the *testimonium spiritus sancti,* what the Spiritualists called the experience of the spirit or the inner light, and what the mystics called the quickening of the divine spark. This experience is the genuinely decisive source and authority, but it is neither simple nor sudden, nor simply supernatural, nor separable from human thought and feeling. It is rather the product of a living interaction between historical influences and the immediate, though relative, religious productivity of the individual. Hence the evidence will be purely subjective and indemonstrable, although this subjectivity will always include within itself a surrender to historical objectivity; nevertheless, this surrender will take place only in the context of an utterly personal selectivity and nuance. This subjectivity constitutes the mystery of contemporaneous religious activity. This is the only way in which a definite synthesis of all these various sources can be achieved; but it remains a fully personal synthesis nevertheless.

LECTURE

We come now to the question: What sources do we use in our *Glaubenslehre* as we go about the task of formulating the consciousness of the community? This question concerns the various layers of sources and authorities we encounter and their uneven critical value. The sources that come to mind are the Bible, tradition, and personal experience.

But first let us take an unprejudiced look at contemporary Christianity and ask whether it can be exhaustively traced to these three sources. There are elements in it that come neither from the Bible nor from the tradition, but neither are they are personal; they are "modern." Among these modern elements, for example, is the peculiarly modern *love of nature*, which has nothing to do with the Bible. This love of nature takes the form of a feeling for the immanence of God in nature, a feeling that need not necessarily issue in pantheism. For many, this is the bottom line of their piety. The same can be said for the contemporary unwillingness to picture God or his abode. The picture of a human race that stands at the center of all things is an image that no longer resonates for us. On the contrary,

> No one for all eternity
>   Will ever grasp God's nature,
> But truly will he bind himself
>   To us forever.[1]

For us, humanity is no longer the only goal; indeed, it is difficult to affirm that it is even the highest goal. To think that, in spite of the immeasurability of the universe, and in spite of how insignificant our existence really is, we bear something of the divine within us—this is a specifically modern thought. It is not the insight of one specific thinker, but a conviction that permeates all our instincts; and almost every modern dogmatics is filled with it.

We now have a picture of the great richness of the Christian religious life-world and can return to the first of its three layers, the *Bible*. The Bible is not for us, as it was for the orthodox, equally edifying at every point. The picture of Jesus in the New Testament

---

1. The conclusion to "In Harmesnächten" (In nights of sorrow), a short poem from the collection *Stunde* (Hour) by the Swiss poet Conrad Ferdinand Meyer (1825–1888). The entire poem could be translated thus:

> Painfully, I often stretch out my right hand
>   In nights of sorrow
> And I feel, unexpectedly, the grasp
>   Of another —
> No one for all eternity
>   Will ever grasp God's nature,
> But truly will he bind himself
>   To us forever.

See Conrad Ferdinand Meyer, *Werke*, vol. I, ed. Hermann Englehard (Stuttgart: J.G. Cotta'sche Buchhandlung, 1960), p. 35.

immediately and self-evidently leaps out before us, and everything else is organized around it. In the Old Testament it is the Psalms and the prophets that stand out, and also the personal element. The third component of the Bible, the apostolic proclamation, has its greatest value for us in the Pauline letters. The older dogmatics was based more on Paul's letters, especially the Letter to the Romans, than on Jesus; but today people can relate better to Jesus than to the starkly dogmatic Paul.

What finally counts, what the Bible means to us, is chiefly a matter of the personality. We see authentic revelation not in sacred doctrines, but in the strengthening of the God-consciousness communicated to us by the great personalities of the Bible as they dynamically agitate and excite us. Their significance does not lie in their scholarly contribution. Schleiermacher was insignificant as a historical and biblical scholar, and Zinzendorf[2] was not critically sophisticated, but his significance, like Schleiermacher's, is based wholly on personal qualities. This is related to the particular path of development that religion has taken. With Jesus, too, it is neither the teaching nor the moral example that is of first importance, but rather the imponderable nucleus of his entire disposition and his unified life. His individual utterances are of much less importance.

It is impossible to understand Jesus in isolation; we must refer to the Old Testament if we are to understand him. He is the fulfillment of the piety of the prophets and the psalms. It is against the epic background of their greatness that we can first appreciate Jesus' heroic greatness without indulging in the mawkish sentimentality that so easily distorts our picture of him. We unlearn the customary frivolous interpretations of his personality and begin to appreciate its true majesty. Paul, too, is equally indispensable. Jesus himself grew out of the context of Judaism, and hence did not make a conscious break with its legalism and messianism. The earliest communities, for whom the spirit of Christ had become completely separated from the Christ of the flesh, completed the break with Judaism by transforming Jesus from a national messiah into the redeemer of the world. This is why we must insist on the complete Bible, and not, like Ritschl, on only the picture of Jesus. Here, in this focal point, we find everything that

2. Nikolaus Ludwig Zinzendorf (1700–1760) was the leader of the important pietist community that lived on his estate at Herrnhut. This community was the beginning of the Moravian movement. (In German, the Moravians are called *die Herrnhuter,* although they themselves trace their heritage to the Hussites of the fifteenth century.) Schleiermacher was educated in Moravian schools, and although he later broke with them, he continued to be influenced by their piety.

30 INTRODUCTION AND PRIOR QUESTIONS

went before him and everything that has come since; for as long as we cannot produce greater depths of religious strength within our own souls, "Jesus" will remain for us the name in which all salvation is to be found.[3] On the whole, wherever contemporary religious life has severed its ties with Christianity, it has produced nothing to compare with the richness that Christianity, despite all its internal conflict and strife, has to offer.

It is not necessary to have a theory of the Bible. The main thing is that the Bible is there and that we learn to read it properly, i.e., without any critical or dogmatic anxiety and without any scientific interference, but simply as religious people. Even theologians must learn to do this. Whoever seeks life from the book of life must find the passages that resonate within their own soul. Hairsplitting may be left to the appropriate specialists.

The second layer that we encounter is the *tradition*. Although Protestantism theoretically does not recognize tradition in the same way as Catholicism, it nevertheless does play a most significant role in Protestantism. We need only consider what would happen if we actually restricted ourselves completely to the Bible. To do that with utter consistency would simply be to eliminate the millennia that lie between us and the Bible. But this kind of faith is utterly impossible for modern human beings; it could, at most, be possible only in sects. This becomes quite clear if we but recall some of the prevalent themes of the New Testament: "The frame of this world is passing away,"[4] that is, we await the hour in which we will be clothed with the heavenly *doxa* [glory], something which can already be experienced, according to the Bible, in the gift of glossolalia. Or remember the demonology of the gospels, which traces all sorts of illnesses to the work of the devil and the like. No sooner do we immerse ourselves in that milieu than it becomes clear that the Christianity of today is not that of the Bible. Catholicism has fully acknowledged this fact. The finest and sharpest of the Modernists, Loisy, insists upon it in his critique of Harnack: The idea that there is one authoritative gospel, he says, is a fiction![5] Catholicism, much more practical and realistic than Protestantism, recognizes that the gospel is only the germ from which everything else has sprung. The development of

3. See Acts 4:12.
4. 1 Cor. 7:31.
5. Alfred Loisy (1857–1940) was a major figure in the Catholic Modernist movement. He was excommunicated in 1908. See his *The Gospel and the Church* (1903), trans. Christopher Home (Philadelphia: Fortress Press, 1976), which was Loisy's response to Harnack's *What Is Christianity?*

Christianity has not been a process of adulteration, but of becoming. Many of our cultural achievements are related to the gospel only by virtue of being its result in some way.

This brings us to the following conclusion: the more settled in the world Christianity becomes, the more thoughts of the return of Christ will recede into the background. The command given to the rich young man[6] could be meant only for a narrow circle of disciples, not for the masses. There are a thousand such things in the gospel that come under the heading of "historically conditioned." Passages like the beautiful saying about the lilies that neither sow nor reap[7] reflect the circumstances of an oriental culture and a different physical climate. For the people of our lands, it should mean: Take care to work hard, but do not set your heart on it! The gospel's demand to overcome everything with love can be realized only on a relatively small scale, in face-to-face human relationships. It is an oriental idea that the world can be made to conform to human will, that angels will protect us, etc.

Moreover, the anthropomorphic understanding of God is the product of an entirely different world; but it is the doctrine of the nearness of the Last Judgment that is most foreign to us. This doctrine signified not the transitoriness of all things, but their end—an end so imminent that Paul counseled against marriage.[8] Hence we find, side by side with the gospel's majesty and power, a countless host of things most intimately and essentially bound up with it, things which we must starkly reinterpret lest we fall into the most precipitous kind of sectarianism. By the same token, there are thousands of things in our modern Christian world that are far from the world of the gospel. Mass society, a rich cultural and affective world that expresses itself in artistic symbols—these were not present then. But even then, the doctrine of the Spirit foreshadowed how the gospel's most authentic inner instincts would be developed in the future. Only after the grain of wheat fell to the ground could the Spirit come; Jesus was unable to give it to his disciples while he was yet with them.[9] This idea has been fully vindicated; the subsequent history of Christianity has not been a deterioration. Development had to take place on Catholic and Protestant soil alike, and we must recognize its value.

6. Matt. 19:16–22.
7. Matt. 6:28.
8. 1 Cor. 7:25–31.
9. See John 12:24; 17:7.

Protestantism has not, therefore, eliminated tradition, but only an inauthentic traditionalism. It refined Greco-Christian dogma, but did not eliminate it. In its own way, it worked out the same sort of relationship with a non-Christian spiritual tradition (Humanism) that the early church had worked out with Platonism. Protestantism rejected tradition only when the councils threatened to become doctrinal legislatures and the popes to become infallible judges of doctrine. It is not really the case that Protestantism returned to the Bible. We too have taken up the tradition, although not in the Catholic sense. That is why we recognize the confessional writings, though not as binding—that would be the Catholic approach. They are to be treated simply as part of the essential, basic stuff of dogmatics.

We now come to the question of how the tradition is to be understood in its particulars. The sheer mass of the material is overwhelming and requires conceptual digestion. This is a task for church history, a discipline that is usually preoccupied with all manner of details, although its true *religious* task is to distinguish between deviation and development. Knowing the details may be necessary for scholarship, but it is the latter task that is necessary for life. A feeling for Augustine, the great mystics, and the Reformers is indispensable. And this feeling must not be merely intellectual; our soul must partake of it.

But if we wish to appropriate the excellences of the past, we immediately come up against the fact that their impact on us cannot be wholly explained in terms of the past alone. Everywhere in the history of Christianity we find all manner of religious simplifications, distinctions, and elucidations that cannot be explained simply in terms of what went before. So, for example, we concur with Luther's emphasis on solace in the midst of sin while we relegate everything medieval and scholastic to the margins of our consciousness—despite the fact that things medieval were still quite important to him. How has this come to pass? What gives anyone the right to simplify things in this way? Schleiermacher's understanding of God and of humanity is saturated with thoughts of immanence: for him, the divine and the human are not completely separable at any point; miracle becomes only another name for the agency of God. In both examples, there is clearly something at work besides the Bible and the tradition: the modern world's own thought and spiritual insight. This is also true of Harnack's beautiful, but quite unhistorical, formulation of the essence of Christianity.[10] His concept of a human social commonwealth is

10. See Harnack, *What Is Christianity?* pp. 93–101 (literally translated, the title of this book is "The Essence of Christianity").

drawn from Kant.[11] Even in orthodox dogmatics we find all sorts of once-important issues that are now retreating into the background. No longer, for example, do the orthodox theologians view the Bible as a textbook of natural history, and its vague references to such matters are no longer treated as decisive. This was not formerly the case.

Now we must ask: Shall we accept the modern world—which has already imperceptibly extended its influence everywhere into the most personal and private elements of our life—as a source for our theology? The answer is yes, and we will do so openly, not in secret like the orthodox dogmatics that sought to preserve the miracle at Cana by explaining it as the fabulous acceleration of a natural process! We will pay the modern world the compliment of taking it seriously. We will investigate it critically, but criticism always implies a prior, conditional acceptance. We will be cautious, but also quite open.

Up to this point, we have said nothing that many others could not agree with; but we now begin to move in a direction that will make it impossible for many to continue with us. Whoever wishes to oppose our *Glaubenslehre* will have to start here. We hold that it is fundamentally wrongheaded to take a merely negative approach to modern life. We should not always be asking just how far we should go in making concessions to modernity. It is rather a question of reading the indicators. Immanence and humanity, for example, are two important and widespread concepts that belong to the modern world. Neither represents apostasy; both are indicators or proposals, even though their meaning—like all religious meaning—is concealed in various systems and difficult to interpret. They are both essential to contemporary religious life. Immanence echoes and reechoes throughout all of modern poetry. This poetry is something altogether different from the religious songs of days gone by or the rather shabby things one finds tucked away in palm leaves. It signifies a different kind of feeling for life, a dynamic sensitivity to the whole. It is not really pantheism—a word that can signify many different things, anyway. It is a sensitivity to the God who lives, moves, and has his being[12] in the cosmos, the God who creates all and receives all. The concept of humanity, likewise, can be interpreted in many

11. See Immanuel Kant, *Religion within the Limits of Reason Alone*, trans. Theodore M. Greene and Hoyt M. Hudson (New York: Harper & Row, 1960), pp. 85–114.
12. Acts 17:28.

different ways. We could call it a most pagan idea—but for Herder it was a Christian concept. It is an extension of the Christian life. We must always remember that these thoroughly modern ideas are not destructive.

Shall we, then, treat the modern world as nothing more than a great apostasy? It is no more apostate than any other era. Every age has had its God-slayers, cold intellectual natures are no novelty, and fools like the one who said, "I am convinced that God must fear me" cannot be taken as typical of the modern era. We can, on the contrary, clearly recognize God's continuing self-attestation in the modern era as well. But if we do grant the modern era access to our theology, we should do so not in secret, but openly, with full awareness of what we are doing. We shall call a spade a spade.

The first point at which these recent developments have made themselves felt is in our new understanding of the value of history. In earlier times, Jesus' life was understood in terms of a cosmic intervention by a higher world, through which God entered into the sinful, lower world, transforming his wrath into love. But for modern human beings, the life of Jesus is part of the fabric of universal history, which never stands wholly apart from God, but everywhere manifests the battle between the higher divine life and the creaturely life with its downward pull. Jesus is not like a meteor that suddenly appears in the heavens and then descends to the earth. He is not separable from the whole, nor can he be understood except as a part of it. This new understanding of history applies to everything else as well. For us, redemption affects not God, but humanity. We believe in a higher inspiration that emanates from a specific center. The God-consciousness of Jesus radiates upon those who stand within his circle. If we are to understand fully the significance of this *transformation in our estimate of history,* we must realize that history was once thought to have no relationship whatsoever with the divine life. But we no longer perceive any metaphysical transformations of the world. It is not God, but humanity that is destined for love through Christ. This change in our perspective is quite instinctive and intuitive, and for that reason quite difficult to prove. It is closely related to the next point, which is another internal religious realization that is utterly positive, not negative, in character.

The second point at which the modern world has an impact on our theology is the *colossal expansion of our picture of the world* as compared with earlier times. Not only Catholicism but Protestantism as well once rejected Copernicus. Melanchthon[13] dabbled in physics as well as theology. According to him, the earth had to be the center of the universe because it was the site of the incarnation. It was inconceivable that it could have taken place on other stars, for then we would have to draw the blasphemous conclusion that the incarnation had moved about from place to place.

No sooner does our picture of the universe undergo this sort of expansion than the question unavoidably arises: Why did the inconceivable happen on this particular planet? It was at this point that Giordano Bruno, Spinoza, and Leibniz drew the unavoidable conclusion that God's omnipresence extends throughout the universe, spelling the end for the unreasonable intimacy with God that earlier worldview had presumed. The end has come for the naive belief that the sun and the stars were placed there simply to help us tell the time. The human race can no longer be thought of as the purpose of the world. The idyllic coziness of the world is gone! In its place now stands the startling contrast between our own insignificance and the immeasurable vastness and majesty of the universe. Against this backdrop we now look like ephemeral insects; but it is precisely here, in the contrast between our own transience and the infinity of God, that we find a new source of inspiration. It summons up religious feelings that were never there before, and because these ideas are no more provable than the old views, they demand faith. This encounter between the finite and the infinite is another one of the truly positive features of our time.

We now come to the third point: the *new meaning of belief in miracle*. Primitive humanity was perfectly accustomed to the idea that this world is penetrated by another world, that there was an order that flowed from that other world into this one. But the forces that flowed from that other world—unnatural forces—could be set into motion only for the highest goals; hence the concept of miracle became central to religion. Today, these presuppositions no longer hold sway over us. This is why the historical criticism of specific miracles is not particularly important; the real question is not whether certain events did or did not happen. What really counts is the abolition of the two-world concept. These two worlds do not correspond

13. Philipp Melanchthon (1479–1560) was Luther's junior colleague at Wittenberg, and the subject of Troeltsch's dissertation, *Vernunft und Offenbarung bei Johann Gerhard und Melanchthon* (Reason and revelation in Johann Gerhard and Melanchthon) (Göttingen: Vandenhoeck & Ruprecht, 1891).

to the unity that we experience in existence. No self-manifestation of God through some abnormal event would convince us of anything. What does convince us, however, is the vastness of creation and the depth of inner experience.[14] Therefore, the concept of miracle must be vigorously harrowed if apologetics is to defend it. This does not mean that belief in miracle is to be abandoned; on the contrary, the world itself is a miracle. And if the world cannot be grasped as a whole, then neither can it be fully comprehended in detail, quite apart from any supposed occurrences of physically impossible phenomena. The real miracle is the inner miracle, wherein we perceive the power of God and his activity. This process, too, is a case of new adjustment, not negation or apostasy. It is not that we now understand everything and hence have no need of miracle, but rather that our experience of miracle has been both internalized and deepened.

But if this be the case, then there can be *no absolute contradiction* between the Christian and the non-Christian, for proof that greater perfection is to be found within Christianity than without is no longer forthcoming; it is simply not convincing. The concept of a world perverted through original sin and then subsequently redeemed has lost all meaning; it has suffered thousands and thousands of desertions. The contradiction between the Christian and the non-Christian remains, but it is no longer absolute; it is now conceived in terms of a relative contrast between the higher and the lower, between the more and the less pure. This is the fourth point at which the change in the times makes itself felt.

The fifth point follows immediately: the change in our attitude toward the *church*. In earlier times, the church was a great, divine instrument of salvation; it constituted the sphere of the miraculous, outside of which stood the "world." The contemporary church no longer really plays this role, and it is out of the question to think of it as a lightning rod for the reception of supernatural powers that strike down from the heavens. It is simply one of the many great organizations with which we, to whom it pertains, cannot dispense.

The sixth point we must mention is our attitude toward *sacramentalism,* which all of us, quite instinctively, are inclined to dismiss. Sacramentalism signifies an intrinsic connection between a material procedure and a supernatural, divine agency. Jesus knew nothing of

14. It is difficult to translate this sentence without recalling Kant's comment in the conclusion to the Second Critique: "Two things fill the mind with ever new and increasing admiration and awe, the oftener and more steadily we reflect on them: the starry heavens above me and the moral law within me," Immanuel Kant, *Critique of Practical Reason,* trans. Lewis White Beck (New York: Bobbs-Merrill, 1956), p. 166.

such a connection, but it was a feature of Catholicism from the earliest times. Protestantism narrowed the concept, but retained it. Sacramentalism presupposes the reality of two worlds: the spiritual, supersensual world and the material world. Miracle reveals the first in the midst of the second by wrenching physical things out of their context—a view that is no longer possible for us today. The blending of Lutheranism and Calvinism today provides additional evidence for the waning of sacramentalism, which had previously been a key issue in dividing them. Baptism is no longer popularly viewed as a sacrament, but as admission into the church. The Lord's Supper is viewed purely psychologically, which constitutes a growing difficulty for the churches. Only a very few continue to believe that it is a miracle taking place in the sure realm of the senses. This issue in particular was closely tied to Luther's own particular pathos, but we live in a different world. Luther was comforted by the idea of the presence of God within the bounds of the senses precisely because it was tangible and conceivable, while we no longer find such tangibility conceivable—or, at least, we can no longer muster the same degree of pathos over it.

The concept of *redemption*—this is the seventh point—has also undergone a transformation, a transformation that addresses a particular deficiency of Protestantism. Protestantism has not greatly emphasized the ethical impact of conversion, but has been essentially concerned with consolation and the forgiveness of sins. It abandons the world and settles down into a sacred repose with God. But for us, the concept of redemption points in the direction of something more positive and practical. When the two worlds merge into one, then the Christian triumph over sin must necessarily issue in new life. Participation in the world and its tasks becomes a duty. Goethe already realized that what is truly Christian is the *deed*. The contemplative side of redemption has now become subordinate to the heroic.

The eighth point deals with the Christian *ethic*. It used to appear as a law, as something finished, fully realized, derived from a realm of unfailing truth—in opposition to the transient world of the human. The Christian ethic was bound up with the other world and its requirements. On the contrary, we no longer fix our vision on law, but on life. Nor do we any longer seek a Sunday ethic for Christians, but rather an ethic that extends to every day and encompasses everything. The Christian ethic is a matter of attitude. Consequently the radical distinction that was formerly drawn between Christianity and other moral principles, which supposedly did not come straight from God like the Christian principles did, is disappearing. Our interpretation is open to comparison with non-Christian interpretations. Here too we see a movement in the direction of greater depth and psychologizing, toward displacement of the transcendent by the contemporary. Thoughts of reward and punishment become ever more unbearable to the ethical consciousness. The other-worldly can signify nothing other than the gradual emergence of the fruits of the higher life, and an ever deeper inner growth in a divine world of spirit. The modern theologian says: The bureau of eschatology is generally closed these days. This is because the ideas that undergird such eschatology have lost their roots.

We come finally to the *modern concept of development* and its effect on the concept of redemption. We no longer think in terms of protoplasmic guilt, but of development. Humankind has not fallen from a state of guiltlessness through its own sin and frailty; it has risen from darkness to light. This is the sense in which the Christian concept of redemption can make use of the inexact word "progress."

Every one of these points—this must be constantly reiterated—is absolutely not negative. The only question is whether we, in acknowledging them, have moved beyond Christianity proper. And we deny that we have done so. Christianity is the only firm religious capital that we have; a new religion is a possibility only in books. If there is to be a living religion among us, it will be not new, but changed. We need not fear for the future of Christianity.

Nothing we have discussed will become effective for us until it does so through *personal experience*. And this brings us to the third level of our sources and authorities. What comes to us from the outside must be made to live on the inside. This means far more than mere acceptance of the given. Behind it there always stands a personal investment, an often unconscious exegesis, a synthesis or a dissolution. What is truly personal will ever be a secret of life. I have received what I am, but I have received it in actual existence. Of course, we must not idealize this process too much; not everything can be internalized, and much remains mere stuff and authority. And this personal appropriation can yield very different results in different people. Many will never manage to achieve unity, while others will reach it only with effort, while still others will achieve it instinctively. But the process by which it takes place will always remain mysterious, even if it is present only in the tiniest nuances. It is not a miracle that can only be passively witnessed. It contains an element of incomprehensible productivity, something unrepeatable and individual. The depths of this process touch the mystery of being itself. This inner reception and appropriation is also the true aim of all prayer and meditation.

The upshot of all this is that personal appropriation is the real and final source. I sense it, not in any passing excitement or agitation, but because I feel the power that comes over me, a power that is stronger than I am—this is the final court of appeal in every debate. It is in authentic experience that we first see the revelation that is personally granted to us. It is rather like artistic experience, where through love and sympathy we may become absorbed in something remote, and yet finally must always return to our most individual level, where we have the surest evidence of a power that prevails over us. It is characteristic of life that a primal or originating experience is the way it is but once; and if that experience is to be overthrown, it can only happen through something personally convincing.

It is only in this way, in the final analysis, that we develop even our hatreds. When a Nietzsche takes the life of the Christian community to be a democracy of mediocrity, that is ultimately to be traced to a personal, prior conviction—just as when somebody else recognizes: there is more here than meets the eye. What we take as objective must first be illuminated by the center of our own life, so that we hearken within our own breast: here and only here do we find what we seek! In precisely the same measure that what we receive becomes our own, to that extent do we receive the capacity to be productive as well. Not as if we could say, "This is a part of me, while that comes from outside of me!" It is rather a matter of mutual interpenetration. In every religious life, something primary is interwoven with something received.

To conclude: We feed on the tradition, but this tradition would be a dead thing were it not for the productivity of the one who receives life from it. This is what the doctrine of the Holy Spirit is about. The Scriptures can be understood only by one whose eyes have been opened by the Holy Spirit. This is what the Reformers meant by the *testimonium Spiritus sancti*. It is a question of *spiritualizing the Bible*. What we have in the Bible must be grasped first in subjectivity. It is the core of what we find convincing, and the stuff out of which we develop our faith. Everything takes the form that it has acquired in us: the personal remains the touchstone.

§3. Revelation and Faith

DICTATION

1. An analysis of the contemporary consciousness of the community includes more than just a historical analysis of the dominant historical facts. It flows instead from the conviction that, just as

Christianity as a whole is the highest revelation of God, so too contemporary Christianity is not merely human opinion and feeling, but
a living organism stimulated and animated by God. This brings us to
a consideration of the place of the *concept of revelation* in theology.
Such a consideration presupposes that theology's authorities and
sources are not more or less interesting human opinions, but results
of the divine life, or revelation.

2. Orthodox theology acted on this presupposition by locating all
revelation in the Bible as a whole. It then construed everything else
that followed as mere interpretation of the Bible; the revelatory
character of this interpretation was traced back to its link with the
Bible.

But to restrict revelation to the Bible in this way has proven no
more defensible than the old view that took the Bible to be a collection of inerrant propositions. Just as we have had to broaden our
views concerning the sources of the Bible, so too will our perspective
on the exclusive revelation of the Bible have to undergo a similar
broadening. Thus Catholicism teaches that there is a progressive revelation in the church and the tradition; indeed, Catholicism refers
revelation to the open-ended realm of ongoing papal decision. On
the other side, all the mystical and pietistic movements have
acknowledged another revelation alongside that of the Bible; they
locate revelation in the inner experience or the work of the Holy
Spirit that is necessary in order to understand the Bible in the first
place. In both cases we find a concept of *progressive revelation,*
although care is surely taken that it never be allowed to supersede
the primal revelation.

3. Such a concept of progressive revelation is possible only if the
available sources are not viewed as mere human opinion. If these
sources are to mesh with the Bible, then revelation cannot be limited
solely to the Bible, but must also be recognized in the other sources
as well. The Bible—or rather the history to which it witnesses—then
becomes the *foundational and central revelation;* the historic traditions of the church and the modern world of religious feeling become
the *progressive revelation;* and contemporary religious experience
becomes the *contemporary revelation.* Revelation therefore exhibits
stages: its history has never come to an end, extending all the way
down to the present day. Of course, this progressive revelation must
be construed such that it displays a *unified principle* and preserves an
inner continuity throughout all its stages. This is to be accomplished
by repeatedly surveying the primal material [*Urstoff*] and constantly
renewing the harmony of the various stages. These are the critical
means by which this revelation-faith remains Christian.

Of course, one may ask whether a progressive revelation might not lead beyond Christianity. This question used to be considered under the topic of the so-called *perfectibility* of Christianity. Given the independence of the practical religious consciousness and its contents from the vagaries of all theoretical knowledge of the world, we must say that today there can be no question of any such development beyond Christianity, and furthermore that no such possibility lies within our historical horizon. However, one must also say that a developmental perspective on history requires us, in light of how it has happened before in earlier eras, to admit that it is quite conceivable that it could happen again. Apart from this, belief in Christianity's unsurpassability flows quite naturally from Christianity's essence and impact, but this cannot be conclusively demonstrated. In conclusion, we must say that all these developments and transformations should not be viewed so much in terms of perfection, but rather in terms of a living adaptation to the present environment.

4. But it is not only with the concept of a progressive revelation that we must reckon; the very concept of revelation itself has come to be understood differently. The old, *mechanical* concept of revelation has been replaced by a *dynamic* concept, something for which Luther himself set a very clear precedent. No longer is it a question of immutable supernatural truths, but rather of an inner awareness that issues from the mysterious connection of the divine and human spirits, which denotes the whole of the inner life, with its religious and ethical convictions and values. It is just such a whole that emerges directly from the great biblical personalities, i.e., the prophets, Jesus, and the great apostles. The Bible is therefore always a revelation, insofar as it presents us with a picture of these historical-personal powers in a way that continues to be effective today. It is a witness to revelation, not the revelation itself; but the same can be said for all the forms of faith that followed, all the way down to present-day experience, with the sole proviso that they stand under the governing influence of the archetypal productive personalities. They constitute the *reproductive revelation* in which there is always an element of relative productivity. As a result, the absolute distinction between Christian and non-Christian revelation falls to the wayside. Instead, we now distinguish between higher and lower revelations, a distinction that even the old church recognized with its theory of the so-called natural revelation, a theory that helped it to blend the ancient world's ethics and religiosity into Christianity. Today, we may likewise conclude that the stirrings of the modern world may be ascribed to God and with equal right be blended into Christian piety.

5. Given these presuppositions, we may say that the contemporary consciousness of the Protestant community, measured in terms of its authoritative and productive powers, is also based on revelation; but the revelation it contains is not the immediate source of our *Glaubenslehre*. Dynamically understood, revelation exists not in isolation and immediacy for itself, but rather in its effects. It can be only indirectly grasped in the founding personalities, for whom it was the ground of their entire world of impressions, feelings, and intentions; but apart from these, it cannot be grasped at all. Yet it is also present in all subsequent developments and contemporary experiences, as well as in the very human and temporal realm of thought and feeling. Revelation immediately transfers from the realm of the human spirit to the realm of human thought, imagination, and will, always manifesting itself only as the inner essence [*Inbegriff*] of the human concepts of God, world, humanity, beginning and end, living values and moral commands—concepts that give every indication of being influenced by time, environment, descent, and upbringing.

This is how the biblical-Christian imaginative and conceptual world took its basic form in the classical revelatory personalities; but it is also the way in which an original, imaginative interpretation [*Vorstellungsdeutung*] issues forth in tradition and contemporary piety. In religious language, this imaginative interpretation is called faith; it is the uniquely religious form of conceptual and imaginative thought. A proper insight into the nature of this faith is therefore a prerequisite for a correct understanding of the task of dogmatics.

6. On this basis, we can now clarify the *twofold* nature of faith: it is, on the one hand, a practical attitude and approach toward the whole of life; on the other hand, it also formulates and conceptualizes religious impressions and concepts. As a practical attitude, faith interprets the inner awakening of a new, living reality (which is the basis of faith), a reality which must be described as a comprehensive disposition and temperament. Faith's conceptual function, on the other hand, consists in explaining and explicating the impulses that the temperament contains. This is why the concept of faith has been misunderstood and disputed.

In fact, both functions of faith belong together; it is just as dangerous for faith to degenerate into empty, thoughtless opinion as it is for faith to harden into rigid intellectualism and become nothing more than mere doctrine and authority. If it is the peculiar tendency of Protestantism to emphasize faith and to think of it as a unified attitude, that must be understood as a reaction to Catholic sacramentalism and ritualism. But that reaction should not lead to a corresponding overemphasis on the other side of faith, that is, an overemphasis on faith as the inner essence of specifically religious conceptions. Faith's relation to this comprehensive *attitude* is what connects it to the *revelatory* impulse. This impulse is properly understood only when we realize that faith is the inner essence of religious concepts and impressions. Faith is equally both, the attitude and the inner essence; but because faith traces this attitude back to the revelation on which it rests, we must turn to a closer inspection of this inner essence. Hence we now take up the question of the essence and *cognitive value* of faith as religious knowledge.

7. Faith is the specifically religious form of knowledge. Psychologically, its essence consists in the expression of basic religious positions in terms of malleable, living perceptions and visions. Perceiving its objects in symbolic and contemplative forms, it uses all the various media that the emerging and encompassing symbolic universe can offer; but when it does become necessary to develop an essentially new religious content, then faith takes these already given media and imparts a new character to them, accentuating some elements and eliminating others, inferring new connections and perspectives. But these perceptions are accompanied by a strongly felt conviction of reality and truth that clearly distinguishes them from mere artistic fantasies or images.

This is how belief in the great *bearers of revelation* and in the central personalities themselves becomes authoritative and decisive for the community at large. The symbolic universe they create, and upon which they leave their impression, is the means by which they convey their religious possessions to their followers and believers. Hence, their conceptual beliefs constitute the enduring and essential symbol of the religious power that radiates from them and influences the present. And insofar as they become authorities for their believers, they themselves become the objects of their followers' own faith-constructions. Thus they, as well the meaning and majesty that believers ascribe to them, are added to the inner essence of faith and its various images. Thus every universal (and no longer simply national or racial) religion is characterized by faith in its God and in its founders. To be sure, this faith undergoes a vast number of modifications, elaborations, and transformations over the course of time, but the enduring faith of the formative, primal era continues to undergird its inner religious content throughout its subsequent development and interweaving with later conceptual worlds.

8. *Rationalism* denies that faith has any epistemological value; it seeks to transform faith into truths of reason, i.e., into necessary

concepts that follow from some kind of ultimate principle. Even less helpful is *positivism,* which ascribes no epistemological value to symbol or imagination and furthermore takes rationalistic metaphysics to be nothing but illusion. Least helpful of all is theological *dogmatism,* which has no interest in a human interpretation of a religious life-content, but rather seeks immutable, divinely assured truths. But none of these objections is convincing. Faith receives its warrant from its underlying religious substance. Faith is true insofar as (1) this basic substance yields practical moral and religious evidence of being the highest revelation, and (2) its conceptual world yields a clear and living expression of this impulse.

Faith's epistemological value therefore depends on the religious significance of its ground of revelation and on the depth and clarity with which it expresses this ground. Its epistemological value is not measured in terms of its adequacy to an objective knowledge; it is rather the adequacy of its interpretation of its basic religious possession that it interprets that counts. Furthermore, faith always remains a matter of *symbolism;* even when it is subjected to scientific elaboration and refinement, its specifically religious character derives directly from the liveliness of its symbols.

9. Faith is therefore always prior to dogmatics and to teaching about faith [*Glaubenslehre*]; it is more original, more alive, and generally more popular. But faith also has important needs: it needs to have the disorderly and excessive growth to which it is prone constantly pruned back to a practical religious foundation. It also needs to be assembled and unified within a comprehensive system of religious and ethical concepts. Finally, as part of faith's interrelationship with other forms of the imaginative and informative life, it needs to participate in scientific dialogue with nonreligious forms of knowledge. That brings us, at last, to the need to formulate faith in a way that makes it accessible to the community for practical, cultic, and pedagogical purposes.

These four requirements make it necessary for theology to engage in *scientific* activity. Theology therefore undertakes the scientific cultivation and regulation of faith, but it does not seek to transform faith into scientific and rational knowledge. Rather, even as it goes about its tasks, it preserves faith's practical-religious and symbolic-contemplative character.

LECTURE

We now take up the question of the revelatory character of our sources. We are concerned not only with the characteristics of becoming and being, but primarily with recognizing those self-authenticating authorities upon which we wish to build our faith. This means that we sense within them something more than the purely finite and purely historical—we sense that they are interwoven with the divine life.

Orthodoxy answers the question this way: Christianity and the Bible are identical. That answer, though, is just as complex as it sounds simple; "Bible" means "biblical interpretation." Hence Catholics are quite right to respond: "The controversy between us is not over the Bible, but over its meaning." As soon as we realize this, we can grasp the difficulty of the Protestant position. In order to say that the Bible is revelation, we must ascribe to it the capacity to interpret itself. But, on the contrary, Protestantism has itself experienced nothing but conflict over interpretation of the Bible. The Bible does not interpret itself; instead, it has turned out to be the book in which everyone can seek and find their own dogmas. There is another revelation that stands alongside the Bible, a subjective element to which the doctrine of the Holy Spirit attests. Hence we must recognize other sources of revelation besides the Bible. We are heirs to a tradition that extends throughout the whole of history down to our own day, a day whose life also flows from God. We hold to the concept of a *progressive* revelation.

The concept of a progressive revelation is self-explanatory to Catholicism. It sees Protestantism as dead because it restricts itself to a single localized book. By way of contrast, Catholicism possesses the flood of the great ideas of history, and, if need be, the dikes to contain this flood. On this point one may compare Cardinal Newman[1] and Father Tyrell,[2] who, incidentally, was one of the purest, most religious characters of our time. He was excommunicated, but in the hour of his death he found a courageous priest who gave him the last rites.

We can give only a partial assent to the Catholic conception of tradition, however, for we cannot accept it as something established for all time. The experience of spirit must finally be a personally convincing revelation. So it is really only we who can say: "We know what revelation is, because we have it." Even the revelation of the

---

1. John Henry Newman (1801–1890) was a leading figure in the Oxford Movement; he eventually converted to Catholicism and was later elevated to Cardinal. Troeltsch perhaps was thinking of Newman's 1845 treatise, *An Essay on the Development of Christian Doctrine* (Baltimore: Harmondsworth, 1975).

2. George Tyrell (1861–1909) was an Irish Anglican convert to Catholicism who became a Jesuit. One of the earliest of the Catholic Modernists, Tyrell was suspended from the priesthood in 1906 and then excommunicated in 1907 for his protest against the encyclical *Pascendi*.

Apostles and the Fathers must be understood in terms of the inner penetration of the spirit. What separates us from Catholicism is a question of magnitude, not principle. Past revelation can be understood only in the light of present revelation. The word is but the remains of life, and not life itself. Taken by itself, the letter kills.[3] It is only when life can be breathed back into the remains that we can have more than mere letters.

Several objections to this concept of progressive revelation are encountered. It is suggested that we are in danger of falling into an unlimited subjectivism. But this danger has not appeared very great for some time now, unless Protestantism itself is subjectivism. The maze of churches and sects that is Protestantism attests all too clearly to the impossibility of a single uniform interpretation, unless it is simply an option that no one has exercised. There assuredly is subjectivism in Protestantism, but only the subjectivism that flows from Protestantism's principle and essence. Moreover, this subjectivism is moderated through the influence of the great biblical personalities that always remain the central revelation as they grasp our life. Life interprets life, spirit interprets spirit. In the second place stands the tradition, which conducts the revelation; and finally, as a conclusion, comes the life of the present.

Amid all the variety, the basic direction remains the same, so that it is possible to bring unity out of diversity. Everything is to be measured against Jesus and Paul, who are the central expression of the faith; they are like a pole to which our compass needle points, drawn to some kind of energy that lies in them. At this point, the task of theology is harmonization—a task begun anew in every age. It is not our job to discover something that has never been found before, but rather to find in our own way what others have found in theirs—but which never can be found once and for all. Unity can be found only in the principle. This is also what the theological side of church history and the history of dogma is all about: identifying the continuity. In this connection, we should mention Biedermann,[4] whose work may be contradicted at many points but who nevertheless undertook the task with all seriousness.

The second great topic connected with the concept of progressive revelation is the problem of *perfectibility,* a term bequeathed to us by the Enlightenment. See the essay by Zeller in the *Tübinger Theologischen Jahrbüchern,* recently reprinted in the third volume of his

3. See 2 Cor. 3:6.
4. Alois Biedermann (1819–1885), a Swiss Reformed theologian.

collected writings;[5] the term is sprinkled liberally throughout. The older theology understood the concept of inner adaptation in terms of perfection. But for those schooled in historical thinking, there can be no such thing as perfected thought; there is only thought that corresponds to changes in the present situation. It is in these terms, and not in terms of perfectibility, that the problem must be formulated. For it is undeniably here, where we recognize the validity of new and changing formulations, that we must earnestly contemplate the serious danger that they may go beyond Christianity and become something utterly different. The question is: Are we still developing in continuity with Christianity, or are we headed into a religious future that will no longer be Christian?

Our judgment on the matter is this: If we are convinced that our inner-practical-religious life (to be contrasted with purely scientific-theoretical inquiry) has a far-reaching impact on the shaping of our character, then we need not fear any new configurations. A completely new religion could develop only if it could demonstrate a stronger religious power to us. This will not come to pass. Christianity has not been surpassed. Theoretical changes have not touched its inner essence; and when we take these theoretical changes into account, we can and must affirm Christianity's religious content, because there is nothing similar, or more profound, on our whole horizon.

Hence the *mechanical* understanding of revelation yields to the *dynamic* concept of a progressive revelation. We no longer have supernatural communications; in their place we find a surging consciousness of the unity of the human and divine spirits. The mystery in this event remains, but now it is the mystery of an inner, living disposition. Wherever there is spirit, there is revelation, in preaching as well as in Scripture. It was never any different with the great religious personalities. But whatever presence characterized their lives should also characterize the lives of those who follow them; and this observation brings us to the concept of *reproductive* revelation.

The concept of reproductive revelation already suggests the image of a spark that leaps from heart to heart, igniting a different flame in each, according to what it finds therein. Productive revelation already carries the reproductive revelation within itself. The latter too is a creation of spirit, reaching into the depths of the spirit's own life:

5. Eduard Zeller (1819–1885) was a highly influential theologian and historian of philosophy. Troeltsch's reference is to Otto Leuze, ed., *Eduard Zellers kleine Schriften*, vol. 3 (Berlin: G. Reimer, 1910–11).

image becomes archetype, intrinsic to the self. The spark comes from the outside, but it is the soul that must be ignited. It is, to be sure, usually a relatively small matter; but even so, it is genuinely productive. Schleiermacher speaks of the communication of Christ's efficacy to the religious consciousness.[6] A whole series of theologians has subsequently affirmed much the same thing according to their own lights—Herrmann most enthusiastically of them all.

At this point, however, we encounter a difficulty: have we not reduced revelation to no more than a spiritual state of mind, making it impossible to distinguish Christian from non-Christian? This is a legitimate question, although too sweeping in this formulation. The material distinction between Christian and non-Christian remains. The Christian revelation is not identical to the Brahmanic [Hindu]. Their differences remain substantial; what has changed is that we, unlike the earlier theologians, no longer depict the former as divine and the latter as human. Generally speaking, there is revelation wherever the totality of an ethical and religious life appears in combination with an awareness that it proceeds from God. This should come as no surprise—for to make a distinction between divine and extradivine revelation where none exists is simply to exchange one futile artifice for another. As soon as we broaden our perspective to include non-Christian piety, the differences cease to be absolute. Plotinus and Paul both possessed immediate communion. Christianity itself could not have begun in any other way; it too must be understood as a mixture of the divine and the human. Neoplatonism put the matter differently: everything is simultaneously divine and human. We certainly make distinctions regarding content, profundity, and majesty, but not between human and divine. The early church did essentially the same thing when it appropriated the concept of a "natural" revelation. It could do so only because it regarded the natural revelation at its deepest level as also a divine revelation.

If revelation is understood in this way, then it cannot be the immediate object of dogmatics, for it takes place in the innermost depths of the personality. It becomes conceivable only insofar as it can be expressed in words; and to express it in words, we must make use of general concepts and images; but these general concepts must be ordered according to revelation's inner, latent impulse. Revelation requires intelligible forms; without language, which is always historical, it could never be passed on. This transformation is universal and

6. Friedrich Schleiermacher, *The Christian Faith* (1830), trans. H. R. Mackintosh and J. S. Stewart (Edinburgh: T. & T. Clark, 1928), pp. 425ff.

unavoidable; we never encounter the revelation itself, but rather its subsequent development and rendering. Development can never exhaust the revelation's inner impulse, but only give shape to its driving power. We call this development and rendering of the revelation "faith"; it transforms an inner experience into a complex of human concepts and precepts. When we appropriate the concepts of faith, they act like a transparency through which we can see the actual impulse itself; and when they resonate and reverberate in us, a genuinely living connection with the divine life ultimately emerges. Revelation and faith are not identical, but they are correlated. No revelation can fail to be transformed into faith, and there is no faith apart from revelation. But a dogmatic exposition of the revelation itself is not possible; what is possible is a dogmatic exposition of faith—which is saturated by revelation. It is through faith that revelation becomes accessible in the first place.

This theory is not new. It is already present in Luther, and quite elegantly formulated by Kaspar Schwenkfeld and Sebastian Franck.[7] Franck, in particular, was one of the most profound spirits of his day, even if now he is forgotten. This is what the distinction between "the spirit and the letter" or "the spirit and the word" is all about. For Jesus too, spirit comes before the word. "Spirit" here means the same thing as what we call "revelation." But spirit can reproduce itself only by means of the word.

This clarifies the twofold meaning of the concept of faith. For some people, faith means submission to the accepted truths of revelation, while for others it means an attitude of confidence. But it cannot be an either/or. The former leaves no room for the religious soul, while the latter fails to answer the question, "Confidence in what?" Confidence always implies acceptance of something as genuinely real. Faith is both: confidence in something, and believing something to be true. Confidence makes no sense unless I know what I have confidence in; and insofar as I *know* it, it is a matter of *knowledge,* of believing something to be true. Therefore, faith consists of both practical and theoretical elements. This leads us to ask the following question: To what extent does the theoretical element of faith yield authentic knowledge of reality?

Faith does not provide any experience or knowledge of things; instead, it provides an interpretation of things in a specific light. That

7. Kaspar Schwenkfeld (1489–1561) and Sebastian Franck (1499–1542) were both important figures in the Reformation. They are often considered heirs of the German mystical tradition and precursors of pietism.

is how it is, for example, with the idea that spirit both flows from and returns to God. Interpretation involves symbolic thinking; it is primarily a product of the imagination, which is seeking to express the inexpressible. The truth of such interpretation depends not on its agreement with scientific thought but on the breadth and depth of the living impulse that underlies it. Faith and its interpretations will not help us build steamships and railroads. Faith is borne of the distress, passion, and exaltation of our spirit, whose highest and fieriest flights are already quite vivid before our eyes. The conceptual world of faith, then, has much in common with symbolic poetic discourse; it differs, however, in that the concepts of faith are not a matter of play, nor are they interchangeable. Faith is a kind of poetry that lives from a consciousness that does not seek to be poetic. Faith intends to express an authentic life, subjection to which is a duty. Its truth is of an entirely different order than scientific truth; but it is truth nevertheless.

The chief opposition to this religious conception of life comes from pure *rationalism*. Rationalism finds this all much too poetic, much too iconic. It would prefer to treat faith as a matter of scientifically demonstrable knowledge. Such a desire is certainly understandable in a person gifted with a highly logical nature. The only objection that we have to this desire is that it is refuted by the facts: it has never happened. With all the internal contradictions of the religious life, with all its depths of despair and summits of bliss, faith has never been successfully transformed into rational thought. No predicate can fully circumscribe God; as soon as we make the shift to scientific discourse, we are confronted by the impossibility of expressing his essence without dividing it. The only thing we can express is what is experienced, not any logical deductions. The opposition between the ardor of experience and whatever contradicts it in thought will always remain; that is what the history of theological controversies is all about. But the conclusive demonstration that religion cannot be reduced to science is this: substituting scientific discourse for religious discourse leads to the dissolution of religion. And if this is the case, then we must recognize that faith grasps something real, and we must allow it the freedom and vitality to express that reality.

Another objection accepts the premise that religion is not the result of rational inference, but warns that science will open itself to all sorts of fantasy and nonsense if it acknowledges that there is any truth in religion. It says: There is nothing transcendent anywhere; all that there is, is firmly rooted on this earth. God, the soul, and immortality are illusions. This is the voice of *positivism*. Positivism thinks of religion as poetry; and positivist philosophy views metaphysics as the great seductress of humankind. For positivism, metaphysics is nothing but poetry grown pedantic. This poses the question: Can imagination provide any genuine knowledge of life, or not? A negative answer to this question would mean a colossal impoverishment of life; it would cut off access to a whole range of hidden realities. The question cannot, however, be decided on purely scientific grounds. All that remains certain is that it is the property of the imagination to express the inexpressible, not simply for the sake of amusement, but to discover things that cannot be discovered scientifically. Imagination grasps that which science cannot grasp—for imagination perceives the whole, which can be represented only through symbols and images.

Yet a third objection is raised by the hard-line *theologians,* who are not interested in having to rescue dogmatic concepts from some twilight of the imagination; they want the firm foundation of revealed doctrine. They say: Since religious images have an immediate grasp of reality, they must be divine communications. Therefore, they should not be understood, but believed. We naturally find this objection just as untenable as the others; for we hold that there is an underlying, objective revelatory impulse which is subjectively interpreted. We have images of faith, not a science of revelation.

In light of all this, we might ask whether it would not be best simply to give oneself over completely to faith, since faith is not a matter of scientific knowledge anyway. There are millions of people who do live on just such a freely sprouting faith, without the benefit of any scholarship. If this is possible, then what need have we of theology? Theology can regulate faith and give order to the wild and luxuriant growth of images. Left to itself, faith has a propensity to excrescence, dissipation, and indifference. One person fantasizes about the last things, another about a love affair with the Savior, while Jatho's God turns up pantheistically in every part of nature and yet remains an object of theistic experience—two things that do not go together. The task of preaching requires that such wild formulations be brought under control. This control must always return to the underlying impulse; it must ascertain to what extent the various images of faith really arise from religious circumstance, and to what extent they lead away from it. Religious experience should always shine through the images. This means that we will need to delete a great many things that no longer have any meaning. Theology can also develop faith's inner conceptual unity despite the contradictions.

It can point, for example, to the inner logic of such concepts as God and world, and it can develop them in a systematic context. This is done not as philosophical theory, but as experience and description of the whole. And finally, theology can stretch the boundaries at the points where faith and science confront one another. All these are tasks that make theology necessary.

Glaubenslehre is neither philosophy nor science, but theology. Yet it does stand in need of scientific knowledge and training: the results of the philosophy of religion and the psychology of religion, the acuity of logic, the observing mind, and the capacity for objective self-immersion. Theology also requires the ability to formulate disagreements and conflicts with science. But the subject matter is unscientific; it is simply given. Theology's conceptualizations are nontheoretical. Schleiermacher's difficult, yet classic *Glaubenslehre*[8] is a masterful model of this approach. No dogmatics since his has even come close to matching his achievement. Among more recent dogmatics, the works of Ritschl,[9] Biedermann,[10] and Pfleiderer[11] stand out, although Pfleiderer's is rather flat and wishy-washy. But even today, Schleiermacher's dogmatics remains the most intrinsic and profound of all.

§4. Faith and Knowledge, Theology and Philosophy

DICTATION

1. The knowledge proper to faith arises from the revelation that it interprets. It is a specifically religious form of knowledge, a disposition toward reality as whole, based on a specifically religious position. This is what distinguishes faith from all scientific knowledge and establishes its *independence in principle* from scientific knowledge. Faith is the religious comprehension, interpretation, and valuation of reality, not a rational, systematic explanation of reality. Hence it follows that the practical religious consciousness, based on temperament, character, and life-style, is independent in principle from the theoretical consciousness, which is based on rationalization and logi-

8. Schleiermacher, *The Christian Faith.*

9. Albrecht Ritschl, *The Christian Doctrine of Justification and Reconciliation* (1881), trans. H. R. Mackintosh and A. B. Macaulay (Clifton, N.J.: Reference Book Publishers, 1966).

10. Alois Biedermann, *Christliche Dogmatik*, 2 vols., 2d ed. (Berlin: G. Reimer, 1884–85).

11. Otto Pfleiderer (1839–1908), *Grundriss der christlichen Glaubens- und Sittenlehre* (Compendium of Christian faith and morals), 6th ed. (Berlin: G. Reimer, 1898).

cal unity. That is what makes it possible for the religious consciousness to continue with the same basic orientation even when the theoretical consciousness undergoes various transformations.

But this only a relative independence; for any interpretation of the central meaning of the faith and its revelatory impulse must still take place in the context of all of life and thought. Moreover, this interpretation must agree with knowledge derived from other sources, or, when it runs contrary to such knowledge, it must substantiate the contradiction. It is particularly a task of the dogmatic elaboration of faith and its images to attend to nonreligious knowledge and to eliminate the most blatant contradictions.

Hence, despite the very real independence of faith and religious knowledge from theoretical knowledge, there is also a significant *relative dependence* on both sides; the practical effects of this dependence can be seen whenever popular religious movements are adopted by intellectual elites, and they can also be seen whenever major upheavals of the theoretical world-consciousness make themselves felt in society. The nature of this encounter between practical religious knowledge and theoretical knowledge varies, however, according to whether it is an encounter with the more narrowly defined scholarly disciplines or an encounter with the broader synthesis of all these disciplines in a universal system, i.e., philosophy.

2. First, faith's relationship to the specific scholarly *disciplines:* the discoveries of every age are stockpiled in these disciplines, and they have a powerful influence on the practical dimension of life. Here we may speak of an almost complete incommensurability and neutrality between faith and the disciplines so long as we restrict ourselves to questions of detailed research in the narrow sense. But these detailed investigations also give rise to the more broadly generalized scholarly disciplines that have a substantial impact on our worldview and world-interpretation: cosmology, geology, biology, anthropology, and universal history. These disciplines have yielded specific results that may be regarded as certain, at least in their main points. Religious faith must now take a positive approach to these results, accepting them but also submitting them to its own religious conceptualization and interpretation. This is one of the most important tasks of modern theology. On this question, the old biblicistic and scholastic dogmatics were closely bound to the popular and philosophical world-picture of antiquity. Faith must detach itself from this philosophical world-picture and adapt to the *new* one; and this new world-picture, moreover, is less the result of philosophy than it is of specific disciplinary research. The contemporary crisis of faith and of theology is to a

large degree rooted in this problem, and it will not be possible for the Christian life-world to reassert itself until this problem is resolved by a new adaptation to the new world-picture. But whether this is possible, and if so, how it can be done, are questions that must be deferred until the detailed execution of the dogmatic task begins.

3. With respect to philosophy in the proper sense of the term, we must rule out any attempt to treat religious faith and knowledge as general metaphysical hypotheses about the unity and ground of the universe. In this respect, religious experience is altogether different in principle from all logically unified knowledge. The former refers to internal and personal appropriation of a most real and vital basis of life which reveals and imparts power; the latter refers to transitory and contingent hypotheses which reflect the endless variety of inconclusive data that are inherent in the quest for an abstract unity. To be sure, their goals are congruous: Religious faith and philosophical metaphysics both seek the absolute, but they understand and seek it in different ways. Faith and philosophy can, at most, converge; they are never interchangeable. Their difference is essential, but so too is their potential for convergence, apart from which it would be impossible to have a religious life-world of any real consequence. Furthermore, a complete rejection of metaphysics is itself a metaphysic, a metaphysic which is, moreover, contrary to faith.

4. The possibility of such *convergence* depends on two other possibilities. The first is that, despite the complete separation of religious and metaphysical knowledge, the latter could be so constituted that the two could coexist in the context of a general view of things. In other words, since religion presupposes the dominion of the spirit and the goals of the spirit over the world, religion can be affirmed only in connection with a metaphysics that is ideological and teleological in principle. This excludes not only materialism and positivism, but also parallelist pantheism (in the proper sense), pessimism, and pure skeptical relativism.

But these excluded positions are all untenable even from a purely philosophical point of view: they are either self-contradictory, or they fail to do justice to reality. Moreover, we find that Christian religiosity is compatible with an *idealist metaphysics*. This idealist metaphysics may take the form of a more epistemologically oriented subjective idealism, or the form of a more speculative objective idealism. Both forms are consistent with the idealist mainstream of modern philosophy that runs from Descartes and Leibniz down to the modern idealists.

5. This gives rise to the second possibility, namely, the tendency for religious teachings and abstract philosophy to amalgamate into a broader *worldview.* This, however, must be distinguished from philosophy per se. A worldview fleshes out the philosophical concept of the absolute with specific *values* drawn from ethics, philosophy of religion, and aesthetics, formulating them in terms of the unifying ground that realizes these values in history. The concept of the absolute then ceases to be an abstract ideal teleology, and becomes an interpretation of the world in terms of specific concrete objectives and goals. This is no longer pure philosophy, but worldview-philosophy, which necessarily goes beyond pure theory and uses poetry and the imagination.

Such a synthetic philosophy is part and parcel of numerous theologies and philosophies. It is the final end of knowledge and the goal of universally inclined minds, but, nevertheless, it is not part of the task of theology. *Glaubenslehre,* with its affirmation of concrete religious values, is a necessary prerequisite for such a synthesis, but it does not rely on such a synthesis. Theology can stand independent of any such systematic worldview; and even when a given theologian presupposes a particular worldview, it will be perceptible only in certain specifics. Theology itself never presupposes or requires a worldview in addition to religious values (which are, in fact, presupposed by the worldview and not the other way around).

LECTURE

One of the things which makes *Glaubenslehre* necessary is faith's encounter with the various disciplines that come under the heading of philosophy. This is where we meet one of the most burning questions, whose chief peculiarity is that the more we pursue it, the more elusive it becomes. What we basically have here is this: a question of harmonizing the differences without glossing over or losing sight of them.

Scholarly knowledge, unlike religious knowledge, does not issue from a practical living impulse. It does not carry out its tasks under the light of the love of God, but rather seeks a pure and strict grasp of physical and mental data in order to achieve a logical presentation of the facts. That is why religiously gifted people never fully grasp the intellectual approach of the sciences. They have an entirely different approach to things. The religious person perceives a whole that is complete within itself, while in science we see nothing but an infinite number of individual details, alongside which there is nothing; and only the most narrowly circumscribed causes for these details are sought in an infinite regression. The subject matter of science can never be grasped as a whole, for it extends to infinity in both time and space. Hence it is utterly impossible to explain the scientific world in terms of the religious world, e.g., to explain the processes of nature in terms of the righteousness of God. Religion can only interpret the world—not explain it. Science, on the other hand, offers us nothing but details. Science can serve as the basis for a technical world only, not a religious one. The future development of religion must be based on religion itself; religion will never draw its sustenance from science.

Religion, therefore, is independent of science. It can long outlive any upheaval in science. Indeed, we could undergo massive transformations in our theoretical world-consciousness without needing a correspondingly radical change in religion. Religion can be overcome only by religion. That is why France was able to break the power of Catholicism within its borders only by means of a state atheism that was laced with a vestigial ethics and spirituality. But even this atheism did not signify a genuine victory over religion. A religion can be overcome only by a deepening of the religious spirit.

The distinction between the religious God-consciousness and the theoretical world-consciousness does not mean, however, that there is no practical relationship between them. Their difference is not absolute, but relative, for no part of our spiritual life is restricted to a sealed chamber. Unfortunately, theology has usually emphasized the contradiction between them while neglecting the relativity of the contradiction. This tendency has intruded even on the Bible. The Bible is permeated with images of the beginning and end of the world: the angels of fire trace the path of the stars, and everywhere there are popular images of the world's and humanity's being. The Bible is also rich in allusions to ancient philosophy.

Consequently, Christianity from the very beginning worked out an agreement between biblical revelation and the "natural" revelation of ancient science, an agreement that lasted until well into the seventeenth century. It was dissolved by two different forces. On one side, it was assailed by the methods of modern detailed research, which assembled a mass of information that called the supposed unity of biblical and natural revelation into question; meanwhile, on the other side, the presupposition that there even was such a thing as a uniform and fully accepted natural reason fell to the wayside. Our era differs dramatically from all preceding ages, for we can no longer take it for granted that there is *any* universally accepted natural knowledge. Even Catholicism recognizes this; that is why its priests must attend anachronistic courses on philosophy in which Aristotle still constitutes the chief subject.

Scholarship today is irreversibly divided between the exact sciences and the moral sciences [*exakte Wissenschaft und Geisteswissenschaft*]. Henceforth we will have to deal with these two formidable entities, neither of which will fail to have an impact on the other. Practical questions are now the stuff of philosophy. This puts philosophy in a difficult situation, but it also allows the winds of freedom to blow in. No thinking person is any longer burdened with the obligation to accept a standard, universal philosophy. Science can no longer be corrected by dogma. This has meant not only a loss for our time, but a gain as well. But no gain takes place without struggle, even if the struggle takes place in our own souls.

The essential difference between these two forms of knowledge remains basic to our inquiry, even if it is only a relative difference. Now we ask, Where does this relativity become visible? If we are to answer this question, we need to know the main positions taken by the newer theoretical understanding of the world. These are not a matter of philosophy. A frequent mistake in discussions of this issue is to treat it as the question of faith and knowledge. If that were all, it would be a comparatively easy matter; because, of course, one can have one's own opinions about faith without the benefit of philosophy. But it really concerns the results of the specific positive disciplines. If we recognize that the cosmos is absolutely unlimited, then the question of the relationship of life to inanimate matter, the question of the origin of life, whether it emerged from cells according to specific laws, whether all living beings share a common ancestry— then these are all questions of fact. The age of the human race is not a question for philosophy: we must dig the answer out of the earth. And these are things that really count. It might be possible to cling to the old ways of doing philosophy; but it is not possible for outdated cosmology, geology, and history to persist. This leaves us with the task of thinking through the new data and interpreting them—pantheistically, theistically, or philosophically. Hence we face a double problem: first, the question of theology's relationship to the specific disciplines, and second, the question of theology's relationship to philosophy.

With respect to the specific scholarly disciplines, we say: Watch out, for we are dealing here not only with precise data, but also with hypotheses that attempt to fill in the gaps in the data. A certain skepticism toward most cosmological theories is not unjustified. The triumphant cry of Darwinism, which was supposed to solve all problems, but which now runs up against all sorts of anomalies, may serve as an example. The old atomistic method is also no longer unconditionally valid. But even as a degree of skepticism is justified, we are still obligated to accept the established facts. Obviously, we cannot evade the consequences of the Copernican system, nor can we shrink from the immeasurable vastness of the universe, in comparison with which our solar system is inconceivably insignificant. The similar chemical makeup of the universe as disclosed through spectrum analysis necessarily eliminates any geocentric or anthropocentric picture of reality. We cannot even find a physical center of the universe any more.

This means that religious experience will have to take on a new and quite different color. The universe that now stands before us is immeasurably greater than the seven days' work of the Bible. The immeasurable majesty of the now limitless universe streams into our religious feeling. We know that our earth was formed by spinning off from another heavenly body; we also know that the total amount of time that life has existed on earth is but a tiny fraction of the age of the earth itself—it is like a breath that briefly fogs up a cold window, only to disappear in the next minute. Science tells us that we appeared at a certain moment in time, and that at another moment, we will disappear—but it tells us nothing more. Just as the earth began without us, so too will it end without us. To put it in religious terms, this means that the end will not be an apocalypse.

This does not yet pose any danger to our religious possessions. The deeper our awareness of the contrast between the unknown secrets of the world and our own transitory, precarious existence, the more profound our experience of the divine life will be when we perceive it even in the midst of this transitory existence, purifying us and edifying us. And even when the historical fate of the human race in its immeasurable breadth and diversity is set before us, we will recognize that every time possesses its own eternity and its own divinity, even though they cannot possibly be normative for all time. To be earnest about all these things does not turn one into a skeptic or a materialist. On the contrary, in the midst of such a universe we will cling all the more tightly to the revelation of God that lies within our hearts and sends out its rays of light. This changed religious stance will not be expressed in words, but felt in a new manner. Our sense of salvation will not be divorced from the Bible, although it will be cut off from the world-picture of antiquity and attached to a new picture of the universe. The new world-picture is by no means irrefragable, but it is probable enough. The faithful cannot ignore this new world-picture; they must explicate their religious heritage in the midst of these transformations. This does not mean something like a "Christian" cosmology; that would be consummate nonsense. What is called for is to transpose religious feeling in the context of a new cosmology. Naumann refers to this in his *Briefen über Religion*[1] with a most characteristic image: We need to peel the ivy off one wall and affix it to a new one. This project is of the utmost importance. Nowadays one hears very little from the theologians about Adam and Eve, but also very little about the new discoveries that have the world in an uproar. That is why it is one of theology's most important tasks to help people develop a religious approach to these things.

The second task associated with the theoretical world-picture brings us to philosophy. We seek a central standpoint that can provide us with an overview of the world as a whole. Inasmuch as such a standpoint actually goes beyond what is given, this task is plagued with a thousand difficulties. It will always be controversial and will never achieve universal acceptance; it will always be possible to find yet another central standpoint someplace else, over here, over there. The peculiarity of the individual is decisive, but this leaves us with a massive unstable quantity. Yet if we limit ourselves to nothing more than the specific disciplines and the facts they can discover, we will be left with nothing but flimsy images that are no more verifiable than our central standpoint itself. Hence countless millions, untroubled by philosophy, concern themselves only with the intrinsically religious and the evidence it provides. This is the natural result of necessity; but it is not so easy to keep religious experience altogether separate. However unstable the currents of philosophy may be, our theoretical thinking strives for unity, and it is impossible to ignore these demands altogether. We must therefore inquire into the relationship between faith and philosophy.

There has been no shortage of attempts to claim that religious knowledge and philosophical knowledge are actually the same thing. The greatest modern attempt to do so was the Hegelian system. For Hegel, religion is nothing other than the affective consciousness of

---

1. Friedrich Naumann (1860–1919), *Briefen über Religion* (Berlin-Schöneberg: Buchverlag der "Hilfe," 1904.)

the unity of the world, which theoretical knowledge apprehends as an idea. Religion grasps God poetically according to our imagination, while speculation grasps him scientifically as abstract form.

To this we must add: Spirit is grasped differently in religion than it is in philosophy. Hence their objects remain the same, but their sameness is by no means unconditional. If we seek to ascend to the theoretical form of knowledge, we finally come to a sphere where the content too seems different. That is why that which Hegel's system united was so quickly and radically separated after his death. D. F. Strauss[2] put an end to this ecstatic union; for him, lions and lambs ate the same philosophical hay. Later on, the identity of philosophy and religion found new advocates, particularly Biedermann and, although less clearly, Pfleiderer.

Such a unity is in fact impossible. Of course, the object of piety cannot be any different from the object of philosophy, but their difference in form remains and makes it impossible to reduce either to the other. Religion implies an intense inward turn and a specifically personal stance toward life, not the conclusion of a lengthy thought-process. A practical stance toward life can never be transformed into theoretical research on the first principles. We must remember that religion is apprehended, not comprehended. Indeed, in religion, we do not wish to comprehend. "Now we see through a glass darkly."[3] But even a precise philosophical system, for that matter, although it tries to deal with the total context of all things, never arrives at the ultimate ground of all reality. We may, to be sure, bring the religious and the philosophical forms of knowledge together as much as possible; but the summits of the pyramids are too high for us to know them as one and the same. Religion remains necessary for life, but not for theoretical unity, and therein lies the difference.

Nevertheless, we must still lay great emphasis on how these two forms of knowledge, for all their differences, remain quite similar. Our philosophy and our faith must both tend in the same direction, lest we sow the seeds of distrust and rend the spiritual world asunder. You cannot be a Spinozist with your head and a theist in your heart; on the contrary, we must postulate that the lines that extend from both sides will ultimately converge. That convergence point, to be

---

2. David Friedrich Strauss (1808–1874) was an influential left-wing Hegelian (a term also applied to Ludwig Feuerbach and Karl Marx). See his controversial *A Life of Jesus* (1848), trans. George Eliot (Philadelphia: Fortress Press, 1972), and also his critique of Schleiermacher, *The Christ of Faith and the Jesus of History* (1865), trans. Leander E. Keck (Philadelphia: Fortress Press, 1977).

3. 1 Cor. 13:12.

sure, remains hidden from us, but we can sense its presence in both forms of knowledge. Moreover, faith cannot be accompanied by just any philosophy; it can coexist only with a teleological, idealist philosophy that refers the highest values of spirit, not to the work of nature, but to the activity of freedom. Hence we see that the essential difference between the religious consciousness and the theoretical consciousness in no way excludes the possibility that they may harmonize; indeed, we must go so far as to say that faith is possible only when accompanied by a philosophy of freedom.

We must therefore not be misled by the pessimism and materialism that hover around us, for our highest and most civilized concepts point in the direction of idealism. The greatest European thinkers—above all, Kant and his successors—affirmed the teleological-idealistic movement. Everything apart from this movement makes us lose heart and despair of attaining the ultimate. Even radical pantheism is no exception: it too issues in despair. Seeking to identify spirit with matter, taken to its logical conclusion, issues in materialism, for if spirit and matter are treated as commensurable realities, then matter will be the stronger of the two. On the other hand, however, if we are dealing with the form of pantheism (which is, after all, a highly variegated movement) that refers simply to the pan-divine life of all, then we in fact are no longer dealing with pure pantheism, but rather with the concept of immanence, which implies the elevation and self-realization of spirit.

If we make this distinction between faith and philosophy, not only can we in good conscience concern ourselves with our own sphere, but philosophy can also be freed from worrying about what theology is doing. Philosophy's duty is to discover the basic laws of the spirit through the study of reality, and it is not obligated to pronounce a religious blessing on its abstractions.

Schleiermacher takes an approach very similar to our own on this question, except that Spinoza's and Schelling's influence pushed him in the direction of a stark monism. Schleiermacher constantly teetered on the brink of pantheism. We therefore find his philosophy untenable and will make no use of it here.

Our *Glaubenslehre* will be accompanied by a philosophy that seeks the key to the highest mysteries in spirit and not only in the blunt facts of mere existence. But if we have these two sources of knowledge—i.e., philosophy's affirmation of the preeminence of the spirit, and religion's affirmation of a holy and gracious God—we will be grasped by the idea that it must be possible for the two to intersect; for that is the only way in which we can arrive at a worldview in the real sense. Such a worldview cannot be based on religion and ethics alone, but must also interpret the brutal givens in the context of divine activity.

This is the takeoff point for the highest dreams of the thinker— but the thinker who dreams them is no longer a philosopher. A vast body of philosophical poetry arises from these dreams, dreams which owe both their appeal and their profundity to the fact that they go beyond all simply personal reflections and offer us a total picture of all reality. Kant is not one of these thinkers; he remained a pure philosopher. But Leibniz's prestabilized harmony, Hegel's system, and Schopenhauer's surrender to Nirvana are all no longer philosophies, but worldviews. A particularly good attempt to formulate such a worldview, which nevertheless recognizes that a worldview is not philosophy as such, is to be found in Richard Rothe's *Ethics*.[4] But such a synthesis is not a task for theology, for a worldview presupposes both religious values with which only theology can deal, as well as other values which do not fall under the purview of theology.

Otherwise, religion and philosophy share a not dissimilar lot. The religious life of our time is like a compass needle that flutters back and forth and cannot find the pole. But philosophy too is plagued today with instability and convulsions, and all the theories in the world are powerless to change this state of affairs.

§5. The Christian Principle and the Organization of *Glaubenslehre*

DICTATION

1. *Glaubenslehre,* therefore, remains a relatively independent, purely theological matter. It raises Christian faith-conceptions to the level of dogmatic-systematic form, simultaneously referring back to the objective world-picture even as it continues to move ahead toward a normative religious vision of the whole. The task of elevating the conceptions of faith to the level of dogmatic precision requires conceptual work: retrieving that which is essential to these conceptions, and giving the most precise conceptual expression to what they instinctively imply. At the same time, these ideas must be compared with one another and placed into a systematic relationship. But for

---

4. Richard Rothe (1799–1867), *Theologische Ethik* (*Theological Ethics*), 5 vols., 2d ed. (Wittenberg: Zimmerman, 1867–71).

that to be possible, the various concepts must instinctively express a solid, unified kernel of religious thoughts. Above all, we must return to this basic kernel, for it—along with the consistency of the whole— is the criterion of accuracy for our dogmatic propositions. So it is our task to highlight and develop this largely unconscious unity through which the basic, undivided religious revelation works. This is how specific ideas of faith are highlighted.

2. This leads us toward a synopsis of the Christian faith and its concepts, a summary formula for its entire religious disposition that can serve as the basis of the exposition. Such a synopsis or formula is called the *Christian principle*. The concept of such a principle issues from the general method of modern historical-psychological thinking; its purpose is simply to bring the whole complex of endless multiple appearances together into a central formula that will express the unifying root and driving force behind the whole. Formulating the principle itself involves a historical intuition that extends over the entire range of manifestations, but it also involves pointing toward the future direction the principle will take. This concept of the principle, like its formulation, is very subjective, but no more so than any other unfolding spiritual development. For objective support, it relies on devotion to history and careful attention to religious experience.

3. Given these presuppositions, we define the Christian principle—which will serve as the basis for all subsequent discussion—in this way: Christianity is the general, decisive breakthrough in principle to a religion of *personality*, opposed to all naturalistic and antipersonalistic understandings of God. The general historical character of Christianity as a religion of personality is particularly visible in its contemporary Protestant form, and it is likely that its future development will proceed on the basis of this idea: human souls, redeemed and sanctified through communion with the living God, raised up to God and bound to a realm that comes from God and is directed toward God, a realm of personalities inseparably bound together by religious love.

This elevation is accomplished by means of a religious knowledge of God and by the will's formative surrender to God, who encounters us with his essence—which grounds the ideal of personality—in the revelation-history of the prophets through its culmination in Jesus, and from Jesus down to the present. Jesus is thus the center of the redemptive self-revelation of God. In a word, it is the principle of a religious *rebirth* or *higher birth* in a realm of spirits infused with God, so that everything that is merely natural becomes a means to self-development and self-production, i.e., a revelation of lower degree. It is the principle of a present, internalized, spiritualized, and yet utterly theistic and personalistic orientation.

This formulation of the principle stands opposed to all others, including: any ecclesiastical and sacramental religion of redemption and incarnation; any religion of the forgiveness of sins and renewal through a divinely ordained, atoning death of Christ; any religion based on the identity of the divine and human spirits (as symbolized in the mythology of the God-man); any didactic and moral-legal revelation of the rational goal of humanity through the authority of Christ; any religion of social renewal of a suffering humanity by means of the potent commandment of brotherly love; or any religion of individual Christ-mysticism through communion with the forgiving, sanctifying, living Savior.

4. If theology consists in the exposition of the principle, then the basic divisions and subdivisions of the material flow from the principle itself. The primary division is immediately evident: the distinction between the *historical*-religious and the *contemporary*-religious elements of faith. The former consist in the vividness and living strength that undergird, anchor, and fortify the Christian conception of God. This means that the basic presupposition is a religious valuation of history—and particularly of its center, the personality of Jesus. This is a presupposition which, to be sure, becomes effective only in the context of an assent to the whole; and it is therefore already conditioned by the whole. On the one hand, then, the Christian principle is an interpretation and evaluation of faith based on the Christian lifeworld as a whole—although this includes the particular moment, complete with its own meaning and function, presentation and foundation, taking the historic power, context, and direction of this lifeworld and making them part of the contemporary world. But, on the other hand, Christian belief in salvation is itself also a relatively independent moment in which the various aspects of the Christian conception of God are given to us both as a present experience and as a task.

This *Glaubenslehre* is therefore divided into two parts: the first deals with the religious significance of *Christ,* while the second expounds the contemporary, active *faith in salvation* that is practiced in the present. The second part is in turn subdivided according to the constituent elements of this faith in God, given here only in its specifically Christian form. These subdivisions are: *(a)* the Christian concept of God; *(b)* the Christian concept of the world; *(c)* the Christian concept of humanity; *(d)* the resultant concept of salvation as a present experience; *(e)* the concept of the community based upon that experience, or the Kingdom of God, and finally, *(f)* the all-embracing concept of the final consummation.

LECTURE

Our task in these new paragraphs is to explain how the stuff of faith will be formulated and organized. The most important thing here is to find the leading idea of religious faith, or the *Christian principle.*

If we examine the matter more closely, we find ourselves standing immediately before a great many diverse conceptions of what contemporary Christianity is. The diversity is so great that no unity seems to lie within it; but nevertheless, it is obvious that some sort of unifying point must underlie it all, holding the various contradictions together. It is the same as with an individual person: there is a general striving of the will, a central drive that produces a unity of life, that holds the myriad fragments of our existence together. In the depths of our unconscious there lies a primal and basic unity, which, despite all the catastrophes that threaten to tear us apart, preserves an inner direction from the beginning—until the day that comes when we learn, to our surprise, that there is just such a unity in our own life, a life in which we have become what we are. There is such a primal unity in Christianity, too, and its development is nothing but the germination of this kernel. That is what we need to analyze. Our analysis shows that the Christian principle is far finer and more subtle than the mere concept of a principle; for since we can derive it neither from the several religious communities nor from the dogmatic or philosophical-historical schools, what remains is for us to formulate its inner point as a wholly personal, spiritual attitude.

This concept of the principle of Christianity will have to be pursued in the greatest depth, and formulating it will be an extremely delicate task. Our *Glaubenslehre* is like a tree whose roots reach down to the point in our lives where everything comes together: history, personal destinies, anticipation of the future. It can never be fully explained, for it is rooted in something entirely subjective—not a frivolous subjectivity, but something that takes shape within us, overwhelming us with an irresistible inner sovereignty. Hence it will never be a matter of proof; instead, it will depend upon evoking the strongest response from our soul. Our decision is and remains a risk, but we do not require the boldness of the gambler who plays the odds first here and then there. What we do need is the feeling that tells us: here is a stream that flows from the depths of God. We know the truth by its fruits,[1] that is, by the strength and the peace that it provides.

Given this presupposition, if we seek the primal form of the seed of Christianity, we encounter it in the totality of its appearance as the *monotheistic* religion of *personality.* Anchoring individual souls in God and uniting souls together through God, that is what Christianity is all about. If Christianity views surrender to God as the highest value and as the final goal of life, saturating the soul with God in a forward drive to inner independence, then surely it signifies neither immersion in God nor loss of self nor disappearance into infinity, but rather the finding of self. The original miracle of Christianity is that it enables the finite soul to be fully surrendered and taken up into the divine life and thereby drawn into its workings. The basic idea of Christianity is not mysticism and affection, but elevation. For to that in our souls which is capable of such elevation, the divine essence appears as an all-consuming encounter with the narrow human spirit. To win the soul in this Christian sense, to save the soul through surrender, is no exercise in saccharine piety, but an experience of being grasped through pain and suffering. Refined in this way, we are brought back to the goal of life.

The soul can find God's love only when it turns the love thus received outward, to others. Swept off its feet by God's love, it must sweep others along with it. Brother-love flows from love of God. It is the fruit neither of humanness nor of an inclination to love for the sake of human nobility; it is rather the love for something which is actually not the self at all. It is love for those who, just like us, are called by God—a love which flows entirely from God. As we love him in ourselves, so also we love him in the neighbor.[2] And even if the divinity that God bears within himself could be obscured, it would still broadcast its sparks from every grain of sand. Every human soul has infinite value, but not a value in and of itself: a human being is born and dies, like a sheep or a flower of the field.[3] It is only insofar as the divine life flows into a human being that the higher self emerges.

Humanity, social betterment, and universal friendship are praiseworthy endeavors, but they are Christian only insofar as they stem from inner surrender to God. They are Christian only insofar as we

1. See Matt. 7:20.
2. See 1 John 4:12.
3. Ps. 103:15.

say, Our love for God would be a lie if we did not love our brother.[4] The elevation of the human personality that Christianity intends comes not through proof, but through an act that grasps the soul in faith and recognition. It depends on an affirmation of God, but also on capitulation to him; we are encountered by him in the great circle of life in which Jesus was raised to his greatest heights and from whence it pours out its stream into our time. This stream is: the principle of rebirth or higher birth. We are not dealing with any "ism" here; the Christian world is much too rich and deep for that. It comes not from the desk, but from life.—

This version of the Christian principle stands opposed to a number of other versions. In Catholicism, the Christian principle consists in the redemption of a world fully alienated from God by means of the gracious institution of the church. The priests, whose hands are, in a way, extensions of God's hands, perform all manner of holy ordinances and miracles to bring about moral purification. The original miracle, however, remains the veiling of the Godhead in flesh and the establishment of a church that also consists of spirit and flesh. To this physical-superphysical process of redemption, Catholicism then adds the moral process of redemption as well.

The old Protestant orthodoxy construes the Christian principle as assurance of the forgiveness of sins, based on divine action; and through the faith that this action makes possible, a new man emerges. The death of the God-man is the central miracle; he carries out the great transaction of redemption, blotting out sin and effecting a divine reconciliation. The entire religion is based on surrender to this event of great redemption, except that now nothing takes place by means of priestly action anymore—everything comes through the proclamation. Significant in its own way, this version of the Christian principle as new birth through surrender remains with us still, except without the death of the God-man in the background.

Another version of the Christian principle describes the being of the God-man in terms of the essential identity of the divine and human spirit, of which we are assured in Christ. His life completely exemplifies this God-man-ness: he is the original, perceivable God-man. This is evidently quite close to pantheistic monism. It remains viable even for those who deny the historical existence of Jesus, for it is of no consequence whether the symbol of this God-man ever lived or not; it is simply enough that the human race could express its ideal in this way. The historical is utterly transformed into the mystical. At

4. See 1 John 4:20.

this point, Schleiermacher's position borders on Hegel's. Here we part company with Schleiermacher. The higher birth of Christianity, which takes place through becoming grasped by God, does not presuppose an already self-existent divine-human identity of which religion only makes us aware. The concept of God-man-ness corresponds to a concept of God as the Infinite that gushes out through the world. Our own position is more theist-voluntarist. We think, not of an identity, but of a creative reality; not of being, but of begetting.

Rationalism and moralism understand Christianity in terms of a supreme moral law of love and purity, proceeding from the authority of Christ. Christianity gains its inner stimulus from him, and from him the individual receives the confidence to act. The Ritschlian school and Herrmann belong here.

The Christian-social movement also construes the principle in ethical terms. Their ethic, however, is aggressive and world-changing. For them, nothing rests on hope. Their eschatology consists in the grandiose proclamation of a new age, emerging from the Christian spirit. Ethics, much like the credo of social democracy, becomes a matter of practical revolution.

Finally, the pietistic version—at its most affective in Zinzendorf— signifies a wholly personal, often quasi-erotic passion for Christ. The passion means everything: peace with God and the capacity for moral activity.

We do not list all these different versions of the Christian principle in order to criticize them, but to distinguish them from our own. We need to give unified expression to personal experience. That is the only way to avoid the perils of dogmatism. The various dogmas do indeed express the principle, but interpreted in terms of the instinctive drive of the individual soul. Once again: Our *Glaubenslehre*'s version of the Christian principle clings to the concept of the higher birth, elevating us above our own narrow destiny, above earthly and sensual passions, and drawing us into the life of God as new creatures, internally pulsing with his power. But, even when it becomes a new creature, the human cannot become an object of love without becoming something more. Faith in a higher birth is faith in the creation of something new, something which does not yet exist. This new creation provides our soul with a home in the midst of an infinite and chilling universe, a home to which our fellow creatures are also destined. We love them because, on the way to God, the lines do not simply intersect—they unite.

This understanding of the Christian principle *organizes* our subject matter. The principle contains a twofold thrust: the constantly repeated process of rebirth is mediated by history. Part One of our *Glaubenslehre* will therefore consist of historical-religious propositions. This does not mean history alone, but religiously interpreted history; not facts alone, but their meaning. Nor does it mean philosophy; it is rather an interpretation of the depths of practical experience. Schleiermacher's historical-religious statements constitute the weakest part of his *Glaubenslehre*. He inappropriately includes historical elements in the second part of his *Glaubenslehre*, where they are lumped together with the contemporary-religious propositions. Ritschl does the same thing, while the orthodox theologians do not even recognize the distinction. Such a distinction would be impossible for the orthodox, because their history is no history at all, but a timeless supra-history, a metaphysical-cosmological act of redemption. For them, Jesus' death is of course a fact, but not a historical fact in our sense of the word—just as the God-man Jesus is not truly historical. He was the disguised Almighty himself, his death here was planned from all eternity and remains in all eternity, effective in every moment, and hence is not a historical-religious matter, but a contemporary-religious one. But for us, the death of Jesus is something historical and psychological, not a metaphysical-cosmological redemption.

Part Two of our *Glaubenslehre* will consist of contemporary-religious or metaphysical-religious propositions; for even though the Christian faith finds its anchor, context, and future development in its history, it also embraces a relatively independent moment as well. The Christian concept of God is a contemporary experience. Part Two therefore will contain propositions about redemption—which is constantly being renewed—about the idea of God to which redemption leads, about the human being who is to be elevated redemptively, and about the final goal. Schleiermacher calls all these things "reflections on the pious consciousness."[5] These reflections then extend to a consideration of the world. The contemporary-religious propositions also contain further assertions about the concept of the world, including beliefs about providence, etc.

Both the contemporary-religious and the historical-religious statements alike are statements of belief; they can by no means be scientific and precise. They are both immanent in the Christian principle, as it is affirmed by faith. On the one side stands history, on the other side the idea.

5. Schleiermacher's actual words were "reflection upon the religious affections." See Schleiermacher, *The Christian Faith* (1830), trans. H. R. Mackintosh and J. S. Stewart (Edinburgh: T. & T. Clark, 1928), p. 127.

PART ONE

JESUS CHRIST AS THE OBJECT OF FAITH

§6. Faith and History

DICTATION

1. A particularly difficult problem of contemporary religious thought concerns the relationship of faith to *historical phenomena*. In contemporary piety, Jesus primarily appears as a historical personality and the historical center of faith. But this has caused new difficulties, centering on the question of the religious meaning and significance of Jesus. This was not a problem for the old christology, or it was dealt with as, at most, an inessential side issue. The old christology had its own problem: how to unite the divine essence of Christ with the traditional historical picture of the man Jesus. The problem never disrupted it in principle, however, because his history of Jesus was overwhelmed by the essence. But now the dialectical-metaphysical critique of the doctrine of the two natures, and, in particular, the historical study of the Bible, have brought history back to center stage, so that the most difficult problem we now face is this: faith and history.

2. The following considerations require a clarification of the relationship of faith and history: *(a)* the fact that the reproductivity and sustainability of subjective personal faith is directly related to the breadth and depth of the content of the religious life and its contents; *(b)* the redemptive character of Christianity, which requires a power to enable humankind to rise above itself, a power which can be found only in historically mediated forces; *(c)* the communal character of Christianity, which as a universal, spiritual religion can find its unifying point only in the personality of a founder; *(d)* the unique character of the Christian cultus, which can function only by making its religious possession contemporary, even though this contemporary possession must be represented in its classical, original historical form; and *(e)* the need to define Christianity's relationship to other religions that also have focused historical origins.

These considerations all force us to recognize the essential and insoluble connection between history and faith, and the need for a *religious interpretation of history*. It will surely become necessary, from time to time, to loosen these historical ties in order to make room for spontaneous religious production, but even this spontaneous religious production will, at bottom, be nothing more than a new orientation to history, a fertilization of the already given.

3. But modern thought responds to all of this with opposition and skepticism. It doubts and rejects the religious value of historical phe-

nomena, particularly in their ecclesiastical-dogmatic form. Modern thought includes *(a)* the modern principle of *autonomy*, which, when it comes to religion, rejects all merely historical authority and insists that belief in anything must proceed from an inner necessity. It includes *(b)* the modern historical understanding of how faith is conditioned by its *environment*, which has explained why orthodoxy transformed the history of Jesus into the supra-history of the incarnation dogma; and by opening the Bible to critical historical research, it has also shown that we no longer have direct access to simple historical fact. Modern thought also includes *(c)* the application of *historical criticism* to biblical history, making faith's relationship to history uncertain; this is because criticism never yields absolutely certain results, questions the boundaries of the tradition, and subsumes the origins of Christian history under the rubric of a universal, never-completed development. Modernity also includes *(d)* the recognition of the historical *relativity* of Christianity, which is the result of its historically conditioned division into various confessions, none of which can be acknowledged as the only true one. Also included here are *(e)* the *history of religions* and the *philosophy of religion*, both of which view Christianity as one great religion among others, with nothing unique about its establishment or growth; hence nothing in the history of Christian origins is exempt from analogy to other histories. Finally, modern thought includes *(f)* the general *historical-relativist attitude* of the present day, which, in light of the extent and duration of human history, dares not locate the absolute center of this immeasurable history in *one* historical appearance.

For all these reasons, the problems posed by history for faith are far more difficult than those raised by metaphysics or natural science. The old understanding of history has come to an end. Human history now consists of immeasurable periods of time, of historical events that are all equally conditioned and finite. The principles of historical criticism are universally established. Now the question is how the relationship between faith and history can be maintained under these circumstances.

4. All attempts to secure the independence of faith are still subject to the psychological facts mentioned under 2 *(b)* above,[1] namely, that every strong and substantial faith comes to the individual subject as the revelation of religious heroes and as the common work of entire generations. Faith occupies, appropriates, and enlists the sympathies of an individual for the fullness of its ethical and religious content,

1. See p. 73.

leaving but little room for spontaneous religious production. That is what makes faith appear redemptive and liberating, and that is why faith can lift the individual subject above its own limitations and bring it into full and living contact with the divine life for the first time. It is through such elevation and empowerment that faith gains autonomy in the first place. Autonomy is not the starting point of religious development, but its high point; and even then, autonomy continues to need frequent recourse to the historical powers that stir up, visualize, and attest to faith.

Indeed, we could say that the relationship of faith to history is simply a matter of psychology; but it is a psychology that is tied to the structure of the community, to the cultus that is so closely identified with the community, to the need for personal support, and, above all, to the concrete content of the faith. A faith without these would ultimately develop into a faith without community or cultus: an utterly individual, personal, and emaciated mysticism, as can be seen all too often in the non-Christian movements of our day.

These basic observations free us from the preceding list of difficulties, as long as we always remember that theology can comprehend nothing more than the highest contemporary religious development, and is naturally incapable of laying down any binding law for the future and its infinite possibilities.

5. *Historicism* and historical criticism unquestionably pose a crisis for Christian thought; but they have, at any rate, authenticated the supreme validity of Christianity and the historicity of its foundations, at least with respect to the decisive impulse found in the personal religious lives of the prophets, Jesus, and the apostles, particularly Paul. It has also preserved Christianity's indispensable relation to history, so that all that is now required is to formulate that relationship anew.

Accordingly, faith should first be described in terms of its inner contemporary truth and power; but we must also emphasize that this contemporary power is bound to the contemporizing and enlivening power of its *historical foundations*. This will not be accomplished through historical-critical research into questions of detail, but rather by emphasizing those historical elements that shape the personal and spiritual foundations; the details of historical research are allowed to fade into the background. Faith assimilates these historical-personal-spiritual foundations, valuing and interpreting them as the summit of divine self-communication and revelation. As a result, our historical-religious propositions are truly religious statements, not historical-critical ones.

6. Formulated thus, our historical-religious propositions fall into three categories: *(a)* the religious revelation contained in Israelite history, or *prophetism; (b)* the *personality of Jesus* as the foundation of the Christian religious life-world; and *(c)* the subsequent *history of Christianity,* regarded as the further development of the revelation. The first two historical categories were already present in the older dogmatics as the distinction between the old and new covenants or the Old and New Testaments; but even the third category was present in the doctrines of the *corpus mysticum Christi* [mystical body of Christ] and the Holy Spirit. Discussions of these three categories follow immediately, with the religious interpretation of the personality of Jesus naturally being the most important topic. Part One will conclude with the doctrine of the economic Trinity, which will link together the historical and supra-historical elements of the concept of God.

LECTURE

The religious meaning of history is bound up for us primarily in the total figure [*Gestalt*] of Jesus; everything converges in this figure as a totality. But Jesus is not the sole object of faith. It is important to make this point against thinkers like Herrmann, whose exclusive interest in Jesus renders everything that comes to us from his isolated form utterly unhistorical. Thinkers like Herrmann make the figure of Jesus look much more like a meteor that fell from the heavens, a contrived picture that is less a matter of history than faith. Even Schleiermacher does not deal with Jesus as a truly historical figure, bestowing predicates on him that do not belong to history. For us, however, the figure of Jesus cannot be wrenched from its historical context. He is not to be separated from the prophets who prepared his way, nor from the magnitude, grandeur, and simplicity of their demands. Indeed, the prophetic spirit culminated in Jesus. His words echo the Psalms as well, and we must have them ringing in our ears if we are to hear him. We would sentimentalize the figure of Jesus if we failed to include this harshness.

The real picture of Jesus consists in his self-testimony, grasped by the faith of the disciples and by the whole of the history that follows, wherein his life always appears anew as the light that shone from within. We can no longer determine his actual words, but we still have access to the life that flows from them. And everything beyond our control that we experience in ourselves (or in books or in people, which is where the most powerful expressions of the Christian life flow) belongs to history—and that is where we catch sight of the divine life we seek. The inconceivable power and meaning of all developing [*werdende*] history carries us in its flow and sustains us.

But this also tells us something about the many serious difficulties associated with the meaning history holds for faith. Innumerable opportunities for sensitivity to the presence of God surely arise within the soul, but they will be crippled if they are isolated from history. And our age is particularly inclined to do just this. Of course, personal faith always remains an individual matter. But inconsistency or emptiness would result if everyone had to draw everything simply from their own self. If such a thing did come to pass, it would scarcely constitute religious progress, and would certainly not be the highest ideal. We can put it much more directly: if we are to partake of the whole Christian life, we must make room for its historical significance. We are certain to find ourselves in situations in which we dare not rely on ourselves alone; in such an hour, the tendrils of our faith will reach out for history.

Nevertheless, we cannot conceal the difficulties that stand in the way of including history in a *Glaubenslehre*. One objection towers above all others: the demand that faith must be autonomous. This objection insists that everything that is idea instead of mere fact, everything that arises from freedom, everything that forms the depths of being—that all these come not from authority, but from the inner necessity of the personality. We may summarize these idealistic objections, championed by Kant, as follows: Nothing can be achieved as the result of external persuasion. Affirmation of God makes sense only when it occurs in a living, personal moment; everything else is mere supposition. Hence history cannot be a matter for genuine conviction, since it is simply part of the universal causal connection of things. Faith can build only on that which belongs to the eternal, and it must divest itself of the historical. Faith cannot be backward-looking. Faith must relate to contemporary and eternal things, not to bygone things that can be known only through a thousand intermediaries. We can believe in the future, in immortality; but if we turn back, we find everything is covered with a thick, oppressive layer of dust.

The objection continues: If Jesus is nothing but the divine become visible, and not a genuinely historical person, then he is timeless and indistinguishable from the Father. Faith can easily find its object in him. Jesus is present as a king in every moment, listening to every prayer. And everything else about him is de-historicized as well. The eternal enters the arena of history, and then and only then can it become possible to grasp the eternal by believing the history. Or: If we were to give Jesus and the founding of the church back to history, they would then become part of the total context of history and hence lose their link to the divine realities. Then they could no longer be proper objects for faith, for our faith would then be based on the temporal and finite instead of on the eternal.

Both these objections—which insist on autonomy and timelessness—have been reinforced by the application of historical criticism to the history of early Christianity. Our knowledge of this history has shown just how finite Christianity is. Criticism can never demonstrate that something happened. It deals only in probable effects, and even when it does succeed in penetrating the veil of tradition, it always remains subject to error. The difficulties associated with all historical phenomena are most pronounced at the point that most concerns us. Christianity arose from the lowest social classes and achieved literary expression only after leaving its most significant original forms behind. But even today Christianity is in no way concerned with precision in the scientific sense; it is primarily concerned with vindicating its faith. Whatever was preserved under various circumstances was subsequently subjected to great elaboration. If we consider all this, we can scarcely avoid the conclusion that not one point is certain. Our faith therefore cannot rely upon the documents alone, or else it will rest on a very shaky foundation. If we had to buttress our faith with Zahn's[2] apologetic, it would not be able to carry much weight.

What all this means is that Christianity has no unity as a whole; it is fragmented through and through. Or is there something in it that could provide a reliable historical basis for our faith? But if we understand that the unity of Christianity consists in a perpetual struggle for truth, then we find that Christianity contains a specific historical impulse, but is only relatively bound to history. If its unity lies in a forward-moving process, then it admits of no turning back. Its unity lies in its future goal, not in the past.

Further: various modern developments have made a purely theological approach to Christianity impossible; instead, we must submit it to the general procedures of the philosophy of religion, classifying it according to its stage of development just as we do with all other

2. Theodor Zahn (1838–1933) was a conservative New Testament scholar who spent most of his career at Erlangen. His work was characterized by a strong emphasis on the authenticity of the New Testament writings. See his *Introduction to the New Testament*, 2d English ed. of the 3d German ed. (1906–7), trans. John Moore et al. (New York: Charles Scribner's Sons, 1917).

religions. Here we encounter the fact that there are all sorts of historical parallels. All religions have divinized their founders' personalities. Hence it appears that there is a law of religious development.
And if there is one, its effect on Christianity can be no different from
its effect on any other religion. Historical interpretation, done on its
own terms, is not radically different for other religions than it is for
Christianity.

Finally, we come to the general historical-relativist attitude of the
present day. Theologians all too readily forget the skepticism that
overwhelms the modern person who contemplates the immeasurable
vastness of time. According to the unanimous opinion of scientists,
our planet has existed for three million years![3] When confronted with
such wild expanses of time, we find it infinitely difficult to think that
all eternity is bound up in this historical moment that we call Jesus,
and to insist that all of humanity must bind itself to him. This is the
where we encounter the greatest difficulties with any and all absolu-
tizing of a particular historical moment.

If we still dare, despite all these serious objections, to maintain a
relationship with history, we must do so differently than in the past.
Such a relationship must be unconditionally maintained. The solitary
mystic, suspended completely in the present, is ineffective, particularly in the realm of ethics; and this ineffectiveness is the result of
mysticism's unhistorical character. To eliminate history is to ensure
the decay of community. Purely internal experience is not to be
underestimated, for it is undoubtedly the flicker and glow of the
central flame; but it holds little significance for the things of this
world. It signifies a religiosity that does need to be nurtured and
cultivated in intentional isolation, but it lacks any concrete direction.
If our faith were oriented solely toward mysticism, it would lose its
Christian character. Of course you could ask, Why not? Everything
has its hour.—

But let us look at the new sources available to our age. A general
mystical sensitivity to the unity of everything with God is, as we have
seen, ethically impotent. We cannot expect it to provide any impulse
for human progress. Many seek a foothold in art; but with respect to
this play of the fantasy, people frequently no longer know whether
they seek art for the sake of the majesty and fascinating sanctity that
it portends, or for the sake of the beauty that it offers to our instinct

3. The text reads "three hundred thousand," but that probably reflects an error in
note-taking, since Troeltsch was relatively scientifically literate, and he does speak in
terms of millions of years elsewhere.

for pleasure. Neither is ethical power to be found here. This particularly needs to be emphasized, for it is where the truly crucial problem of the present lies. It is unconditionally true that there is no new religion in our future. Or if there is, it will be a religion of impotence, siding now with Schopenhauer and now with Nietzsche, unable to impart any strength; for no matter how earnestly it may be felt, it will never be able to organize itself. But if this is so, and if without history we stand immediately before the end, then there must be some other approach to the issue of faith and history.

Here, above all, we must take note of the psychology of religion[4] and its important insight into the difference between productive and nonproductive natures. The vast majority of people come under the latter category; above them, at the summit, stands the personality that forms its own religious power directly, drawing from the complete historical agglomeration. But this personality's impact is actually the work of an entire generation, in comparison with which the individual person is always the weaker. Neither is world-assessment nor ethical direction to be achieved with a single stroke. Whenever religious community can no longer be held together by the state, it finds its cohesion in the personality of the founder. The interpretations of this personality may change, but the personality itself retains its central location. The cultus, too, is bound to the founder's personality; the cultus looks up to it. As the significance of sacrifice wanes in the higher religions, emphasis shifts to the common sanctified community, built on the personality of its founder. Someone who thinks the cultus is superfluous may be right about some given particular case (although the cultus does not consist simply in going to church); but a community that is built on nothing more than shared knowledge will never be universal.

We must further observe that the modern concept of autonomy does not mean that everything must be self-produced. That would quickly put an end to all mathematics! We would all fall back into barbarism. Instead, autonomy signifies a certain *sort* of consent. It does not signify any unthinking cramming of something down someone's throat, but rather a person's grasping what it is that makes something so right. Autonomy signifies not dead, passive reception, but understanding. To transform something is not to produce it, but to make the unfamiliar into a part of one's own life. We newly create none of our great cultural achievements. If we could, all education would be superfluous—the young could do their own education

---

4. The text has "philosophy of religion," but "psychology of religion" makes better sense.

themselves. Autonomy enables criticism, but not production, which is a matter of further cultivation; and further cultivation presupposes something to cultivate. Here we say, Think with the dead, for their thoughts are many.

Similarly, religion never begins with autonomy; instead, autonomy is the *goal* of religious education. It would be the pinnacle of nonsense to rear little children as autonomous beings. To attain an autonomous faith is to enter into the domain of history and to recognize its foundational significance. The Reformation indeed demanded a personal, individual religious life; but it was something to be won from authority, not from an isolated subject. Modern Christian thought also seeks a personal, individual life; but what it seeks to do is to transform history subjectively, not to slash the ties that bind.

To reply to the *second* objection: To be sure, we cannot make something from the past into an object of faith; but the thing from the past with which we are here concerned should be understood to include something supra-historical in its inner essence. It is not a matter of submitting to some historical fact that is over and done with, but rather of something that proves itself to be supra-historical and nevertheless still inseparable from history. History makes itself contemporary by producing historicity in us. That is why it will never be possible to put the idea on one side and history on the other. What seems to be mature autonomy today will someday be seen as the product of a limited historical era, within the limits of a specific culture. We can never conceive the eternal in the abstract, because life is never abstract.

There is no religious idea to be grasped apart from history; but there is also nothing historical that is not also more than historical. Wafting over history is the fragrance of supra-history, inextricable from the unity of the divine life. By "historical" we mean not that which is merely past, but the divine that is contained therein. This objection would make sense if history were exhaustively a matter of time. But history is everywhere bound up and intermingled with what lies behind it. We refer to the *meaning* of the fact, which can never be separated from the fact itself. But this does not mean that we look backwards! What really counts is the ideal, spirit-saturated concept of history. The same holds true for all church history as well: it is not the mere fact that counts, but the meaning that reveals itself in the historical fact. This search for the pure idea, this rationalistic ideal, is a delusion!

The *third* objection stems from the relativistic attitude to which the fragmented state of Christianity gives rise. Here too we say: There is no pure idea by which we may sort out the human confessions. The divisions within Christianity are to be understood thus: We are not dealing with something finished, like the seamless robe of Christ, which simply needs to be preserved intact. What we have is a truth that is *becoming*, always in the process of approximating, something that can never fully empty itself into human life. The truth lies in the goal, not the starting point![5] If it did lie in the starting point, we would find ourselves in the dreadful circumstance of having once had the truth, but not being able to find it any longer. But what we do have is a truth which is now always just taking form, so that divisions are to be expected. We say, Not that I have already attained it: but I press on.[6]

With regard to including Christianity in the history of religions and the philosophy of religion, we say, We must learn to see the light that shines from God, the revelation of God, in the whole of history. When we do, we will no longer view the profusion of religions as a hindrance. Revelation is not limited to Christianity; similar revelation and divine seizure is to be found everywhere. But when we see the great Light working itself out all over the earth, we will then no longer be able to understand why the great profusion of religions should be any cause for alarm. It remains an offense only to those who continue to see nothing but darkness in the non-Christian world. But these are the people for whom there will be no true joy in Heaven unless everyone who believes differently burns in Hell.

The *final* group of adversaries brings us face to face with the relativity of history as a whole. And it is true: anyone who walks— even once—through the great prehistoric collections of one of our museums, who sees the endless rows of display cases filled with the remains of ancient times, will scarcely be able to avoid asking whether a similar fate awaits our civilization as well. Could the poles shift some day, causing our entire culture to sink once more into the night of an ice age? If we take such possibilities seriously, the nothingness of all historical being overwhelms us. There is no evading the fearful impact that this has on us, as long as we have nothing more than the facts and still want to say: Christianity must be the eternal religion! But as soon as we see that the human race bears the light that flows

---

5. It is difficult to translate this to English without recalling the words of William James: "Our great difference from the scholastic lies in the way we face. The strength of his system lies in the principles, the origin, the *terminus a quo* of his system; for us the strength is in the outcome, the upshot, the *terminus ad quem*." William James, *The Will to Believe* (1897, reprint, New York: Dover, 1956), p. 17. Troeltsch was familiar with James's thought.
6. Phil. 3:12.

from the divine life, then we will no longer need to repress the terror and fear we feel for own day in history. Every cultural circle lives out and possesses what its highest revelation means to it. And if what our revelation means to us is someday lost, we nevertheless still have it and what it means for us today. But whatever there is in our culture that truly comes from the divine life will also be true for any time or culture.

We can safely leave to the future the question of what form the divine life will take in cultures and eons that are yet to come. All that we need to know is that it is no accident that we have these ideas, that what we have in our own particular form is something that always was and always will be. To think about our own day in history can, as we have already conceded, cause us great distress, particularly as our knowledge of history continues to grow. The problem of history in general poses more serious difficulties for the Christian faith than does natural science. But rather than make the typical response to the problem—that we are on a path of progress that will lead, without interruption, to a golden age—we need to consider the much more sobering possibility that progress will come to an end. But here too we must not yield to terror and start throwing everything overboard. Whatever happens to the world is in God's hands; and everything, whatever comes and whatever might come, are his self-revelations, which can never fully diverge from what we already have.

We must also consider the difficulties that arise from our uncertainty concerning the facts. We are already prepared for this with respect to the history of Israel: Even in conservative circles the practice of criticism needs no defense when it comes to this. We are now used to being uncertain whether Moses actually lived or not, for it poses little danger to our common religious heritage. The profound, illuminating greatness of the ancient prophets cannot be lost; indeed, it becomes all the more pronounced as we realize that historical research can never challenge it. Is there anything about the alterations that we have had to make in our portraits of Augustine, St. Francis, or Calvin that has made our energy less certain? No, as long as our picture of a historic personage still retains its effect and its transformative power despite the changes. The only sticking point is the person of Jesus.

Research into the life of Jesus has recently become a battleground of contradictory opinions, with emotions rising to a fevered pitch on both sides. One side seeks to preserve the Christian faith, the other to bury it. Drew's thesis that Jesus never even existed would not be championed so energetically if it did not mean the death of Chris-

tianity, were it true.[7] This is a dreadful thesis! If it were true, it would
mean that thousands of years have been lived under a lie; a more
ominous thesis could not be conceived.

Let us attempt to take a completely dispassionate look at this
issue by focusing first on St. Francis of Assisi. We are convinced that
we know the main points of his life, despite the legends. After all,
criticism is not a game; it aims at knowledge. But why is it not possible to do the same thing with Jesus that we can do with Francis? It is
only necessary to exclude the passion, hypercriticism, and nervous
apologetics of the present time. There is much of which we can no
longer be certain; the historical origins of Christianity cannot be fully
illuminated. But to say that we know nothing of Jesus' life is a
monstrous utterance that would require us to hold that the Pauline
letters are inauthentic—which is utterly impossible. Despite all
vacillations and obscurities, we can still know the person of Jesus
with great clarity. And for the purposes of religion, it is not necessary
to know more than that. We see his human form in his personality
and his sanctity, and we, like Paul, are touched by his inner meaning.
And it is just this inner sense that remains free from all criticism! It
is a purely personal matter of overcoming values determined by
nature: the communion of the soul with God is what is at stake here,
and nothing else! And on this point we can dispense with any uncertainty. We can cheerfully turn the details of Jesus' life over to the
researchers.

Turning, then, to the history that commands our attention, in which
Jesus is the most important point but not the whole, we divide the
material into three parts: (1) the religious significance of the history
of Israel; (2) the religious significance of the person of Jesus; and
(3) the religious significance of the subsequent history.— The subdivisions were also present in the old orthodox dogmatics, although
under different titles: "The Meaning of the Old Covenant," "The
Meaning of the New Covenant," and "The Continuing Work of the
Holy Spirit."

7. The dispute to which Troeltsch refers centered on a book published in 1909 by
Arthur Drews (1865–1935), *Die Christusmythe,* which argued that Jesus had never even
lived, that the Christ-myth had actually developed *before* the pseudo-historical stories
of the Gospels, which had been composed later with absolutely no basis in historical
fact—not even a historical man named Jesus of Nazareth. The appearance of his book
unleashed a storm of popular controversy in Germany. Drews was a member of the
Monistenbund, which had been founded by Ernst Haeckel (see above, p. 22 n.16). See
Arthur Drews, *The Christ Myth,* trans. C. Delisle Burns (London: T. Fisher Unwin,
1910). For more about the controversy and Troeltsch's response to it, see
B. A. Gerrish, "Jesus, Myth, and History: Troeltsch's Stand in the 'Christ-Myth'
Debate," *Journal of Religion* 55 (1975):13–35.

§7. The Religious Significance of the History of Israel[1]

DICTATION

1. To acknowledge Christianity as the highest divine revelation is also to recognize the religion of Israel as its prior stage and presupposition, for without it, Christianity is incomprehensible. It is always necessary to comprehend Christianity in terms of its rich background in the Old Testament.

2. The first task is to establish the essence of Israelite religion as a religion that burst the boundaries of nature religion in every sense and became an ethical religion of the will: in other words, *ethical monotheism.* In this it is absolutely unique. All other possible analogies in the history of religions are weak and unclear by comparison. The religion of Israel, through the agency of the prophets, marks the separation of God from nature and the placement of God over all the world as a creative will. This signifies *(a)* the antirationalist and antinaturalist concept of an inconceivable, living will that is beyond human measure, which includes the concept of *creation.* The content of this will, however, is then *(b)* directed to the recognition and veneration of God in moral obedience. This recognition of, and participation in, the *divine holiness* by means of moral obedience becomes the essential goal of the human race. Such a view stands opposed to all merely cultic and ceremonial religions, to all mundane, eudaemonistic versions of the human vocation, and, finally, to every merely contemplative pantheism and acosmic mysticism. Since the distinguishing characteristic of this view of God includes the concept of an ethical goal which is established for the creature, we find *(c)* a greater use of examples drawn from *history*—the personal lives of the prophets and the fates of great peoples—and a correspondingly lesser use of all examples drawn from nature, particularly those referring to nature's abstract regularity.

3. In these three respects, prophetic monotheism is an original religious creation, distinct from the rest of the world. These three characteristics comprise the germ of the definitive, humanized, and ethical religion of *personality* that Christianity became. The *limitations* of Israelite religion lie in its nationalism, which was never fully overcome; in the legalistic shawl it drapes over the ethical religion of humanity; and finally in the resultant narrowness of its religious vision

---

1. The title given in the Table of Contents is different: "The religious significance of Israelite prophetism."

of history, with its limited horizon, its nationalistic-apocalyptic goals, its massive belief in miracles, and its tendency to eudaemonistic ethics. But Israelite religion lacks nothing when it comes to its single-minded, purely voluntaristic concept of God and the way in which it takes the unity and connectedness of the world up into the concept of God, all of which sharply distinguish it from the Indo-Germanic religions.

4. Despite its limitations, the continued religious significance of prophetism is such that the record it has left in the so-called Old Testament has become a Christian document. We express this in the formula that prophetic religion is the old covenant, Old Testament, or old decree of God, which prepares the way for the new covenant or new decree. This assessment is still justified; it excludes the nationalistic elements of the Old Testament at the same time that it elevates the prophetic. The prophetic elements, in all their simplicity and power, continue to inform Christianity's simple, basic ethical idea, as well as to guard against any degeneration into sentimentality, subjective mysticism, or intellectual dogmatism.

LECTURE

Among us, the Old Testament suffers from the wholly unhistorical view that the most important things about it are the various predictions and the impossible accounts of the genesis of the human race that are found in it. But the history of Israel has much greater significance for our historical realm, and this is just as true for Islam as it is for Christianity. Israel's struggle with its fate reaches a peak in the Psalms and in prophetism. The Psalms, in their strong, pure voices, along with the stringent, earnest, and solemn grandeur of the prophets, who sought to purify the Yahweh-religion and to make it non-Jewish, constitute the background against which we must view Jesus. To be sure, the concept of God is not yet as thoroughly spiritualized as in Christianity; but it is therefore quite free of the sentimentality that so easily manages to insinuate itself into later, more sophisticated conceptualizations. The clarity, power, and gravity that continually flow from the Old Testament into the Christian conceptual world are unmistakable. For now, however, we are compelled to omit detailed treatment of this topic, referring instead to the exposition of the Christian concept of God in Part Two.[2]

2. Pp. 111–94 below. Gertrud von le Fort included a note here referring the reader to the essay "Glaube und Ethos der hebräischen Propheten" (The faith and ethos of the Hebrew prophets), in *Gesammelte Schriften*, vol. 4, *Aufsätze zur Geistesgeschichte und Religionssoziologie* (Tübingen: J.C.B. Mohr, 1925).

§8. The Significance of Jesus for Faith[1]

DICTATION

1. The person of Jesus is the center of Christian history. This makes it particularly important that we distinguish purely *historical* matters from their interpretation by *faith*, even though this is a particularly difficult and involved task. First of all, we need to emphasize that the determination of the historical facts must, from the very beginning, be strictly separated from religious interpretation. For scientific theology, the former is strictly a matter of historical-critical research. Research into early Christianity, however, has created an increasingly important historical problem. The use of customary historical-critical methods has made it impossible to know what happened where the sources are silent.

But historical knowledge can, either directly or indirectly, influence faith and its interpretation. Hence, at this point, Christian belief is dependent on historical research, just as it is also linked to other forms of scholarly research at other points. Of course, this dependence applies only to the specifically scholarly discussion, and not to simple lay faith. The latter can rely on its instinct for the historical essence of the evangelical tradition, confident that it has grasped what is decisive, even if it cannot prove it scientifically and must remain reticent about specifics. But in order to guarantee this instinctive judgment, it is necessary for historical scholarship to reach a clear consensus about the history in question.

2. But now these historical investigations, because of the nature of the sources, have encountered the most serious of difficulties. And because of the importance of the subject, they have also engendered the most passionate contradictions. This is the direct cause of the great uncertainty that afflicts the present situation. Hence we must certainly both anticipate and seek greater clarity and specificity from historical research. But we already have clarity on the chief points. Today the *central* question is whether the apostolic community's belief in Christ and redemption can be traced back to the impact of Jesus and is consistent with his inner person; or whether their belief in a savior-god and his redemptive death was appropriated from some non-Christian mystery cult and grafted onto the more or less vague remembrances of a Jewish rabbi. The struggle over whether Jesus

---

1. See also Ernst Troeltsch, "The Significance of the Historical Existence of Jesus for Faith" (1911), in *Ernst Troeltsch: Writings on Theology and Religion,* ed. and trans. Robert Morgan and Michael Pye (Atlanta: John Knox Press, 1977), pp. 182–207.

even really existed—a monstrous idea—is simply the most provoca-
tive expression of the latter hypothesis. With respect to this idea, it
should be said that the myth which is supposed to have been grafted
onto the memory of Jesus has never been identified, and that all the
proposed candidates have borne only an external resemblance to it;
furthermore, there is no evidence in the sources that such a grafting
ever occurred, and such an occurrence would be utterly without
parallel.

But if this is the case, then the development of the Christian belief
in salvation and in the saving death of Christ must be traced back to
the impact of the person of Jesus himself, i.e., to the resurrection
faith and the messianic Christ-cult that arose from his impact. The
resurrection appearances and the high messianic descriptions of
Christ, for their part, must be traced back to the extraordinary impact
of his personality. His profoundest impact—his religious and ethical
proclamation of the value of the soul and the Kingdom of God in
brother-love, as well as his extraordinary consciousness of mission
and his struggle for a divinely induced world-renewal—all these are
clearly historical. The only thing that remains questionable is the
extent to which the image of Jesus in the gospels, and particularly the
image of Jesus' messianic self-consciousness, was influenced by the
community and its image of Jesus in the Christ-cult. We have not yet
achieved clarity about that, and, by the nature of the case, clarity will
be difficult to achieve. It will also be difficult to determine how the
Christ-cult arose within the community, and how it came to resemble
the cults of the mystery religions (a development that must, somehow, have taken place among some pagan converts to Christianity).

3. This assured body of facts, however, is sufficient to confirm
religious faith in its *interpretative* task; we only need to clarify what it
is that such a religious interpretation of these historical facts can do.
It cannot establish any facts, but it can interpret them. Yet this interpretation cannot be an arbitrary exercise of the imagination; it must
proceed from the historical meaning and spirit of the facts themselves. To be sure, however, one does not simply interpret Jesus'
history and the formation of his character in isolation, but rather
must approach them with reference to the previous history that culminated in them, and the subsequent history that developed their
results. Hence a fullness of living reality streams into the fact that is
to be interpreted, proving it to be more deeply rooted and more
richly developed than its narrowly circumscribed historicity would
suggest. But even if the interpretation of this narrowly circumscribed
historical fact can be extended in this way, it nevertheless is bound to

historical and psychological connections and effects; and it must therefore interpret them by analogy with the general interpretation and evaluation of historical personalities. That is why we are concerned with Jesus' historical and psychological effects and with their significance for our religious life. Such an assessment will never be able to speak in terms of cosmic or metaphysical transformations, but will refer rather to the transformation of souls through Jesus' impact on them. In particular, the only meaning that can be attached to his suffering and death will be historical and psychological—the effect it has on believing souls.

This interpretation of the significance of the historical personality of Jesus, then, yields the following categories: *(a)* the foundational and original revelation of the Christian life-world in the entirety of his personal life; *(b)* the inauguration of the possibility of Christian redemption through surrender of the faith and the will, whereby the soul surrenders itself to the God who is revealed in Jesus; and *(c)* the gathering and concentration of the community around its head, joining his life to an inner life of community and continuity.

4. An interpretation of Jesus in these categories stands in the dogmatic tradition of the doctrine of the *three offices of Christ:* prophet, high priest, and king. This doctrine was the result of an instinct that was thoroughly sound, although its development was, of course, conditioned by the orthodox mythical doctrines of the divine nature and the atoning death. Now, however, the orthodox doctrine of the two natures has been weakened, if not altogether eliminated, by the impact of the historical-psychological viewpoint. We now interpret these offices in this way. As prophet, Jesus is the one who reveals God: not, to be sure, as a lawgiver who legislates doctrine, but as one who reveals an ongoing personal life. As high priest, Jesus is the one who leads us to God and mediates salvation and wholeness; he communicates the clarity and courage necessary for the soul to believe in his revelation of God, as well as providing the soul with the conceptual world in which it can find and experience God. This priesthood must, of course, be sharply distinguished from every ancient and sacral priesthood, and purged of all supposed magical manipulation of God. Finally, as king, Jesus is both the head and the original image of the community that gathers about him, calls itself by his name, confesses him as its unifying point, and celebrates his presence in its devotional cultus.

It is precisely this gathering around a *personality,* and *not* a dogma or an idea or a moral law or a miraculous community founded by Jesus, that constitutes the central focus of Christianity and provides it with the means to propagate itself. And this is precisely what makes it a religion of the spirit, freeing it from both dogma and priesthood, and providing it with a purely inner spiritual bonding, expressing itself (or it ought to be expressing itself) in a spiritual culture.

The most important of the three concepts is that of the king or lord through whom everything—all revelation and all priestly guidance to God, as well as the gathering of the community about Christ as its head—streams ever anew into the lives of the faithful. This is how Schleiermacher and Ritschl construed the religious meaning of Jesus. But if we prefer more modern terminology, we may substitute the following language for the old dogmatic offices of prophet, priest, and king, respectively: the original image of the Christian-personalist life, the foundational and continuing embodiment of the Christian principle (i.e., the living and effective symbol of faith), and the central and foundational personality of revelation. This is how the terms "Redeemer" and "Savior" are to be understood. "Redeemer" signifies both the original image and the authority of faith's redemptive certainty, so that "Redeemer" and "Revealer" mean the same thing.

5. It is likely that faith will also attempt to construe this historical personality's significance in *metaphysical* terms. This poses for us the task of formulating more precisely the communion with God that Jesus' personality offers, i.e., a doctrine of Jesus' relationship to God. This, in turn, leads us to consider various propositions concerning the presence, or specific indwelling, of God in Christ.

The early church accomplished this task first with the help of messianism and later with the help of the doctrine of the *incarnation;* but contemporary theology, for the most part, formulates the relationship of God and Christ in terms of a unity of will, not an essential unity in substance. The revealing and redemptive presence of God in Christ's human personality is then conceived as the *specific indwelling of God in Christ.* Furthermore, this particular unity of will results in a particular place for Jesus among human creatures, which can also be metaphysically formulated. It suggests the concept of the Second Adam[2] or the central human being, who is the spiritual son of the human spiritual world. This, of course, is bound up with the concept that Christianity is the absolutely final and everlasting religion, the religion that will gather all human beings unto the end.

Finally, one could also try to put the historical life and work of Christ into cosmic and metaphysical frames of reference. These would include the central renewal and *exaltation* of humanity that comes

2. See Rom. 5:12-19.

through the influx of a higher life—a forgiveness-assured, and God-filled life. The doctrine of the church, meanwhile, would then consist partly in the founding of the church and partly in the reconciliation of the divine wrath—working together, in a metaphysical sense, for the effective redemption of a sinful world that would be lost without Christ. This too would presuppose the central place of Christianity and its definitive capacity to unify the human race.

But whoever cannot share in these certainties will find all such predicates questionable, and will instead be satisfied with the foundational meaning of the *personality* of Jesus as the *revelation* of God, the head of the community, and the effective symbol of saving and healing religious power, for as long as the Christian life-world endures. At this point, the concepts of the *corpus mysticum* [mystic body] and the *caput mysticum* [mystic head] will suffice. This theological standpoint remains a viable option, even though the most important theological schools will continue to strive after the higher predicates for Jesus in order to adhere as closely as possible to the traditional teaching of the church.

LECTURE

Our primary concern is the distinction between the historical and the religious, i.e., we recognize that faith surely interprets historical facts, but has no part in determining what actually happened. Thus our faith is markedly dependent on history. The kind of picture that historical research draws of Jesus—whether as the abrogation of all messianism, or as a Jewish rabbi who generally taught nothing different from what other rabbis taught, or as a fundamental breakthrough to something specifically un-Jewish—makes a difference in our religious attitude. And particularly when the research has a bearing on whether Jesus even existed or not! If it could be proven that he did not exist, we would have to give up his place in our lives. That is what makes the struggle so bitter! Our faith is by no means independent of the research. This problem was already known in Lessing's time, and was later grasped thoroughly by D. F. Strauss.

The most important modern theological antagonist of our distinction between religious research and religious interpretation is Herrmann, who argues that we thereby make faith dependent on professorial debates. This, he continues, would be unbearable for the religious person. There is a historical certainty that needs no method, for we possess an instinctive certainty: Jesus must have said this and nothing else! Faith must be able to understand the main events of history correctly—not by relying on others, but by means of an instinctive judgment. Whoever denies this, according to Herrmann, does so out of a lack of the congeniality of faith. And this lack of congeniality constitutes the surest proof that scholarship leads only to skepticism, while faith leads to certainty. It is precisely this conflict between faith and knowledge that demonstrates, according to Herrmann, the superiority of a knowledge constituted by faith.

To the contrary, we insist that Herrmann's position requires a fundamental contradiction between scholarship and faith. It says, I believe it because it is absurd.[3] This may have been true as long as criticism busied itself with peripheral concerns, but now that criticism has insinuated itself into ultimate and final matters, things have changed. Whether Jesus actually spoke this one word or not, that is supposed to be a matter of faith? All our collective historical hairs stand on end at this idea. And Wobbermin's distinction between *Geschichte* and *Historie* offers us little help with this problem as well.[4] It is impossible for faith to establish facts of history. Neither enthusiasm nor apathy can express how difficult it is to own up to the monumental challenge that historical criticism poses for faith. For Herrmann's position, any allusion to the dependence of faith on criticism has a powerful, severely shocking impact on the soul.

Nevertheless, on closer inspection, we find that the concept loses much of its terror. We do not depend on the thousands of details, but only on the general results of the research. This holds true not only for our relation to Jesus, but for everything in general. Our relationship to God and the world also cannot be sheltered from the results of scientific research; we cannot evade the implications of a single point. If the Darwinian theory of evolution were fully demonstrated, it would have an impact on our faith. Faith cannot determine how long the human race has been on our planet. This does not mean that every believer must read a commentary on the gospels. The individual will already have a sure instinct for what is decisive. When he hears that the gospels are popular traditions that are not altogether free from adulteration, it will just make the matter easier for him: he will cling only to that which enlightens him. But the laity will be able

3. A famous gibe of the Latin theologian Tertullian (160?–230?).
4. Georg Wobbermin (1869–1943) suggested a distinction between two types of history, *Geschichte* (the usual German word for history, which, literally translated, means "what has happened") and *Historie*. *Geschichte* was, for Wobbermin, experienced history, while *Historie* was the subject of scholarly historical investigation. The latter was the concern of faith, the former the concern of scholarship. See Georg Wobbermin, *Geschichte und Historie in der Religionswissenschaft* (Tübingen: J.C.B. Mohr, 1911), pp. 5–15.

to do this only when scholarly circles rid themselves of the notion that *everything* in the tradition is unreliable; otherwise the people will eventually cease to trust their own instincts. We turn now to the traditions that lie before us. Are they essentially reliable? This question has provoked bitter debate during the last ten years. Strauss himself had already concluded that the available materials, although surely subject to criticism, nevertheless pointed to the facts pretty well. It is only in the immediate past that we have seen the most passionate attack on the sources. This is not only the result of the broadening of our horizons and our growing knowledge of Judaism and the cults of antiquity; it is primarily the fruit of the efforts of a party that has set itself against Christianity. Nietzsche saw Christianity as a "slave morality" that glorified mediocrity. We need not offer any further judgments on Nietzsche's thought here; all that concerns us now is the observation that he gave birth to the wish that the human race could, with a single stroke, be rid of Christianity. And this could be best achieved by demonstrating that its foundations are illusory. Whoever rejects the sense and spirit of Christianity will also turn against its history (Kalthoff).[5] And then one could go on to eliminate the letters of Paul, tracing everything back to the oriental penchant for mythmaking (Lublinski).[6] Maurenbrecher, in his book *Von Galiläa nach Golgatha (From Galilee to Golgotha)*, mounts a more sophisticated attack.[7] These writers all view Christianity as a religious disease of the age, something which must be mortally wounded if religion is to be saved; and they are all passionately committed to this goal.

In light of these assaults, it is no longer questions of detail that are at stake. The problem is this: Do the newly discovered differences in the texts, the difference between the ethical personality of Jesus and the cultic worship of Jesus as the one who was and is and will be—do these differences mean that there are two very different things standing behind the texts? Is it likely that the synoptic Jesus was a Jewish

5. Albert Kalthoff (1850–1906), *The Rise of Christianity* (1903), trans. Joseph McCabe (London: Watts & Co., 1905).

6. Samuel Lublinski (1868–1910), *Der urchristliche Erdkreis und sein Mythos*, vol. 1, *Entstehung des Christentums aus der antiken Kultur*, vol. 2, *Das werdende Dogma vom Leben Jesu* (Jena: E. Diederichs, 1910).

7. Max Maurenbrecher (1874–1930), *Von Nazareth nach Golgatha: Untersuchungen über die weltgeschichtliche Zusammenhänge des Urchristentums* (From Nazareth to Golgotha: Studies on the connections between Christianity and world history) (Berlin-Schöneberg: Buchverlag der "Hilfe," 1909). Maurenbrecher later played a role in founding the German Church Movement in the 1920s, a forerunner of the infamous German Christian Movement of the Nazi era.

rabbi, while the Christ of Paul and John is a figure that arose out of the ancient idea of the god-man—an idea that is to be found in the cult of Mithra and other similar non-Jewish cults? And is what we call Christianity actually the result of a combination of the Jewish rabbi Jesus with the cult of the god-man? What relationship did the Christ-cult of Paul's congregations have to the rabbi Jesus? These questions constitute the horns by which we must seize the proverbial bull.

The beginnings of the history of Christianity are shrouded in mist in the same way that the beginnings of other movements are obscured, e.g., the first stirrings of pietism or social democracy. We have no sources other than the testimony of the communities themselves. Non-Christian descriptions do not begin to appear until Christianity, already firmly established, comes to light in reports sent in to Rome by government officials. It is therefore foolish to hope that we will find documentary evidence for the genesis of the community. The community naturally describes itself in honorific and uncritical terms. And our sources are, in fact, comparatively good. The letters of Paul remain genuine, even if they raise as many riddles as they resolve. Only a violent blow could damage the credibility of Paul's letters. As far as the synoptic gospels are concerned, they contain traditional remembrances. They are therefore not accurate word for word in matters of detail, and they have been reconstructed here and there, but their account is still essentially reliable. The oldest historical account of the community, the Acts of the Apostles, is about as reliable.

Now we ask, Do these sources project the image of a Jewish rabbi that was grafted on to a non-Jewish cult by Paul? Did the mysterious mantle of the god-man that was floating around come down, so to speak, on to the rabbi Jesus? Maurenbrecher, Wrede,[8] and Gunkel[9] have tried to resolve this question: the yawning chasm between the synoptic Jesus and the preexisting Christ of the Pauline communities need be the result neither of an inner Christian development nor of a non-Jewish grafting.

The problem gets more pointed when critics assert that the really essential thing was the cult of the food and the blood, and that its hero, Jesus, was invented only in order to make it more colorful by

8. William Wrede (1859–1906), *The Origin of the New Testament* (1907), trans. James S. Hill (New York: Harper & Brothers, 1909).
9. Hermann Gunkel (1862–1932), *Zum religionsgeschichtlichen Verständnis des Neuen Testaments* (Göttingen: Vandenhoeck & Ruprecht, 1903).

the addition of a cultic legend. This point is repeatedly urged upon us; but it is a point honed so fine that it breaks. In the light of the available sources, this thesis is utterly impossible. It could be possible only if the Pauline letters and the whole of early Christian literature were inauthentic. And besides, if anyone had ever tried to invent such a cultic hero, they would surely not have come up with such stark contradictions between the hero and the image worshiped in the cultus. The other thesis, the one about the grafting, does possess a relative right in light of the contradictions, but it too is impossible for the following reasons.

First of all, the non-Jewish redemption cult that was supposedly grafted on to the rabbi Jesus is unknown to us. We generally know that there were many redemption cults at that time, but the cults of Mithra, Attis, etc., have nothing to do with the cult of Christianity. We would therefore have to presume the existence of a cult entirely unknown to us; and to reconstruct this supposed cult on the basis of the evidence we do have would do such violence to the facts as to be out of the question. Second, we would have to locate where this influx of non-Jewish faith took place. But we search for that in the Book of Acts in vain. And this supposed influx would have had to happen very quickly indeed, since its supposed effects were already in place by the time of Paul. Maurenbrecher has worked very hard on this thesis in particular. The widespread acceptance of foreign cults that took place during that age is just about the only piece of evidence that he has found. Otherwise, all that he has managed to achieve is nothing but the most dubious constructions. Such an influx as he proposes would be most improbable, since it is utterly without parallel. Indeed, comparison with other religious founders indicates the opposite. Thus the thesis that tried to connect the sun-myth to the invention of the person of the Buddha has long since been discarded. The analogy of St. Francis also suggests itself here. His disciples enshrouded him with all sorts of miracles, but we can still clearly and perfectly recognize the image of this particularly fascinating person. Nowhere do we find that a foreign cult settles down on such a figure, but rather the reverse: the cult settles down on a figure that has already been established, as in the Catholic veneration of the sainted Francis of Assisi.

But if all this is true, we then are left with the opposite thesis: that the admittedly different understanding of the person of Jesus found in the early Christian communities is the result of first an *intrinsically Jewish,* and then an *intrinsically Christian* development, all of which can be easily understood in terms of the age in which Christianity arose.

In the midst of all this agitation over the figure of Jesus, we must above all recall his insistence on the infinite value of the soul, in comparison with which all else is insignificant. *"One* thing is needful!"[10] And we must remember the community of love that Jesus intended, where humankind is bound to God, everything is viewed *sub specie aeternitatis,* and all earthly things sink down to the ground. Yours, says Jesus, is the Kingdom of Heaven that already comes here to earth—when the *infinite* value of the soul is recognized, and when love reigns where selfishness, war, and unrighteousness now rule. These ideas are completely original, pointing far beyond rabbinical wisdom. Nor is it, moreover, to be doubted that healings of the sick proceeded from Jesus. In addition, there was his extraordinary consciousness of mission: "Something greater than Solomon is here."[11] And finally, the tragic end and the story of the resurrection! Historical research has nothing to say about the latter. For ourselves, we solve the problem by reference to the devotion and surrender of the disciples, which convinced them that Jesus lived. But no insuperable difficulties stand before those who wish to hold that there was a real spiritual vision.

All these extraordinary circumstances and effects, however, make the process whereby belief in the Messiah came to be transferred to Jesus and underwent subsequent alterations quite understandable. We can see how this belief in the Messiah, once it got connected to Jesus, could transform Jesus, the revealer of God, into the object of a cult. Since what Jesus was and wanted was so thoroughly different from all rabbinicalism, it was impossible for the community that bound itself to him to remain Jewish and nationalistic.

Nor did the cultus that grew around the figure of Jesus honor him as a cultic god after the manner of the mysteries. The Christian community remained every bit as monotheistic as Judaism. The person of Jesus, now elevated into heaven, became transparent to the one God that was visible through him. While pagans may have referred to a "Christ-god," such expressions were banned within the community itself. The community said, We have *God in Christ,* not In Christ we have a new God.

10. Luke 10:42.
11. Luke 11:31.

Of course this explanation leaves us with several problematic and unexplained points. Thus we have the question: To what extent is the picture of Jesus portrayed by the witness of the community already conditioned by the community's faith—particularly with respect to his messianism? Or, How much of the idea of Christ's return can be traced back to his own words? These questions cannot be answered decisively. Mark already writes from the point of view that Jesus is the expected Christ. In just the same way, the rapid expansion of the Christ-cult will remain a riddle; even Paul's teaching, in its main points, is taken from pre-Pauline sources. We do not know how the doctrine developed that Jesus was already present in the creation, equal to God, and then descended into wretched human life. We do not know how the Lord's Supper grew out of the last supper that Jesus shared with his disciples. But we do not need to know everything. The main points, the person of Jesus and the worship of Christ, stand firm; and they must be grasped in their inner continuity. Therein lies yet another proof of faith's need for history. We have taken care to keep faith distinct from history, but we do not need to seek out extra conflicts to go along with the unavoidable ones, nor do we need to set our pride against the results of scientific historical research.

The question that distinguishes faith from history is not, *Which* facts? but What do the facts *mean*? We still have the truism that a figure like Jesus could never have been invented; yet the tradition alone cannot guarantee its truth. But now we have established the historicity of Jesus' preaching and consciousness of mission, and they suffice as a kernel. This is where faith begins its task of interpretation. If these facts resonate within us and call forth agreement from us, then they have value for us. Is there here, for us too, a flowing life in these facts, a life to which we willingly and unavoidably give our consent—or do our waters flow from some other source? This question is to be decided here, and the answer to it is no longer a matter of scholarship, but of personal, living decision. If through Jesus we know the Father who calls us all and determines us for a mutual community of love in him, that is to take a specific ethical-religious stance. We must ask our own inner selves whether we wish to be conquered, humbled, and elevated by the God that Jesus brings; and whether he shall fill us with the trust and heroic courage that are necessary if we are to surrender to this religious life-world.

For this decision to be possible for us, it is necessary to extract the *meaning* of the traditions which come down to us from Jesus. One's

interpretation of these traditions, however, may not be simply whatever one likes. There are utterly pantheistic interpretations of Jesus,
whose creed is the full unity of the divine and human, for which it is
supposed to be possible to appeal to later church dogma! Nothing
could be more foreign to the facts than to make Jesus into a symbol
for this sort of pantheistic unity. We are not talking about ideas that
we project on to Jesus, but ideas that should be drawn from him. But
this is most certain to occur if we appropriate the meaning of the
facts. We may then be sure that we know the meaning that his personality lived and bore; and then we will have what Schleiermacher
called the "the power of Jesus' God-consciousness" which is transmitted to his faithful.[12]

But religious interpretation is not concerned with Jesus and his
history in isolation; rather, in him we see a vigorous religious life that
extends from him down through two millennia to us. In order truly to
understand Jesus' personality, it is just as necessary to recognize its
subsequent impact as it is to take note of its previous background
and preparation. The whole of Jewish prophetism clings fast to Jesus,
and the entire development of Christianity proceeds from him. What
came from him must also have been present in him. We cannot see
him simply in terms of his appearance alone; it is only in the stream
of his effects, in the light of a Paul, an Augustine, a Luther, that we
fully understand him. And here it is not a matter of concerning ourselves with an uncertain philology. We can grasp him in the same
sense that Luther did. We can see him as the source of our inner
freedom, the heroic courage that dares to take the cross upon itself,
despite the cross's contradiction to nature; and we can liberate the
greatness of his wooing from its first narrow interpretation. In him
we can see what the millennia have drawn from his fullness. It is fully
justifiable to ask what Jesus would say today; it is fully justifiable to
formulate the picture of Jesus freely. All that is required is that we
attribute nothing to him that is not apparent from his essence.

The decisive thing about such an interpretation, therefore, is that
it recognizes the enduring, living capacity of Jesus' personality, a
personality whose impact was thoroughly historical and psychological. Abelard already taught that the significance of Jesus was not
cosmic, but rather lay in his soul-transforming impact. Likewise, the
death of Jesus entailed no effect on God and the devil, but was

12. Friedrich Schleiermacher, *The Christian Faith* (1830), trans. H. R. Mackintosh
and J. S. Stewart (Edinburgh: T. & T. Clarke, 1928), p. 425.

rather the great example of a certainty in God that could not be shaken by senseless suffering, that was able to overcome all darkness. And so it enabled others to share this certainty in God:

When I this life must depart,
depart thou not from me![13]

As his life revealed divine power, so too did his death. God remains the redeemer. What I experience before his countenance bestows courage and elevation, and that is redemption! I experience this redemption in personal communion with God; but the courage that enables it, I owe to the revelation in Jesus. He leads us to God, he unveils God's grace through the confidence that flows from him and brings us close to God. And finally: If Jesus is the leader and the mediator, he is also the point from whence the community arises—not merely as a matter of historical fact, but also as the symbol that binds everything together. The community lives not by commandments, but by a personality that has a personal impact! Its path will always lead back to that personality. Without it there can be no Christian community, without it no highest life. The Christian community's only cultus will be to enwrap itself around the image of its founder and to let that image work upon it.

This threefold characterization of Jesus' impact coincides with the old orthodox titles of prophet, high priest, and king. Of course, there are many differences: the high priestly office was the most important, and the kingly office included Christ's lordship over nature, i.e., his cosmic-metaphysical lordship in union with God. But we can still put the titles themselves to good use. For us, the high-priestly and prophetic offices refer to how the individual soul is led to God: the individual soul, supported in its own sphere through Jesus' powers,

13. From the ninth stanza of "O Haupt voll Blut und Wunden" (O Sacred head, now wounded), by the prolific Lutheran hymnist Paul Gerhardt (1607–1676). The entire stanza may be translated:

When I this life must depart,
  depart thou not from me.
When I must suffer death,
  then come thou forth instead.
And when the greatest agonies
  afflict me in my heart,
Then let thy pain and suffering
  remove from me their dart.

Herbert Lang, ed., *Paulus Gerhardts geistliche Lieder* (Bern: Herbert Lang, 1974), p. 32.

attains victorious certainty. The kingly office refers to his lordship over the community, the *caput mysticum* of the *corpus mysticum* [the mystical head of the mystical body]. We are the beam of the search-light, through which the light-source shines ever anew. The kingly office is now the preeminent one. The point of Jesus' life was to create a community, and the community plays a decisive role in the goal of leading human beings to God. The other offices presuppose, and are subordinate to, this preeminent office.

Other expressions for Jesus are "the living symbol," "Lord and Master," "foundational personality of revelation," "redeemer." This last expression provokes misgivings: it smacks a little of cosmic trans-mutation. It is better to say: Jesus was the possibility of redemption. God remains the actual redeemer. Even the word "Savior," because of its associations with the saccharine sentimentality of pietism, is not altogether unobjectionable.

Behind all these attempts to understand Jesus stands the desire to explain his personality in the context of a far broader horizon, to see it as something more than the personality who relates God to us in the most striking fashion. It is conceivable that many will not be satisfied without more than this. The secret of Jesus' personality lies not only in the impact that he had, but in how he came to have it. A purely metaphysical solution to that riddle may be attempted. The ancient dogma pursued the metaphysical path vigorously, believing that the true solution lay in its doctrine of the incarnation—the unique relationship between God and this personality. More recent theology construes this unity, not as an incarnation, but as a unity of will.

This same problem has also given rise to speculation about Jesus' place in the universe. This is the source of expressions like "essence of reality," "central human being," "central sun of the spirit," "begin-ning of a second order of humanity," "Second Adam." By no means are these speculations to be forbidden, but they are questionable. They always imply the difficult claim that Christianity is the center of history. For us, personally, matters are such that we will restrict our-selves to that which is accessible. We take our place in the power of this personality and recognize it as our mystical head. Whoever in good conscience is able to go beyond this psychological interpretation should do so. He will find it easier to make contact with orthodoxy, for he will find it possible to speak, in a certain sense, of the deity of Christ. But when it comes to such metaphysical interpretations, we owe one another nothing but forbearance.

§9. The Religious Significance of the History of Christianity as the Development of Revelation

DICTATION

1. If the religious significance of Jesus rests on the idea of a *corpus mysticum,* then the latter also constitutes an object for religious interpretation. And since the *corpus mysticum* consists in the *historical development* of Christianity, then faith's attitude toward Jesus must be tied to an attitude and faith in the history of the living religious community that proceeds from him. This brings us to the third set of historical-religious propositions. The religious evaluation of the history of Israel as a preparation corresponds to the religious estimate of the history of Christianity as the impact of Christ. Here too, historical research must be distinguished from religious faith and its judgments, just as with all previous history.

2. Historical research into these matters falls under the topics of church history, the history of dogma, and the history of ethics. Now that these disciplines have been completely freed of all dogmatic and ecclesiastical preconceptions, they are free to take up the whole history of Christianity in an organic-institutional and spiritual-ethical perspective. As a result, the interweaving of Christianity's development with the general history of culture grows ever more clear. We can therefore illuminate the history of Christianity by reference to the history of culture, and vice versa. The most significant things here are the great questions of the origin and spirit of the early church, the medieval church, and finally and most importantly, Protestantism.

3. In the old orthodox dogmatics, the religious interpretation of Christian history was completely subsumed under the concepts of the *church* and the *Holy Spirit.* Jesus' impact on history consisted in a unified life that proceeded from the gospel; and this life served as the objective basis of the sacraments, the clerical office, and the Word of God. The church was the objective organization that preserved and continued the miracle of the incarnation in the context of a divine-human institution. The Catholic concept of the church consolidated this view, tracing the sacraments and the Word of God back to Christ, the first priest; both divine and human, Christ established the hierarchy and instituted the sacraments as the material means of infusing his redemptive power, which is now entrusted to the priests. The Protestant concept of the church reduced this objective element to the Word of God, or the consciousness of the forgiveness of sins

that was brought by Christ and recorded in the Bible; this was the kernel of the guarantee that faith will always lead to community. In both confessions, the Holy Spirit is always bound to the objective means of the church's instruments.

But modern sensitivities and recent dogmatics have transformed this concept: now the church is a free, purely spiritual, living nexus that emerges from Christ. Its objective content lies ultimately in the continued impact of the Spirit of Christ and in the community's shared relation to the person of Jesus. But this can have a wide variety of cultic expressions in all sorts of entirely different individual groups. Hence the religious interpretation of the history of Christianity is no longer determined by the concept of the church, but by the concept of a freely worked-out tradition that is shared in a common spirit, or the Holy Spirit. The concept of the church has been replaced by the concept of the *common Christian spirit* as a religious *living unity,* or the developing Kingdom of God. But to describe the history of Christianity in this way—as the pathway to, and the realization of, the developing Kingdom of God—is purely a matter of faith, based on confidence in the effectiveness of the Christian spirit. And insofar as we can characterize this spirit as the Holy Spirit, then the Holy Spirit is not bound to any clerical, sacramental, or dogmatic objectivity as it works itself out in history.

4. If this living Christian nexus is what constitutes the continuing effectiveness of the revelation in Christ, then it must also be understood as a genuinely *continuing development* of revelation itself. This is why the history of Christianity holds such significance for faith. Its great manifestations must be understood as stages in the unfolding of the Spirit of Christ in the life of the world. It must therefore be revered, in all of its subsequent junctions and personalities, as a continuing revelation. In particular, the Reformers should be seen as a new stage in the Christian revelation; and the great changes taking place in the present and future should also be seen as a continuation of the revelation of God. Our entire previous discussion of the authority of our sources was based on this interpretation.

5. Insofar as we view the Christian community as the continuing effect of the Spirit of Christ or the Holy Spirit, then it also constitutes the link between the historical Jesus and contemporary individual rebirth and redemption. It is through the congregation and the community that Jesus becomes contemporary and his spirit effects individual power, communion with God, and the concomitant victory over the consciousness of guilt, evil, and suffering. In this way, *indi-*

vidual revelation, enlightenment, and rebirth are all embraced in the continued working out of the revelation in the community: a work of the Spirit of Christ or the Holy Spirit, in which the living Christian substance produces an ever new and individual reality, thereby continuing to develop within each individual.

LECTURE

We can deal with this material only very briefly. The distinction between historical research and religious interpretation remains fundamental. The former is to be given over without remainder to church history and the history of dogma, while the latter remains the task of *Glaubenslehre.* The older dogmatics began this task with the doctrine of the church as the vehicle of the Holy Spirit. The element of truth in the doctrine is this: Whenever any redemptive power proceeds from Jesus, it is not individuals who produce the community; the community produces them.

The modern world has liberated this concept of the Holy Spirit from the church, transferring it to the whole of the Christian life-world and its spiritual context. Interpretation of the history of Christianity has therefore gone on to acknowledge increased possibilities for various groups and stages; as a result, every particular formation of the Christian concept is to be based on, and affirmed according to, its own particular version of Christianity's living ideal and saving value. Hence the Greek Orthodox Church reflects the world of declining antiquity and the Roman Catholic Church reflects the world of the Middle Ages, while the various versions of Protestantism reflect the differentiation of the modern world. Henceforth the history of Christianity will possess the character of a continuing revelation. This history is an interpretation of faith, for it attaches to faith in the living Spirit of Christ, which is always finding and filling new forms.[1]

---

1. Gertrud von le Fort included the following note, to which we have added data of translation and publication: For further elaboration, compare the following works by Ernst Troeltsch: *The Absoluteness of Christianity and the History of Religions* (1902, 2d. ed. 1911), English trans. by David Reid (Richmond: John Knox Press, 1971); "What does 'Essence of Christianity' Mean?" [1903; in *Ernst Troeltsch: Writings on Theology and Religion,* ed. and trans. Robert Morgan and Michael Pye (Atlanta: John Knox Press, 1982), pp. 124–181]; and *Der Historismus und seine Probleme* [Tübingen: J.C.B. Mohr, 1922].

§10. The Doctrine of the Trinity as the Link between the Historical and the Religious Elements in Christianity

DICTATION

1. Historical-religious propositions are principally religious in character. Their religious significance consists in the way that they fill out the concept of God with concrete Christian perceptions. Hence the concept of God itself reflects these propositions. The idea of God must be conceived in such a way that the *historical* self-revelation of God can be seen to proceed from the *divine essence itself.* These historical-religious propositions are reflected in the doctrine of the Trinity, a doctrine which is nothing other than an attempt to establish an inner correspondence between the essence of God and his historical revelation. The primitive community met this need with its messianic belief, which, through the subsequent mediation of the doctrine of the Logos, later developed into the doctrine of the Trinity. The doctrine of the Trinity says nothing about the actual spiritual content of the Christian concept of God; it only links the divine essence to its historical revelation. This applies to the highly abstract Athanasian-Augustinian form of the doctrine as well, which minimized the historical elements of the doctrine as much as possible, but nevertheless retained its christocentric sense.

2. We begin with the ancient formula that combined God the Father, Christ the Son, and the Holy Spirit. In the apostolic world of ideas, the purpose of the formula was to give a brief expression of the Christian faith in God who was revealed in the miraculous personality of the Redeemer, and who was effective in the community through the outpouring of the Spirit. Its purpose in apostolic theology was to connect that which is both eternal and contemporary— i.e., faith in the redeeming Father—to the historical revelation in Christ and the miraculous, continuing proofs of the Spirit. This is the formula of the *economic Trinity.*

This apostolic formula subsequently developed into the *immanent Trinity* of the *homoousian* [consubstantiality].[1] The immanent Trinity had a twofold function: first, it expressed the philosophical difference between the Christian-monotheistic concept of God and the Neopla-

---

1. *Homoousian* is a key term in the Nicene Creed, where it is usually translated as "of one substance": "And I believe in one Lord Jesus Christ, . . . being of one substance with the Father." It is also translated as "consubstantial."

tonic theory of emanations; and second, it reinforced the apostolic linkage between the historical and the religious. It performed the first task by identifying the Logos with the Father in terms of the *homoousian,* the second by its doctrine of the two natures and the incarnation of the Logos. The *homoousia*[2] [consubstantiality] of the Spirit that follows is simply its fully realized equality with the Father and the Logos, derived from the common use of the formula. This is where the historical connection enters in, through the Spirit's relationship to the illumination of the community.

Finally came Augustine's purely speculative construction of the substance of God subsisting in three *hypostases,* wherein the living riches of the divine inner essence are deployed. But even here, the historical elements continued in the forefront, along with the incarnation of the Logos and, of course, the inspiring Spirit.

3. But now that ancient cosmology has been eliminated from theology, and with the accompanying emergence of a human-historical view of Jesus, the Christian concept of God has grown independent of this basically Neoplatonic formula. The contemporary material exposition of the concept of God is developed purely out of Jesus' proclamation of God; but this makes it impossible to explain Jesus' religious significance in terms of the incarnation of the Logos. And this, in turn, spells the end for the patristic, immanent doctrine of the Trinity. But the concept of a redemptive revelation of God, in Christ and through the Holy Spirit, still remains the most succinct summary of the Christian faith; and so this three-ness remains. But no longer can it be understood in terms of the immanent Trinity—only in terms of the so-called *economic* Trinity.

4. Understood this way, however, the Trinitarian formula provides us with a brief summary of Christianity: the revelation of God, given in Christ, and made effective for us in the Spirit. *God in Christ,* and through the *Spirit of Christ,* in *us.* Stated in this way, the Trinity remains the enduring classic formulation of Christianity; all of theology can be expressed in it. The doctrine of the Trinity expresses faith in God in terms of its bond to Christ, and in terms of the confidence from the Spirit which grasps and transforms us. The economic Trinity, then, provides the transition from the doctrine of the Christ in Part One to the doctrine of the redemptive faith in God which Christ communicates and empowers, in Part Two.

---

2. The word *homoousia (Die Homousie)* is a mistake; there is no feminine form of *homoousian* in Greek.

LECTURE

We come now to the conclusion of this section. Our historical-
religious propositions continue to be truly religious propositions; the
higher their meaning, the more impact they have on the center of all
religious ideas, the idea of God. God must be conceived in such a
way that historical self-disclosure is a necessity for him. Christianity
drew this conclusion quite early, seeing in Christ and his teachings a
revelation of God that went beyond the Jewish Yahweh. Thus Christ
attained the status of Lord, not as a new God, but as the highest
revelation. As a result, the picture of Jesus quickly moved much
closer to the picture of God, to the image of the Son and the Father.
The highest, truest essence of God was no longer to be found in the
prophets, but in Jesus. Through him, as the mediator, God became
visible. This is how the early development of the dogmas is to be
understood.

Christ continued to be elevated until he became virtually indistinguishable from God, except that he remained a subordinate who
would finally turn his dominion over to the Father.[3] This di-unity led
to the great battles of the early church, which were the result of
attempts to determine Christ's relation to God more precisely. The
overriding monotheistic interest required whatever appeared to be
divine in Christ to be identical in essence with the Father. Hence the
mediator, filled with divine powers, united with God, became Lord
and Creator. Christ became the Logos become flesh. But this consubstantial *di*-unity was not yet a *Tri*-unity, or Trinity. The Trinity came
about in this way: In the apostolic sense, the Holy Spirit is the Spirit
of Christ, which attests itself in charity, glossolalia, courage, and the
breaking of the natural self. This Spirit proceeds from Christ, in
whom God reveals himself. The next step was to draw the Spirit into
connection with God and Christ; and once this development came
into contact with the popular ancient interest in threes, it was only a
short step to including the Spirit in the unity of essence. The Spirit,
just like the Logos, became identical in essence with God. Thus did
the di-unity become a Tri-unity, by way of the *homoousian*.

This *homoousian*-Trinity differed from the apostolic formula,
which intended only an *economic Trinity*, in correspondence with the
divine world-ordering. According to this economy of salvation, God
revealed his love in Christ, who, having departed from the world,
bequeathed the Spirit to those who believed in him. At this point the

---

3. 1 Cor. 15:28.

historical and the religious are on a collision course. The immanent Trinity, as opposed to the economic, stands for something utterly timeless and outside of history. It refers to an eternal division of the Godhead into three, a three which must nevertheless be thought of as one. Within the divine substance the Godhead eternally moves through three potencies. Thus the historical moment becomes an eternal moment, and the original purpose of the doctrine appears lost. But this is only an appearance. Even the immanent Trinity preserves a historical moment: The essence of the Logos reaches into time with redemption, and the essence of the Spirit is present in every illumination of the community.

The problem of trinitarian dogma is thus quite clear; the only question is whether we can find a satisfactory interpretation of it. To that we reply: the immanent Trinity belongs to the concept of incarnation—God becoming flesh in a moment of time. It also belongs with the concept of redemption as apotheosis attained by means of the sacraments. It entails Neoplatonic cosmology and metaphysics. Yet now we no longer ground our faith on incarnation, but on revelation instead. How this revelation came to pass is, for us, the basic mystery of personal life. That problem will remain. A new solution would be simply to return to the apostolic concept of the economic Trinity: the one God who was in Christ and who, through Christ's Spirit, is in us. We could surely adopt this formula.

Our final conclusion, therefore, is this: If we conceive history as proceeding from God, then our faith in his highest revelation binds the eternal and temporal close together. We can say: I believe in God the Father and in the Son and in the Holy Spirit; for we believe in the eternal Lord of the world, who was miraculously revealed in Jesus, and in his Spirit, which rules in history and leads us farther and farther into all truth.[4]

4. See John 16:13.

PART TWO

1

The Christian Concept
of God

§11. The Place of the Concept of God in the System

DICTATION

1. In our systematic religious exposition, the various concepts of faith are viewed as reciprocally conditioned and complementary parts of a system, so that each implies the whole of the Christian faith. Each concept includes within itself the whole of this faith: the religious and ethical idea of redemption and personality. Only the exemplification changes.

The concept of God, therefore, embraces the whole of the Christian faith: its origin in God and its striving for God. But at the same time, Christian faith in God is but one moment of the entire Christian approach to life. The concept of God stands alongside all other concepts of faith; and these concepts, in turn, express the totality of the Christian faith only in combination with the concept of God.

2. Ours is a *descriptive* theological method: we describe the Christian disposition and the religious concepts or beliefs contained in it. This means abandoning the deductive method that takes the concept of God as an objectively established fact and deduces everything else from it—beginning with creation and preparation for redemption, and then moving on to redemption and its effects—as objective statements about events in the world. On the contrary: dogmatic statements actually express the preconditions and contents of the Christian consciousness of faith, i.e., a living, practical-theoretical

orientation to God, the world, and humanity. Hence the dogmatic concept of God analyzes our thoughts about God, not God himself.

3. Therefore, our discussion of the Christian concept of God is not to be measured against any so-called *natural* knowledge of God. There is no such thing as a generally accepted and logically compelling natural knowledge of God. What is usually meant by such "natural knowledge" is one of the various attempts that have been made to grasp the essence of God, most of which are more or less strongly influenced by actual religion and, therefore, are not genuinely scientific matters. Instead, the first thing we should do is to construct the Christian concept of God and to compare it with the non-Christian concepts of God found in the great universal religions, all of which possess their own practical religious intuitions of the whole. We will discover both positive and negative relations, both connections and contradictions, between Christian and non-Christian concepts of God. But in this process, Christian faith in God consistently proves itself to be the consummate religion of personality, in comparison with both the less developed religions of personality as well as with the wholly impersonal religions.

4. A brief survey of the territory before us yields the following starting points for the exposition of the Christian concept of God. First comes the task of highlighting the characteristic essence of the Christian concept of God in contrast to all non-Christian concepts, particularly in terms of the strong connection it draws between the *divine will and essence.* The second task is to call attention to the peculiar way in which the Christian concept of the will culminates in the concept of the *divine holiness.* The third topic is the consummation of the concept of holiness in the concept of the *holy love,* which fully clarifies the sense and purpose of the concept of holiness at the same time that it embraces the full meaning of the Christian concept of God. The fourth thing is the great problem of how this belief that there is an intentional love and goal for the world can be reconciled with the empirical character of the world and its countless manifestations of ateleology, or the problem of so-called *theodicy.*

LECTURE

Part Two of our *Glaubenslehre* has the task of providing a comprehensive summary of the contemporary religious consciousness and its concepts. We think here, above all, of the *concept of God.* Our sensitivity to God is not a matter of history. God is immediately present to us; concealed in our most deeply hidden feelings, we have a permanent self-relation to him. But this leaves us with a whole series of questions.

We have to consider the concept of God with respect to the heights and depths of our souls. Our sorrows and joys grow out of this world; we are combatants in a struggle. Entangled in the world, yet hoping to transcend it, we are compelled to ask: What do we have to say, religiously, about this world? How do we protect ourselves from its terrors, how do we align its values with those of the higher life? Or: What, religiously, is a human being? Seized by God in the midst of the world, the human being experiences the elevation that we call redemption. But what do we mean by that? How much of it is a triumph over pain and guilt, and how much an elevation of moral power? And further: Whatever this elevation brings, we know that it is something greater than the individual, something that binds individuals together in a living unity. What is this unity—or, what is the Kingdom of God? And finally: It does not yet appear what we shall be.[1] What then is our final destiny?

Thus do we move from the concept of God to the concepts of the *world,* the human *soul, redemption,* the *Kingdom of God,* and the Christian *consummation.* These are all contemporary-religious questions. But they are also all intrinsically related to the historical-religious statements considered in Part One; for it is from historical powers that we garner the courage to make these contemporary-religious affirmations.

Before we take up the specific theme of this section, I should make a few general remarks about my own approach. It is not easy to specify what is unique about my position. It has much in common with other views. But there are differences, even if they are not readily apparent. I will mention only one: no other contemporary theologian stays as close to Schleiermacher's method and approach, nor feels himself in such inner agreement with him. The only thing that separates us revolves about a single point: Schleiermacher's futile, although admirable, struggle against monism. But despite his struggle against it, Schleiermacher's dogmatics is everywhere saturated with pantheistic thinking, shot through and through with an atmosphere that breathes heavily of Spinoza and Goethe—an atmosphere to which our own present day also stands very close, albeit more as a caricature. In contrast to Schleiermacher's, our *Glaubenslehre* will not exhibit the slightest tendency to monism; it will be personalistic through and through, characterized everywhere

---

1. 1 John 3:2.

by an undiminished emphasis on ethics and will. But with respect to
Ritschl, although our approach acknowledges his great importance, it
has nothing to do with him in its inmost soul.—

We turn now to the Christian *concept of God*. We must immediately emphasize that we are dealing here only with our thoughts
about God, which is the only way that we can appropriate God's
impact on us; it will never be possible for us thoroughly to plumb the
depths of the divine life. This point must be vigorously stressed: for it
is unthinkable that we should attempt to grasp and define the reality
of God. Such an undertaking would be enormously beyond human
ability. We can speak of nothing save that which touches our own
human sphere, alongside which there are spiritual realms, no doubt,
whose existence we do not even suspect; but we will never have the
opportunity to reach God through them. Similarly, there must also
be a relationship between God and the subhuman creatures, and
even a way in which the sleeping and the semiconscious are drawn to
him. Here too we have no more to say. We have only the beam of
light that falls upon our own soul.

Henceforth we will be able to formulate and express our concepts
about God only insofar as he lives in us through the impact of Christianity and its effects. We will remember that our formulation will
never even come close to exhausting the depths of God. Somebody
once asked Richard Rothe, in reference to his *Ethics*,[2] whether he was
afraid to analyze God. He answered, "I analyze not God, but my
thoughts about God." But thoughts, of course, which we are convinced originate with God! This is the one thing that we are able to
affirm. It is only with fear and trembling that we can try, here, today,
in Auditorium 5, to ascertain what God is! We know that he is the
light that no one sees, the light from which a few sparks fall upon our
souls. But even if we come at our task in this way, we are still very
much in earnest. There is much that is intensely personal in our
attempt to grasp God on the basis of these sparks in our soul, a grave
and perilous venture. But we must dare to interpret that which lives
in our hearts!

Another objection to our procedure is that this particular dogmatic formulation of the concept of God treats it as one concept
among others. Doesn't this reduce it to the same level as the other
concepts and deprive it of its true force? Doesn't the concept of God
possess so much energy that it exhausts all of faith without remain-

---

2. Richard Rothe (1799–1867), *Theologische Ethik,* 5 vols. (Wittenberg: Zimmerman, 1867–71).

der? Calvinism, for example, insists that the system as a whole is already contained in the concept of God. The Calvinistic method is quite majestic in its own way. But it becomes impossible as soon as we recall that theology gives us information only about ourselves. Calvinism derives the world and everything else directly from the essence of God, objectively formulated aright with the help of the Bible and reason. But the concept of God only expresses the whole perimeter of Christian piety, the concept of the world expresses only our religious attitude toward the world, and so forth. The whole of our subjective religious life is contained within every concept. We will therefore illuminate specific points by referring to the always identical whole. But since we can never grasp the whole, we must circle about the orb if we are to form a picture of it.

Our propositions will therefore take the form of descriptions of the pious frame of mind, but in terms of a different exponent or exemplification for each concept. We have a theology of consciousness instead of a theology of facts. This is no mere finesse. Behind the theology of facts lurks the wish that reason, at least, might be able to do what the eyes cannot—make everything as precise and compact as possible. But, on the contrary, for a theology of consciousness that harks back to Schleiermacher, these things can never be known apart from subjective experience. They can be seen only through the cloak [*Schleier*] of our inner life, never directly or tangibly or apart from the subject—in short, they can be had only indirectly. But they are nevertheless really *had,* just because they are matters of subjective experience. "Subjective" here assuredly does not mean a matter of arbitrary taste, but a subjectivity which is saturated with God.

Schleiermacher's method is also possessed of a religious significance, because it inclines us to be more generous when we see different people drawing different conclusions. We can be more understanding of differences if we are free of the need to insist on objective correctness.

If this is how the concept of God is derived from our faith, then the evidence for doing so rests on this, that we perceive this faith as something which forces itself upon us. It is only natural to wish that objective confirmation could be added to this subjective certainty. Great religious personalities have no need of this, but intellectually gifted persons will always seek to illuminate the subjective side of life from the objective side. All religions are subject to the desire for philosophical evidence, something like faith insurance, so to speak. Medieval and Protestant scholastics alike labored with a double concept of God, religious and scientific, each of which complemented the other. It was a procedure that stood in direct contradiction to a truly religious life, but it was possible in the context of a shared horizon that included a natural concept of God. But this held true only for the Middle Ages and, in part, for the age of Protestant orthodoxy. There could be a philosophical knowledge of God then. It consisted in the Aristotelian doctrine of a spiritual and teleological monotheism, something which Christian doctrine could easily put to its own use. The Stoic concept of God, which culminated in the goals of an ethical spirit, was also part of this philosophical complex. And finally, Neoplatonism's concept of God as the last, highest, and most spiritual inner essence, surging through the depths of the finite, sinking down to the level of the animal, and returning back again—through thought—to its origin, was added to the mix. These Neoplatonic and Stoic concepts were easily combined with Aristotle and, when taken together, served as a self-evident knowledge of God.

For us, the situation is altogether different. The emergence of modern philosophy marked the end of the generally accepted monotheistic-spiritual-teleological conception of God. Today we encounter entirely new currents of thought and difficulties that were unknown to ancient philosophy. Even today, Catholicism refuses even to acknowledge that the situation has changed, believing that its superiority to the modern world consists in its retention of a twofold basis for its concept of God. A Catholic cleric recently pronounced all moderns "Titans" for resisting the natural knowledge of God for no reason. Well, Titans we are not, but this much is true: Modern philosophy is no longer in a position to offer us any support to fall back on, for the simple reason that there is no scientifically demonstrable, objectively based solution to the problem. The more formal that logical deductions become, the more removed they are from experience. There is of course a type of philosophy that penetrates the depths of the ground of the world, but it is not a product of scholarship; it is rather mediated by a religious energy. This is where Leibniz, Hegel, Lotze, and several others belong. Schopenhauer liberated himself through religious impulses, mediated through Buddhism.

The concept of God can no longer have a double support. We must now have the courage to risk it on the basis of our decision. When it comes to this, it is no different for the philosopher than it is for anyone else: he too, at bottom, owes his knowledge of God to his inner life and disposition. But this is not only a loss—it is also a gain. Religion is more free, more alive when it does not always need to keep looking back at its philosophical sibling. Religion loses its tendency to abstraction and proof, which have often rendered it laborious and onerous. Religious knowledge can result only when life breaks out in assurance and passion; and the oftener it does, the purer it will be. Henceforth apologetics will find its tasks, not in connection with the concept of God, but with other matters.

Our discussion of religious faith and its self-certainty leads, in turn, to a consideration of non-Christian forms of faith. In all universal religions, religious faith always implies a sovereign certainty. This fact frequently eludes the theologians. Herrmann, who stakes everything on Christian self-certainty, is unaware of the problem this makes for him: other subjective forms of faith approximate the same sort of self-certainty. And this is very significant. The contemporary situation in philosophy leaves us no alternative but to illuminate the various Christian concepts in terms of their opposition to other religions. But their relationship is not one of mere opposition alone. Religious systems such as Neoplatonism, Brahmanism [Hinduism] and others exhibit both kinship and opposition. Instead of referring to a philosophical horizon, we now find ourselves looking to the history of religions. There, we find that the more we scrutinize the wide world and its future possibilities, the more essential our differences appear. This corresponds to the situation in which Christianity finds itself, pressing forward and conflicting with foreign religions. We may anticipate a decisive battle between the religions in the future.

The only remaining question is whether, practically speaking, we need to devote more attention to non-Christian religions or to *not-yet* Christian religions. This is particularly relevant to the sciences, which have done more than anything else to make the apologetic task difficult. Popular Darwinian theories and antispiritual [*seelenfeindliche*] psychology reduce all spiritual occurrences to psychophysical processes, frequently blocking our access to souls. The various philosophical systems, the vast majority of which are known only to a few, and then often only at tenth hand, are of much less concern. There are some figures, however, such as Schopenhauer and Nietzsche, who have had far-reaching influence. But theology is not primarily apology. The tenacity and durability of its own world of ideas is the main thing; and positive and direct proclamation is its task. This is accomplished primarily by the strength, conviction, and profundity of the personality itself, although it cannot be effective apart from a genuine, positive, and comprehensive perspective.

Naturally, some supplementary defensive work will be appropriate. Many theologians make the mistake of ignoring the great questions of the evolution of the earth, etc. This leaves the field wide open for the nontheologians. In England, natural scientists openly take religious positions and offer opinions on the extent to which some biological or other sort of theory invalidates Christianity. These scholars enjoy the surpassing great advantage of being believed by everyone, while no one believes the theologians, because the theologians are never free to say anything different from what they have always said. But in Germany, the nontheological scholarly world is characterized by an overwhelming and unjustifiable laziness and smugness in this regard. It is not a question, however, of doing a little theology, but of strengthening people's faith, of keeping open the wellsprings that the modern theories of unbelief threaten to strangle.

For apologetic purposes, Lotze's *Mikrokosmos*[3] and Jäger's writings[4] are to be recommended. The Catholic church has also, in its own way, produced some very good apologies.

But now let us turn to the task of subdividing and classifying our subject matter. We can do this if we take an overview of the whole. If we take it as our task to describe this living whole, quite unpretentiously and without scholarly finesse, we come *first* to the creative, altogether free *will* which knows no necessity. This is the dominant theme of the Christian concept of God. God is life, God is the Lord, his ways are higher than human ways,[5] he is the potter whom the clay cannot question.[6] And yet this absoluteness does not signify arbitrariness. We are convinced that this will is directed to a goal intrinsic to itself: hence the concept of the will leads, in turn, to the concept of a *goal*. The last and final reality cannot express itself in a motley series of arbitrary acts by the will, but only in purpose and intention. This, in turn, suggests the term "essence," or that which is necessary in itself. The will and the essence of God are in fact central to every discussion of the Christian concept of God, although it is not necessary to use these terms.

This two-pronged concept of God in Christianity contrasts with the one-sided concepts found in other religions. The Jewish concept emphasizes the arbitrariness of God, stressing the chosen people who are chosen for no reason. In other religions, such as Brahmanism [Hinduism] and Neoplatonism, God is one-sidedly construed as

3. Hermann Lotze (1817–1881), *Microcosmos* (1856–64), trans. Elizabeth Hamilton and E. E. Constance Jones (New York: Scribner & Welford, 1886).
4. This is perhaps a reference to Paul Jäger, *Zur Überwindung des Zweifels* (Tübingen: J.C.B. Mohr, 1906).
5. See Isa. 55:8-9.
6. See Rom. 9:20-21.

essence: he is selfsame for all eternity, he is the one apart from whom there is nothing. The Christian God, in contrast to the latter, directs himself to an eternal goal and an eternal meaning. But what unifies this goal and meaning among things? Christian thought answers: the realization of the *holiness* of God. For when he encounters us in the majesty of his holiness, writing his "Thou shalts" in our heart, he demands not only fear and devotion, but surrender as well. What God demands is a pure heart.[7] This is the *second* standpoint from which the Christian concept of God is to be understood.

If we pursue the concept of holiness further, we come to the *third* standpoint. The divine holiness is no moralism. God did not give the world his law and then abandon it; instead, he searches for the creature with *love* and *passion,* creating the very holiness that he demands. Here we find no cold law, no crushing commandment that seeks fulfillment in human compliance; we find a holy love that embraces us and incorporates us into itself,[8] thereby bringing us to faith. This divine love is not to be understood as eudaemonistic in any sense. Its purpose is not to assist every creature in pleasing itself, as if we were to say, I can see that existence has meaning, because things are going well for me. Divine love has nothing to do with that sort of thing, for it seeks to elevate human beings to the level of its own higher reality.

At this point we immediately encounter the question: How can we reconcile this point of view with the actual state of the world? All that we can see in the real world is the brutal dominion of nature, and a spiritual life shattered into a thousand pieces. This is one of the most difficult questions in all of theology, one which can be answered only hesitantly and haltingly. Leibniz used the term "theodicy" for it.

The exposition of the Christian concept of God, therefore, has the following divisions: (1) God as will and essence; (2) The holiness of God; and (3) God as holy love.

§12. God as Will and Essence

DICTATION

1. What we describe, then, is not God himself, but our thoughts about God. Our sources include the Bible and the consciousness of

---

7. See Matt. 5:8.
8. "[Eine] heilige Liebe, die uns sich selbst einverliebt."

the community, but also the modern intuition and picture of the world, and, finally, the personal struggle for meaning and value in life. By no means can the concept of God simply be based on a few Bible verses. We may also expect, as a matter of course, that the concept of God will both contradict and confirm reality in a variety of ways. Hence there will always be a substantial remainder of that which is logically inexplicable in the concept of God.

2. Jesus' concept of God fulfills the prophetic concept of God, and therefore can be understood only in connection with it. In comparison with the most highly developed of the non-Christian concepts of God, the first thing we notice about the Christian concept is that God is, first of all, almighty and creative *will*. This will manifests not only the unity and oneness of God but, above all, the personality of God. And if the concept of the will is preeminent, so too is the concept of the *goal* which is to be realized. God's honor, self-glorification, life, and power all manifest themselves as a goal. But this means that the essence of reality must be understood to subsist in this will, and to constitute the basis of this goal. God, therefore, is always living, always creating. He is truly manifested not in being, but in *becoming;* not in nature, but in *history.*

But there is also a significant dimension of irrationality to this will, insofar as it constitutes the groundless power of creativity in the whole world and in every individual. God is the ground of all grounds; hence God cannot be grasped on the basis of some other ground, but is rather the highest fact of all. Not that the plan of the world is merely too high for human reason to grasp, but rather that it is simply not even commensurable with reason itself, for it contains within itself a creative power that produces new beginnings and realities from no other basis than itself.

This is why history is the real means of the revelation of God, while nature remains the presupposition and basis for spiritual-religious values; nature provides only a general revelation of the greatness, majesty, and regularity of God's creations and truth. This, of course, presupposes that the concept of history has been extended beyond the bounds of mere human history: just as the Bible broadened its horizons by thinking in terms of realms of angels and demons, today we, now that geocentrism has come to an end, must speak in terms of a plurality of spiritual realms.

3. On the other hand, the concept of God cannot be fully expressed in the concept of an absolute will, which, taken by itself, is liable to lead to the religiously impoverished concept of God as a merely arbitrary will. This happened repeatedly in Judaism, and particularly

in late Judaism's theology of history. It is this same concept of God as mere arbitrary will that makes Islam such a meager religion.

To avoid this, we must emphasize the enduring eternity and unity of God, or the *eternal essence,* over against the absolute will. This is precisely the point at which Jesus went beyond the prophets. The prophets' goal was a holy, chosen people, who would serve as ruler and prophet for humankind; Jesus' goal was the dominion of God everywhere in the human will and soul. That had already been implied by what the prophets said, and some of them had drawn that conclusion from time to time. But it is in the preaching of Jesus that it is fully and consistently attained for the first time.

Jesus understood God as will in the same way that the prophets did; but Jesus understood this will as internally present to all human beings, closely bound up with God's essential goal, manifest to every simple, childlike mind. For the prophets, everything was tied to the separateness of the people of Israel, and hence to nationalism, finally coalescing in the concept of a revealed law. For Jesus, God dwells within the soul, working an outwardly effective knowledge of the good within it. God's *immanence* in the soul, along with the turn to the human soul, replaces Israelite nationalism. The goal is now nothing less than the will of God, glorified through his creatures in surrender and worship.

This surrender, however, is free, inward, and voluntary; the surrender of the human will to the holy will of God. The goal is religious insofar as it signifies the creature's surrender to God. But it is also a moral goal, wherein the moral will is united to the holy will of God by means of surrender. The result is the ethical *elevation* of the individual who is simultaneously bound together with other individuals in a *moral disposition of love.*

This is what Jesus' proclamation of God as Father means: a Fatherhood that is the result neither of his power as creator nor of his covenantal relationship with the chosen people; it is rather the result of the fatherly love he directs to all human beings, seeking to make them children of God. This is also what Jesus' proclamation of the *Kingdom of God* signifies: he expected a miraculous transformation of the world, but this transformation was no more than a true, genuine, and free surrender to the will of God and the God-pleasing brotherly love that results. The Kingdom of God is no arbitrary miracle, but should realize the essential goals of the will of God. From this perspective, then, the eternally unified will of God illuminates the inner significance of the arbitrary will (which leads us to patience) as directed toward values realized in communion with God.

4. This is what differentiates the prophetic-Christian concept of God from all others. Judaism and Islam stand closest to it, since they issued from the same root; but they both emphasized the will of God over the essence of God and henceforth became progressively more shallow and meager religions. The differences are even more pronounced when it comes to polytheism, which has no absolute divine will; polytheism recognizes only multiple and fragmented wills: wills which are, moreover, bound to particular natural phenomena and can only slowly and with difficulty come to an essential fulfillment.

Equally clear, however, is the much more important contradiction between the prophetic-Christian concept of God and all those monotheisms that are based, not on will, but on the entirety and totality of being, subsuming all individual being under the whole. These are the pantheistic-monistic religions, which, like Brahmanism [Hinduism], simply permit the illusion of individuality to submerge into the all. But they also include all those religio-philosophical systems that likewise construe the essence of God in terms of the all-encompassing context of things, locating it in the natural law of the whole. The most significant examples of this kind of thinking are the Eleatics and Spinoza, for the ancient and modern worlds, respectively.

The uniquely Christian-prophetic concept of God, as opposed to all these other concepts, is *theism*. But this word must be taken in its full sense, signifying both will and essence; it may not be rationalized simply in terms of a personal-teleological-anthropomorphic idea of God.

There is, to be sure, an *inner tension* within the Christian concept of God. Again and again this tension has come to the surface throughout the entire history of Christianity, sometimes taking a more voluntarist-predestinarian form, other times taking a more substantial-rational form. The tension has increased in the modern spiritual environment, where the substantial-rational version of the concept of God is now reinforced by the logical, predictable character of the laws of nature, which further contribute to a rationalistic view. But this tension belongs to the nature of the case; no concept of God is without some kind of tension, because even the flattest sort of rational monism must come to grips with the problem of contingency.[1] Indeed, one of the distinguishing characteristics of the Christian concept of God is that it has *enhanced* the tension, emphasizing both sides very strongly. The only way to overcome the tension is to

---

1. See Ernst Troeltsch, "Contingency" (1912), in *Encyclopaedia of Religion and Ethics* (New York: Charles Scribner's Sons, 1912–15).

attribute the entire rational world of laws and values to the will of God itself.

We are left, then, with this vision of the whole: an absolute creative power has established a rational and orderly world, such that through the creature's free surrender both within the world and beyond the world it may be raised to the level of a relatively creative spirit; so that the creature, through its free surrender to that which is necessary and binding, can be elevated above the merely factual and come to share in God's creative power. Formulated thus, this is the *God-concept of freedom* or, if we take the stronger meaning of the word "spirit" (as distinguished from the ordinary inner life of the soul), we may call it a *spiritual concept of God.*

In this way, the Christian concept of God stands out in the history of religions as the most central and characteristic concept of God. But more than this, it has also proven to be the religious idea that consistently fulfills all the tendencies of religion, and, moreover, corresponds to the meaning of our objective knowledge in many ways. With respect to fulfilling the tendencies of religion: We see that the presupposition of all religion is the inner separation between God and the soul, and that our religious tendencies can be fulfilled only by a divine will that has both the initiative and the real, living power to grasp souls, to transform them fully, to cause new power to flow into them and to incorporate them into the process of attaining the world-goal. With respect to our objective knowledge: we see that, despite all the rationalization of reality, the problem of irrationalism continues to surface both in particular and in general. Thus the acceptance of the modern concept of nature into the Christian concept of God has provided it with the idea of an all-encompassing, universal objective causal nexus as the presupposition of spirit; yet spirit can never be collapsed into this objective causal nexus, nor can God's living unity be collapsed into the total context of nature.

5. Our discussion of God as will and essence necessitates special consideration for the question of the *personality* of the concept of God. This personality derives not only from the concept of will, but also, in particular, from the religious-ethical concept of the goal of the world. The latter concept necessarily implies that the kernel of the divine essence must be conceived as similar to the highest human religious and ethical strengths. Insofar as such personalism unavoidably leads to anthropomorphism in the idea of God, we encounter several objections which must be reviewed in turn.

a. The first objection holds that the effect of this approach is to *diminish God;* but no such diminution is either intended or achieved, for it is no more than a characterization of God, based on an analogy drawn from finite human being. And no concept of God can dispense with analogy. The only question is, from what part of the human spirit shall we draw our analogy? From its capacity for logical unified thought, from artistic fantasy, from moral law, from animal instincts, from unconscious affections, or from the freedom that is shaped through a necessary truth? It will depend on our view of what constitutes the highest human activity, or what is most in harmony with the supra-human. Hence it will depend on how we rank the various spiritual values. Now the highest of these values is moral freedom, and hence the concept of God should be described as analogous to it; other analogies may apply to specific aspects of the work of God, but they are not central. Applying the analogy of moral freedom to God signifies no diminution, but rather the establishment of unconditional values by the divine will. It does not ascribe finite will to God.

b. The second objection holds that such a concept of God introduces a *dualism* between God and the world, whereas both religious and scientific thought alike seek a final unity. But here we must sharply distinguish the unity that religious thought seeks from that which scientific thought seeks. Religious thought can achieve only a practical resolution of the contradiction between God and soul, never a logical one. Hence, from a purely religious viewpoint, this objection carries no weight. Such an objection can be raised only by the scholarly disciplines, which always seek the greatest possible logical unification of experience. From the standpoint of epistemology, this is the unity of universal law; from the standpoint of metaphysics, it is the unity of universal substance. But universal law is only one among many explications of reality—there still remains a *plurality* of different conceptions. And it is utterly impossible to subsume the whole manifold of reality under a mere unity of substance. Pure science by itself never issues in pure monism. But this renders the objection that theism means dualism meaningless, particularly since the Christian concept of God entails no *external* dualism between God and the world or between the body and soul, but rather an *inner* contradiction: the contradiction between the merely existent natural life and the spirit that arises from it and against it.

c. A third objection holds that this concept of God is impossibly *teleological,* particularly in the way it divinizes finite human goals, giving rise to an utterly impermissible anthropocentrism. To this it must be replied that the concept of a goal cannot be eliminated from the concept of God without also eliminating religion itself. Its teleological character as such is not subject to objection; what can be questioned is where the goal is located. But by no means does the Christian concept of God locate the goal in the human race and its fortunes in the world, but rather in the spiritual-personal, God-uniting life of the creature, which emerges in human beings only upon surrender to God. And this goal is not limited to the human race; it is a universal, spiritual, and rational goal. We understand it clearly only in the case of human beings, but it is the goal of all spirits in whatever realms they may be found. The concept of a goal, therefore, has nothing to do with any finite sensual eudaemonism, but rather with attaining and fulfilling the spirit's unity with God. It signifies not humanization of the divine goal but *deification of the human goal.*

d. The fourth objection refers to the idea of *freedom* that this theism necessarily implies: the absolute freedom of God, and the relative freedom of the creature. The former, it is argued, is a non-concept, while the latter is supposedly contradicted by determinism and by the concept of the all-encompassing causal nexus of the world. We may concede that the concept of God's freedom is irrational in the sense that any and all attempts to trace the universe back to a final ground will ultimately come up against irrationality. Further-more, no matter what significance one wishes to attach to the regu-larity of the universe, the divine life cannot be identified with this regularity, for this regularity only subsists on real life; it is not life itself. And it is equally impossible to subsume the spirit's *elevation over nature* under the laws of nature, for it signifies elevation and triumph over precisely those laws. But if all this is true, then the irrationality of the world-process, like the irrationality of the spirit's elevation above it, remains sure and steadfast alongside all causal rationality, and will never be eliminated. To be sure, this leaves us with the question of how this causal regularity is related to the liveli-ness and creativity of the life that it can never exhaust. But that is a question that may never be answered, and at any rate we will never be able to answer it here.

LECTURE

The Christian concept of God perceives God as absolute, utterly free, and unconstrained will, but also as a will that includes a unified essence within itself. We do not formulate these ideas out of Bible verses—the relevant passages are innumerable—for, although the concept of God can be illuminated by single words, they can never exhaust it. The Bible as a whole breathes this concept just like the air and storm clouds that swirl throughout it; and it is this totality of the Bible upon which we must build. But the Bible is not our sole source of light. Present-day consciousness, and our own personal struggles in particular, will have something to say. We seek to uncover our thoughts about God, sensing him in our depression and our elation, in our prayer and in world events.

Turning to our first source, the Bible, we see this in the New Testament: the people to whom Jesus speaks already know what God is. Everything essential is already presupposed. So we turn from the New Testament to the prophets, whose utterances constitute one of the most important developments in all history. Their proclamation made it possible for a people as small and insignificant as the Jews to have such a remarkable impact on world history. And this prophetic proclamation still expresses itself with great clarity. Again and again the refrain is repeated: Yahweh is the living Lord, your God, beside whom there is none other. He has created everything: whatever exists, exists only through him. There may be other gods who rise above human beings, but none who can rise to the level of the Almighty; in comparison with the true God, they constitute nothing but folly, idol, and abomination. Yahweh has been seen by no one; he permits no likeness of him to be made. He is not confined to the temple; for the world is his, and the heavens his garment.[2]

All these utterances are animated by this powerful idea: God is creative will. Whatever he commands comes to pass. God formed everything purely by himself. He is the will that can make something exist. This is the unfathomable miracle: he can make something exist! This concept is inexpressibly superior to those religions that instinctively and self-evidently take the given at face value, construing their gods as mere individuals and never as creative will. Their gods are conditioned by that which is already given—the gods may well change it, but they did not bring it into existence. Their gods depend themselves on the matter to which they give shape. But the God of Israel is not limited by the given; neither is he identical with being as a whole: all being is grounded in him. The final secret of the world lies in a will whose motives cannot be fathomed. This constitutes a radical break with polytheism: If God is absolute will, then he cannot share his lordship with other gods. This alone is what made it possible to rise above the level of the demonic. It is not the oneness of

2. See, e.g., Isaiah 40–44, esp. 42:5-9.

God per se that matters so much, but rather the absoluteness of his will, which his oneness expresses.

But we moderns no longer struggle with polytheism; our battle is with *pantheism*. Pantheism's piety consists not in the exaltation of the divine will, but in the self's recognition that it is merely the gateway through which the being of the world flows. The prophets never encountered pantheism. The first Christians encountered it in the form of Neoplatonism, while today we encounter it in Buddhism and monism. This makes it important to emphasize the prophetic-Christian concept of God, i.e., the *personality* of God—in analogy to that which we call human personality. This does not mean, of course, that we are to understand God as something like a super human being; rather, it means that, in our deepest ethical intentions, we intuit something of the creative divine will. Where else could we find even this limited understanding if not in ourselves? The only question is what side of ourselves we will choose for our analogy: from the dark twilight of our life-instincts, from a lucky intuition, or from our creative understanding and moral will? Many find that they can best conceive the All in terms of the instincts of life, in terms of the musty unconscious. But Christianity seeks to construe God as personality.

This is not to say that God is a personality, but only that the key to our understanding of God lies in creative power. The analogy is not to the subspiritual, nor to the natural side of our essence, but to our highest aspirations. At the same time, we see that personality is everywhere bound to a physical substrate of consciousness. Hence we may seem to be saying that the concept of God is just another expression for the heart of the world. But the believer does not have the world-process in mind when he says: The Lord your God is a living God! Rather: Person-like-ness [*Personhaftigkeit*] is the utterly natural consequence of the divine will, although we know personhood only in an enormously diminished form in human beings. Whoever wishes to deny the person-like-ness of God will have to try to conceive him in terms of being; and the usual result of such a quest is the sort of being about which we can say no more than this: it is. But how can this whirling confusion be identical with God? And is not being already a product of the will? In Christianity, being appears reducible to will. Hence the faith of Christianity attaches, not to mere being, but to becoming, to the always-new. From this time forward, history attains a significance that is found nowhere else.

Another consequence of this person-like-ness is that the concept of absolute will becomes unthinkable apart from a concept of the goal. If God no longer coincides with the world, he then coincides with his goal. And so we come to the difference between God and the world. That which is created is not identical with the creator, but is, in its totality, only God's means.

This distinction between God and the world is basic to the Christian concept of God. The biblical sense of nature sees it all as revealing the divine majesty. "Day and night change before the Lord."[3] "The heavens are telling the glory of God."[4] This powerful, awe-inspiring sense of nature knows no goal that consists merely in the happiness of the individual creature, unlike the boor who thinks that God must have no regard for his life if some poor little wish of his is not granted. That is not how it is at all. The biblical concept goes much deeper than this. It leads to the point where God's self-glorification consists in his creation; and this self-glorification is his most noble goal.

Such a concept of the divine will is absolutely *irrational*. We are dealing with something that rests on no other foundation. There is, to be sure, something ultimately irrational in the pantheistic-mystical religious attitude as well, but in an altogether different way. For we are not restricted to the mystery of mere being; we find an answer to the mystery—an answer that lies in an antecedent will that cannot be questioned. The final ground of all grounds is the fully groundless divine will. This is what is specifically irrational about the Christian concept of God. Other religious attitudes cling to a general law, or to the general in general. But for the Christian-Jewish concept of God, the general is inconsequential. We focus not on what is general, but on the will that brings forth the whole. That is its depth!

We go back behind being, to a power, an energy that is expressed in being: it is immeasurable, an absolutely supra-rational fact, but not a brute fact; rather, it is something that bursts forth from the inconceivable depths of the will. This refusal to stop at mere being constitutes this concept's greatness! For this mere fact of being, the fact that anything exists at all—this is the real problem! Is it not equally likely that nothing should exist? There is no rational reason that there is anything at all; not because of any deficiency in reason, but because of the divine will itself. This will is the ground of grounds, the law of laws; its Why knows no reason. We say this in deepest humility. We submit to this last will, honoring in inexpressible devotion that which creates for no reason at all; which, moreover, creates its own ground and necessity.

3. See Ps. 74:16: "Thine is the day, thine also the night."
4. Ps. 19:2.

If this holds true for the whole, it also holds true for *individual*
entities. Throughout the latticework of rationality we feel this
groundless creative will and nature of God surging through every
pore of reality. Everywhere we look, we see that which cannot be
explained on the basis of what went before it, but is new in every
respect, flowing from the eternal power of productivity. We distrust
all attempts to explain rebirth or higher birth merely as the result of
various chains of events: for in those chains of events, and beyond
them, we always see the act of creation. We recognize every great
personality not only as the product of its circumstances, but also as
the product of divine creativity. For us, the emergence of any new
organism always signifies a new being, something that was not there
before. Above all, the productive character of this creativity comes
into the foreground; it has enormous significance for the liberation of
human beings from the organic sequence of life that precedes them.

At this point, one could ask whether what is true for the whole
also holds true for the individual: that to acknowledge the emergence
of the new is to acknowledge miracle. Indeed, there can be no objection to thinking of miracle in this way. The basic thing is always this
question: Why is there anything at all? This is why we should never
be taken aback by the explanations offered for various chains of
events. In general, conflicts in popular thought resolve nothing. When
the Bible speaks in wonderful terms of the incalculable, unfathomable depths of the divine activity[5] that surprise us again and again
with ever new self-disclosures of the divine life, it is not a defect of
the Bible, but its greatness. It is at just this point that Christian
thought about God probes more deeply than anything else we know.

This concept signifies that the revelation of God is not changeless,
but rather a great creative power; and hence the proper medium of
revelation is *history*. Here we must take care to remember that the
Bible will not admit of any narrow anthropocentrism. For the Bible,
the spiritual world created by God consists not only of human beings,
but also of an invisible realm of spirits above and beneath the human
race. However, the world of angels and demons later retreated into
the background, leaving us only with the world of human beings. But
this retreat also led to the contraction and impoverishment of the
world, an impoverishment that needs to be overcome by the concept
of a plurality of spiritual worlds. The divine will has been confined to
too narrow a frame. As soon as we recognize that we live in a truly
valuable land that is, when it comes to the spirit, nevertheless only

5. See Rom. 11:33.

one among many, the idea that history is the medium of revelation will lose all its offensiveness. But it can cease to be objectionable only from this point of view; for the disparity between us and the immeasurable is too great to think that the divine will can be set into motion for our sakes alone. History as a whole cannot be limited to mere human history. The idea that we will be purified in order to come to a higher spiritual essence is not entirely foreign to the Bible. Indeed, the possibility that we already have contact with other spiritual realms cannot be altogether ruled out. If the concept of a plurality of spiritual realms stands, then the idea of a present intercourse with them cannot be ruled out as impossible and absurd.

Let us return once again to the starting point of these reflections: the recognition of God as creative will. This does not yet circumscribe the concept. Given only what has been said thus far, the divine will could be construed as mere *arbitrariness*. But this is not the Christian concept; for Christianity, God's will does not break forth first here and then there without any rhyme or reason. To be sure, this notion occurs often enough in the Old Testament, where it is put in this way: Now God wills that this should happen! There is also an element of arbitrariness in the election of Israel; God could just as well have chosen the Philistines![6] Later Judaism viewed the Law simply as the product of God's arbitrary choice: Do not seek for the reasons for this Law; it is enough that God gave it to you to serve as a boundary against the Gentiles! This is how Jewish eschatology is to be understood: The God who has chosen this people and then humbled it and made it serve foreign nations, can, whenever it pleases him, return them to power and restore the throne of Solomon. This is what makes Judaism so alien to us. But wherever God is understood exclusively as will, the result is a pronounced tendency to nominalism and an undiscriminating passion for miracles. This is not true, however, of the prophetic conception of God. In fact, the ruling opinion of the Old Testament in general is that God does not desire observances of feast days and cultic ordinances, but rather a pure heart that humbles itself before him and shows justice to widows and orphans.[7]

The stunning energy with which the Old Testament, on innumerable occasions, attacks everything external, means that the will of its God revolves about a central point. The goal of the world is not simply to reveal the power of God, but also to reveal a will that

6. See Amos 9:7.
7. See Isa. 1:12-17; Amos 5:21-24.

desires the good. Indeed, the good is exactly what the will of God is. This is how the concepts of essence and will are brought together. The arbitrary election of Israel fades into the background, while this simple idea comes to the foreground: The will of God is the moral law of the heart, and all who acknowledge this law have a share in God. This is Judaism's contribution to individualism and to the turn to the individual soul. Nevertheless, the Old Testament still permits the concept of essence to be swallowed up by the concept of an arbitrary will.

Jesus' proclamation of the Kingdom of God, despite all legalistic and apologetic attempts to obscure it, remains the plainest and clearest summary of the divine essence. For Jesus, the Kingdom of God signifies the full lordship of God within human beings. God demands complete surrender: not the external, mechanical obedience of simple submission, but rather the inner affirmation of a holy moral law. The human and the divine must become fully one. The gospel proceeds on the tranquil and childlike conviction that the intentions of the human soul must be realized in terms of the complete lordship of God. The gospel does not deny the faith of the fathers, but focuses its attention on the individual soul instead of the people, demanding an unconditional break with everything external. This is all easy to demonstrate and easy to understand, but difficult to achieve, for it means simply this: The essence of God is the essence of the good; and since God is perfect, the soul shall be perfect also.[8] Your soul shall be like his; for it is worth more than the whole world. And your soul shall come to God with other souls who have likewise surrendered. You shall be united to them in unconditional brotherly love, which loves the other because it too is directed toward the same goal.

Universal love corresponds to *radical individualism*. This is what is authentically new in the proclamation of Jesus. Essence continues to presuppose will; but now the goal is not the divine sense of honor, but rather an inner circle with the Kingdom of God at its center. This Kingdom of God is completely different from the Old Testament's idea of the restoration of the Kingdom of David. To be sure, the image of the kingdom is somewhat reminiscent of the Kingdom of David, but what the Kingdom of God is becomes clear only with Jesus. It is on this basis that the designation of God as Father is to be understood. God is described as Father already in the Old Testament and even outside Judaism; but, in Jesus' proclamation, "the Father" refers not to the creator and sovereign of the Old Testament, but to

8. See Matt. 5:48, but also Lev. 19:2.

an internally perceived unity of the divine essence and character, which, in turn, requires a childlike capacity for surrender on the part of human beings.

Let us now undertake a comparison with other religions in order to elucidate the Christian concept of God further. First we encounter Judaism and Islam, which spring from the same roots as Christianity. They are not altogether alien to us, but they differ from the Christian concept of God in their one-sided emphasis on the will. The great will of God, alongside which nothing else can stand, is the great pathos of Islam. Islam grants conditional recognition to Christianity and Judaism: Jesus is a forerunner of the Prophet. But Islam's ethical commands correspond to its relatively narrow formulation of the divine essence. It requires the faithful to fight for the honor of the faith, to practice prayer, and to treat one another humanely; but there is no universalism that would draw all souls into communion with God. It does not speak of a Kingdom of God. The grandiose concept of the will overwhelms everything. Before this will, there can be only fear, sacrifice, and uncritical acceptance. What a narrow and impoverished soul results! God leads everything; but his directions make no sense, and hence Islam forfeits all warmth and life. It is the starkest monotheism on earth; it judges Christianity to be somewhat polytheistic due to its doctrine of the Trinity and the veneration of Mary. Islam's starkness is expressed in the doctrine of the absolute omnipotence of God over everything, which renders the concept of the divine essence weak and insignificant.

The same holds true for Judaism: a stark monotheism dominates here as well, the result of an overpowering concept of the will. Also like Islam, Judaism believes itself a more monotheistic and hence a purer religion than Christianity. And pure it is; but formal, too. The idea of a love that issues from the inmost essence of God remains alien to Judaism. A similar point of view is to be found in the related, but nearly extinct, religion of Parsiism [Zoroastrianism].

Each and every form of polytheism, no matter how refined it may be, manifests the exact opposite of these conceptions of the will. The only remaining form of polytheism today is that of surviving peoples. Except that, now and again, one finds paradoxical people even today who think that polytheism is not such a bad thing after all. According to them, polytheism actually corresponds to reality, which looks more as though there really were numerous divine powers locked in a struggle with one another. Hellenists are of the opinion that all polytheism is tolerant. It even builds an altar to the unknown god.[9] Others today are enthralled with the idea that each solar system has its own spirits. And there are even those curious persons who think that ancient Germanic polytheism can be revived in earnest. Back to Wotan![10] they cry, demanding that the Edda[11] be taught in the schools. Their number includes a few devoted fanatics of Wagner's pre-*Parsifal* works. The apostles of many of these theories are at least able to enjoy the satisfaction that comes of having stirred up a good controversy.

In response to all this, we must make it clear that the advantage of monotheism lies not simply in having only one *God*, but rather in the universality of having one and only one *will*. Polytheism weakens religion, for it relativizes the divine will. Unquestionably, there have been pious polytheistic people, such as Aeschylus, for example, who have striven for a thoroughgoing unity. But it is impious to splinter the divine will and to bind God to the powers of nature. The power of God is thereby exchanged for the powers of nature, which are more powerful than they are spiritual. Therefore, we must continue to maintain the sharpest possible opposition to every polytheism.

A much more pressing concern is the need to differentiate Christianity from the monistic-pantheistic universal religions. If, in Judaism, we can trace a line of development which leads from polytheism to the concept of an ethical will, there is also a second line, outside Judaism, one which also begins with polytheism but develops instead into the major forms of religious pantheism. The most potent representative of this development is Brahmanism [Hinduism], but there are other examples in history. Even the Greeks were familiar with various forms of extreme pantheism, such as that of the Eleatics.

Pantheism can be characterized thus: The Godhead is unconditionally the One, over against which all separate individuality is mere appearance and delusion. In truth, we are eternally one with the eternally unmoved. The religious paradigm for pantheism is just this Oneness, in opposition to all human claims of uniqueness. The ego is sacrificed to the divine being, which is all that really exists, the All. Buddhism adds an ascetic dimension to this sacrifice to the All. For Buddhism, I-ness is a sin, just like every natural zest for living and all consciousness of individuality. The self attains peace and blessedness

9. Acts 17:23.
10. Wotan (or Woden or Odin) was the supreme god of the Germanic pantheon.
11. A collection of ancient Norse myths and legends of gods and heroes, found on a manuscript dating from the eleventh century. It is the most important source for our knowledge of ancient Germanic religion.

through a will which has been freed from all self-seeking. Here polytheism is utterly eliminated, but its place is not taken by the ideal of
gaining an active life interwoven with God, but rather by sacrificing
one's own life to the Unconditional. There is great religious power
here, but it is altogether different from that which is found in Judaism
and Christianity.

For a clearer understanding, we need to return to the concepts of
will and essence. There are two possible paths that lead out of polytheism. One elevates the will and then seeks the germ of essence
within it, so that the divine will is tied to an ethical goal. But there is
another path: to emphasize *not* the divine will, but rather the divine
essence and its interweaving with all material being. Being takes the
place of will; and since being is divine, it can in no way be limited and
therefore poses no more conceptual problems. It is clear that this
absolute being must then be intertwined with all the individual differences of our particular being; otherwise, these peculiarities would be
both inside and outside God. The result is that the ego, along with all
its goals—including its ethical goals—is completely interwoven into
the All. The goal is not something in God, but the dissolution of
personality in him. This constitutes Buddhism's overwhelming pathos:
Its greatest achievement is not to gain the soul, but to lose it! Every
power, even the greatest, must remain silent. But such a religion, in
which all that remains is this blessed annihilation, is pessimistic to the
core; for it engulfs all particular being, not only in respect of sin, but
in every respect whatsoever. This way of thinking shatters even the
highest strivings after personality into fragments of illusion. The contradiction to the Christian world becomes radical at this point.

The choice between these two alternatives is by no means a scholarly or scientific decision. Both suffer from various logical difficulties. For the prophetic-Christian concept of God, the problem is this:
How is divine omnipotence to be reconciled with the existence of
other self-acting, goal-setting essences? In the starkly monistic systems, on the other hand, it remains inconceivable that the world of
appearances could even come to be in the first place, since nothing
should exist alongside this timeless and spaceless being. Even the
process by which individual will is dissolved is itself an individual
thing, and therefore only an appearance too! Therefore, in either
case, the decision can only be personal, immediate, and practical.
Here, where we are grasped radically and intrinsically, where we feel
our greatest religious awe—that is where our decision must lie also.
And here, now, we choose this: Despite the awe-inspiring character

of the great religions of the East, the real power to regenerate the human race is to be found in Christianity.

Many people think that these voices from the East are very far removed. But Buddhists send us missionaries. There are already small Buddhist congregations in London and America. But even more significant is the fact that the very same religious contradictions that we are discussing here are to be found in our midst, springing from our own sources. We have philosophical systems that lean toward the religions of will, such as Kant's and Fichte's, while on the other hand we have systems such as Spinoza's, which clearly side with the religions of being. Schelling, among others, attempted a reconciliation. In his later period, he held to a completely pantheistic understanding of God, yet acted in accord with an understanding of God as a will who leads souls through the world-process back to himself, i.e., back to infinite, undifferentiated being. This is also how Hartmann's and Drews's campaign against Christianity should be understood. Both of them seek to unite pantheistic being to a teleological will in the world, leading ultimately to the disappearance of all individuality. All these decisions rest on massive differences in attitudes toward life. Spinoza's approach was largely determined by his own mystic capacity for self-obliteration, while Kant's was shaped by his own strong personal and ethical will. But those who seek to mediate between the two are really pantheists, for whom will serves only as an intermezzo.—

We turn now to the task of pulling together the various motifs of our God-concept as they emerge from the Bible. The term that suggests itself for our position is *theism*. It originally signified, like "deism," a rational belief in God. Later, during the time of Kant, it was used to describe the specific essence of the Christian belief in God as opposed to pantheism. Now it has become a catchword for the position that identifies God as more than simply the essence of the world, i.e., as will—not just any arbitrary will, but a will that imparts its own goal to itself. In other words, it signifies a person-like conception of God; and so we find ourselves face to face with the dispute over the personality of God. The word "personality" is dangerous, however, and in order to facilitate our discussion, it should be replaced by the word "person-like-ness" [*Personhaftigkeit*].

We must always insist that to speak of God is to speak of *absolute* will. Every human will is set in motion by some external motive. But with God there can be no question of motive; for what external thing could possibly set an absolute will in motion? And if we are in earnest about this being an absolute will, then we must also be in earnest about its being an absolutely irrational will as well. For it is only a tautology to say that the divine essence is the self-definition of the divine will. If God sets forth a goal, he does so not because he must, but for no reason at all—or, his reasons are valid only because they are self-produced. How God's will comes to be is unfathomable to all thought; in this respect, God is utterly incomprehensible, crushing, mortifying, immeasurable. Our science can grasp only that which can be traced back to something else, but here there is nothing to be traced. This also implies that God is not bound to any obligation. There is no moral law that he must follow; that is only for finite creatures. The only foundation for God is the irrational.

Theism implies irrationality. To be sure, theism is often trivialized into a rational-necessary knowledge of God: concepts such as creation out of love, providence, self-revelation, and even immortality are, like everything else, all deduced from the idea that God is bound to follow the law of love. Rationally formulated in this way, the concept of God is reduced to little more than a platitude. Nevertheless, for many, this is the only way that the concept of God can be made approachable. But whoever drinks deeply will feel differently. What a ridiculous idea it is to have an absolute will that nevertheless stands under the law of love and requires another essence! How self-contradictory it is to have a divine love that is bound to a law of love, as though love came *before* God and bound God to itself! No, theism makes sense only in terms of a groundless divine will.

This is where theism decisively surpasses pantheism. Its superiority consists in this, that the concept of an irrational will makes us aware of how fantastic, mysterious, and terrifying the concept of God really is. Theism thereby comes to grips with a problem that pantheism does not even acknowledge. Pantheism simply grasps being without asking what it is that being exists through. Theism probes much more deeply on this point. A famous French mathematician has said that the basic problem of all thought is the question why anything exists at all. The only way to answer this question is by reference to a groundless will. Reality is, in its inmost essence, irrational; that is why every theism devoid of irrationalism is bland. Descartes and Augustine expressed this most clearly.

With respect to this problem, the history of Christianity has exhibited extreme variations. At one point we encounter a one-sided concept of will, while at another we meet a concept of essence without any will. Calvin taught that if God chooses to make someone an idiot, God cannot be called to account for it! We are what we are, and the world is to be accepted in the deepest humility. God made the world, and he could have just as well not made it if it suited him not to do so. We are stricken dumb and senseless when it comes to this, and we just have to take it as it is. And if we are destined to eternal damnation, then we will be made to prove his wrath, just as we would otherwise be made to prove his grace.—This is the pinnacle of irrationalism, simply dispensing with all theological difficulties. On the other side, God has frequently, during the history of Christianity, been incorporated into the world. We need both concepts, will and essence; and this is best accomplished by a concept of God as *freedom* or *Spirit*.

A concept of God as freedom does not signify something identical to human freedom; this freedom applies to God alone, while all creaturely freedom is merely patterned after his divine freedom. The concept of creation hangs on a God-concept of freedom. Creation means: a pure, free positing of the divine will. God is *act*—living, creative act! But just as he gives the creature the task of participating in his essence, so too he presents the creature with the task of participating in his freedom. But given the creature's sensible limitations, freedom for the creature means—insofar as the creature partakes of it—freedom from sensuality. Not that the creature *is* free, but *will be made* free. Human beings partake of the divine creative power only when they achieve a new, i.e., reborn, essence.

The concept of God as Spirit provides us with another vocabulary. It is used in the Gospel of John and, frequently, by Hegelians. It does not refer to the immaterial essence of God. It does not mean that we can neither see nor touch God. In fact, we can affirm that we touch and see God in a certain sense: for he is everywhere, and he lives in the real world. What this concept is really about is productive power. The concept of God as Spirit differs from the concept of God as freedom in that the latter emphasizes more the will, while the Hegelian terminology emphasizes the centrality of spiritual values. But the question of the origin of these values takes us back to the concept of will. Spirit is never to be understood as simply what is there, but rather always against the background of an act of the will. For the doctrine of the Spirit always signifies for us human beings what should be, the doctrine of that which is yet to be attained in order to impart shape to nature. Spirit therefore presupposes the free will through which Spirit generates itself, just as it presupposes nature. Otherwise, the taunting criticism that the Christian God is some sort of ghost who stands in need of a material world would be justified.

We come now to the question of how far this concept of God, as we have portrayed it, is not just one of several possible God-concepts, but the one that we *acknowledge* and *accept*. This question deals with the whole of the Christian faith. The decision is a purely religious one. Just as the decision whether Raphael or Rembrandt achieved the greater art can only be made on the basis of a subjective sensitivity, so too here with this decision. We can make any variety of strong, moving appeals to the temperament and the imagination of those who see things differently from us, but we can never prove that the opposite of what they decide is true. But subjectivity by no means signifies arbitrariness, for we believe that there is an inner necessity, albeit one which can only be felt subjectively.

And so now we ask, What illuminates the roots of our essence most deeply? Let us, quite unpretentiously, consider the final wish of all religious searching: to be freed from oneself, to be lifted above the individual ego. Where can this quest come to rest? We answer: in a God-concept that shows God to us as a real power that reaches out to us, that binds us to a truly vital, higher life. But whoever feels differently, whoever sees redemption as consisting in mere submersion into the divine All, he too will surely be free from all care and sorrow, and he cannot be contradicted, except perhaps through clarification of what it really means to have the religious quest fulfilled. According to our decision, however, there can be no doubt that a specifically religious judgment must decide for the living God who creates life—not only as an eternally self-identical All, but rather as an ever higher consequence of himself, purifying and elevating humankind, making it participate in eternity.—

Further: How does this relate to the realm of *objective knowledge?* To be sure, religion springs from religion and not from objective scholarship; nevertheless, we continue to make certain references to the latter that are important for faith. There is a widespread opinion abroad in the land today that a radically pantheistic conception of God is better adapted to our scientific world-picture than the Christian concept of God. But science is not all of a single piece; there is no complete unity, and for science just as for all knowledge, the question of why there is anything at all remains open. When it comes to this question, science too stands face to face with the irrational. Therefore whoever makes the irrational a constituent of his worldview cannot encounter wholly irresolvable difficulties.

Nevertheless, the bitterest of conflicts rages over precisely this point. There are four main objections that have been raised against the Christian concept of God. First: that the person-like conception of God is finite and anthropomorphic. Second: that the Christian concept of God is dualist—i.e., it implies a dualism between God as a will that is directed toward a goal, and the world in which he realizes himself. Third: that the idea of a goal is inseparable from the intrinsic contradiction involved in all teleology. Fourth: that the concept of God as freedom is posited without cause, and is incapable of being derived from anything.

To the *first* objection we must concede that a person-like conception of God does involve some anthropomorphism. The only question is whether it can be avoided. The only thing we know that comprehends plurality and change in a single unity is the human person; we have absolutely no other analogy on which to draw. The only remaining question is, From what part of human life will we draw our analogy? One could, like Aristotle, choose thought. God would then ultimately appear as a concept that thinks itself, an *actus purus,* a pure spirit. With respect to the question, Where, then, does matter come from? Aristotle answers: from the realm of abstract possibility, formed by God, the concept that thinks itself. But this too is a monstrous anthropomorphism, one that actually renders God finite. A law that no one has ever even thought of is nonsense, and furthermore, requires a matter to which it can be applied.

Another analogy seizes on the imagination as that which makes it possible for the human person to be a unity. God would then be the limitless imaginer of the world, who brings forth everything from himself and fills it with life. But how should one conceive of this great world-poet, who simply produces matter absolutely from himself? Our imagination is bound to thousands of givens. The poetic fantasy proves to be separate from its work: the work of art is distinct from the poet. But this distinction between the creator and the work brings us back to anthropomorphism.

Still others seek an analogy in the concept of life itself, in some dark principle of the inconceivable. The world is the eternal life-process of God—one hears this all the time. But this analogy also fails, succeeding at best in grasping a similarity between human beings and plants and animals. And then: What, really, is this life? It is nothing but a simple grasping of preexistent stuff which is then implicated in a mysterious principle, an organizing principle which is nevertheless bound to something which drives toward unity [*etwas Zuvereinheitlichendes*]. Hence this position is always thinking of a life which is struggling to move forward, which necessarily implies a struggle with other lives. This too is nothing more than another form of anthropomorphism.

Finally, Eduard von Hartmann struggles with an analogy that is even more vague. He says: Our conscious life is, to be sure, bound to the finite world, but this conscious life itself emerges first from the unconscious. God is the unconscious! But since we do not know this unconscious, the transference of God to the unconscious must remain hypothetical. And so we are compelled to describe God as the unconscious that becomes conscious in some way or other. Then the world-process becomes God's return to the unconscious. And this brings us right back to anthropomorphism. The emergence of conscious life, and the desire to submerge oneself in something greater than consciousness, draws on a human analogy.

It is not only the Christian concept of God, therefore, that makes use of analogy! The only difference is that the Christian concept of God proceeds on the basis of its own particular analogy, namely, the analogy of moral freedom. And we are completely within our rights to make use of this analogy, for this is where the strongest link between the human and the supra-human is to be found. We seize on an analogy to that which is most capable of being godlike, where the human being breaks out of mere existence and achieves devotion to intrinsic values.

Therefore, we view God as person-like, active will. But that will not help us avoid conflict over the concept of infinity. Our analogy leads us to conceive of tensions within the divine life. But contradiction and tension belong to the essence of the finite. The problem must therefore be stated thus: Is infinity the proper measure for the concept of God? If it were, we would then be unable to avoid the conclusion that any concept of God that acknowledges tensions in the way that we have is untenable. And thus we must straightforwardly reject the idea. Here the concept of infinity signifies nothing but the absence of all predicates. If we were to do away with everything that tension and limitation signify, such as the differences between good and evil, will and essence, all that would remain would be the concept of a deity with no object, a deity that is absolutely unpredicated. No matter what else we might say, even the simple ascription of existence signifies limitation! For to exist means to be understood by an intelligence; anything else would be a contradiction! A concept of supra-being [Übersein]—a being that is no being— has been advanced. The Gnostics and Neoplatonists spoke of the great ultimate, before which one can only keep one's silence. But keeping one's silence makes sense only when there is something to stay silent about, or else we are drawn into the sphere of nothingness. But God is the highest reality. As such he bears all tensions within himself. And the tensions are really there! Anything else is a false ideal.

Infinity in time and space, however, is an entirely different matter. It has absolutely nothing to do with the concept of God, but rather with our finitude. It is linked to the givenness of the world of space and time in experience; it bears an antinomian nature within itself. The world of space and time extends to infinity both forward and backward, but this infinity consists only in points and limits that can be further enumerated.

A third position joins Spinoza in saying: Infinity consists in absolute necessity. And since the character of world-substance is to be necessary in everything, all that remains is the question of its own necessity. But the world-substance itself is only a fact. When one says that God is his own cause, that signifies irrational self-establishment through his own will. But nevertheless, it remains indisputable that there are new, emergent, and unreckoned creative realities, which cannot all be understood as the necessary result of the totality of the world.

Infinity, therefore, does not provide us with the means whereby we may grasp the concept of God. In any case, it is essential that we draw a sharp distinction between religious infinity and mathematical-philosophical infinity. The former signifies the supra-human, creativity, holiness, and the utter and complete absence of proportionality. This sort of infinity may apply: but never philosophical infinity, which signifies a complete absence of tension, nor mathematical infinity, which is implicated in space and time. This is a point of enormous significance. We will be left helpless if our concept of infinity is drawn from mathematics or philosophy. We can approach the subject only by means of inference.

Fundamental to this is the concept of the microcosm that mirrors the divine macrocosm, even if only in the most elementary points. This is Leibniz's concept. Just as the microcosm is the concretion of the divine, so can the divine be conceived only by means of inference. These great questions extend throughout a struggle which is centuries old. The Neoplatonists taunted the Christians with the charge: You lack the infinite! The Christians defended themselves by showing that a complete absence of tension, taken to its logical conclusions, issued in a being that was being no longer. Tensions that are present in the microcosm must stem from the macrocosm. It is characteristic of Christianity to seize on the analogy of moral freedom to illuminate the concept of God.—

The *second* great objection is constituted by the problem of monism, something one hears a lot of crowing about everywhere— crowing which largely is done by people with the brains of a crow! According to this point of view, the dualism of the Christian concept of God is inadmissible, since dualism is irreligious, and since no respectable human being would have anything to do with it anyway. Science admits of nothing except complete and utter unity. Religion, according to this point of view, requires the substantial unity of the divine and human spirit in the same way that science requires a unified conception of things according to the necessary principle of an all-encompassing law. Pantheism satisfies both these requirements, and it is the source of the strongest modern opposition to Christianity. It draws its energy from this combination of science and religion. But these two areas are fundamentally quite different, and it is quite senseless to combine them. Religious pantheism has an entirely different basis from scientific pantheism. All religion, no matter what, is essentially dualist.

Religion is always concerned with wretchedness of the soul that subsists solely in itself, with the knowledge that there is something higher, and with attaining the blessedness that comes with surrender to this higher reality. This dualistic starting point is lacking only at the lowest levels of religion, where, for example, God is still thought to be limited, so that the contradiction between the finite and the infinite has not yet emerged. Nevertheless, even these lower forms of religion strive for elevation to something higher, and so there is dualism in them as well. The only question is where this dualism lies. In theism, we have the contradiction between wills, that is, the contradiction between the supra-human will and the finite will from which the former demands total surrender. Theism ultimately leads to a convergence of these wills, so that its dualism is only a starting point. The triumph of this convergence is achieved through the elevation of the partly yearning, partly resisting will. It comes to pass through conversion and surrender, whereby the human will is not annihilated, but rather adjusted to the divine will.

Pantheism's starting point is equally dualistic. There is, on the one hand, the partial being that does not yet know itself, and, on the other hand, the All-being. The root of this dualism is the false self-estimate of the individual who thinks that he is something, when, in fact, there is nothing besides the whole. This contradiction between the individual and the All is not overcome through conversion, but by thought. Our will clings to the illusion of individual being. As soon as we realize that we have no individual or particular being, our will fades away and the veil of illusion is rent. This is what Richard Wagner sought to express with the word *Wahnfried* [peace from illusion]: "Here, where my illusions find their peace . . ."[12] The upshot of pantheism is therefore a painful and deeply felt dualism as well; the only difference is that pantheism, unlike Christianity, believes that dualism is rooted in intellectual illusion. It is a dualism between appearance and reality, to be overcome by submersion in the All. But there remains a basic riddle in all of this: How did this illusion come about in the first place?

Thus pantheism leads humankind to its redemption by way of a path that leads through the harshest dualism. While theism is basically optimistic, holding out for the elevation of the finite will and not its mere negation, pantheism is deeply pessimistic. Everything, everything is illusion, and is to be recognized for the illusion that it is, so that the ego may be not elevated, but forfeited. Richard Wagner's development—which, at any rate, is not to be taken as particularly profound or instructive—illustrates the pantheistic concept of redemption in the *Ring*, while the Christian idea of redemption by means of being taken up into the divine will is depicted in *Parsifal*.

Therefore, it makes no sense here to speak in terms of an unconditional monism; it is rather a case of finding where the dualism lies, and clarifying the difference in how it is overcome. Moreover, both approaches presuppose the irrational: the Christian-theistic approach relies on the irrationality of the divine will, while the pantheistic approach refers to the irrational separation of being and appearance. But when it comes to the intelligibility of the two positions, we find ourselves in the same situation both hither and yon; one would have to have a powerful antipathy for Christianity in order to find pantheism any more intelligible.

As soon as we put purely scientific considerations to one side, we find that every religious position is dualistic through and through. But every religious position is also filled through and through with a longing for the complete dissolution and reintegration of this dual-

12. *Wahnfried* is the name Richard Wagner gave to his villa at Bayreuth, built in 1874. It could be translated variously as illusion-peace, peace from illusion, fantasies at rest, fancies at rest, dream-peace, etc. At the entrance is the following inscription:
Hier, wo meinen Wähnen Frieden fand
WAHNFRIED
Sei dieses Haus von mir benannt.
"Here, where my illusions find their rest, be this house named by me Peace from Illusion." This translation is from Ernest Newman, *The Life of Richard Wagner*, vol. 4: 1866–1883 (New York: Alfred A. Knopf, 1946), p. 419.

ism. In this sense we are all monists. But we ask only this: Are we really and truly individual wills that are destined to unite with the divine will, or are we appearance and nothingness, doomed to mere submergence?

Pantheism's adherents, however, claim that their position can be reinforced by the addition of the scientific method. But the scientific method holds very little significance for the religious world. Even the brightest scientific method throws no light on the question of whether the world is to be understood as the result of divine will or as illusion. The more sophisticated pantheistic systems realize that they have nothing to learn from scientific apothecary-monism. These things are not to be found in the botanist's specimen jar, but come from years of immersing oneself in the problem.

We turn next to the more subtle *scholarly objections,* based on theoretical philosophy. The first of these is this: the essence of logical thought dictates the need for a firm, unbroken context for the world of experience. This, however, supposedly points to an unconditionally and universally monistic law of the world.

Even if we were to concede that the logical character of scientific thought truly demands this, the only thing that it establishes is the scientific-causal form of judgment. Alongside this there still stands an entire range of different possibilities, such as, for example, the form of judgment based on moral commandments, which has nothing in common with scientific-causal judgments. There is, further, the aesthetic approach to reality in terms of the laws of sublimity and beauty; and it too is every bit as necessary as science's thoroughgoing rationalization. There is also the teleological approach, i.e., the investigation of reality in terms of the goals that are realized in it, another approach that is not based solely on what is given. Thoroughgoing rationalization, therefore, is but one form of judgment among many; namely, the one with which we attend to logical necessities. But our spirit uses other forms of interpretation to attend to necessities which are every bit as substantial. We will never achieve a full understanding of reality by means of the scientific-causal approach; only that which is amenable to logical investigation is accessible to it. We will never arrive at a monism that is capable of bringing the whole of reality under *one* law.

And so we are utterly given over to pluralistic views, no matter how much the ideal of unity may remain. Other ideals demand that we look to the interiority of the All, so that the only question now can be how the plurality of interpretative principles is to be unified. But under no circumstances can this plurality be subordinated to the scientific-causal principle. There is not a single reason why we should think it is the highest principle. There can be no question of making a unified world-principle into an object of religious feeling. Similarly, it does not by any means unconditionally follow from the ideal of logic that everything must be primarily conditioned by a universal law. Who is to say that there are no real breakthroughs, that nothing new freely takes place at specific points? When it comes to these possibilities, it can only be a matter of hints and intimations that simply indicate the difficulties associated with this problem and demonstrate that there is nothing here that requires a monistic position.

The only difficulty for our position lies in the way that modern human beings are possessed of a certain sense for the All. And so it is extremely simple for them to be led to the conclusion that this All should be the true object of religious veneration; and it is correspondingly difficult to make them see that this universal law is ultimately inconceivable, and that other conceptions have just as much right. Again and again one finds that the conversation begins with muddled expressions like "I venerate this universal law; it is God." Public discussions of the question that start with this sort of comment are all quite unproductive, despite their present popularity.

So far we have discussed only the finer, and hence rarer, form of monism. The grosser form of monism is the *dogmatic-metaphysical* variety. This type of monism says, We rely on no more than our senses and our measurements of sensible reality. Using them, we find that we have the unity of matter and the unity of law. We have the sum total of the innumerable elements of energy, and we have their behavior with one another. And so we find ourselves in possession of a simple and imposing idea. What more do we need? We have comprehended and explained everything.—The advocates of this point of view are quite convinced that their knowledge is most edifying: seeing the whole of life comprehended in a single unity provides a certain religious satisfaction. It is also very difficult to have any impact on this point of view, for the ideas that would make it possible to criticize it presuppose a deeper level of interest than is here to be found; this point of view simply rests on altogether superficial thinking, devoid of all spirit.

We cannot go into all the details at this point. The most important issue is this: If it is true that there is nothing but tiny particles and the laws that regulate their motion (presuming for the moment that these monists can deal with the incomprehensible difference between energy and matter), then our thoughts and perceptions too are nothing but naturally governed movements. But that would make it impossible to make any distinction between true and false judgments. What I am saying now, I say because the law of nature makes me say it! Haeckel, to be sure, is of the opinion that truth is determined by correct brain function. But how are we to distinguish between correct and incorrect brain function, if it is all a matter of natural necessity and nothing more? A Helmholtz and a simple idiot are at most to be distinguished by the fact that the one man's output is useful, while the other's isn't?! Even if we could open up the skull and inspect the brain, we still could not thereby determine what constitutes "correct" brain function; for the criterion of correctness would have to be determined in advance. Hence, when it comes to the capacity to think, there is no monism, but rather a dualism of matter and validity. The law of thought can *never* be transformed into a law of nature. The law of correctness, and the law of actual development, is dualist, and so it will remain for this system. And that spells the end for the majesty of monism. The gentlemen among us who praise its majesty fail to grasp the elementary distinction that the laws of physics are something different from the rules by which we determine questions of truth.

Now it remains for us to formulate properly the dualism we have endorsed. The popular form of dualism is impossible, for it thinks in terms of a spatial and temporal duality: God is high above the world, separate from it and opposed to it. The world will last for a time, and then God will make a new one. This is the dualism of the older piety. In contrast to that, we mean something which is neither spatial nor temporal, but rather internal. It is expressed in the pious feeling that we are in God, but not indistinguishably identical with him. Once again the irrational rises up before us: Each has his own life in God, not next to God, but really in him. This is not conceptually intelligible. We can only picture it. Just as our own thoughts are both within us and are yet simultaneously artistic creations that stand apart from us, so too are we a *part* of the divine all-life, distinguished from it just as a *work of art* is distinguished from its *creator!*

In our experience, this contradiction is quite simply resolvable: We sense the entire world—everything in which we find ourselves— as the divine all-being; and at the same time we sense that we our- selves have a separate existence, no more identical with God than we ever were, so that unity with God is a task to be achieved. This unity can be achieved only by making a break with selfhood; a break, however, that signifies not the destruction of the self, but its eleva- tion. As soon as this unity is achieved, the human self, now yielded to

God, is no longer obstinate in will; yet in such a way that God's will is experienced as the self's own. Not monotony—that would be unbearable—but something else: The whole of this motley existence is part of the immeasurable divine life, the primal mystery that finite things are of and in God in every moment of their existence, simultaneously identical with and separate from him; products of his will, but not God himself. Beneath all this lies the concept of panentheism, as opposed to pantheism. It attests to the way in which the being of each and every thing is included in God; but it also attests to each and every thing's peculiarity. This particularity will be really overcome, not through recognition that the world is an illusion, but rather through surrender.

We come now to the *third* objection to the personalistic concept of God. This objection focuses on the concept of a goal, a concept which, it is claimed, always imposes limitations on God. The concept of a goal suggests an analogy with the human will, which is never free from opposition, and which attains its essence only when it finally achieves its goal. How then, it is asked, can a personalistic God be conceived other than as capable of achieving his essence only when his purposes are finally realized? Is the Absolute then incomplete, working on something independent from it? With the Absolute, everything is supposed to be necessary. Just as we need no more than the mere concept of the globe in order to know what a globe must look like from any perspective, so too, when it comes to God, everything must be complete. According to Spinoza, any alteration whatsoever would destroy God's majesty. The objection continues: If we inquire after God's goals, all we have in view is, at most, either human prosperity or the following of his law: God is thought always to busy himself with this obstinate human creature. Lessing concluded that it is very bad manners to attribute goals to God.

This objection poses two questions: First, can we even speak of God in terms of his commitment to goals? And second, can we see these goals in the human race? The answer to the first question is this: The very idea of God cannot even be thought apart from some kind of goal. To do so would be to kill precisely what religion is all about in the first place. A concept of God without any attainable blessedness would be utterly unthinkable. Its very significance consists in this: that we grasp a higher life, that there is a meaning to existence, and that we affirm this meaning in our religious experience! God is surely not to be thought of as merely necessary. All attempts to construe God as mere necessity eventually come back to the idea of a goal in some way. Spinoza's *amor intellectualis* is no different. The concept of blessedness signifies no lapse in religion, but its essence.

The only question, then, is where this goal is to be sought. What characterizes Christianity is that it locates this goal in the elevation and divinization of the finite creature. But this is not to say that the human race and its well-being are the only divine goal. Given that our planet is nothing but a speck in the universe, it is conceivable that humankind is simply a variety or species. Augustine supposed that human beings were not foreseen in the original world plan, but became necessary as a result of the fall of the angels. They were a sort of breeding stock of replacements for the fallen angels, which is why it naturally made no difference to Augustine whether or not millions of people were lost.

But there is a very different way in which human beings can be construed as the goal. Countless people, in complete naiveté, think that their own personal good constitutes God's highest goal, and they lay the blame for the whole miserable mess at God's feet as soon as things do not go the way they want. If they cannot figure out why things are going so badly for themselves—other people's fate is not such a pressing concern for them—then they no longer wish to believe. The same sort of thinking frequently occurs, although somewhat less egoistically, as a response to global distress. And any one who has lived through such a disaster will scarcely be able to avoid such thoughts altogether. Nevertheless, they are based on a serious error. If we take the concept of a goal to signify human blessedness, then we refer not to the sensible-natural life, but rather to something that is yet to be.

The blessedness that Christianity envisions consists not even in so noble a eudaemonism, but rather in something higher than our legitimate sensible-natural needs. It is the higher birth that counts. Not the sensuous, but the spiritual human being is what matters. The divine world-goal and the self-communication of God refer to the spiritual self alone—never a higher animal, but rather the divine human self whose birth comes through sorrow and sacrifice, through separation from nature and surrender to the divine life that grasps us. But the blessedness of the higher self can shed rays of joy on us even in the midst of the deepest night of a senseless fate. This is why we speak only conditionally of human blessedness as a divine goal. It is a matter of the divine within us, and its value is universal and trans-human. Every creature of which we can conceive must have the same goal: to have the divine spark be struck from them. And so we say, in the specifically theistic sense of Christianity: Meaning and goal lie in the blessedness of the creature.

But this surely does not mean that we limit everything to the human race; rather, we think of that which binds us to all conceivable spirits. The goal of union with God is completely universal; by no means is it bound simply to the human race. We are not thinking of something small and narrow, limited to us alone; rather, we think in terms of ourselves only insofar as we can break through to that which is higher than ourselves. In this form, the idea of a goal cannot signify the least limitation on God.

At this point a further question intrudes upon our discussion. The process by which creature becomes spirit is, to be sure, the highest goal of divinity and of the world-process; but is it also the only goal? There are billions of human beings, and countless of them will never make a complete break with the animal level of existence; they are perhaps even incapable of doing so, due to being dreadfully restricted by spiritual and physical defects, subhuman circumstances and sur-roundings, and the like. And the entire spectrum of subhuman crea-tures comes into question here too. All higher developments are preceded by millions of prior stages. We all live in purely material, even deathlike bodies. Are we to think of the inanimate, latent beauty of plants and their simple power to take nourishment as a prerequisite for the creature's capacity to become spirit? If, for a moment, we think of an isolated valley high in the Alps, where countless numbers of tiny plants cling to the sides of boulders, plants whose beauty and perfection will never be seen by the human eye, then the question strikes us in its full force: Is all this only a detour on the way to the highest goal?

Countless mysteries remain at this point. One might say: These entities are known to us only by their appearance; we know nothing about their soul. And it is thoroughly conceivable that this motion-less beauty constitutes the bodies and organs of invisible spirits, that these bodies hold the same significance for these spirits that our bodies hold for us. And the existence of these unknown (to us) spirits may enable us to think that the whole natural world is destined to disappear once the process of becoming spirit has been completed. For those who believe this, the whole of the unpersonal world con-stitutes a stimulus to similar thought.

But the problem may also be approached through the observation that there is a whole series of subordinate goals that stand alongside the highest goal. One of these goals could be an outpouring of the superabundance of divine power into subhuman creatures, a self-outpouring of God into the subethical, where, naturally, the tasks imposed could no longer be ethical ones. In addition, the infinitely important function of the aesthetic is difficult to subsume completely under the spiritual and ethical. The poet elicits a fullness of life from nature, a fullness which is beautiful only in the poet's own singing and ringing. The only thing we can say with certainty here is this: The spiritual goal is the decisive thing *for us,* no matter what other goals there may be in addition to this central one. Otherwise we would remain unaware of the ultimate unity of life, and in our meditations, even as we surrender ourselves to the heights, we would have to stand on the verge of the depths.

And now for the *last* objection! It is the focal point of all objections to Christian theism. Its emergence coincided with the appearance of several different religious viewpoints, all of which sought to associate themselves with its scientific connotations. Hence it is often quite difficult to gain clarity on this matter, since we are not dealing with pure science, but rather with various combinations. The issue at stake is theism's insistence on freedom. The concept of freedom signifies the complete inconceivability and groundlessness of the divine existence. God is—through his own freedom. That is the point; for whatever is true of God's existence must also be true of all events in general. Just as the whole is a sign of creative freedom, so too is the individual. God's freedom reappears in the creature. This, in turn, signifies the *new,* that which is not conditioned by what has gone before. And this corresponds to the concept of rebirth. Rebirth is a creative act, not the consequence of circumstances or a mere reshaping of the given. We therefore interpret the concept of creation in terms of the concept of freedom. And *this* is what is assailed by opposing sensitivities and scientific orientations. Pantheistic piety as a whole is far removed from any concept of freedom. It prefers firm, unbroken clarity over any sort of unpredictability. It characteristically insists on the unalterability of the divine will, a concept which sacrifices all individual being. Here too, as before, only a truly religious feeling will be capable of affirming or denying the concept.

We hold that pantheism consists in a virtual dread of the new; that is why it seeks to restrict religion to the sphere of unchangeability. On the other hand, if we acknowledge the freedom of God, we also thereby acknowledge all reality, which means in turn that our religious thoughts are incomparably stronger.

On this basis, we can respond to the scientific objection in the following way. All scientific thought rests on the attempt to unify and connect the whole of reality in terms of cause and effect, to replace the irrational with the verifiable. The reduction of all reality to immutability will therefore satisfy the demands of scientific thought. The uniformity of the scientific method does manifest a certain kinship to pantheistic thought, but it is ultimately altogether quite different. The question here is this: To what extent can this conflict be resolved? All theology and philosophy of religion are fundamentally involved in this question. And here and now we must say, The conflict is irresolvable. We are confronted with an irreconcilable contradiction: on the one side we have the irrational, on the other the quest to find a reason for everything. The question can only be whether science is the primary approach to the comprehension of reality, i.e., whether the whole of reality is exhaustively reducible [*verknüpfbar*]. If it were, we would then have to admit: We are not very far along on that path, but it is our goal.

But does it make sense to say that the whole world must be scientifically understood? I am still not able to inquire after the causes for God in the same way that I do for water vapor or lightning! To do so would signify the complete breakdown of the scientific method. Spinoza was aware of this breakdown and sought to address it by saying that God is his own cause. But that is to say nothing more than this: God is inexplicable, he is the Ground of all grounds— irrational, primordial being. Hence science is incapable of comprehending the fact of God and the world as such. God is God through his groundless will. At this point, all science runs aground.

We can therefore only ask whether each and every thing in the reality which now exists is bound by rigid logical rules or not. This brings us to the difficult question of the sense and meaning of the principle of causality, detailed investigation of which is a matter for philosophy, not theology. But let us consider for a moment the possibility that it really is the case that one thing is always grounded in another, and that every event is therefore already contained in what precedes it. This would mean that nothing new could ever happen in the world, since each and every thing would be nothing more than mere extrapolation from what was already there. The decisive thing is the question: Is there anything new? We can certainly concede that every new thing has connections to that which precedes it; the question is whether the new is simply given without remainder by what precedes it, so that it is not really something new, but old. That would be the same as to say: Change is illusion. For every transformation would, on this basis, be incomprehensible. But if we acknowledge even at a single point that there is something new, then we immediately have something irrational.

The new is not scientifically comprehensible, for it raises this question: How does something which was not, come to be? The advocates of necessity say: It was present in the ancestors, in previous animal stages, even in the atoms! Thus we are referred ever further back. But irrational uniqueness is the essence of every individuality. And no necessity-fanatic can get away from that by claiming, That must be an illusion. You can actually read sentences like this: "Individuality is unscientific." But, in all our peculiarity and interiority, and despite all inheritance, we are *now* and not then. Each of us is an other, an individual, a new self. No matter how many similarities and resemblances there may be, the "Nameless" [*Anonyme*] of which Goethe spoke will always be present. Individuality can be experienced but never explained. It signifies the dominion of the new; it is effective in the new birth. Here we have a full right to speak of the "new man."

But how is this standpoint to be reconciled with the equally legitimate demands of science? We must answer, We do not know. The difficulty at this point is immeasurable. We could cut the conceptual knot and say, We will simply make everything rational. Or we could cut the knot by saying, We will not concern ourselves with the demands of scientific rationality. Both responses are equally impossible. But which theoretical approach should we adopt? Once again, we do not know. Only one thing is clear: Both starting points are valid. Things are reducible to their causes; but the presence of the irrational in them is equally unquestionable.

§13. The Holiness of God

DICTATION

1. The preceding discussion of God as will and essence leads next into a discussion of God as a will that is eternally directed toward, and faithfully and personally embodies, the *good*. This good is the goal of the divine essence; and moreover, it presupposes the divine will, since the good, according to its nature, must be willed. Will and essence are therefore united in the concept of a will directed toward the good, or *absolute holiness*. This concept of God's holiness and completeness corresponds to the basic concept of biblical religion and also constitutes the center of Jesus' preaching. We must insist, therefore, in direct contradiction to numerous misinterpretations, that holiness is the central concept.

This central concept of holiness, however, leads to an entire series of further concepts that are also contained in the preaching of Jesus. These concepts are, to be sure, often included merely as presuppositions or illustrations, but they still require conceptual formulation. They are the concepts of the *absolute completeness* of God, the *moral law* of God, the *moral world-order,* and *moral freedom.* They also include the *contradiction between God and evil,* as well as the contradiction between God and all merely self-satisfied and stationary natures. This concept also impels us once again toward dualism: the dualism of God and world, nature and spirit, will and essence, all of which bear the essential imprint of Christian religiosity. Finally, these concepts culminate in the idea of the divine *judgment* that is already at hand for the soul in every moment, and will ultimately culminate in a final judgment on the complete worth of its personality.

2. These basic concepts have a decisive impact on Christian piety. What makes the concept of God truly God-like is not some connection to the merely external powers of nature, as in polytheism, but rather its inmost essence and connectedness with the world-goal. But on the other hand, this concept of God does not consist in a transformation of the moral law into an abstract, self-sufficient law of nature or the universe, as is so often the case when monotheism develops out of polytheism by way of philosophy, as it did in Stoicism and Confucianism; instead, in Christianity, the moral law is directly infused with the living spirit of the personal, demanding will of God. And finally, this concept of God is removed further still from the essence of the pantheistic-pessimistic religions of the East, which forfeit the moral dimension altogether in religious self-annihilation or in a quietist will, so that the moral element is eliminated from the concept of God, leaving us only with the duty of religious self-deception. In opposition to this, prophetic-Christian piety includes the moral demand in the concept of God, so that the image of the will of God is the archetype of the good. For human beings, this means that religion is incorporated into the moral will, and conversely, that the moral will is grounded in, and directed toward, religious concepts.

The peculiar character of *Christian moral law* comes from this intrinsic connection between moral and religious consciousness: a radical and austere understanding of the unconditional will of God; a pure and temperate disposition that stands under the demands of the divine will; and a religious spiritualization of the moral law that transforms it into a requirement to surrender before God, elevating this commandment above all others. The hallmark of such a moral law—and the hallmark of the Christian concept of God—is its tension with the world, the world's culture, and all intra-worldly goals. The Christian moral law and the goal of the divine essence constitute an extraordinarily lofty, rare, and pointed ideal. That is why it is understandable that the Christian concept of holiness can, on the one hand, become sectarianized and restricted to ever decreasing numbers of people, or, on the other hand, be seen as unachievable due to the universal reign of sin, a reign that can only bc neutralized by the forgiveness of sins.[1] But in either case, it becomes difficult to maintain that holiness is both God's essence *and* his goal for the world.

In fact, however, the New Testament concept of holiness as something opposed to the world is only the most extreme form of the prophetic-Christian concept. Its radical nature results from its connection to the New Testament's eschatology. Where this eschatology does not dominate, as it did with the prophets, then all moral activity is sanctified and drawn into the sphere of religious holiness; and when eschatology returns to the foreground, as it did in the emergence of Christianity, it poses the task of constantly developing and renewing the inner relationship between holiness and the general moral consciousness of life on earth. This, in turn, poses the task of the religious sanctification of all moral will, or overcoming this fundamental tension through the *sanctification of earthly life.* Since all life on earth can be traced back to God's creation, it must be possible to transform it into both the matter and the agent of the sanctifying will. This is the task of ethics. All that is necessary here is to describe the holiness of God and the sanctification of the finite spirit as the goal of the world, a goal that indeed comprehends the world within itself.

1. This reflects the widely influential typology of sect and church developed by Troeltsch and the sociologist Max Weber (1864–1920), which Troeltsch discussed at length in *The Social Teachings,* trans. Olive Wyon (New York: Harper & Row, 1960). According to Troeltsch, the *sect* (e.g., the Anabaptists) holds to a *heroic,* perfectionist ethic, to which only a few people can attain; the sect therefore must *withdraw* from society and the world, and hence can have little impact. The *church* (e.g., the Catholic or Lutheran church), on the other hand, emphasizes the forgiveness of sins instead of moral perfection, and therefore holds to an ethic that can be attained by most people; therefore, the church can remain in the world, but its impact is also limited because of its pessimism about the universality of sin.

In addition to church and sect, Troeltsch also described a third type of Christianity, mysticism, which consists of a purely personal and internal experience, with a very loosely structured community. Although mysticism is not mentioned in this particular discussion, it is evident that mysticism had a great impact upon his thought in these lectures.

Troeltsch's discussion is still considered a standard in the sociology of religion, even when it is disputed. See *The Social Teachings,* pp. 993–94, and also pp. 328–49.

3. But as clear as these concepts are, and as pronounced as their connection with moral and religious experience proves to be, they involve difficulties and obscurities that are equally pronounced. An entire series of major disputes connected with the Christian concept of God arises here, and they must be resolved insofar as possible.

a. The concept of God as the *absolute good,* complete and holy, merely expresses the way in which everything that is absolutely necessary and valuable is rooted in God, so that the essence of God cannot even be thought apart from absolute goodness. This is the source of the famous controversy over whether something is good because God wills it, or God wills something because it is good; but it also raises the question whether any moral predicate abstracted from human being is not utterly incommensurable with the goodness of God, since such predicates are always drawn just as much from our goodness's contradiction to evil or nature as they are from our communion with God in opposition to evil. Instead, these predicates cannot be viewed as anything but images for the divine perfection. The only abstract expression available for the latter is nothing but the most general formula for the moral character, namely, the *self-establishment of the person through freedom.* It is here and only here that an analogy between human morality and divine holiness can be drawn.

b. No less serious are the difficulties which the concept of the divine moral law poses. The moral law is by no means set or codified in its content. This is implied by the concept of moral autonomy and its rejection of *every statutory legalistic heteronomy.* It also implies freedom from every biblical moral code, whether drawn from the Old or New Testaments. The moral law is a free, internally necessary self-legislation of the human spirit, as Kant correctly described the Christian ethos.[2] But this autonomous moral law must also be understood theonomously, as a divine moral law. And this, in turn, is possible only if the divine and human spirits are essentially related to one another, so that the latter's self-legislation can simultaneously be seen as the outpouring of the divine spirit on the human spirit. This highlights the real greatness of Christianity over against all statutory morality and all purely utilitarian eudaemonism.

But this poses yet another difficulty, that of specifying the *content* of the Christian moral law. Its content cannot consist merely in the

2. See Immanuel Kant, *Religion within the Limits of Reason Alone,* trans. Theodore M. Greene and Hoyt M. Hudson (New York: Harper & Row, 1960), pp. 139–90, esp. pp. 163–73.

formal, subjective activity of the conscience, but must provide a specific, material direction to all activity, a direction provided by a combination of moral and religious goals. This signifies, in turn, that the content of the moral law is a *task* which must always be undertaken anew. The subjective conscience must always regulate and reformulate the moral will anew in terms of the final religious goal of communion with God; hence the moral law must always be re-formed and reformulated in every general context. The moral law then becomes an active, variable entity, for which the temper of the subjective conscience and the objective direction of a religious goal are the only firm motifs. This is the only way in which we can enable an *intrinsic relation* to the life of the world—something from which the moral law of the New Testament completely retreats, but which the present age unconditionally demands.

c. The Christian approach to the moral law is, furthermore, closely linked to the ideas of *freedom,* the *potential for evil,* and *guilt.* In the preceding section, we have already discussed the idea of freedom as a general metaphysical principle. Here it is a question of its specifically moral significance and its connection to the divine holiness. This is where the concept of freedom derives its central meaning: the freedom of the finite spirit, that is, its capacity, under the impact of the divine Spirit, to begin new undertakings—for both good and evil. But this brings us face to face with the sharpest contradictions. First, there is the religious and dialectical contradiction that such freedom would restrict and condition the omnipotence of God. Second, there is the scientific objection that the ethical life, too, belongs to the deterministic order of nature as much as anything else.

To the first objection we may reply that it has force only if a pantheistic piety is presupposed. No intrinsically religious contradiction is involved in holding that the divine creativity is communicated to finite spirits that continue to draw their being from God. And if the reality of the finite spirit is presupposed, then this creative act of God within it can only be God's own act, that is, the demand to surrender in freedom. Everything is simultaneously grace and deed, divine action and human surrender at one and the same time. But this also includes the possibility of the finite spirit's self-refusal of the divine initiative, and hence the potential for a truly evil reality as such. To affirm the reality of evil, however, does not detract from religious feeling; indeed, it strengthens it. From a purely religious standpoint, then, there can be no objection.

The task of making a detailed response to the second, scientific objection, belongs to ethics. All that can be said here is that the moral feeling itself certainly demands only that moral motives be distinguished from morally indifferent motives. However, if moral activity is considered from the highest point of view, then the peculiarity of the moral motive cannot be conceived without the metaphysical concept of freedom.

  d. Now, at the same time, the moral-religious person stands in the context of nature, under a propitious necessity that extends not only to his spiritual self, but to all of his life and perception. Hence it is necessary to maintain a firm relationship between moral value and the course of nature, a relationship that will finally and completely satisfy the demands of the *will to live.* The Bible first did this by correlating moral value and disvalue with reward and punishment. In light of the difficulty involved in maintaining that such a correspondence actually takes place in this world, the Bible began to lay increasing emphasis on the other world, the Last Judgment, and the new world of the Kingdom of God. The Bible then transferred this idea to its view of the end. For the Bible, the concept of the end is not a purely spiritual triumph of the Spirit, but rather the totally satisfying bliss of a living will that is united with God. The sinful world of the present, however, stands under the rule of the devil and is filled with suffering; here the divine world-ordering can be seen only fragmentarily. After the Bible, the church went on to develop these ideas into a rich eschatology of heaven, hell, and purgatory, all in an attempt to answer the questions with which we are here concerned. And while belief in these other worlds continued to grow, the significance of this-worldly reward and punishment also came to play a greater role in church doctrine than it had in the New Testament.

  But these very popular beliefs—which were closely linked to the popular metaphysics of the ancient world—have now been completely transformed, first by the impact of Greek philosophy, and now in particular by modern scientific thought. First of all, the concept of reward and punishment has been replaced by the concept of a *moral world-order.* According to this concept, positive or negative consequences can be related to moral or immoral activity only in a general way; they are the intrinsically necessary consequences that flow from activity as part of the general nexus of reality, and by no means do they always unconditionally come to pass. Positive or negative consequences do not always happen specifically to the individual, but rather to the general nexus of living reality. The concept that goodness will prevail by means of the intrinsic moral regularity of reality has replaced the idea of punishment and reward by specific divine intervention. The whole theory of reward and punishment strikes us as a Jewish idea today; and insofar as it is found in the New Testament, it appears as a remnant of Judaism that must be abandoned. Jesus himself decisively broke with it.

Second, even the specifically Christian version of the concept of reward and punishment, which is modeled on the contradiction between earthly life in the realm of the devil and the wonderfully blessed life of the Kingdom of God, poses insuperable difficulties. For us, the entire biblical picture of devils and demons has faded away. For us, the limitless, enduring world is not some preliminary stop on the stations of the cross, but rather the arena of struggle and higher elevation.

In conclusion: blessedness cannot be understood as an altogether new state of affairs that abruptly and miraculously ruptures into reality, but must rather be conceived according to the ruling idea of an organic development: as a continuing development of the higher life, beginning with regeneration and extending beyond death, where the goal is at last attained through developments of which we know nothing. But even this goal cannot be construed as an other-worldly final reckoning of reward and punishment, but rather as the consummation of an organic development—already begun in this world—of the higher life. For the same reasons, the Last Judgment can be understood only as a symbol for the final completion of developments already begun on earth.

Finally, the whole question of the *cosmic victory* of the good, like the attendant question of the fulfillment of the ethical and natural will-to-live, is answered by the New Testament with fantastic images—the coming of the Kingdom of God, the heavenly Jerusalem. The church further elaborated on this with its threefold eschatology of hell, heaven, and purgatory. But today these teachings are all nothing more than symbols and images that are, in part, no longer even conceivable. What we have today are faith-postulates that allow both the ethical-religious will and the natural will to live to reach their goal; for God, as Lord and Creator of nature, must also bring these wills to their goal as part and parcel of the soul's consummated communion with God.[3]

LECTURE

Our discussion of the concept of God grows ever more specific. But we must let the controversies fade into the background in order

---

3. This entire discussion, and particularly this mention of "postulates," recalls Kant's Second Critique. See Immanuel Kant, *Critique of Practical Reason*, trans. Lewis White Beck (New York: Bobbs-Merrill, 1956), pp. 111–53, esp. pp. 126–28.

to allow the concept to come before our eyes once again in all its simplicity, greatness, and majesty. We have seen how our faith depicts God for us as creative will, and how this will is illuminated by its essence and goal: this, in turn, led us to a consideration of the divine essence. Now for the first time we encounter the concept of holiness. Only those who are holy may draw near to God. He is perfect, and all finite creatures shall be perfect as he is perfect.[4] Again and again the Bible resonates with this mighty summons: You shall be holy, for the Lord is thrice holy! "He has shown you, O man, what is good!"[5] And it is not only in the Old Testament that the essence of the divine will consists in overwhelming holiness; it holds true for the New Testament as well. We particularly emphasize this because of the sentimental approach to the New Testament that dominates today: God is love, the forgiveness of sins, the "haven of rest," and so forth! These are all, of course, genuinely Christian; but the first thing upon which all of Jesus' preaching insists is this: Whoever is a hearer of the Word must also be a doer![6]

We encounter a strong, pungent flavor everywhere, quite free of all the customary sweetness. There is no mention of any merely quiescent reconciliation that would relieve us of the task of being holy. Jesus was consumed by the will of God; he lived it and breathed it. He was neither soft nor mellow. His demand for a righteousness which exceeds that of the scribes[7] is both delicately human and yet powerful and earnest. God desires the *whole* human heart, and so Jesus, like the prophets, asks not for rites and sacrifices: I do not look for the words on your lips,[8] but for a purified life, given to God, free from selfishness and the enticements of the world. "You shall love the Lord your God with all your heart and your neighbor as yourself."[9] Alongside the demand stands the promise: If you fulfill this, then you shall enter the Kingdom of God. The only thing that is mild and restrained about this is that it does not require torturous hairsplitting over specific demands; but it nevertheless lays claim to the entire soul, energetically urging it on to practical application.

It is no accident that this demand is interwoven throughout the entire Bible. Its appeal is to the most sublime depths of the human soul: the soul's capacity to yield to God, to renounce its own righ-

---

4. See Matt. 5:48; Lev. 11:44.
5. Mic. 6:8.
6. See Matt. 7:24; Luke 8:21; but also James 1:22.
7. Matt. 5:20.
8. See Matt. 15:8.
9. See Luke 10:27.

teousness, and to yield everything in this bond to God—even though we are already bound to him in everything. Paul likewise exalts this demand for holiness. And he also says that love of God is to issue in love of the brother.

But this leads to another entire series of concepts. God not only demands the good, but himself is the consummate good. Furthermore: As soon as we liberate our soul from everyday distractions, we hearken to the conscience as an emanation of absolute holiness. We possess no revelation of the moral law apart from the revelation within us. The still and quiet sanctuary of the soul, whose voice is so seldom heard in our everyday activities, is precisely where the will of God appeals directly to us. But he also compels us to an unconditional recognition of the moral law within us; for it is destined to triumph. The moral law is revealed in our inner life, but it does not remain a merely internal concern.[10] Nor is it a simply spiritual matter; its purpose is to subdue the world. "Thy will be done as it is now in heaven!"[11] That implies the concept of a moral world-order in which the good self joins the *good* in victory over evil. The righteous person is only temporarily under siege; God must always restore him anew. The Bible enthusiastically believes in this, in the coming Kingdom of God, in the triumph of the divine holiness. The great importance of the moral world-order is that it also implies the triumph of thought over and beyond nature, signifying, in turn, confidence in the unity of life. Here there is no division. It is a triumph in, and over, the sensible world.

The concept of personal human responsibility is closely related; indeed, thoroughgoing responsibility is one of the dominant themes of the Bible, far too little appreciated by the insipid interpretations that favor the forgiveness of sins or similar comforts to the exclusion of the great seriousness of moral responsibility. In the Bible, it is the wholly personal will that is of primary concern. "No one else can take your place." It poses the pointed question, Do you want this, or not? All this is easy to say, but hard to do. Our eternal destiny relative to God is a matter decided within the soul itself. Jesus expressed it again and again: I tell you, genuine righteousness is entirely personal. Whoever decides against the good does not belong to God. Whatever does not proceed from the whole will, whatever is mere afterthought, whatever is mere participation in collective work, has no value.[12] Responsibility can never be shifted to anyone or any-

10. See Rom. 2:14.
11. See Matt. 6:10.
12. A reference to Matt. 5:21–6:18?

thing else. This implies a colossal individualism; yet it does not reflect enthusiasm for individualism as such, but for responsibility.

With moral freedom comes moral struggle. It requires the complete elimination of all illusions, of everything that is human instead of divine, of everything that can be satisfied by halfway measures. It requires a struggle against the merely natural human self! The idea of outrage over evil corresponds to the idea of holiness. In the Bible, this outrage is manifested as the wrath of God, directed against every sinful thought that detracts from the divine glory. This holiness scornfully strikes down every lunge toward darkness, every self-seeking gesture that stands in its way. It is just as disdainful as it is demanding. This is visible in the concept of the *judgment*, in the present judgment of God that is already with us just as much as in the related concept of the Last Judgment, in which one's true value is shown for what it is. All these concepts signify the dominance of the biblical concept of the essence, and it is only when we know this that we can understand God as love; for in the Christian sense, love is *holy* love.

The difference between Christianity and other standpoints can be clarified by this concept of a holy, unconditionally demanding will. Other such standpoints are by no means devoid of warmth and passion, but they are based on unity, the cultivated appreciation of beauty, and the dissolution of the self and its needs. The demanding will of God differentiates Christianity from all merely religious inclinations. All higher faiths, to be sure, possess ethical concepts. Even the polytheistic divinities have moral predicates; but since they have control only over certain specific spheres of nature and power, they remain subject to what they control. The gods of polytheism are nature-gods and political gods who take the morals of their corresponding peoples under their protection. Apollo's original character is scarcely even known today; what we know today is only the purity and nobility of a later transfiguration. As long as we have a variety of gods before us, they can absolutely never sustain the ethical idea in its full sense; for morality, just like divinity, remains divided among them. Full divinity is possible only for a single God whose almighty essence expresses itself in holiness.

Nevertheless there is no dearth of potent moral development and expression outside of Christianity. The Stoics taught a thoroughly ethical monotheism, and Confucianism made use of the great, universal moral law of widespread education, which was traced back to the will of Heaven. In both cases there are certain approximations to the Christian God; but the difference in both cases is that the moral law is in the foreground while religion is in the background. This is particularly true of Confucianism in its highly cultivated forms: there the divine will never truly touches the soul. For the Stoics, moral law is cosmic and universal. Natural law takes the form of the moral law in human beings. Just as it is given to the tree to blossom, so the ethical command is given to human beings. For Stoicism, however, morality is the highest form of the natural law, and it is divine only insofar as God is identical with the law of nature. God is to a certain extent subsumed under natural law, even identified with it. Stoicism was the original, unrefined pantheism. God is law, but not a will that grasps the individual soul in a Thou-Thou relationship. The same thing can be detected in similar developments today in our own culture. Here too we hear that the moral law as such is what constitutes divinity. This is supposed to be the only scientifically tenable understanding of God. It is possible to read Kant in this way. The earnest character of such thought demands our closest scrutiny; but what is missing here is the personal, ethical cleavage of the whole human being. The particular character of the Christian concept derives not from a universal moral law, but from personal contact.

Even more dramatic is the contradiction to all pantheistic and monistic, i.e., *quietist* orientations. Where both individual essence and individual will alike are mere illusion, there is no place left for the moral law. For it is precisely in the individual will that the ethical is concentrated and established. To whatever extent we undo the separation between us and the One, to that extent will ethics collapse. For then God is not conceived as the bearer of the moral law, but rather as substance, as the absolutely real, without judgment or decree, timeless, unpredicated—he just *is*. Nothing is left for the human being except to submerge into the substance of the divine All; and ethics, therefore, consists in nothing more than the very limited task of overcoming egoism and illusion. The first moral imperative is to "de-preciate"! Act only so as to undo your action through your action, whether in ecstatic submersion or peaceful serenity![13] There is

13. Perhaps reflecting Bhagavad Gita IV, vv. 18, 20:
   Who sees inaction in action,
      And action in inaction,
   He is enlightened among men;
      He does all action, disciplined.
   Abandoning attachment to the fruits of action,
      Constantly content, independent,
   Even when he sets out upon action,
      He yet does nothing whatsoever.
The Bhagavad Gita, trans. Franklin Edgerton (Cambridge: Harvard University Press, 1972), p. 23.

moral demand here, but one that calls only for knowledge as contemplation, and so the real center of religion is missing. The demand—and it is an enormously difficult demand—is posited, not as coming from God, but rather as the first step along the human path of coming to know God.

This stands in the sharpest contradiction to Christianity, where we find that all essence is radically referred back to God. In Jesus there is not the slightest hint of the sort of mysticism that strives for the slow asphyxiation of the authentic self; instead, we encounter the heavenly Father's clear moral demand, which is nothing other than holiness. There can be no union with God, it must come through the will! There is no unity in substance, only a unity of surrender and action! Of course, it is impossible to choose between these two views on any scientific basis. Here, we can only speak for ourselves: Despite pantheism's great poetic and persuasive power, inner truth is not to be found where God is perceived only as a substance into which one is submerged; the truth lies rather in winning the soul by losing it.[14]

We must now attend to the further consequences of the Christian concept of holiness. When it is God who is making demands, he has the right to demand the entire heart. Hence all commandments are finally not a matter of duty, but are rather a *link to the divine essence*. And it is this inner linking that makes Christian morality such a serious matter: Each demand constitutes a revelation of the divine essence. We perceive God's pull and attraction therein. But this signifies more than the simple observation that ethics flows from God. It also means that ethics leads back to God. The divine spirit is present in every moral demand. And not only that; in every submission to the moral demand, in every fulfillment of its commandments, we take a step toward God. We are not dealing here with some abstract law of reason; it is the voice of the living God. He is not only our source, but also our goal. All moral activity leads to self-healing, to self-consecration for the sake of God. The Christian ethos therefore includes a certain other-worldliness. The meaning and purpose of all activity is to mirror the essential clarity of God in the resoluteness of one's own person. Even the commandment to love one's fellow human being is not realized in a philanthropy of some kind, but in light of the common determination of all souls for God.

The Christian ethos subsumes everything beyond this religious foundation under its relative indifference to all ordinary good and bad fortune, and its complete indifference to all cultural goals such as

14. Luke 17:33.

the state, possessions, and the like. About these the Christian ethos has nothing to say. Jesus' proclamation is directed only toward God and is, as a consequence, complete in its radicalism; alongside this, everything else fades away. We must recall that, for Jesus, God's devouring presence was completely bound up with the imminent end of the world, so that all that was needful was to endure until the Kingdom would come. An awareness of Jesus' unbounded radicalism must inform any unbiased reading of the gospels. But the thousand-fold artifices of the theologians have finally managed to transform the command "If any one takes your coat, give him your cloak as well"[15] into a solicitation for charitable contributions! In the same vein, warfare is utterly out of the question as far as the New Testament is concerned; patriotism cannot make any appeal to Christianity at this point. Luther knew this well when he said that anyone who finds that the war is unjust should willingly accept the penalty for refusing to serve.[16] The Christian ethos is indifferent to everything that concerns gain, profit, and success in the world. "Take no thought for the morrow" and "Seek first after the Kingdom of God, and all things needful shall be given unto you."[17]

Therefore, the concept of holiness also entails a highly significant counterpoint, which refers all activity to the final, highest goal. This implies sharp opposition to the world, an opposition that culminates in Jesus; and it further implies that this radical opposition involves something that cannot be completely subsumed under the content of the moral law, or which can be subsumed only so long as we await the imminent appearance of the Kingdom of God. Not only do Jesus' demands exceed human ability, they also exceed the human situation. Taken consistently, they rule out the possibility of the continued existence of the world. It is only in the extremely narrow confines of the *sects* that Jesus' radical demands can be understood as the goal of the world—and the sects, for their part, have failed to appreciate the gospel's universalism. There have been frequent attempts to neutralize these demands by reference to the concept of the forgiveness of sins. But this is achieved only at the cost of sacrificing the indispensable concept of the divine holiness.[18] Hence we are left with the task of mediating—insofar as possible—between the demands of Jesus and those of the present, dedicating the world's goals to God. But to

15. See Matt. 5:39.
16. See Martin Luther, "Whether Soldiers, Too, Can Be Saved," in *Luther's Works*, vol. 46 (Philadelphia: Fortress Press, 1967), pp. 130–31.
17. See Matt. 6:34, 33.
18. See above, p. 154 n. 1.

mediate is not to reconcile. Jesus is still the salt of the earth![19] The concept of divine holiness always implies a tendency toward other-worldliness, and a continuing tension with the world that can be ignored only at the cost of superficiality. It is limited only by the need to carry the radical Christian demand into the world. This is where the great tasks of applied ethics lie. But there are also profound, difficult problems in the concept itself, problems that do not admit of conceptual resolution. To them we now turn.

The idea that God is the primal image of all goodness already poses certain difficulties. We can see this as soon as we ask wherein God's goodness consists. We know the good only in terms of obedience to the moral law that grasps us and overcomes us. All human virtue presupposes working on, and overcoming, one's own self. Now we could never say that God obeys the moral law in the way that we do. Our virtues and moral imperatives cannot be transferred to him. To be sure, we speak of his goodness, truth, and righteousness; but there are other concepts that pertain to our virtue, such as bravery and moderation, that would be absurd if applied to God. This means: if the fine distinctions customarily applied to the various virtues are applied to God, they cannot refer to any ethical activity or achievement. With God it can only be a matter of expressing his essence, an inner self-consistency that has nothing to do with what we perceive as moral.

The scholastics asked whether the good is good because it is willed by God, or whether God is good because he wills the good. But this is sophistry: to posit a criterion against which God is to be measured is a manifestation of superficiality in religious thinking. We must, however, acknowledge a difficulty with respect to the depth of God. To think of God as good means that we must also construe the moral law as an expression of his essence. But we do not know how the goodness of God is related to itself. Nothing can be said about how God makes his essence known in the moral law. The law tells us nothing about the goodness of God apart from its relation to us.

At this point we also frequently encounter the objection that this constitutes anthropomorphism. To this we reply, If we transfer the predicates of human morality to God, it is only because we perceive inner moral necessity as being in the closest possible connection to the concept of God; for in Christianity we understand God first of all on this basis [inner moral necessity], not as a unified substance. The only analogy which remains open to us is this: Just as the inmost

19. See Matt. 5:13.

essence of finite morality is to elevate the human self to the rank of a self-created (and not merely inbred) personality, so too the goodness of God signifies God's own self-positing [*Sich-selbst-Setzen*]. The human person is analogous to God—or, as some say, God is analogous to the human person—in this: becoming a *new* essence through freedom. But for us, human personality is the image of God and not the other way around.

A *second* difficulty touches on the moral law itself. The demands of Christianity are not externally revealed by means of written words on two tablets of stone, as they are for the Jews. Christianity makes only a pedagogical use of the decalogue. Even the words of the Lord contain no law. The demands of Christianity are, as Paul says, purely spiritual,[20] sensed only by the conscience, and altogether inward. It is the autonomy of Kant's moral reason, which gives its orders in correspondence to the situation. But how then can the conscience be the divine law? How can it be understood to demonstrate the divine holiness? Only by presupposing the supra-sensual presence of God in the human person. In that case the moral law would become something purely pneumatic. It is always a matter of personal human decision, proceeding, not from some sort of self-contained reason, but rather from the mysterious bond of the human and the divine spirit. Then it would only occasionally be necessary to distinguish the voices in accordance with the saying, "You think as men think, not as God thinks."[21] This is the Christian concept of the soul, a concept not everyone can grasp. But whenever we make any reference to the Christian moral law, we are also saying that human moral law is simultaneously divine in origin; and furthermore, we are also expressing the metaphysical statement that God is present in us. In Christianity, *autonomy* is *theonomy*.

But this still does not answer the question: In what does this auto-theonomy [*Autotheonomie*] consist? What content are we to give to this moral law that we freely shape on the basis of our own interiority? Or should we simply renounce any content at all? Is it just an act of freedom and nothing more? Herrmann holds that the conscience is constantly required to formulate the moral law anew. And still the sense remains that everything is not unconditionally free, that we still must reckon with altogether specific requirements that are, despite their specificity, difficult to define: requirements for stringent self-

---

20. A reference to Gal. 5:18 ("But if you are led by the Spirit you are not under the law")? See vv. 16–23.
21. Matt. 16:23.

surrender before God, separation from the entanglements of the world, and, most emphatically, love of the brother. So there *is* a content to be discovered. By no means do we hold that there are no restraints whatsoever. Jesus' demands are to be taken as revelation. Purity of heart that achieves what is needful, love which is not mere helpfulness but rather a genuine bond in and through God—these are absolute requirements. They define both the starting point and the ending point. But both the goal and the beginning lie in God. He himself constitutes the freedom of the conscience. Now we can put it correctly: the Christian moral law is always formulated anew, but it always has a specific goal on its horizon as well. The basis of it all is the metaphysical premise of the interpenetration of the divine and the human, and the corresponding premise of a free law with a given goal and direction. Ethics embraces the individual.

Now we turn to a *third* difficulty. The concept of God as the one who is holy and who grasps us in our morality defines the characteristic freedom of Christian action. We have already dealt with the freedom of God. Now we come to the question of finite freedom, that is, *human* freedom. We understand freedom to include the capacity for evil, that is, for self-denial of the good. Divine powers never work like natural processes, but rather in contrast to them. In God we are elevated to a higher life; but we have the capacity to refuse it. Therefore: Not some monstrous process of spiritualization that bears souls higher and higher all by itself, but rather a demanding will and a real foundation for a new will! For even to reject the demand requires a new stance of us no less than does surrender to it. The persistent tug of the will of God always leads to something new. It produces something higher, or something lower, than what was there before. Along with the moral law comes the impulse to a truly new creation. This is where freedom happens, this is where there is a parting of the ways; the entire Christian life-world hinges on this point. That is why there are so many objections to it, and not only deterministic objections (which are almost synonymous with modernity), but religious objections as well. If finite creatures possess freedom, it means that humankind possesses a relative independence within the context of the divine life, a freedom that is by no means fully circumscribed by God. We are therefore dealing with something that comes to us first as a demand, but which also entails a moment of human freedom and thereby signifies a corresponding limitation on God.

Let us take up this latter point and make ourselves clear: we are talking about a limitation on God! And is that not, from a religious point of view, intolerable? And do not its dialectical contradictions unravel the concept of God? We have described God as absolute will; how then can we assert that finite creatures have freedom? Do we not thereby make them into little gods? Doesn't this make us, and not God, the masters of our own fate? Isn't all of this more moralistic than it is religious? Schleiermacher responded that all these objections must be incorrect. If the proclamation intensifies, and if the moral law flourishes within us, they will enhance the divine majesty only if sanctification is an actual *deed* and not merely identical with the universal world-process. It is not that the creature must be creative in the same sense as God, but rather that the divine life takes initiative in the creature.

Every thought that surfaces in us comes from God; and if he does not compel us the way that the powers of nature do, then both agreement and disagreement must remain real possibilities for us. Surrender is meaningful only when it is voluntary! The divine initiative is not the same thing as the act; it is a demand that can achieve its goal only when a finite will takes on the risk—as its *own* risk—of surrendering to the demand. The problem can really be put only in this way: How is it possible that the almighty will of creation can produce these relatively independent spirits? And this is the fundamental enigma, one which goes all the way back to the elementary difference between finite and infinite spirit. If we deny this elementary reality, the entire concept of holiness falls away. The seriousness and greatness of theism depend on the affirmation of God as the one who separates the finite creature from himself and thereby makes it possible for the creature to grasp its freedom. The decisive difference is the difference between the finite creature and God.

Another question is, How is this freedom of the finite spirit related to the demands of *science?* Here we must, above all, emphasize that freedom cannot be scientifically demonstrated; science deals only in necessity. If the concept of freedom implies that some new reality can arise without a logical ground, then it affirms something that is scientifically inexplicable. The only remaining question is whether something that is logically unprovable can be conceived to exist. But all being, in its inmost essence, is inexplicable; and part of this inexplicability is that the finite spirit can attain to a higher life. Ethical power offers no explanation, but it does lead to the question: Whence comes this ethical power? Is it already present, or is it an irrational act of the will? To this we say, It is an utterly unjustifiable and illusory presupposition to think that everything unprovable is also nonexistent. All individuality is inexplicable! Scientific objections to freedom are therefore out of the question. There are things that cannot be overcome by scholarship because they are not objects of scholarship. As a matter of practice, this is now more widely acknowledged than ever. Contemporary psychiatrists [*Nervenärtzte*] enthusiastically seek to discount determinism and to make people believe once again that they have a will of their own.—

This brings us to the *last* point in this train of thought. The human self is not merely a spiritual essence that obeys the command of sanctification. It remains a *natural* being as well. If we were to say that the divine essence's goal for the world is a holiness that renders everything else irrelevant, we would find ourselves left with an attitude of complete indifference to nature. But that would mean that spiritual consummation and chaos could coexist simultaneously in the realm of nature, that the moral spirit could be saved in the midst of the greatest brutality and misery. But such a view runs directly contrary to our instincts. The human will to live seeks to satisfy its needs in all realms of existence. There can be no spiritual consummation apart from the corresponding natural prerequisites.

The first of these prerequisites is life itself: even the philosophers cannot evade this point. The human self must first *be*, and that includes eating, drinking, and a great deal more besides. Nor will a mere minimum suffice. No one who must struggle simply to maintain mere physical existence will have any strength left over for the tasks of personality. Material circumstances are necessary to foster and to support spiritual health. This is grounded in the warp and woof of being. The divine world is not merely spiritual. A large measure of its majesty and beauty is rooted in sensual bodiliness. And even if we could really deny all that is natural about our person, nevertheless we would still face the question, relative to the world, What is the link between the two? Biblical conviction answers thus: Religious faith signifies not only the attainment of ethical goals, but also blessedness and satisfaction in the whole of life. It is precisely in its religious life that the soul says Yes to life, seeing itself fulfilled and drawn to a goal. Images of such blessedness permeate the entire Bible: the fallen house of David shall be restored,[22] the Messiah shall bring about the fulfillment of all desires. Or the images of blessedness are referred from this-worldly images to an other-worldly realm, whether in a heaven that comes down to this earth or in eternity itself.

22. Amos 9:11.

Thus does the Bible, with naive fantasies, portray the fulfillment of all existence. The good person calmly awaits the good that will come to him. Yahweh will exalt the lowly and make him righteous! The Beatitudes of the New Testament are only the logical extension of this faith. Blessed are those who weep now, for they shall be comforted, they shall be satisfied, not only with righteousness, but satisfied on all counts![23] Everything you lose shall be restored seventyfold. The same is to be found everywhere in the Bible. It is only at a few extreme points that we find words like these: "Though body and soul both languish, you are still the comfort of my heart and my portion forever."[24] That is an emotional climax. Upon careful reflection on the constitution of the human nature, however, such resignation cannot prevail. Humanity strives for success, or to put it in a more exalted and purified way, humanity strives for blessedness.

The great problem here is the question of how God binds that which is natural to the highest goals of the spirit, or the question of the relationship between the *spiritual world* and the *laws of nature*. And this is an enormously perplexing question. We are unable to say, This is of no concern to us, for we are interested only in holiness. God himself is not based solely on holiness, but also embraces nature within himself, in unity with his holiness. It is a matter of interpenetration in the divine life no less than in human life; the only question is how. The problem is not purely conceptual. Its greatest difficulty consists in that it is an experiential problem, not in the sense that both sides of the problem merely *could* relate to one another, but that they really do.

For its part, the Bible speaks in terms of reward and punishment against a background of a correspondence between the moral law and nature. But even the Bible realizes what difficulties such a concept of reward and punishment poses, and compensates for it by transferring it to the other world. Here and now is the time for suffering, but there everything will be different. The final reconciliation will consist not in the glory of the naked spirit, but in the complete fulfillment of all being. The Bible is far removed from any cold spiritualism that would refuse to countenance success and happiness or blessedness.

For us it is a question of reformulating the concept. We too say, If God is Lord of all things, there must be a harmony between moral values and the natural course of the world. The Bible's concept of

23. Luke 6:21.
24. See Ps. 73:26.

reward and punishment is very popular and simple, but it elicits grave objections. Experience teaches us a thousand times that moral achievement affords no protection against suffering; on the contrary, victory often goes to the stronger. Such great contradictions in experience lead humankind to call upon the divine righteousness; and if the divine righteousness fails to manifest itself, everything is all too often thrown overboard. And not only are we confronted by this practical difficulty, but by a religious one as well. The concept of reward and punishment requires that we must think of God as constantly preoccupied with every little human weal and woe, handing out praise and blame like a schoolmaster. But it is a debased understanding of morality that takes it to be nothing more than reward and punishment. Truly moral activity is done for the sake of the majesty of morality itself! Difficulties arise from the natural side once again as well. It is impossible to imagine that the law of nature is continually broken for the sake of punishing sinful cities with tidal waves and other outbreaks of nature, when nature itself is incapable of making any distinction and sweeps away the innocent along with the guilty. And it is equally impossible to think that the continuity of nature is being broken in the positive sense in order to bless good people with rich harvests and the like. The opposition that comes from the side of nature is modern. But we can also no longer accept the concepts of reward and punishment for the religious reasons already cited. Indeed, we must ask, Is there any connection whatsoever between the moral good and good fortune?

And now for the answer. Yes, we may unquestionably speak of the benefits of the good. Benefits spring from every good person, not only for himself, but for others as well. Thus health is often the purely natural result of a morally temperate life. But in a life that is drawn to God, good is done for the sake of God's moral dignity and not for advantageous results. This frequently becomes apparent to children and grandchildren when their parents cease to enjoy the outwardly prosperous life they once had. "God's millstone grinds slowly, but exceedingly fine." But here we must realize that results are not the same thing as reward and punishment. Every activity takes places in a particular context, and whoever possesses sufficient vision can see results that extend through millennia.

Hence the concept of reward and punishment should be replaced by the concept of a *moral world-order.* It is in this sense that we are justified in appropriating the verse "Righteousness exalts a nation."[25]

25. Prov. 14:34.

We must only be clear that this excludes any idea of immediate intervention by God; we are dealing with an *inner* sequence of events. No firm relationship can be drawn between the magnitude of one's beneficence and his moral accomplishments, there is no immediate relationship to the individual. What I achieve through self-sacrifice can benefit many thousands of people, as the death of Jesus shows. And so this concept of the self-sustaining results of moral activity can also explain how the good fortune of the godless is inseparable from the misfortune that proceeds from them.

Nevertheless: We may not refer all good and ill fortune back to the moral world-order. Incidents of mass misfortune occur simply because of the causal regularity of nature; they happen to whomever they happen. We can no longer ascertain any connection to moral activity. We are rather confronted by the fact that even though we are everywhere embedded in and connected with nature, nevertheless a great measure of its activities bear no relationship to what we do. It is surely conceivable that, from the viewpoint of some final, highest perspective on the world—a standpoint no human spirit can attain—there is a connection between nature's activities and ours. But such a perspective is denied to us. There will always remain an element of fate over against which we are powerless to do anything, save to meet it with the courage and unshakability of faith.

We need not ask, God, why did you do this? Even Jesus refrained from interpreting great disasters;[26] his religious instincts led him back to the will of God. We also find no reckoning of reward and punishment in Jesus; that is the point of the parable of the workers in the vineyard.[27] Paul subordinates the theory of reward and punishment to the concept of grace. Nevertheless, the idea of reward and punishment continued to exercise a limited but real dominion, and this is one of the points at which we have gone beyond the New Testament. In the New Testament, the theory of reward and punishment was broken for this world, but it continued to be applied to the other world and its ultimate outcome. This world was the domain of the devil, and that is why there could be no clear correspondence between morality and success on earth. But the devil has already been bound, and on the day when the Kingdom comes, everything will be evened out, as portrayed in the parable of the rich man and Lazarus.[28]

26. See Luke 13:2-5.
27. Matt. 20:1-16.
28. Luke 16:19-31.

Here too we find that we are confronted by ideas that we can no longer accept. We cannot imagine that there will be some sudden equalization apart from other developments leading up to it. To our way of thinking, every future destiny must develop in inner continuity with that which precedes and that which follows it. We envision no miracle, but becoming within a context. It is only in this way that we should think about immortality and the process of holiness that leads to it. The final consummation can consist only in the soul's development beyond the external, natural, and fated, until it reaches the point where our higher self emerges from all these and returns to God. The ultimate destiny of evil persons can be conceived in terms of their self-dissolution, the ultimate result of persistent, self-destructive opposition to God.

There still remains the postulate of a great final reconciliation between that part of our experience we interpret as natural and that part we interpret as moral. But we have already laid the foundation for this; for if the soul returns from nature and destiny to God, then both nature and destiny must be reunited in God, the Lord of all things, as well. This is, however, only a postulate. It signifies the final unity of that which is now painfully separated, a unity to which our deepest instincts attest. No matter what stages of purification we must go through on the way, the end can only be that we shall have *all* in God.[29] Nor is there any naked spirituality in God either; indeed, ultimate satisfaction may take the form of immersion in the fullness of life as a whole. All our convictions compel us to admit that we can conceive no form of being that is wholly immaterial; for our convictions themselves subsist in the context of an interpenetration of nature and spirit that is given to us as a contradiction to be overcome. But to overcome a contradiction does not mean to eliminate one of its components!

These are deeply penetrating questions, the answers to which, as for all questions concerning nature, are no longer to be sought in the Bible. This much is certain: What we are today, creates our future; and no power on earth can bring forth a tomorrow out of nothing. The concept of blessedness ultimately signifies not only holiness, but also the blessedness of the entire will to live. Humankind is not solely a moral essence and its goal cannot be attained solely through morality. Our spirit's interpenetration with nature must refer back to an ultimate interpenetration, an interpenetration to be sought in the depths of the divine life.

---

29. Perhaps a reference to 1 Cor. 15:28, "God will be all in all."

And now one more thing: If we assert that there is a correspondence between morality and the moral person, how does that relate to our experience? We must concede that such a correspondence cannot be substantiated in a large number of cases. There are fortunate occurrences that cannot be linked to any moral value; there are people with rich potential for moral achievement that never put it to good use, and, conversely, there are cases where the best people are destroyed by unrelated strokes of fate that impair or destroy their moral-spiritual abilities, such as in the case of a debilitating or fatal disease. There are brutal natural disasters that snatch away thousands of people at a time without distinction. Every daily newspaper confirms that fate is no respecter of moral worth.

What can we say to that? We can only express a personal conviction here: spiritual value and natural value do manifest a positive correlation in the nexus of the world as whole, but not with respect to individuals. There is surely a general teleological connection that rules over everything, but right now there is also a battle that rules over everything, a battle that can be conceived only as a struggle with fate, a struggle that is one of the conditions of the world's becoming. We cannot conceive of any spiritual life free from misfortune and loss as long as it remains enmeshed in this battle. But a battle is a matter of life and death, where courage, daring, and personal risk are more than mere words, and where casualties, both dead and wounded, are to be anticipated. The question is, Does the creature have a categorical right to demand good fortune and the realization of its goals? A full discussion of this question belongs to theodicy, but here we can say this much: No, the creature has no such right! The clay cannot call the potter into question:[30] God is not to be called to account! Whenever a human being is borne upwards on the divine life, there is cause for thanksgiving—not for making demands.

§14. God as Love

DICTATION

1. We have not yet exhausted the topic of the holiness of God; for there is more to the concept of holiness than simply God's relationship to the absolute moral law. In relationship to the law, God appears simply as the source of all moral reason and the basis of the agreement between the natural order and the moral order. However, just

30. See Rom. 9:20.

as the moral law itself is not a mere norm, but is realized in the achievement of a blissful summit of spiritual value, so too Christianity conceives God not merely as the source and archetype of all norms, but also as the love that is present in these norms, communicating itself at the same time that it enables the good. God not only commands the good, but also creates it in us through the presence of his Spirit. To be sure, this good can be created in us only through the experience of being profoundly shaken. The divine holiness must shatter all natural selfishness, illusory self-righteousness, and stubborn evasiveness.

Hence holiness has a twofold task of humiliation and exaltation. Both functions are comprehended within the concept of a *holy love* which enables community only by way of shaking and disruption. In this way, children of God are transformed into trusting, triumphant, and self-confident personalities, who together constitute a united kingdom of love. This is the deepest meaning of Christianity, expressed in the preaching of Jesus in these terms: children of God, Kingdom of God, and fatherly love of God. It simultaneously includes God's readiness to forgive sins without requiring anything more than faith—confident self-surrender. It is of the essence of God's fatherly love that the finite, sin-burdened spirit is shaken, but only so that it may be forgiven, elevated, and purified.

This brings us to the *ultimate secret* of creation and the world's existence: the *loving act* of God whereby his essence is reproduced and multiplied [*vervielfältigt*] in innumerable realms of spirit, and in those very realms reclaims itself. God is thus construed, in terms of a universal theism, as the one who allows the light of his goodness and love to shine upon all spirits in their several contexts and circumstances; and this is most clearly and vigorously revealed in Christianity. Such a faith in God, of course, has no need of a vicarious atonement. What we have instead is a holiness that is formed by, and subordinated to, a creative and instructive love. Any idea that requires a work of atonement to coordinate righteousness with grace, holiness and love, annuls the inner unity of the idea of God. Instead, a thorough clarification of the matter reveals that this holy love—which creates everything, and which enables what it requires, requiring only that the soil be prepared for the creation of what is required—this holy love is what *grace* is. Undeserved grace, which on its own initiative creates and imparts and fulfills its own demands for holiness by shaking and refining the soul—for the Christian concept of God, this is the last word.

2. At this point we encounter the decisive difference between

Christianity and all non-Christian religions. The higher polytheisms generally had various ideas about the gods and their favor, kindness, and friendship, a view which generally accords with the person-like character of God we advocate. But the grace and favor of the poly-theistic gods remained essentially eudaemonistic in character, based on unpredictable whims that resemble the ancient and long-standing indifference of nature. The monotheistic developments that arose out of polytheism bear traces of the idea of the goodness and grace of the All, but they remain bound to an abstract legal conformity. In pantheism, the person-like-ness of God is completely lost, and sensi-tivity to the unity of the All replaces the idea of grace. Only in Christian theism does the idea of grace come to its rightful place: anti-eudaemonistic, and tied to the moral value and health of the soul. Church dogma, however, has given the concept of grace a very uneven and disjointed treatment, relating it primarily to the forgive-ness of sins and the atonement, and then trying to connect it to moral renewal as much as circumstances would permit. But forgiveness of sins and the atonement were, in turn, referred back to the separation of righteousness and love that resulted from the Fall into sin, so that grace could not arrive until the atoning sacrifice of Christ overcame their separation.

3. The idea of God as love and grace lies so utterly *beyond* all scientific knowledge of the world, and is so completely and purely a matter of *religious* certainty, that no new philosophical-metaphysical problems arise here. The problems encountered here concern the prerequisites of the concept of love, as developed in (1) and (2) immediately above. All that we need to say here is that this concept of love is not analogous to human love and, therefore, does not render God finite; for the love of God is neither affective nor sen-sual, but is rather a matter of unity and community in objective values in the spirit. In fact, the real analogy to the religious ideal of love in the Kingdom of God lies in God's supra-human love for all creatures. All images of fatherly and motherly love are just that—images.

On the other hand, this idea of grace and love raises a number of difficulties with regard to practical and actual matters, where it is very hard to see everything in terms of grace and love. The first contradiction arises from the observation that love is a goal achieved only with relative infrequency; this has led to the concept of a love that does not embrace everything, or the doctrine of particular *pre-destination*. The second contradiction arises from comparing the con-cept of love to the suffering and brutality of nature and the power of evil, or the problem of *theodicy* so-called. Dogmatics has dealt with these problems in a variety of ways.

a. The question is whether the divine love of the creature is *universal* or *particular*. Now it is fully clear from ordinary experience that in the midst of earthly life, at any rate, the potential for elevation possessed by various objects of the divine love varies greatly. Inferior and uncultured races, spiritually stunted or diseased individuals, lives that are cut off in earliest childhood, and, finally, diverse endowments for the religious and ethical life—these all demonstrate that all are not equally destined to such a life. The realization of love's goal, therefore, is surely a particular matter. It has been asked whether this diversity can be reconciled with the righteousness of God. But this is not a purely religious question, for the creature has no claim on God and God has no corresponding duty to be righteous; finite entities can make such claims only on one another—not on God. Instead, the essential goal of becoming children of God is to be reckoned only as the highest goal, to which other goals are subordinate. The doctrine of development after death is of no help here; it is impossible to think that a breakthrough could come in the course of repeated reincarnations, for any development that takes place after death must start before death.

A more difficult question concerns the relationship of this particularity to *freedom*. In light of all that has been said, a deterministic understanding of particularism must be ruled out. Particularism signifies only the beginning of the possibility; its realization depends on the individual's will to surrender. So, within the wider circle of those who are called to salvation, we find a narrower circle of those who have grasped it. There is therefore no double predestination to heaven and hell, but there is a predestination that comes via the offer of the possibility of salvation; and, within the latter circle, there is a narrower circle of those who realize salvation in their own surrender to grace. But as for those who do *not* surrender to grace and salvation—a grace which is by no means limited to Christianity, but does find its highest expression there—about them we have absolutely nothing to say.

b. This interpretation of the divine essence as holy love poses a still greater problem, namely, the metaphysical question of how this divine love relates to the immeasurable physical and moral misery of the real world. This is the problem of *theodicy,* a very serious problem for every religion, but a burning issue for Christianity in particular, given its emphasis on the divine essence as love. Church doctrine came to terms with this problem in a most childlike and popular mythical fashion, simply referring all sinful corruption and all natural evil, all suffering and death, back to the Fall; and everything that could not be explained in this way was blamed on the devil and demons. All suffering was explained as the just punishment for original sin. Ancient philosophy of religion—from which the church theologians often borrowed—attributed everything to matter and its darkening of the soul, thereby elevating matter to the status of another principle alongside God. This solution—which was unworkable to begin with—has now become utterly impossible, given our insight into the unlimited expanse and regularity of nature and the biologically conditioned struggle for survival among the various organisms; and this also means that the doctrines of original perfection, the Fall, and original sin have become equally impossible.

If we are to find a different solution for this problem, we need to start with two observations. On the one hand, we have the spiritual world and the redemptive powers that are present in it; on the other hand, we have the universal regularity of the natural order in its self-limiting reciprocal activity, along with the dominance of evil and its consequences. This twofold circumstance must be traced back to the divine essence itself, which embraces within itself the battle between the goals of holy love and the data of nature, between the goals of the spiritual world and the aberrations of the spirit. But the *unity* and *absoluteness* of God can be preserved only if this struggle itself results from the essence of the divine love. The way in which spirits are interwoven in a purely actual world—a world which they must cultivate, and where they must suffer—this, like the possibility and even necessity of sin and error, must flow from the essence of the divine love. Hence creation must also involve *God's own self-submission* to the concomitant *suffering* of nature in its manifold actualities, as well as his own self-submission to the spiritual and moral errors involved in the process of elevating the spiritual world to him. This would mean that, for the Christian life, it would be religiously and ethically necessary that complete surrender to the grace of God involve the obliteration of creaturely obstinacy and egotism. God's activity in the world would then be constituted in the elevation of spirit from the limitations of creation to divine communion, while the spirit's redemption would consist in its return to God. This, in turn, would mean that redemption is also, in the final analysis, *God's own self-redemption,* God's own return to himself. Hence the general foundations of the concept of redemption would have to be completely developed and deployed in the context of the concept of God, since the essence of religion itself consists in redemption, and since the consummate religion must also be consummate spiritual and moral redemption.

   c. The creation and cultivation of personal spirits so that they may partake of the divine life is a concept that ultimately implies that the divine life itself has the capacity to grow: the *self-augmentation of God* by means of constant, newly generated spiritual life. Thus the personalities produced through this process take on the role of God's assistants, cultivated and produced by him to aid in his work of spiritualizing the world and forming personal life; they function as co-workers, who in their work, sacrifice, and responsibility help realize the divine goals. They cooperate with God in his task of spiritualizing and ethicizing the world. But these ideas involve a whole series of *metaphysical difficulties.* If God can grow and augment himself, then it is difficult to speak of him as infinite. If he cooperates with the spirits whom he has cultivated, then he is conditioned by his own creatures; and the entry of souls into the divine life signifies that finite life and becoming have significance for God himself. And finally, there is the question of the *ultimate significance* that these cultivated, spiritual personalities hold *alongside God:* whether these personalities, even though begun in time, can become eternal and timeless in the end.

   The Bible of course gives us no answer to any of these questions implied by the theistic-Christian concept of God as love; but neither does a dialectical discussion of these questions resolve any of these issues. Even the idea of God's growth and self-augmentation by means of a constant re-production of essence can be understood only in relative terms, for all such new developments originate solely in the divine essence and are therefore previously conditioned by it. It is conceptually impossible to resolve this contradiction, which is in fact another manifestation of the contradiction between will and essence. The corresponding question of the ultimate significance of personality is beset with similar difficulties. Here we can give only an approximate answer: Freedom consists in surrender to God, surrender to that which is necessary and binding; and to the extent that this happens, freedom is elevated to the level of necessity, or to the level of its self-abrogation of freedom as decision and choice. This is similar to the idea that insofar as separate existence alongside God is overcome and unity of wills is achieved, the goal of separate existence is to return to the divine spirit. God's self-reproduction and self-enrichment are accomplished only via finite life-processes; and the regathering [*Wiederaufnahme*] of finite spirits into his essence fulfills this process. But this regathering in complete unification of wills may nevertheless not signify that individual particular existence will be altogether dissolved. At these points, however, religious speculation is incapable of conceptually reconciling the truth-claims of *theism* and *pantheism*. All concepts finally break down at the concept of God, although those concepts which help us begin our formulation of the concept of God retain their relative right. Hence we take leave of all speculation and return once again to the starting points of Bible, history, and inner experience.

LECTURE

We have seen that the divine essence reveals itself to us in the idea of holiness; and we have seen that the ruling concept here is not the idea of *is* but the idea of *ought*, which destines us to action and to more than mere submersion into the divine All. But holiness is nevertheless not the last word in the Christian concept of God. There still remains a kernel hidden inside the essence of divine holiness, and now we must uncover it. God is, to be sure, the moral law; but this moral law is permeated by a power that is more than simple demand. Augustine said, "Give me what you command."[1] God is a piercing will, but he is simultaneously an inner warmth, an empowering power through which we realize the moral law. Perfection is no dead formula, but gives life. The point of the moral law is unity of will and life, meaning, in turn, inner success and *blessedness*. Morality is no sterile compliance with demands; it is a shining law that is also a communication. God gives at the same time that he demands—that is the profoundest thing here. The Christian faith believes that finitude is drawn up to the divine life; it holds that the demand is empowering, that law is not letter but spirit. The comprehensive word that suggests itself for this is *love*, divine love, a holy love, a love that awakens the moral law within us, penetrates us, and—when it possesses us—creates goodness within us. Morality is the most visible evidence of this love. Holiness and love belong together. Holiness is not a goal and purpose in itself, but the means whereby the will to love overflows us. At its most profound, holiness radiates the love and root of life that binds the creature to divinity.

Now this is not the customary account of the relationship between law and love. They are often treated as opposites, and the concept of

---

1. See Augustine, *Confessions*, Book Ten, Chapter 29, in Albert C. Outler, trans., *Augustine: Confessions and Echiridion* (Philadelphia: Westminster Press, 1955), p. 225: "Give what thou commandest, and command what thou wilt."

the atoning death of Christ is deduced from them. But any intrinsic contradiction between holiness and love was quite unknown to Jesus. For him, God always desires the holy, and yet is also always the heavenly Father whom we should emulate.[2] For Jesus, true righteousness is a manifestation of love. To be sure, Paul saw grace and law as opposites, but by no means did he mean to imply that grace is independent of the good; for the essence of grace is to awaken and to empower us to do the good. Grace can never be separated from the demands of holiness; grace, indeed, is what makes holiness possible. That, and that alone, is what Paul thought! The truly good never comes from law, but from union with the divine will. So here too there is no chasm dividing goodness from the law, but rather a goodness that comes by grace; not holiness apart from grace, but grace issuing in holiness. The *new self* signifies a life *derived from grace*— that is the *center* of the whole New Testament.

Of course, this is not to deny that holiness must first humble and prepare the human heart for the creative work of goodness; and this is not something that flows from consolidating our powers, but from complete surrender. Our initial experience of holiness does not consist in the sense that love is approaching us, but in a feeling of being *shattered*. This is no contradiction; for we are dealing, not with human love, but with a love that is determined by an eternal content. It is not sentimental love. God is not engaged in choosing a sweetheart, but with elevating humanity to true goodness. Such love cannot suddenly overwhelm us with a downpour of blessedness and favor. First it must startle finite beings; that is why it initially appears as a destructive, torturous law. Our hard shell must first be cracked, and this shattering love is the chisel that cracks it. The image of destructive, torturous law is but the image held by the self-seeking person, an illusion that will persist only so long as we persist in our finite limitations. Eventually we discover that this torturous law is *only* a starting point, only the dark entrance to understanding the divine love. God takes no pleasure in shattering us; but the fruit of this shattering is surrender and belief. Surrender is the goal, even if it is not the initial result. The concept of holy love therefore has a twofold significance: destruction and surrender. Through the latter we attain to creative love, by which, in turn, we come to know this self-giving love.

For Jesus this goal was revealed in *being a child of God* and in the *Kingdom of God,* both of which refer back to God as Father. This

2. See Matt. 5:48.

does not mean trusting in the sort of benevolent divine power that ensures that all will go well for you! What Jesus meant was this: Renew your intention! Free yourselves from yourselves, and enter as children of God into the Kingdom of God! The Father's love will care for the children; and since it is a holy love, it will reach them even in pain and self-hatred—not for the purpose of assuring us that nothing will trouble us for long on earth, but for the purpose of assuring us that we are "beloved of God," that is, destined for his Kingdom. It is not primarily a matter of our fate and life. When it comes to these, even human fatherhood stands on pagan soil. It is not the *word* as such that is decisive, but the *meaning*. And it means this: holy love does not aim at good fortune and prosperity, but rather at inner awakening, communion with God in eternal, highest values— a communion with God and with all souls who find themselves in him. For the idea that we are all brothers and sisters derives its meaning only from Jesus' understanding of the name of the Father.—

This brings us to the concept of the *forgiveness of sins*. The divine power that terrifies us is greater than the human heart. Even the preaching of repentance does not proclaim destructive wrath, but rather the God who searches in love. But this love can awaken life only if it has the ability to shake our self-confidence and transform it into God-confidence. The holiness that brings us down is simultaneously the forgiving love that lifts us up—God's own self-communication. It is extraordinarily important not to isolate this point; we should rather see it in its entirety as essential to the concept of God. We do not have a God who is essentially a holy, condemning judge, a judge who only sometimes, and then only under specific conditions, suspends his holiness and judgment. On the contrary, it is specifically as holy love that God both shatters and elevates. His disposition to the forgiveness of sins must be conceived as part of his essence, something there from the beginning. God made the creature so that it should go through sin and be awakened by him; it is precisely the creature who is humiliated that will detect God's strong and gentle goal, it is precisely the creature who is humiliated that God draws up, indeed, it is only into such a creature that the fullness of God's power can be poured. This can come to pass only when the creature is simultaneously humiliated and awakened in confidence, when God's love becomes part of its essence and animates its inmost will. There is one thought that is in all and through all. The basic concept is that *holy love draws the creature up to itself.*

This contradicts numerous dogmatic viewpoints. According to the old school, God was the essence of righteousness, and only Jesus' substitutionary sacrifice for sin could mitigate God's righteous condemnation of humanity and transform divine punishment into mercy. But Jesus held no such view. The prodigal son, finally yielding in childlike fashion, says only, I will arise and go to my father.[3] Jesus reproves all who disapprove of God's generosity. Paul too acknowledges no such transaction between righteousness and grace. His interpretation of the death of Jesus is particularly difficult, worked out almost in terms of the destruction of flesh-dwelling demons. The doctrine of redemption with which we are familiar, on the other hand, is a product of the Middle Ages. It posited a division within God and thereby dissolved the unity of righteousness and grace in him, only to reunite them through the vicarious sufferings of Jesus. But this is both ethically and religiously untenable: ethically untenable because it requires that one who is innocent shall suffer; and religiously untenable because the meaning of holy love includes the forgiveness of sins.

The love of God requires no special arrangements; it *is* grace. It presupposes nothing more than self-surrender, for its work can be done only when the soul is completely open to it. It is undeserved grace, it cannot cease to be grace. And it is grace that produces both faith and the resultant certainty that arises from a renewed strength for life. *Grace is the last word in the Christian concept of God.* It sheds light on his entire being. And if "grace" is the last word in the concept of God, it is also the ultimate meaning that creation has for us. The living will to love pours itself into creatures in order to bind itself to them. The person-like-ness of God seeks that the creature become person in order to mirror the divine essence. But this can be attained only when the creature permits itself to be drawn upwards. One can achieve personality only through God; for we are only because God is. With this observation we come to the end of this line of reasoning. The mystery of being compels worship, but we do not worship theories; we worship in surrender, in the conviction that we experience this mystery.

The concept of grace also provides us with the consummate distinction between Christianity and other religions; for grace is the key to Christianity's *personalism*. For those who are bound by inner experience to the divine holiness, the kernel of this experience is the person of God. Whoever rejects this belongs to an entirely different *type* of religion, one whose creative powers must remain altogether foreign to us. This is the mother lode of Christianity, the

3. Luke 15:18.

source of our great religious fate; we may not let ourselves be deceived about it.

To be sure, some of these ideas are to be found in ordinary human feelings, and, therefore, in all religions. But in the polytheistic religions, grace is something more like a temperate disposition on the part of the deity. Goodness as such does not permeate the essence of polytheistic divinity, for the gods are supra-human powers of nature that could erupt at any time, with unpredictable and gruesome results. The gods fear human presumption. There are also eudaemonistic gods whose task is to look out for human well-being. Christianity first elaborated the concept of love in its inmost sense, where God seeks communion with the finite spirit. There are also monotheistic religions like Stoicism, for example, in which the concepts of providence and a divine world-order are viewed as the product of a good God. But Stoicism, like Platonism, lacks a love that grasps the soul. They say, May the gods grant it to us to become like them. But what is meant is only submergence into the world-law, not a personality sought by God. It is much the same with pantheistic monotheism. Just as the All-God devours ethics, so too does every thought of love break down before the All-life. Humanity is nothing, deity everything. The one truly human act is to seek the unity behind all human searching. A remnant of love glimmers in this unity of the All. Yet this All is not grace, but an All-substance that swallows up everything. The concepts of love and grace can attain their full meaning only when personal character comes into its own.

During the development of Christianity, grace has been understood in many different ways, and today the differences to be found are great. Catholicism locates divine grace primarily in the establishment of the church and its magical-sacramental works. This is altogether different from our view of grace as seeking out the individual. Protestant orthodoxy views grace in terms of restoration and correction. Grace initially appears after the Fall of Adam in the form of propitiatory sacrifice. But our concept, in opposition to both the Catholic and the orthodox Protestant understandings, signifies a purely spiritual idea, one which requires no historical event to make grace a possibility. The idea has its basis in the modern antianthropomorphic concept of world events, which cannot be strictly proven here. It is the result of a transformation in religious feeling. Earlier times had no problem with thinking of grace as a phenomenon magically bestowed on human beings. We now find ourselves in agreement with our contemporary picture of the whole of things, which demands both unity and continuity in the divine life of the

world. The ultimate ground for this position is an instinctive opposition to any separation within God. The same aversion is already to
be found in Meister Eckhart. On this point we find ourselves in
agreement with the mystics' interpretation of the divine love.

We return again to *theoretical difficulties,* this time focusing on
those posed by the relationship of the concept of divine love to the
world. And here we stumble onto a particularly thorny path. First
come the properly philosophical-conceptual objections. These are
rather trivial; for as soon as one affirms the personalist-ethical concept of God in general, all the conceptual artifices and dialectics that
were once used to reconcile it with the demands of logic are left far
behind. There is also the objection that the concept of love is
anthropomorphic. But grace is more than love: grace is not anthropomorphic. This objection forgets that there is no vestige of affectivity
in the divine love, including any vestige of the sensual elements that
pertain to human love—not only the love between a man and a
woman, but all human love. What is meant here is only the inner
unity of will. The love of which the Christian world speaks is *theo-
morphic* love, the exact opposite of anthropomorphic love: not the
satisfaction of personal needs, but an objective common surrender to
the supra-human. That is why the Christian idea of love is often
assailed as a "utopian love" or "ascetic love" that kills all emotion in
the soul; and this criticism is far better justified than the charge of
anthropomorphism. For it is of an altogether different character than
all human love; it is the unification of the holy and the absolute. The
result is the theomorphizing of humanity.[4]

The real difficulties lie not here, but quite elsewhere. They involve
the contrast between the thoughts that soar to the greatest heights of
faith and the daily course of events—the riddle of the everyday. Daily
events often seem to stand in the bitterest contradiction to the concept of divine grace. This is a truly difficult question; but it is even
more difficult to avoid. Here we can do no more than strain and
search for an answer. Everyone is finally faced with the task of finding a solution for themselves. But it must be done, and we will offer
our verdict, as good or bad as it may be.

If we take it as given that holiness is also love, then we face the
question, To how great an extent is this love realized? Here we must
say, It remains unrealized for anyone who does not want it. But then
the question arises, Is everyone *capable* of wanting this love? Here
there is no end of puzzles immediately evident to anyone who thinks

---

4. Or, "divinization of humanity."

freely and broadly enough about the matter. There are millennia of history! We see the wretched pottery and tools of prehistoric peoples, and we ask ourselves, Weren't these peoples overwhelmingly, indeed, exclusively preoccupied with the struggle for survival? Or is it really so foolish to think that they too had the potential for holy love? Anyone who feels a burning desire for this love can easily overcome the barriers to achieving it for themselves. But what about the prehistoric peoples who were still overwhelmed, if not by their still close kinship to the animals, then by their submission to nature? Or again: How do we answer this same question when it comes to the inferior races of the world today? Nor do we need to wander so far from home: in our own midst we meet people with thousands of various physical and, in particular, spiritual impairments that make it impossible, as far as we can see, for them ever to have ethical and religious capacities. There is no more oppressive experience than a visit to an insane asylum [*Idiothaus*]. For there one finds not merely damaged wills, but hereditary weak-mindedness and inferiority; not that there is no moral impulse to be found, but rather that it is so weak that we cannot speak of its attaining the goal of divine love. But here too we do not need to go so far from home. Stillbirths and early deaths pose the same problem. Those who are trapped in the countless circumstances of want and misery face such severe difficulties that we can scarcely expect them to rise above their considerable limitations. To be sure, there are those whose nature enables them to break through, but the vast majority are incapable of so doing.

There remains the fact that spiritual aptitudes do vary. Bad influences and neglect may always play a part, but the important role of natural aptitude is beyond dispute. There are purely practical natures in which the ethical and religious elements are minimal. And there are other cases, where perhaps a spark of the higher life has been struck, but some unfortunate incident cuts off all hope of further development. Of course we will never be able to prove that the higher life is strictly impossible for anyone, but it nevertheless remains clear that there are very great differences in disposition. But if we concede this, then we must ask, Are all really destined to the higher life? There is a minimum capacity sufficient to make it possible to ask, Can God's goals for spirit and love be achieved?

Another difficult point concerns the human relationship to the animal kingdom. An animal is no machine, but a spirited [*geistiges*] organism. But if animals are not mere automatons, then we must ask, What is the relationship between the spirited power incarnate in animals and our concept of the highest goal? The answer that animals exist for the sake of human nourishment will not suffice. Theologians, of course, are not supposed to ask these sorts of questions, but this does not make them any less necessary.

All these forays ultimately lead to this question: Is the highest goal exclusively *particular?* If it appears that not all human beings are capable of partaking in the highest goal, does that mean that the goal of salvation is not meant for all, and that *no guilt* attaches to this? *Predestination* looms on the horizon. The evidence points to particularity. This has often been expressed in Christian doctrine, most bluntly by Calvin. He never tired of repeating: "God is not obliged to lead everyone to the highest goal! The animal could just as well ask why it is not a man, or the man why he is not an animal."[5] There is enormous truth in this. The one objection that can be raised is that it contradicts the divine righteousness. But that is not a religious objection. What does "righteousness of God" mean? Against what power is God to be measured? Does he have a moral duty to be righteous? God cannot be thought of like the state, which is created for the purpose of giving everyone their due insofar as possible! We cannot in any way free ourselves from the idea that it pleased God to determine the fate of living beings in this way or that. We too have been allotted different talents, energies, sensitivities, and thousands of other things. Why did you not make me smarter? Why did you not give me a higher position? We have no more right to call God to account on these matters than we have to ask, Why did you not call everyone to the highest goal? To be sure, the idea of predestination is monstrously difficult, but a true religious sensitivity will nevertheless struggle with it.

Of course, this concept has no immediate practical application. For wherever the question is posed, a movement of God has already taken place; and whoever perceives no such movement we must commit to God's hands. Otherwise, here too it is a personal decision that everyone must make on their own. But there is practical evidence for the concept of particularity, evidence which is, moreover, deeply religious, for it frees us from the need to question our God. Here, in this *Glaubenslehre,* we take the position that salvation is particular.

5. See John Calvin, *Institutes of the Christian Religion,* ed. John T. McNeill, vol. 2 (Philadelphia: Westminster Press, 1960), p. 933: "Let them answer why they are men rather than oxen or asses. Although it was in God's power to make them dogs, he formed them to his own image. Will they allow brute beasts to argue with God about their condition, as if the distinction were unjust?"

There are still a few more alternatives, particularly the doctrine of *reincarnation* widely disseminated by contemporary theosophy. The idea behind it is this: The world is the spirit's training ground for supra-sensual life. The difference among spirits consists in how quickly they are able to break through to the higher level. In every generation only a few succeed; the rest must submit to new incarnations after their death and return to the same task. The process is repeated until breakthrough is achieved. In this way it is possible that all will attain the highest goal, even though most will take a very long time to do so. This idea, which is quite attractive, comes from universalistic Buddhism. It eliminates the objectionable features of a consistent doctrine of predestination and is not, of itself, impossible. But it would nevertheless require a strong imagination to make it conceivable. We would need to believe that there is a finite number of souls, and that the number of souls on earth will become progressively smaller until all achieve breakthrough.

Another alternative is to believe in a development which continues after the death of the body. But this concept is also of very little help. The idea of a development that occurs beyond this life is natural enough; for even under the best of circumstances we never fully achieve the goal here. But it is difficult to apply this concept to beings who did not begin the process of development at all when they had the chance. That would deprive life on earth of all meaning. And so we are left with the particularity of grace.

This way of thinking apparently leads to determinism, but only apparently. Particularity does not have to be understood deterministically. We are speaking only about the possibility of a breakthrough, but that does not mean that when such a breakthrough occurs it must be achieved in a deterministic fashion. All that we *can* say is that in many cases the possibility does not exist. For those who are called, there remains the decision whether to follow the call or to reject it. And this decision is ratified in a second choice, whether to surrender oneself or turn away. At this point we thoroughly separate ourselves from the doctrine of predestination, which damns guiltless people to hell and exalts others to blessedness apart from any choice on their part. There can be no talk of a hell for those who are excluded. We cannot say what becomes of the life-energies of those who fail to achieve higher development.—

Theodicy is another sensitive problem. In the midst of our struggle with ourselves, we also find that we are threatened by nature in hundreds of ways. Any random accident can erase the most illustrious and moral person. A dumb stone that falls from a roof can kill the most generous person. The most significant spiritual hero can be weakened by any sort of infection. Minute foreign organisms are capable of infecting us for life. Nature's sheer disorder and disruption can only be partially controlled through technology and science. And, for the religiously and philosophically inclined person, we must also add the colossal power of human evil and baseness to the shattering, sinlike forces of nature. The most illustrious things are contaminated by petty and egotistical emotions. A few rabid egotistical fellows could someday manage to unleash a world war [*Weltkrieg*] in which thousands would lose their lives.[6] But the criminal characters are not as vexatious as the little wretched devils who will not let the good come out. That is why the greatest human beings rarely die without succumbing to a deep cynicism. Bismarck and Frederick the Great can serve as examples.

This issues in practical difficulties that are particularly urgent. Many have thought they needed to make themselves look bad in order to preserve God's love, thereby making some sort of sense out of the situation; they attribute sin to themselves in order to exonerate God. This theme is given powerful expression in the Book of Job. What does church teaching have to say about this? It has always been aware of the full severity of the problem and developed its theodicy accordingly. The word "theodicy" smacks of something like "God-justification," as if there could be such a thing! But what it means is simply this: What are we to think in light of all these difficulties? Church teaching answers, The world and nature would have been free from suffering, sin, error, and death if only humankind had followed God's command. This answer involuntarily conjures up memories from our childhood, when we explained these things to ourselves something like this: The human race could not, to begin with, completely forget its earlier deathless state and could only very hesitantly reconcile itself to dying. That explained Methuselah's great age and also the giant prehistoric animals that could almost never be killed. Such things were, to be sure, vestiges of the deathless age that went before.—Church teaching then continues: Suffering and death are the result of freedom, both human and demonic. Punishment for sin extends to animals and plants, for all have sinned along with Adam and thereby share in his infinite guilt. Each receives its due: our portion is suffering and death in the world, which has now become a place of punishment where we must yearn for the future life.

6. This comment was made about one and a half years before the outbreak of World War I.

The ancient world tried to solve the problem in a rather similar fashion. It sought the cause in the contradiction between spirit and matter. Creatures had fallen from the spiritual world into the material world by means of some mysterious, prehistoric fall into sin; and with the appearance of material sensuality came disorder, desire, and suffering. Late antiquity's religious goal was to overcome sensuality through bodily asceticism and logical thinking. This doctrine was acceptable because the modern concept of nature had not yet developed. Antiquity reckoned on the basis of a dualism between the purely spiritual and the purely material. But it is impossible for thinkers schooled in Christianity to adopt this framework, for a remnant of polytheism remains in it. There are two world-principles in such a dualism, resembling two divinities: logos and sensuality. Neither can we adopt the church's solution, which was heavily influenced by the world of antiquity. It is enormously difficult to see how sin could overthrow the divine order.

In response to the church doctrine as well as to ancient teachings, we say: Nature is not something to be tossed about hither and yon as you please, and sensuality does not signify dullness of mind; they constitute an orderly and regular whole. We are threatened by the regularity of nature, not by sin. No matter whether the pressure of steam drives a machine or levels a volcanic peak, it still obeys the same law. The same powers that make life possible also destroy it. Nature is not hostile; it is the presupposition of life. Our bodies would be unthinkable apart from the laws of chemistry.

But these same laws work our destruction in countless ways. Under this presupposition, our spirit's embeddedness in nature appears in an altogether different light. Given our knowledge of the body, it is laughable to say that death is the result of sin; for everything is subject to the cycle of matter, everything is subject to the laws of nature. Birth and death stand in the closest connection. Neither is the struggle for survival the result of sin, for it is simply part of existence. All beings have their survival instincts, and the result is a profusion of unavoidable conflict and competition. A never-ending struggle among the tiniest organisms takes place even within our own bodies; and the same struggle goes on everywhere.

And finally, with respect to error: it is not to be thought of as the result of the Fall, either. For us, truth, like the spiritual life as a whole, is a struggle. Correction realizes itself through error. We distinguish justifiable egoism from unjustifiable: it is only against the excesses of the life-instinct that ethical objections may be raised. It is

part of the law of our being that our sorrow and our joy spring from
the same source. Now it is much easier to say why the old solution is impossible
than it is to find a new one. Leibniz brought his great genius to bear
on the problem; but even what the greatest mind has to say on this
question remains utterly subjective. It only remains for us to
acknowledge the twofold character of our reality. Life derives its
strength from the powers of nature. On the other hand, it remains
certain that we are trapped in a world that is indifferent to the final
goal of the human spirit; for even though the world, on the whole,
proves agreeable to the goal, it continually clashes with it in the
particular.

The conflictual character of being also derives from its character
as *becoming*. We are caught in a battle between the brutality of a
boundless nature and a struggling spiritual life; and here, as in all
battles, there will be injuries and suffering. One cannot deny materialism in the name of supra-idealism, nor supra-idealism in the name
of materialism. But if both are present, then both must be objects of
the divine love; they must both express his will and must both have
been placed in a suffering world by him: a world that does not *merely*
suffer, but will also rise up through suffering. For the spiritual life
becomes deeper and purer under the conditions of struggle. Hence
sorrow is to be traced back to the divine will itself after the manner
of Jakob Böhme.[7]

Further: If all this suffering has been established by God, then it is
also suffering *for God*. We have arrived at the concept of God's own
self-submission to the suffering he wills for the struggling spirit.
Redemption is then God's own *self-redemption*. Unless we want to
ignore the whole problem, we will have to accept other similar conclusions. The concept of divine love can be perfected only if we do
not give ourselves over to the illusion that God does not suffer. It is
essential to the concept of holy love to say that God undergoes suffering himself. This is not a merely intellectual issue; we suffer differently when we feel that suffering itself is no accident, but part of
what makes the world make sense.

More recent dogmatics, including Schleiermacher's, remain silent
on this point. Kant takes the victory of the good principle as his way

---

7. Jakob Böhme (1575–1624) was a German mystical thinker who was particularly
concerned with the relationship between God and nature. His emphasis on regeneration, in opposition to the doctrine of justification by imputation, brought him into
conflict with the authorities.

192 THE CHRISTIAN CONCEPT OF GOD

out of this problem.[8] We could accept Kant's limitation, but even his position demands that we spell out just how we are to conceive of this victory of the good principle, which is a very difficult thing to do. The world gushes harmony only on the optimists, and when something goes wrong for them they comfort themselves with the thought that every picture requires shadows, or else the tragic dimensions of life would be overlooked. Goethe was a master at that. He knew the tragic dimensions of life well, but was not uneasy about them. Pessimism, on the other hand, is overwhelmed by the reality of the tragic; hence the bitter opposition between Schopenhauer's followers and Goethe's. When radicalized, pessimism says, The world is torment, and the only thing that can save us is a cessation of the will to live. Maeterlinck,[9] who is neither a pessimist nor an optimist, seeks a provisional solution to the problem by deepening the harmony of the soul so that the soul can clearly see that it is not only a part of nature, and hence can be blessed in itself. All profound thinkers are occupied with this problem. Our solution is related to that of Jakob Böhme, who, for his part, manifests kinship with Neoplatonism.

One last concept remains to be considered. If we follow the concept of holy love to its conclusion, we are confronted by the idea that God, in calling the creature to himself, actually *grows and multiplies himself* as the result of the *creature's* own activity. This thesis is absolutely unavoidable. Something is added to the life of God, something new. God is actually growing. This conclusion results from theism, which affirms the broadening of the divine life, as opposed to pantheism, which denies it. God raises up helpers for himself from among the finite spirits, which is how the spiritualization and ethicization of the world will be achieved. He reckons us as part of the household of his creation. We hold significance for him, for to omit the individual creature is to deny universality. What enables us to be helpers in this process is the freedom of the creature, which is no superfluous adornment that may or may not be put to use. Instead, if we refuse to use this freedom, we interrupt God's development.

These ideas have great practical and religious value, but they also entail extraordinary theological difficulties. If we speak of God's actually being extended, then we are speaking of a finite entity; for

8. Immanuel Kant, *Religion within the Limits of Reason Alone,* trans. Theodore M. Greene and Hoyt M. Hudson (New York: Harper & Row, 1960), pp. 85–128.
9. Maurice Maeterlinck (1862–1949), author of *Pelléas et Mélisande* (1893), was a Belgian poet, playwright, and essayist. Affiliated with the Symbolist movement at the turn of the century, he was influenced by Meister Eckhart and Jakob Böhme, and took great interest in mysticism and the occult.

only finite things can grow. And moreover, this growth is not a natural process. It comes from the freedom of finite spirits; and no matter how much they are grasped by God, they still remain only relatively creative, given the interpenetration of grace and freedom. But this too would signify a limitation on God from this side. Despite these objections, however, only thoughtlessness could prevent us from reaching these conclusions.

Now there remains the question, Wherein does the goal consist *for God*? The emergence of the higher life in the finite spirit must also be thought of as a form of divine growth. To God Angelus Silesius[10] says, "Apart from me you cannot be." Thus thinks the mystic. God happens where a finite consciousness believes: not in the sense that God is discovered, but in the sense that God grasps himself. The upward struggle of the finite spirit is a moment in the life of God himself. God fully becomes God first through being believed and loved by finite spirits.

Let us consider this. Can we conceive that those whom God cultivates as co-workers will become timeless and eternal? To say yes is to affirm the inner essence of blessedness. But in truth, this idea, that those spirits who have become independent become timeless as well, is terrible; although we cannot exactly say just what it is that makes the idea so revolting. If we accept timelessness, we surrender the idea that God will finally be all in all.

Christian thought at this point reaches conclusions that are anathema to pantheistic thinking, and the result is a radical confrontation between them. But an element of pantheism's relative truth emerges in this confrontation. We must grant a certain right to pantheistic feeling at this point. Nevertheless, it is also at this point that pantheism encounters massive dialectical difficulties, particularly the questions of how particular existence could even come to be in the first place, and why effort is required when everything is mere appearance. The conclusions of both sides are so stark that we recognize once more the need to work out a synthesis.

As Loisy says, all discussions, all concern about the inspiration of the Bible and similar matters are insignificant in comparison with the question, Do individual beings have real existence, or is everything only a dead All-life, with no individuality? That is the really great problem! If we lean in one direction, our feelings incline toward

10. Angelus Silesius (Silesian Angel) was the pen name of Johann Scheffler (1624–1677), a widely read and loved German mystical poet who was influenced by Eckhart and Böhme, as well as by the Mennonites he met during student days in the Netherlands. His poetry describes God pouring himself into the soul.

pantheism; if we lean in the other, they incline toward theism. The connecting link between them is hidden from our view in either case. For contemporary praxis we hold to theism; pantheism emerges for us only in the logical consequences of our thinking. And yet for that reason we must affirm their connection. But we cannot figure out what this connection is. Every human concept ultimately runs aground on the concept of God. For it still holds true that:

> No one for all eternity
>   Will ever grasp God's nature,"

which is why we must also remember the conclusion:

> But truly will he bind himself
>   To us forever."[11]

And this "binding" begins where the concept of God raises human beings above the level of animals. We must courageously leave the rest to the great Inconceivable.

11. From "In Harmesnächten" by Conrad Ferdinand Meyer (see above, p. 28 n 1).

2

The Christian Concept of the World

§15. The Place of the Concept of the World in the System

DICTATION

Naturally, it was impossible to discuss the concept of God without making constant reference to God's relationship to the world; but there the emphasis was on the world as it proceeds from God. However, religious language also includes concepts that move in the opposite direction, from the world to God, expressing faith in terms of a perspective on the world. These concepts are those of *creation, world-governance* or providence, and *miracle*.

Here too, as with the concept of God, we must emphasize that the concept of the world is not a scientific theory, but a *religious idea*. Science utilizes the concept of a unified world only as a presupposition of knowledge; otherwise, science is content to allow the antinomies associated with the concept to remain. The concept of the world can emerge as a self-contained and real unity only in connection with the concept of an ordering world-reason, or a creative divine will. It is utter nonsense to hold a concept of the world and a unified world-order apart from the correlated concept of a unified divine will.

But this still leaves the question of how we should conceive the *relationship between God and the world*. This question was already decided in general terms in chapter one.[1] Now we need to apply our

---

1. "The Christian Concept of God," pp. 111–94 above.

observations on the concept of God to the concept of the world considered in itself; that is, to describe our *religious sense of the world* and our attitude toward the world. Here in particular it is important to emphasize that no religious attitude can solve any scientific problem; cosmology and natural science therefore fall entirely outside the purview of religion. Revelation offers us neither a sacred cosmology nor a sacred physics, but religious strength and a religious approach to the world as a whole, independent of any scientific approach to the world. Scientific theories come into play only insofar as they may have a tendency to confound certain religious positions.

Faith's certainty in its own inherent right to exist—a right which nature as a whole also enjoys—will protect it from the invidious consequences of science. The concept of nature, therefore, must, at a minimum, be construed in such a way as to leave room for a religious interpretation of nature. Apart from this, religion will find it necessary to adapt to the portrait of nature that experience and scientific knowledge provide. The modern concept of nature—which is altogether different from the ancient, biblical, and medieval concepts—will naturally have an impact on theology.

The religious view of the world was customarily discussed under three major concepts: the concept of *creation,* which signifies that the world is grounded in the will of God; the concept of *providence,* which signifies the guidance of the world toward the divine goal; and the concept of *miracle,* which signifies the creative liveliness of God in every moment. We will elaborate upon all three concepts.

LECTURE

The concept of the *world* is not scientifically precise; it can neither be seen nor proven. What the world is, is a matter for thought, and only in connection with the concept of God; for the unity implied by the concept of the world must derive from a spiritual principle. It is impossible to dispense with the concept of God and still retain the concept of the world. The concept of the world is thoroughly religious, a concept of faith that is correlated with the concept of God. The only question is how their relationship is to be conceived.

We begin with an intrinsic distinction between God and the world, but construed in such a way that the world proceeds from the divine essence. The Christian approach to the concept of the world has, in principle, nothing to do with natural science. It is not our purpose to seek agreement in all things, but rather to express a religious stance toward the world. According to this stance, and despite the world's appearance of unlimited profusion and multiplicity, we see a living unity that arouses the feeling that the world is an expression of creation. The Christian concept of the world is therefore a stance, not an explanation. There is no such thing as a Christian cosmology or physics; there can no more be a Christian theory of the stars than there can be a Buddhist one. (There once was a sacred botany, concerned with such matters as the Tree of Knowledge.)

By and large, then, we concede that a religious doctrine of the world will not provide us with answers to scientific questions. We renounce all attempts to arrange a shotgun wedding between Moses and Darwin by counting each of the biblical days of creation as millions of years! Except that not everybody subscribes to this renunciation just yet. Again and again the attempt is still made to reclaim the biblical concept of creation as an account of the world's beginnings. But that is not what it intends to be! It is a poetic, intuitive description of how the divine will is executed. Orthodox dogmatics sided with Aristotle at this point, interpreting the world not in mathematical-mechanical terms, but rather in terms of an underlying idea. Yet today we find ourselves in an entirely different situation. A Christian point of view yields no scientific conclusions; we take only a religious stance toward the world, viewing it as a whole that is willed by God. We therefore remain independent of all cosmologies.

This independence, however, should not be overstated, as though we need have no concern with natural science. On the contrary, all our statements must be formulated so as to avoid conflicts with science. But independence from scientific research also implies that we are no longer restricted to some religious preserve. We cannot simply shut our eyes to science; rather, we must present our religious conceptions in such a way that they are adapted to the modern scientific picture of reality. The modern scientific picture of the world is absolutely and unquestionably authoritative in its broad outlines; hence, as a practical matter, conflicts are bound to arise. The difference between religion and scientific research holds true only in general terms; several particular issues remain to be resolved. Two matters of particular concern to us here are: (1) the difference in principle between religion and science and (2) the question whether contemporary scientific research and our attitude toward it are compatible with the belief that the whole of reality is guided by God.

This material in this section breaks down into the following subdivisions: (1) The concept of creation, which expresses in general terms that the world is grounded in God, that it is from him and in him, not from itself and for itself. (2) The concept of world-governance, which views the events of the world as generally in the service of divine goals, goals which are, in turn, viewed as the highest and final goals. The concept of creation deals with the ground of the world, while the concept of providence deals with its goal. (3) The concept of miracle, which deals with the creative life of God; it signifies that we are not dealing with a lifeless sequence of events, but with a God whose creativity breaks forth in every moment.

§16. The Concept of Creation

DICTATION

1. The concept of creation is central both to prophetism and Jesus. It establishes the claim that the power of the holy God extends to all of life; and it also provides the basis of a sense of the world's relationship to the divine omnipotence, holiness, and separation [*Weltunterschiedenheit*]. It is clear that the preaching of Jesus presupposed God's internal relatedness to his creation in the same way that prophetism did. His preaching thereby agreed with the conception of the world found in the Indo-Germanic religions, which had emphasized the kinship between the divine and the natural as well as the way in which the world's order mirrored the divine harmony. This is the source of Christianity's *twofold* principle of *transcendence and immanence* in its world-concept. Over the course of Christianity's development, sometimes the former has received greater emphasis, and sometimes the latter. This is how, during the Middle Ages, the Christian-biblical conception of the world came to merge with that of ancient philosophy.

But the problem of binding transcendence and immanence has entered upon a new stage with the coming of the *modern concept of nature,* with its implication of the immeasurability of the world in time and space, the natural causal necessity of all events in the world, and the unbroken, all-embracing context of the world. Every discussion of the concept of creation must take note of this concept of nature. We can, therefore, say nothing here concerning the origin of the world and of time, nor how the world was made and is preserved. We must utterly surrender the anthropomorphic-poetic and mythical character of the biblical account of creation.

2. Given these presuppositions, the concept of creation is that aspect of the world-concept that expresses the *grounding of the world's existence as a whole in God*. This signifies the strongest possible *differentiation* of the world *from* God, as something grounded

in God's will; but it also signifies, on the other hand, the strongest possible *relationship* of the world *to* God, so that it can in every moment subsist only in him, and proceed only from his essence. Creation is the *eternal* manifestation of the world as based in God's will, not the formation of a completed world in time. Creation is not an action in time, but the basis of space and time. Nor is it the merely accidental work of divine arbitrariness, but rather an expression of the essence of the divine will, a will that eternally defines itself as a will to produce the world. Both sides—differentiation and relation—are expressed in the concept of the eternal and timeless creation of reality as a whole.

This concept has nothing to do with *natural science,* for it is concerned with the totality of the all-encompassing context of the world, about which natural science has nothing to say—and never can have anything to say. Nor does this concept provide a scientific explanation of the world's beginnings, which would be impossible anyway. The various scientific attempts to explain the origin of the solar system have nothing to do with the question of the origin of the world; they concern only the beginning of our particular cosmological system, which took place in the context of an already existing world [universe]. Hence they have no bearing on a religious concept of the world.

3. But the concept of creation, as a purely religious concept, is central to the Christian faith; and as such, it possesses great *practical* significance. It heightens our consciousness of the world as rooted in a supra-worldly, irrational ground. It implies, in turn, that the world is neither self-sufficient nor self-explanatory, that it steadfastly points beyond itself and its rationally interconnected constituents to the impenetrable mystery of an unfinished, living productivity. This excludes, then, all of the following: deification of the world, equality of God and the world, reducing reality to the sum of its parts and their behavior, and purely immanent optimism *or* pessimism.

On the other side, however, even now the world reveals the divine essence, wisdom, and majesty. For that reason, the world is capable of evoking a *religious sensitivity to nature* that recognizes the world as an organ and expression of a divine will that it nevertheless cannot contain. This sensitivity likewise leads the *artistic spirit,* not to pagan sensuality and nature worship, nor to artistic self-absorption, but to recognize within itself the revelation of an always productive and ongoing divine life—present in artistic creativity, but never exhausted by it.

This practical duality is, to be sure, an expression of the inner

conceptual duality of transcendence and immanence. It is logically
insoluble, one of the *antinomies* of religious thought. But, in this
regard, it must be noted that every conceivable treatment of the
relationship between God and the world will have its own antinomies.

4. Belief in creation is therefore concerned with God's *eternal*
activity of positing the world *as a whole,* not with the world's beginning nor with any individual point in the whole; for every individual
point borders on the whole and stands within the all-encompassing
context of the whole. When, however, despite this, religious language
does apply the terms "creation" and "creative" to individual events
within the world—such as the origin of organic life, the origin of the
human race, and the emergence of new historical phenomena—it
constitutes a particular application of the concept of creation to
individual events in the world and therefore represents a different
issue, one which will be considered in the discussion of miracle.[1]

LECTURE

Alongside the Old Testament prophetic proclamation of the holiness of God stands the proclamation of God as the creator. Everything that *is,* is not from itself and through itself, but from and
through the same holy will that makes itself known to us in moral
commandment. The same idea carries over into the New Testament.
For Jesus, too, the world and everything in it is the work of the
heavenly Father. In his hand are the lilies of the field and the sparrow on the roof and every hair of our heads.[2] All life and reality rest
in him alone. Things are not final in themselves; rather, they bear the
imprint of the secret of the eternal.

Now it is repeatedly and correctly observed that, along with this
stringently monotheistic concept of creation, Jesus also viewed God
as having an extensive and intimate sympathy for the world and the
things in it. Jesus was no theorist; he read God and his divine will
everywhere from the textbook of human life and the existence of
things. He did not give these things conceptual formulation, but
rather sensed the extraordinary nearness of God to his creation.
There is a quiet shift in the direction of a more immanent sensitivity
to God. The Old Testament's severe transcendence is nuanced and
deepened. Transcendence is still presupposed; but God is increasingly felt and perceived in terms of his characteristic communication

1. Below, pp. 214–23.
2. Matt. 6:28-31; 10:29-30.

with the soul. An abrupt monotheism certainly remains the background of Christian belief, but now it is interwoven with more supple elements. Immanence tempers transcendence.

But this also implies a duality. It cannot be denied that Christian piety includes an element of divine transcendence: God is differentiated from the world. But to deny immanence would be to lapse back into Judaism. The entire Christian world oscillates between the two ideas, emphasizing now transcendence and now immanence. A Francis of Assisi, for whom the holiness of the divine command is everything, senses God in the "Hymn to the Sun" as the one whose love is visited upon us in all living things. There is the childlike sensitivity to God one finds even in the smallest children. These things are to be learned from practical expression, not from leather-bound tomes of theology. All mysticism is saturated with the God who bestows himself on everything and on us, the God of whom it is said: "In him we live and move and have our being."[3] This oscillation is expressed everywhere in free verse, next to which dogmatics looks very much like religion in captivity.

Today, as a result of the emergence of the modern concept of nature, this oscillation takes place under an entirely different set of circumstances, with the result that the idea of immanence has undergone a considerable augmentation. At the center of the modern concept of nature lies the complete immeasurability of the world, which means that the idyllic way of thinking that accompanied the old picture of the world has been overthrown. We may consider the laws governing the movements of the stars irrelevant, but we cannot deny that the world has now become immeasurable. Astronomers now reckon distances in terms of the constellation of Orion. Orion is so far away that it takes the light of its stars a thousand years to reach us!

So it has become impossible to think of God as external to the world. He can now only be conceived as flowing over, into, and throughout this incredible world; and the difference between him and the world must be an *inner* difference. All attempts to fix the beginning and end of the world in time are now swept away into immeasurability. This brings us, in turn, to the second point: The modern concept of nature recognizes one homogeneous law of causality that extends throughout the whole world.

Taken religiously, this all-embracing rhythm—which science abstractly clarifies as causality—is a self-revelation of God, the impact

3. Acts 17:28.

of God on things. The world is no chaos, but rather the emanation of the divine will, from which it must be sharply distinguished, even though they are intimately connected to one another. The world is no accident; it radiates from God's will and expresses his essence. The creation of the world is not to be understood as an event in time, but rather as *eternal* creation in the sense that in every moment the world is set forth anew by God. This liberates us from the necessity of inquiring into what was happening before the creation. God is by no means to be thought external to the world, enthroned above the creation; we cannot imagine him timeless before time and outside of space! These categories do not apply to God; they become nonsense if applied to him. They make sense only when applied to the world.

Our task is not to determine how something came to be! *How* God makes something be must be left up to him. Religion can undertake a religious interpretation of reality only from here, from the standpoint of the world. It is self-evident that this interpretation must come from faith. Hence we need not fear any clashes with science. The latter presupposes the world as given, and links its pieces together by means of universal, logical principles. It is concerned with the parts and not with the whole. The *whole* is a concept of faith, and faith alone can interpret it.

Sometimes it appears as though science here and there does concern itself with the world as a whole. One thinks, for example, of the attempts to explain the origin of the world, such as the various theories about the origin of our solar system. They presuppose the clouds and gases that later condensed into the stars or the various planetary bodies that spun off from the stars—and in doing so, these theories presuppose the world as well. They concern the beginnings only of a tiny part of the whole and not the whole itself! All they can possibly explain is the planetary system to which we belong.

Hence such theories need not alarm us. They have nothing to do with the world as a concept of the intrinsic *whole*. Science too must be shaken by its confrontation with this monstrous vastness. And this vastness is terrifying for us as well; but what is truly critical for us is the impact it makes on our feelings. The more immeasurable the world's extent in space, the more shaken we are by the insignificant size, not only of our own existence, but of all organic life upon our earth as well. It is, therefore, all the more necessary that we conceptualize and believe this: Everything is an expression of God! Nothing falls from his hand, even the remotest thing is grounded in his will. This is the only way in which we will be able to overcome the otherwise crushing impact these images have. For a religious interpretation juxtaposes the immeasurability of the world with the inner vastness of the soul. I, along with what is divine within me, am called to grow upward toward the divine life and thereby to overcome the infinity of space. As the poet says, "But friends, the Infinite does not dwell in space." Whoever denies this faith will find himself uprooted, foundering in the dust of this oppressive meditation.

This has enormous practical significance. Only when we acknowledge, in faith, that this world is to be conceived as posited by God, then and only then will it be possible to keep sight of the deepest ground of reality in the midst of its endless issue. Only then will we always remember that there is something ultimate above and behind that issue. It is impossible to find our rest in the world! An optimism confined to the contours of the world would be unable to satisfy our fullest instinct for life. But this also eliminates pessimism, which would be difficult to avoid if we restricted ourselves to the world. If we but lift our eyes to the hills,[4] then victory over pessimism will be within our grasp; for this world is not the last word. And it is only in this way that victory is possible. Whoever surrenders transcendence and nevertheless continues to speak of a good universe, like D. F. Strauss, forgets that its goodness can come only from an underlying foundation.

These things are all clearly expressed in the Christian sense of nature. God is in nature, to be sure; but nature does not exhaust his presence. This gives birth to a characteristic form of artistic expression. Art is, to be sure, a matter of the senses; but art that corresponds to the Christian worldview is opposed to every pagan form. No matter how great and majestic the latter may be, it still identifies the divine with the sensual. The self-contained beauty of pagan art is so thoroughly saturated with sensuality that no room remains for the divine. That is what strikes us as so strange about antiquity. But Christian art is not exhausted in sensuality. It is directed toward that which is more characteristic and expressive. It touches the soul. It never forgets that there is something behind the sensual, and thus it imparts a new dimension to art. A much greater transcendence, a mysterious tension becomes perceptible. Facial expressions reflect trans-sensual depths, while mere physical beauty is perceived as unintelligible, even unbearable. Compare Carl Neumann's discussion in his exquisite book on Rembrandt.[5] This demonstrates that these

---

4. Ps. 121:1.
5. Carl Neumann (1860–1934), *Rembrandt*, 2 vols., 2d ed. (Berlin: W. Spemann, 1905).

matters have very practical consequences. If life is oriented to the personalistic ideal, then everything will be oriented to the personalistic ideal.

If we pursue this concept of the interpenetration of transcendence and immanence, we will find ourselves on a collision course with some severe logical difficulties. It has always been an antinomian concept. But wherever we have a concept of God, we will also have antinomy: the concept of God can *never* be reduced to a logical formula. This can be clearly seen from the example of Spinoza, who wandered astray when he tried to do so. What counts here is not the logical, but the practical. Nevertheless, despite this conviction, there is one serious difficulty that we cannot avoid. To speak of the whole is to speak of an idea. However, religious language speaks quite freely not only of the whole, but also of the individual. It views the creation of life as a *new* reality. That is very important: It shifts our thinking from divine creativity to divine productivity, something we will consider under the concept of miracle.[6]

§17. The Divine World-Governance

DICTATION

1. Alongside its belief in creation, prophetic-Christian piety also universally holds to belief in a meaningful divine world-governance and providence. Trust in God and leaving all one's cares to God is a leitmotif of Christian piety, one of its greatest strengths, expressed in thousands of different ways at different times. But we must first observe that this trust in God, in the purely biblical sense, is primarily concerned with the objective victory of the good. In the Old Testament, it is trust in the final victory of Israel and the messianic kingdom, which will bring with it the triumph of the righteous. In the New Testament, it is trust in the coming victory of the Kingdom of God, which will mean the end of everything else. Trust in God also implies that suffering is part of an earthly destiny grounded in God's unsearchable will, and which can be overcome only by faith. A powerful drive toward individualization can be detected in the movement from the Old Testament to the New; but the individual's certainty and trust in God remain essentially related to participation in the final goal: the victory of the good, and of the divine love.

6. Below, pp. 214–23.

This attitude of trust in God aims not at any eudaemonistic well-being, but toward the believer's participation in victory of the Kingdom of God; and this is intensified by the *modern concept of nature.* This concept makes it impossible to understand finite destinies as the result of various arbitrary interventions and supervisions. On the contrary, these finite destinies emerge within the all-embracing context of nature and are conditioned by it. Under this presupposition, divine world-governance can refer only to the ordering of the whole context of things in terms of their comprehensive goal; and the salvation of the individual is therefore constituted by participation in the victory of the comprehensive goal. This is where the only tenable contemporary version of the concept begins.

2. Accordingly, belief in providence signifies a *teleological* view of the world, just as belief in creation signifies a view of the world as grounded. The latter religiously interprets the world as a whole in terms of causality, while the former interprets it from the viewpoint of the end. Belief in divine world-governance therefore also refers to the side of the religious concept of the world that religiously interprets and senses the whole world as directed toward an absolute meaning, that is, salvation in communion with God. Hence it is a purely religious belief, belief-fully and confidently evaluating the whole in terms of the divine love that is working itself out in the world. This rules out any *temporal* distinction between creation and world-governance. Creation is not a finished work of art in time, nor is world-governance the mere preservation, moderate improvement, and repristination of creation. Speculative ecclesiastical theology has already given up the distinction between creation and preservation, a simply and naively anthropomorphic distinction. Nor is creation to be subordinated to the divine world-governance that functions as a *world-plan* and *decree,* thereby making creation the mere execution of this plan; this would be the same as interpreting the concept of world-governance in predestinarian or deist terms, which would also be blatantly anthropomorphic. Creation and world-governance can be distinguished only conceptually, not temporally. God is always fully present in the world-process, both as eternal world-governance and as eternal creation.

If belief in divine world-governance is a religious belief, then it can by no means serve to explain the world; therefore, it does not infringe on the *scientific* explanation of the world. This belief has nothing to say about how divine world-governance works, how it draws individuals to its goals, or how it assimilates the relative independence and freedom of the creature. All scholastic speculations about the relation of the *prima causa* to the *secunda causa,* about the *concorsus divinus* or the way in which predestination realizes itself in the form of a sense of freedom, or about deistic precalculations of the course of world events and the convergence of causality and finality—all these are worthless. It is impossible to analyze the work of world-governance, and belief in it will serve neither to explain nor to clarify empirical events.

Furthermore, faith's absolute teleology of the world has nothing to do with the teleological concepts of natural science. Teleological concepts will not be lacking in natural science, particularly in biology. But they constitute only a relative teleology that demonstrates how, under particular circumstances, the formative goal of life organizes the material available to it in certain organisms [*bei bestimmten Wesen*]. The question of the final goal—of salvation and communion with God, of salvation's relationship to the world and the world-process—falls outside the purview of natural science. Science's relative teleology is bound to its particular presuppositions, to the natural goal of animal life; it is subject to limitations and anti-goals [*Zweckwidrigkeiten*]. This relative teleology can surely be regarded as a reflection of the world's goal-orientedness, just as the world's regularity and order can be regarded as a reflection of the divine truth; but it is nevertheless only distantly related to a *religious* teleology of the world in the absolute sense.

Moreover, the natural sciences characteristically function so far as possible *without* introducing teleological concepts, drawing them only as conclusions based on concrete natural reality, explicable on the basis of general laws. The natural sciences do not thereby deny the metaphysical existence and validity of a world-goal, nor of goal-orientedness in general; but their methods of attaining knowledge are not directed toward knowledge of a goal, which is a subject that lies outside their boundaries. The sciences are concerned only with expounding universal and regular causal connections. Where teleological concepts are unavoidable, as in biology, they come under consideration only as the most general and typical sort of impetus toward organization, not as divine goal and intervention.

3. Just as the concept of the goal is much more important, rich, and nuanced for human interest than the concept of cause, so too belief in divine world-governance entails more questions than does belief in creation. Moreover, these questions are of generally greater practical significance: for they pertain to the question whether that which faith acknowledges as the goal of the world—salvation or

ethical communion with God—can be construed as the *exclusive goal* to which everything else remains subordinate. But this is absolutely impossible for subspiritual creatures, and this impossibility, along with our expanding knowledge of the magnitude of the universe, has grown ever more significant. In addition, and for the same reason, it has become increasingly impossible to construe humankind and its salvation as the center of belief in divine world-governance.

Both objections anticipate the realization that: (1) there must be a *multiplicity* of spiritual realms besides the human one; and (2) that the *subspiritual* creature must also have a goal, a goal that includes both the revelation of divine power and the realization of its own life-instinct. This goal must, in turn, be the prior form and presupposition of the spirit's highest goal. We can know that the divine world-governance's goal for the human race is higher and ultimate; and that implicates humankind in a far richer and greater context than it knows, but through which its place in the world and its destiny are surely co-conditioned.

4. The individual person is also confronted by the question of the extent to which each individual is destined to this highest goal, which brings us to the already-mentioned problem of *predestination*. Finally comes the question of the extent to which this goal can be realized within the context of earthly life for the elected human soul, which, in turn, also raises the question of *eschatology*. All these questions require faith in divine world-governance, not merely in order to deal with a series of difficult metaphysical problems, but also to specify more precisely the *religious feeling for nature* and the *artistic sense* which corresponds to it. For this nature-feeling distinguishes goals according to their various levels; and it is also the means whereby the highest goal of the spirit, in its otherness, realizes a wide variety of relationships with the various levels of reality. This feeling also achieves an inner relationship to taciturn nature, alongside the highest spiritual values. In this, Christian artistic sensibility and nature-feeling approximate Neoplatonism and its doctrine of levels; except that the ground, starting point, and goal are not perceived as some undefined infinity, but rather as a living, personal, holy love. That is what made the historical confluence of Christianity and Neoplatonism possible.

5. In all of this, the concept of divine world-governance relates back to the all-encompassing context of the whole. But here too, as with the concept of creation, we encounter the question whether the love of God, which in religious terms is related to the whole, does not also make itself felt and known *in the individual*—not merely

through mediation of the all-encompassing whole, but in individual events as such. Religious concepts like *providence, divine guidance, prayer,* and the *communion of the soul with God* seem to suggest as much. Indeed they do; but this particular issue requires a separate treatment of the relationship of individuality to both the concept of the divine world-governance and the concept of creation.[1]

LECTURE

We turn now to the concept of world-governance or *divine providence.* The term "providence" is not biblical; it comes from Stoicism. It sounds a little anthropomorphic, almost like rational calculation, like making sure that nothing unforeseen happens. Hence the term "world-governance" [*Weltregierung*] is preferable. But the idea itself is eminently biblical. The concept of divine world-governance completes the concept of creation: God brings things to pass on behalf of his goals. This evokes the phenomenon of trust in God—the faith that there is, hidden in the midst of this overwhelming power [*Allgewalt*], an ultimate loving purpose. He who carries the form of the world in his hands, who rules the stars and commands the winds in their course, he also has hold of the person who is ensnared in want and fate and allows him to partake of his blessedness. "Do not worry about anything"[2] is the leitmotif of this faith.

But alongside this it must also be emphasized that the Bible is full of the struggle for survival, often speaking of the triumph of the unrighteous. This message is intermingled with a victorious tone in the prophets, but struggle and care are to be found in them as well. Paul speaks constantly of suffering, yet says that the meaning of this suffering is that "in all these things we are more than conquerors!"[3] Trust in God is no child's play, but a struggle. And more than a struggle: it can never be reduced to a mere matter of personal well-being; it is out of the question for us to say that nothing can go wrong for us. The soul's salvation is at stake, and that is where righteousness finds its triumph. The individual will not always experience the victory of the good; but, deeply moved, will fling himself on the hope and faith that the triumph of the Kingdom of God will be seen by later generations. The Psalms repeatedly lament the fate of the righteous person: His day will come, but for now he must cling to

---

1. Miracle. See pp. 214–23 below.
2. Phil. 4:6, which the King James Version translates "Be careful for nothing."
3. Rom. 8:37.

that which is true and divine. The New Testament, to be sure, says that "Not one sparrow falls to the ground without your Father."[4] That is to say, the sparrow falls indeed, but falls into the hand of God. The point is this: Biblical trust in God is no eudaemonistic means to self-fulfillment. It promises participation in the divine goal; its blessing consists in communion with the will of God. All things strive for this final, highest goal, for a spiritual communion with God. What we aspire to is not good fortune. This is such an infinitely important matter because it is the point at which the Christian religious approach to the world diverges: first in its submission to the external life that can be overcome only heroically, and then in its certainty that "all things work together for good for those who love God,"[5] namely, the good of the soul. Human faith certainly strives to hope that God will bestow external well-being, too, but experience constantly refutes such a desire, directing us back to internal, and not external, well-being.

At this point we must once more clarify our relationship to the *modern concept of nature.* The modern view of nature consists essentially in this insight: that our fate is dependent on the entire context of the far-flung causal nexus of reality. Good health is a gift from our ancestors, not the result of personal intervention by God. Every one of us in this room is a product of those who came before us. Ancient peoples knew nothing of this universal context. They thought that their fate depended on more or less discrete actions. But now we are aware of the general interconnectedness of things, so much so that one can go so far as to say, If I stamp upon the earth, the impact can be felt on Sirius.[6] Even the most minute entity results from innumerable connections, and it cannot be altered without also altering the whole. If, millions of years ago, the earth had veered in a slightly different direction, we would not be sitting here today. God has put me in this place where I stand, but not directly; it is only as the result of, and as part of, the all-encompassing context of reality. Whether this all-encompassing context is open or closed, we cannot think about our destiny except in terms of the interconnectedness of the whole. Nothing stands in isolation.

But this means that we cannot be certain that any given moment will issue in the most fortunate possible result for us. It is incomprehensible that anyone would require themselves or anyone else to

4. See Matt. 10:29.
5. Rom. 8:28.
6. The brightest-appearing star in the sky, 8.6 light-years distant. It is also called the "Dog-star," since it is located in the constellation Canis, the dog.

believe that God will heal a loved one who is ill in order to prove their trust in God. That will be as it will be. Belief does not make destiny. The *whole* is our destiny! A religious attitude has two tendencies, one inclined toward patience while the other strives after the highest goal; and both lie beyond eudaemonism. We must reconcile ourselves to an unshakable resignation! Our task is only to shape our lives within the situation; the situation itself is unconditionally given to us to bear, in both its most difficult and most sublime moments. We must struggle both within and against the situation to reach the objective beyond it, where we leave all this behind, and the highest goal of the world emerges.

If we wish to define belief in divine world-governance in these terms, we arrive at this formula: Like belief in creation, belief in divine world-governance is *a general view of things as being directed, albeit not manifestly, toward the goal of the soul's salvation.* It views things in terms of their ultimate meaning. The question is, Does the world make sense, or is it nothing more than an eternal process of desire- and starvation-through-gratification? We find ourselves occupied in all sorts of activities, the results of which are mostly indifferent, along with some scattered dead spots and a few moments of enthusiasm. On the whole, it is impossible to ask, Why? All desire appears, at its deepest levels, condemned to be nothing more than mere self-deception, for every fulfillment falls short of the wish. That is the opinion—unprovable, to be sure—of many.

But the Christian position is just as unprovable. It is a feeling, an interpretation of things. It views things in this way: The world does make sense, but its sense lies in that which all this suffering and unsatisfactoriness will yield: namely, communion with the Spirit of God. But this can be seen only in the inmost center of the soul, in the light of an essential, personal relation to God. Just like the idea of creation, it is a belief. The ideas of creation and divine world-governance are two sides of one and the same Christian concept of the world, and neither makes sense apart from the other. Each presupposes the other, and can be distinguished conceptually but not intrinsically. Just as the world as a whole is grounded in God in every moment, so too is the world directed toward his divine will to love in each and every moment.

Dogmatics did not make this distinction heretofore. Instead, it said this: First the world was made; and now that it is here, it is ruled. God was conceived as the one who was here before the world and calculated it in advance. Before the world came the ideal of the world, the *decretum absolutum*. The foreseen answer to every foreseen prayer had already been calculated from all eternity, all with the effect of leading to the highest goal. That is what Calvin thought. According to Newton, the world was created according to mathematical principles, and God was the Great Mathematician. Even all the deistic dogmatics included a temporal distinction: The world is the execution of a plan that existed beforehand. This is anthropomorphic thinking, and to us it smacks of the trivial and mechanical. We can no longer continue with temporal concepts and distinctions at this point.

We can no more gain insight into how God makes the world than into how he rules it. Of course our dogmatic textbooks are full of attempts to translate Christian beliefs and to show *how* God really rules the world. Such attempts may be alluring, but they are unthinkable. Our faith inspires and illuminates everything, and explains nothing! The old dogmatics attempted it with the *concursus divinus,* that is, the theory that all finite causality worked according to its own laws while simultaneously concurring with divine causality. But this view ran into inextricable difficulties. In the story of the Fall, for example, this would have meant that the divine causality had to concur with Eve's evil will. Nor does the concept of predestination offer any help here: We either have no predestination,[7] or no individual events.

In the face of this problem, all that can avail is this conviction: God penetrates all and animates all. *How* that can be, faith does not say. This belief does not interfere with the natural sciences. It adds no supplementary, supernatural knowledge, it cannot explain the world, and hence it does not compete with science. Faith looks toward the divine life, believing that the world has an ultimate meaning, hoping that the deepest life-instinct of humankind will be realized. Natural science cannot dispute this, for the question lies beyond its horizon, indeed beyond the horizon of nature itself. Once this is clear, there will be no more attempts to prove the truth of the Christian faith by scientific demonstration—but also no more being misled by natural science, either.

We should also recall that science as a whole is not concerned with looking for goals. Whether such goals exist or not, they are not its concern. The task of science is to explain the processes of nature in terms of universal and regular causes. The concept of a goal has nothing to do with the question of how the various components of a

---

7. This seems to contradict Troeltsch's affirmation of predestination (see below, pp. 213–14, 273, 288, and 304). Here we should probably read "predetermination," which he denies, for "predestination," which he generally accepts.

stone, for example, relate to one another. There may be a goal, but I will surely not discover it by analyzing the components of some gas. Naturally, the scientific method must, for its part, go as far as it can; but the soul should not be confined to the precepts of the scientific method. The error on the scientific side is to think whatever the scientific method cannot find must not be there. Granted, it is important to have a thorough understanding of the chemical laws that govern the human organism, but no more will ever come of this than that which chemistry is capable of conceiving in the first place. But we could never say that a rose, for example, is nothing but an aggregation of diverse materials! A rose can be enjoyed without the slightest knowledge of its components. Otherwise we would have to say that only the chemist understands the rose, not the poet.

Natural science is consummate abstraction. Science abstracts whatever it can from the object, but there is always something left that cannot be abstracted. One surely does not think about one's father or wife in terms of physics. We do not say, You utterly fail to know your father or your wife if you do not know, for example, the names of all their bones. The great illusion is to think that an object is nothing but that which can be grasped through chemistry and mechanics. Chemistry and mechanics are only part of a much richer reality. We should not let ourselves be led astray by their methods, which are really concerned with altogether different things. Life itself shows us what exists; science is no substitute for reality, but rather an abstraction from reality. Reality cannot be reduced to a sum of tiny bits; true reality is that which we *live!*

There is one science, however, from which the concept of a goal cannot be altogether excluded: the study of organic life. Hence biology is greatly beloved of the theologians, for there the concept of a goal appears almost indispensable; indeed, it even seems as though biology could provide us with a precise empirical foundation for the metaphysical-religious idea of a goal. But the biologists, for the most part, remain wary of the theologians, thinking them akin to the devil: give them the little finger, and they will take the whole hand.

Hence we must ask, Just what does the biological concept of a goal signify? Does it really mean that there is a goal that rules over the world? We believe that this is the case. The organic realm can scarcely dispense with the idea of goal, since the procreation of organic life cannot take place apart from the will of the individual. Those who attempt to improve the human race through hygiene do not administer their nursing bottles mechanically; at the very least, they work through the will of the *physicians* who administer them.

There is an organizational drive at work in the arrangement of cells. This is not a trivial item of knowledge. We have before us, as a matter of fact, something in natural science that cannot be reduced to the mere workings of chemistry and the like. The general concept of a goal can surely be seen reflected in that.

But we must also not overestimate the significance of this knowledge. Alongside the biological evidence that supports our thinking, we also find evidence to the contrary. Biology is concerned with entities that are always only *relatively* goal-oriented: that is, beings directed toward only their own goal. But whether it is conceivable that there could have been even better goal-oriented creatures is another question. A camel is quite well adapted to its goal, given that there are camels in the first place. But would it not have been much nicer if there had been no deserts at all, which would have meant that there would be no need for camels? And as for human beings: Couldn't the conditions of our adaptation have been better conceived? An optometrist once said he could have designed a better human eye. Now of course the optometrist cannot even make an eye to begin with, but there is truth to what he says nonetheless.

The most that can be said is this: Under the given circumstances, everything is what it is and accomplishes what it must. The plant that knows how to live on highly marginal soil may be a wonder of adaptation and goal-realization; but does the simple fact that such wretched plants have to eke out a meager existence in this way manifest any goal? After seeing the struggle that extends throughout all of existence, and after contemplating the way in which organisms devour one another, one could well say: there may be some kind of goal here, but could it not be achieved with less suffering? We are often astonished at the truly impressive way in which life maintains and establishes itself under the most disadvantageous of circumstances, but all life still presupposes the struggle. And, finally, might it not have been better for all such beings—even if they are oriented to some kind of goal—if they had never even lived their miserable lives? This question puts us back on religious soil. Biology cannot show that life as a whole makes sense. Biology may well help convince us that there are goals that dominate the movements of organic life, but biology can never demonstrate the ultimate, universal goal of love. The concept of an absolute meaning belongs to faith alone.

There are other problems associated with the concept of divine world-governance, particularly this: Can this belief be so construed that every human being will win a share in the final goal? The doctrine of *predestination* surfaces again, for it can scarcely be contested that there is a separation here; and this separation has been called "election." We must also consider the question of the extent to which the final goal can be attained in the world. The power of the divine goal surely prevails in manifold ways over the distress and disorder of life, but the goal is still a matter of struggle, not fulfillment. It is difficult to affirm the idea of a full attainment of the goal if we seek its realization in that which here lies before our eyes; because everything here depends on the exercise of power, because everything here still lies in need! If, on the other hand, we believe that the realization lies in the beyond, it must still have some connection to the present. In that way, the goal is nevertheless realized in the present, even if only as promise.

Finally, the concept of a goal also compels us to formulate the *Christian feeling for nature* more precisely. A particularly important question here is whether the ultimate, highest world-goal of Christianity also constitutes the goal of the individual. Here we must say that, for Christianity, the goal of nature does not lie in nature itself, but rather in the highest, divine goal which lies behind nature in the first place. This results in a highly characteristic feeling for nature, which need not be the "earthly satisfaction in God" [*irdische Vergnügen in Gott*] of which an old song speaks. This "earthly satisfaction in God," which can probably be had by any grasshopper, is dreadful! Dull unconsciousness has its own charm and beauty that this "satisfaction" could never express. Life, poured into the world, has its own subordinate goals, leading through the stages of revelation, as discussed above. It expresses itself quite *simply* in countless manifestations. A feeling for this unconscious need not be pagan; it is pagan only if one sees the meaning of nature only in its mere existence, instead of seeking for the power which everywhere wells up from it and is not satisfied with it alone.

This means that belief in the divine world-governance is not solely concerned with human salvation. The spiritual-personal realm is only one alongside many others. A world-governance that was concerned with only the human race would not be truly great!

§18. The Inner Life of God, or Miracle

DICTATION

1. The third point that we need to consider under the Christian concept of the world is this: While belief in creation and world-governance relates to the totality of things, religious language and

thought also bear a significant relation to *individual events* within the all-encompassing context of the whole. This is expressed in the affirmation that relatively new creations do emerge within the totality of the given world, as well as in the recognition that new, creative events take place within the peculiarities of personal experience, particularly religious experience. It is also expressed in the individual experience of being led, of providence, and of a personal communion with a responsive divine life. All these things signify a concept that is very important to the Bible, the concept of the *living* God. This concept in all its various forms is what evokes the proclamation of divine creation and world-governance. The Bible and the Middle Ages particularly reckoned *miracle* so-called as part of this proclamation. For ancient sensibility, miracles were neither peculiar nor odd, but were rather the self-evident result of the thought of the age when applied to the life of God. Where Greek philosophy had an impact, the concept of an ordered cosmos limited and focused this belief in miracle; but, given Greek thought's teleological bent, it could still tolerate the belief well.

It was the impact of the modern concept of nature that first made miracle problematic. And not only miracle, but everything else that depicted God as *living*—as opposed to the strongly mechanical connection between cause and effect that governs the universe, and as opposed to the logical connection between antecedent and consequence—became problematic as well. Now miracle in the strict sense can no longer be recovered, for, in Jewish and Christian history, it has been undone, not so much by metaphysics and natural science as by historical criticism. Neither Leibniz nor Spinoza was responsible for the decisive critique of miracle; it was Hume.

But there are other expressions of the living God besides these historical miracles. These expressions belong to the inherent feeling and expression of religion in every age, now just as much as in the past; and they are particularly characteristic of prophetic-Christian theism. To speak of "belief in miracle" would be suitable and materially correct if it simply expressed the antirational character of these certainties. But the established specific meaning of the word "miracle" has rendered the word impracticable and misleading. It might be better to speak of a "belief in immediacy" [*Unmittelbarkeitsglaube*] in order to differentiate it from the beliefs in creation and world-governance, which are always mediated through the all-encompassing context of the whole. Of course, this belief in immediacy is still bound to respect the universal connectedness and continuity of things. It refers to the creative and ruling activity of God in the midst of the whole, an activity which is never reducible to the logical interconnections between events.

2. This enables us to formulate a *conceptual definition* of the belief in immediacy. It is a belief that points to another side of the world-concept. We have already discussed the concept of world as signifying that the world *as a whole* is grounded in creation and divine world-governance. But the world-concept also signifies that *individual* events in the world, along with their mediate grounding, also possess their own characteristic *immediate* grounding in creation and divine world-governance. Just as the world as a whole is purely irrational, so too is the individual. Hence the individual always has a twofold relation: to the whole that mediates it, and to the divine creation and world-governance that are immediately present to it. Just as the whole arouses feelings of the divine greatness, majesty, wisdom, and purpose, so too the immediate presence of God enlivens a religious feeling of inner personal warmth.

This immediate presence is felt, first of all, in the personal experience of an ever new and immediate reality: in the *new creation* of the *inner life,* in the *guidance of personal destiny* [*Schicksalsleitung*], and in the *communion of prayer.* But its impact is also seen extending to the rest of the world; particularly important junctures in the development of the world are perceived as *creative acts,* leading to the conclusion that the fate of humankind is guided by providence. This feeling, then, is nothing more than the particular expression, at particularly prominent points, of the immediacy that is active everywhere, but whose importance is particularly conspicuous at certain junctures. This makes it possible to speak of the creation of life, the creation of humankind, the new creation of the inner life, the influx of divine powers into prominent individuals, revelation, and redemption.

3. Belief in immediacy is likewise a *purely* religious matter, a belief based on religious experience. It is an essential part of prophetic-Christian theism. In the various polytheisms, this belief remained bound to the aimless arbitrariness of the divine powers, while in the pantheistic-mystical religions it was absorbed into the unity of substance that swallows up all finite things. Nevertheless, this belief in immediacy has also developed outside of Christianity, wherever energetic religiosity is present. Traces of it are to be found in Stoicism, Neoplatonism, and later Buddhism. Now, as a purely religious faith, this belief cannot possibly explain or demonstrate its conviction. Its conviction cannot be supplemented with any scientific metaphysics; the How remains completely unknowable.

Insofar as this is the case, this belief can neither infringe upon, nor agree with, natural science. Hence the *contradiction* between *religious certainty* on the one hand, and all purely *logical and rational interpretations* of the world on the other, finds its sharpest expression at this point. Purely rational thinking always links one individuality to another according to the principles of logical necessity; it thus rationalizes reality, either mathematically-logically or causal-mechanically. If this rational tendency is followed without reservation, it leads to a *universal rule of law* and a *monism* that recognizes nothing new, irrational, or immediate. That is the tendency of rational thought, and we must not interfere with it insofar as practicable. But it is not unconditionally practicable to do so. In natural science and historical science alike, this tendency is simply an inference from those instances of reality that are susceptible to such rationalization. But the actual instances themselves always remain far richer than what can be rationalized from them. The fullness of the purely *factual, contingent,* and *irrational* will always endure. Hence the limitations of radical rationalism and monism will also remain.

To be sure, the limitations of radical rationalism do not constitute proof positive that belief in immediacy is justified; but they do, at any rate, put an end to the often-heard demand for an all-embracing rationalism that leaves no room for the immediate. And just as the logical fact of contingency and irrationalism correlates to the religious belief in immediacy, pure rationalism tends to pantheism when it seeks religious support and fulfillment.

LECTURE

Belief in divine world-governance is oriented toward the whole, and it comes into contact with the individual only insofar as the individual is part of the whole. Now we must ask whether we cannot also have an immediate, personal relation to the basic declarations of the Christian faith. We come to questions which touch on matters of prayer and individual destiny.

There has been something missing in the foregoing discussions of creation and world-governance, something that belongs to the discussion not only from a logical point of view, but from a religious one as well. We experience ourselves as something more than mere wheels and bearings that receive and transmit various forces. For the soul that surrenders itself, there is the possibility of an immediate relation to God's ruling goodness; indeed, for the religiously sensitive person this is the heart of belief in world-governance. All pious persons express the sense that their own destiny and personal character development are guided by God, apprehended in prayer as his response and answer. These all pertain to what is personal, not to the all-encompassing whole. The idea of a God who judges the individual, who follows the development of each and intervenes in the destiny of each, runs throughout the entire Bible. So we have come to something of greater *religious* importance than that which has gone before, something for which the struggle with science is even more momentous. We stand before the possibility of the *soul's immediate communion with God:* the possibility which is *the* miracle, *the* inconceivable thing.

First, let us take up the concept of miracle in the narrow and proper sense. Naturally, any inner experience, whether it be that of prayer or of being led, can be described as a miracle to the extent that we are speaking of experiences that proceed from the immediate impact of God upon the individual. But these are not expressly singular or extraordinary things. Wherever the divine life is, there miracle is poured out. And the word is frequently used in this way: Everything is brimming with miracle! Every gifted thought, every flowering of the higher life—all are miracle! Broadly formulated in this way, the idea of miracle is identical to the idea of world-governance. But this is not the concept of miracle in the technical dogmatic sense. When dogmatics uses the term "miracle," it thinks of some utterly particular event that stands in absolute contradiction to what is given. Dogmatics thinks of immediate realities of a much higher order, realities which (it thinks) are particularly well suited to demonstrate the creative, living power of God. We must also further distinguish miracle in this technical sense from the inconceivable that takes place everywhere but does not make things appear paradoxical. Which of these two concepts of miracle addresses our interest in the living God, or do they both?

For countless numbers of people, the idea of an unfettered God who comes forward and shatters the rules is altogether essential to their faith. Catholicism is to this day so imbued with a sense of miracle that it is certain that Luther could not have been sent by God because he performed no miracles. The ancient church acknowledged miracle without reservation, even miracles performed outside its own sphere: Simon Magus and the Roman Caesars performed miracles; Trajan was particularly known for his miracles. Miracles could be performed by the power of demons as well as in the name of God. Throughout the whole of antiquity, miracle was the dearest child of faith. Only in Protestantism was miracle restricted to the Bible, because Luther counted the Bible as the only authority and therefore refused to acknowledge the miracles of saints and popes. Then came the modern era with its scientific knowledge, which consummated the denial of miracle.

Now even from a scientific point of view, it is certainly possible that there are concepts of nature apart from those known to us, and they could play a role in the interpretation of nature. And no one can prove on the basis of the laws of nature that it is impossible for them ever to be broken. It is just an enormous improbability. Likewise, it cannot be proven that the sun will rise again tomorrow. Hence the possibility of miracle cannot be denied on scientific grounds. But the challenges to miracle that come from the study of *history* are far more serious. All ancient chronicles teem with reports of miracles, thanks to the human fascination with the unusual and fantastic. It is also well known that when three or four people tell the same story, each will embellish it to some degree, whether consciously or unconsciously. And wonderful things do happen. A large proportion of the healings at Lourdes are indisputable; the only question is whether they are miracles caused by the living God, or the result of influences on the nervous system. Are phenomena such as stigmata the result of autosuggestion? And we must also ask, With what right are miracles outside Christendom disputed, while Christian miracles are still strongly affirmed? Or, with reference to the Bible, why are some miracles sacrificed to criticism and not others? For critics have laid their hands on several of the biblical miracles, and even when the facts have survived such an investigation, their character as miracle has not.

The upshot of all this is at least that a decisive emphasis on miracle can no longer be maintained. What the facts were, is another question. The healings performed by Jesus, for example, are not to be denied. But the difficulties culminate in the resurrection accounts. We personally take them psychologically, as a vision; and by no means do we particularly aspire to convince everyone to accept fully this most delicate and central point of the belief in miracle. What is required of us in practice, rather, is the greatest restraint. You may confidently call this confusion and halfheartedness, but that is completely beside the point! It is not necessary to disturb people with cheap radicalisms, but rather to be concerned for them.

What is really important is something completely different. Faith attaches to things far more real than miracle. It attaches to that which can be experienced in every instant. It concerns itself with the immediacy of the divine life, made present in prayer and in personal life: The *all-embracing faith in the presence of God* is what belongs in the forefront! Then our souls no longer rely on miracle in the technical sense, and it will cause no rupture in our faith if such miracles slip away. This calls to mind one of Kutter's books, titled *The Immediate*,[1] which pursues the idea of the inconceivable, insisting that all phenomena are more than mere consequences. The mediate is the realm of science, but the "immediate" breaks the context, alters the individual, and returns it to the nexus as something new. The botanist Reinke at the University of Kiel also favors the idea of the immediate. Here we appropriate Kutter's term "belief in immediacy" [*Unmittelbarkeitsglaube*]; for the expression "miracle," which already summons up visions of swimming axes and the like, needs to be replaced.

One of the most difficult struggles for the contemporary religious person is being waged over this point, a struggle which conditions the very tone of our piety. As long as we could follow the religious instinct apart from the impact of science, then it was simply self-evident that we could feel the living power of the divine, not only in the fates of great peoples, but in every individual thing and event. But where the impact of science has been felt, there faith has clung to little more than a religious interpretation of the whole of reality. But that is not what belief in miracle is truly about; the point of this admittedly difficult belief is the anti-intellectual character of the individual life's personal relation to God. Anti-intellectualism is a bad thing when it leads to the neglect of scientific and logical thought as a whole; that cannot be denied. But the anti-intellectualism of which we here speak—belief in the immediate—is necessary nevertheless. The inconceivable surely lives within the nexus of reality. We stand here before one of the most important of all practical matters, one of today's urgent, burning issues. It was not even a problem for the Reformers.

Hence: Belief in immediacy, or belief in miracle in the widest possible sense! This is one side of the Christian concept of the world, but it does not detract from the other. The two sides can be separated only in abstraction, where it is not possible to say and think everything at once. This is the side of the world-concept wherein the individual feels like a part of the all-encompassing whole: not swallowed up by it, nor a simply a product of it, nor determined by

1. Hermann Kutter (1863–1931), *Das Umittelbare, eine Menschheitsfrage* (1st ed., Berlin: G. Reimer, 1902; 2d ed., Jena: E. Diederichs, 1911; 3d ed., Basel: C.F. Spittler, 1923). Kutter, a Swiss, was also known for his fervent interest in social democracy.

background and environment. It is rather the sense of having sprung immediately from God. Thus we have here a different picture from that which belief in creation evokes. The impact on us of the immeasurability of the world, the unlimited abundance of life, the spacelessness and timelessness of God—these all proceed from the all-encompassing whole as a whole. The eternal question can only be:

> Who dares Him to name? . . .
> Name is but sound and smoke![2]

This too is a concept of the greatest religious significance, a significance that will continue to grow.

Nevertheless, our interpretation of the world remains one-sided as long as we concentrate only on the flow of the whole. The greatest miracle of religious experience is this: that, despite all my insignificance, God still chooses to know me in an entirely personal way; and that within me there grows a new self who is the result not of things that I have done but of that which God has done in me. But that which has come to pass in me through God's active creativity, must also be everywhere. I can sense it in every concrete creation, down to each and every plant and animal; alongside the universal there stands the immediate, effective power of God. I sense it at those junctures where the emergence of life persists as a problem in the sciences; for even though it is in the midst of continuity, something New springs forth there, at a specific point. No matter how many preparations there may have been for the emergence of humankind, humanity is still something quite different from the stages which preceded it. And we have every right to view the emergence of the human race as a creative act. This holds equally true for the emergence of the individual. The processes of nature cannot explain how it is that a new

---

2. Johann Wolfgang Goethe, *Faust* I, 16. These two lines do not appear together, but are about one page apart. They are spoken by Faust to Magarete in response to her question about his religious practices and beliefs. In context, they appear thus:

> Who dares Him to name,
> And who dares to proclaim:
> "In Him I believe"?
> . . . .
> Then call it, what thou wilt—
> Call it Bliss! Heart! Love! God!
> I have no name for it!
> Name is but sound and smoke
> Enshrouding the glow of heaven.

Faust: Eine Tragödie, in Goethe, *Die Faustdichtungen* (Zürich: Artemis-Verlag, 1950), pp. 250–51. This translation is adapted from Charles W. Eliot, ed., *Harvard Classics*, vol. 19 (New York: P.F. Collier & Sons, 1909), pp. 144–45.

human being comes to be with its own passions and its own soul, for here the Immediate holds sway.

It is interesting to trace the career of this belief in immediacy. It breaks out again and again throughout the history of thinking and believing. Neoplatonic teaching, despite its pantheistic tendencies, was completely directed toward the individual soul and its cultivation.

But now we need to clarify this belief as an authentically religious belief. We stand before the question of its relationship to the scientific approach to things. We encounter the difficult clash between the religious view of the world as living and the scientific view of nature as orderly and predictable. Science manifests a tendency to rob the individual of its individuality and to understand it only in terms of the whole. Everything becomes a consequence of the whole, and the immediate is excluded. Those who have given their total allegiance to this logical connectedness no longer have the heart to affirm immediacy. This is the real tension between science and religion; and many people resolve it simply by rejecting religion as mere fantasy. Since they hold that it is impossible for the All to have any relation to the individual, they seek to take comfort in seeing themselves as part of the whole. All this results in a monistic view that unites many different trends. Of course we could try to resolve the conflict differently by saying, The entire concept of nature is an unbearable tyranny to which the human race has bound itself. Even some research scientists have said as much. But the theologians usually offer no more than the impoverished assertion that our individuality is assured by inner experience. That is a very cheap answer. To be sure, the problem is enormously difficult, but that does not justify laying down one's arms.

Above all, we must here say this: Belief in immediacy does not constitute an attempt at explanation. We cannot say how God brings his reign to the individual. We have no theory about the How of events, but a religious interpretation that only substantiates the feeling. All pious persons will agree that this is so. Against the view that holds the course of the world to be exhaustively univocal and rationalizable, there will always be an abundance of moments that defy rationalization: the contingent, the merely existent. Only specific portions of reality are susceptible to scientific conceptualization. What we experience is concrete. We can single out individual moments from the concrete—chemical, biological, and the like—but they cannot exhaust it. There still remains that which is accidental, the individual that cannot simply be comprehended under the general—not to mention the inexplicability of the world as a whole.

Now this contingency, a concept of such enormous importance in this connection, naturally cannot serve as a proof of divine activity; it only shows that there is that which does not admit of scientific resolution. But we have proven that a remnant of the irrational is everywhere, and this remnant shows once more that it is vain to imagine that any rational, monistic legal regularity—an idea that is so inimical to us—can exclude all immediacy. A positive demonstration of this immediacy-belief cannot be realized; it remains a religious belief. But the monistic belief in law and regularity, which necessarily issues in determinism and in the substitution of a universal law for the idea of God—which would leave the religious person unable to begin anything ever again—this monistic belief is shown to be something less than unconquerable and almighty. It is noteworthy that several scientists are themselves dubious of this faith in law and regularity, particularly since the revolution that this area has undergone as the result of the new discoveries concerning electricity. English researchers in particular are now less inclined to be rationalistic. We need therefore suffer no anxiety on this point. What we have in science is an attempt to rationalize the world, but nothing more than an attempt! We need not let it deter us from belief in immediacy, which is so indispensable for personal religiosity.

The point at which this belief in immediacy is most vital and has its greatest impact is *prayer*. If we felt ourselves to be nothing more than a fixed point in the whole, then prayer would be senseless. An impact on God can be conceived only if we assume that the soul's surrender has an impact *on God*. It is only in this way that it can stream back into us with a flow of power. For the immediacy of prayer does not consist in effecting an external change—such would, in any case, be of secondary importance—but consists rather in the prayer itself: in communion with God, in purging our passions and ourselves before his countenance, and in the disclosure of his own essence, to which even our own wishes, whatever their weakness, belong. How prayer can influence its object is not a matter for scientific research. The act of submission itself is the heart of the matter. Everyone can think as they will about how it takes place. But even the way in which our wishes are expressed confirms that the essential thing is the act of submission. There is no offering of petitions in prayer but that some will fall to the wayside. Before the face of God, we recognize that some of our desires are senseless.

This concludes our treatment of the Christian concept of the world.

3

The Christian Concept
of the Soul

§19. The Place of Anthropology in the System

DICTATION

1. We have described the world as grounded in God and led by God. One part of this world is the *human person*. Despite humankind's pettiness and preoccupation with its own existence, the human race has already assumed a position of partial superiority over nature. For this reason, and because it draws everything in its immediate environment to itself, the human self is a particular concern of piety; for it is through the self's communion with God that it is relatively distinguished from the world and elevated above it. This is particularly true of Christian piety, which, with its understanding of God as holy love, elevates the human self above the world in principle, raising it up to God through freedom and grace. It thus sets humanity apart from nature and the world more sharply than do any of the lower religions; and it is this point in particular that distinguishes Christianity from all pantheistic religions. Hence the need for a *Christian anthropology*, a religious interpretation of the origin, essence, conditions, and goal of human being on religious grounds. The concepts involved are just as purely religious as those involved in the Christian cosmology: that is, they presuppose a Christian-religious faith in God, and they draw their conclusions solely from this faith in principle.

2. A purely religious treatment of anthropology is possible because the topic with which it deals, i.e., the *soul* as *spirit and personality,* is not a concept of the exact sciences. The idea that the soul in all its manifestations is embraced in a centralized ego or "I" is, in its broadest sense, a supra-empirical idea, one which can be neither proven nor scientifically construed. On the contrary, it leads to antinomies similar to those found in a purely scientific evaluation of the concept of the world.[1] There is therefore something supra-empirical about the soul from the very beginning; that is why belief in the soul already played a great role in the primitive religions, giving rise to ancestor worship, doctrines of transmigration, belief in Hades, doctrines of reward and punishment in the other world, and the like.

In prophetic-Christian theism, the soul, just like the world, is clearly and completely distinguished from God and subordinated to him as his creature. The soul belongs completely to the world God has created; but within that world, the soul, precisely through faith in God, is imparted a supra-human ethical and religious quality, so that we can nevertheless speak of the soul's eternal significance. The mystical religions, on the other hand, consign the soul back to the world in the all-ness of God. Hence theology does not deal with the soul as an anthropological or psychological concept; it deals with the soul as the subject of the personality and its religious destiny which unites with God.

Hence it is clear that the religious concept of the soul has absolutely *nothing* to do with scientific anthropology and experimental psychology; it is rather an object of faith. Such a faith lies at the center of all speculation concerning this concept. As far as the exact sciences are concerned, the religious concept of the soul presupposes such an anthropology and psychology as will leave room for the development of the personality in communion with God; but religious thought is not involved in anthropology and psychology as such. This limitation of our inquiry to the purely religious concept of the soul, however, does not rule out the possibility of a positive relationship to scientific anthropology any more than cosmology can dispense with a relationship to natural science. Religious statements concerning the soul must be adapted to the general context of anthropology; they cannot correct anthropology on a solely religious basis. This means that the biblical myths of *creation and the prehistory of the human race,* and biblical expressions concerning spirit and

1. See Immanuel Kant, *Critique of Pure Reason,* trans. Lewis White Beck (New York: Bobbs-Merrill, 1956), pp. 384–483 (A409–A565), esp. pp. 396–421 (A454–A460).

flesh, death and afterlife, are not scientific conclusions. The Bible and the Christian world of ideas are concerned only with the religious valuation and conception of the soul; they offer no scientific conclusions concerning the origin and constitution of the human race. The *latter* in particular is to be derived wholly from the modern science of man and only then illuminated by a religious interpretation and valuation of the soul. This is a decisive departure from traditional scholastic dogmatics.

3. This provides us with the various subdivisions of this topic. First comes the religious concept of the soul: as that which freely unites with God and thereby becomes a personality elevated above the world, or the *infinite value of the soul.* Second comes the relatedness of the soul, in principle, to God, or the *image of God* and original perfection, which the old dogmatics discussed in connection with the human condition before the Fall. Third comes that which interferes with this communion with God, or sin as a universal human destiny, which the old dogmatics dealt with under the doctrine of *original sin.* Fourth comes the religious interpretation of the historical development of the human race, or what the old dogmatics discussed as the divine *decree of salvation* and the history of salvation.

LECTURE

We have already distinguished God from the world of creatures as a whole; but there still remain great differences within the world. Hence we relatively distinguish the human race from nature. The human self is, to be sure, a part of the whole: a small, weak, part of the world, constantly bubbling up from the world. Yet the human self still perceives itself as separate from the world. It perceives itself as one to whose service the world is—to a certain extent—dedicated, and as one whose ethical power constitutes its superiority over the world. It perceives itself as the microcosm in the macrocosm.

Religion intensifies this universal human separateness from the world, enabling the human person to elevate itself above the world through union with divine powers. For all religion is an attempt to elevate oneself above the world, and this is particularly true of Christianity. "Be of good cheer, I have overcome the world."[2] In Christianity, this signifies a transition from the world to God, where the soul, filled with eternal values, grows into God's life and partakes of him, so that it is enabled to say, "If God be for me, who can be

2. John 16:33.

§19. The Place of Anthropology in the System

against me?"[3] This unbroken soul, this refusal to be overcome by good fortune or bad, by glamour or ignominy—this comes from faith. For this is the *twofold image* of the Christian soul: to be *purely of the world* and still to possess something that *points beyond the world*. The world and simultaneous victory over the world express the subject of Christian theology at this point.

How shall we deal with the details of this teaching? Above all, we must be clear about this: The Christian-religious concept of the soul is a faith-concept, analogous to the concept of the world. We do not have an objective concept akin to the objective concept of the human person found in the sciences, as in medicine, for example. What we have to do here is to take an inner attitude toward the human person, insofar as the person appears in a new light. The methodological point remains the same: Faith-concepts are interpretations in light of the life of faith.

On the scientific side, somatic anthropology and psychology concern themselves with the human person in a purely natural-scientific and physiological sense, devoting none of their resources to what we call "soul." They deal instead with the soul's appearances and data. The sciences divide up the life of the soul into little pieces, which they then strive to bind together into logical and regular connections. The soul that concerns us here does not even come under serious consideration in the sciences. The only way in which the soul, as we understand it, is even discussed in these two sciences is in the question of whether it even exists. The emergent ego, which first comes forth as the result of being infused and filled by God, is supposed to be an impossibility, because it is not recognized by psychology!

Here we must answer, This ego, this "I" of which we speak, cannot be laid on a dissecting plate so that we can then point out the various tissues, here and there, in which it lives! The soul can only be thought, not empirically displayed! This unified center of the personality, where life joins forces with moral freedom, is an *idea!* To think it is to think something that cannot be made visible (contrary to the spiritualists, whose beliefs obscure their own souls and everything else besides). No person's consciousness can grasp his soul in its entirety; the soul as a unified whole is something that can only be thought. But there is also a certain experience of it. At birth, a human being comes into the world as nothing more than a bundle of diverse characteristics. He achieves the true self or "I" only through the formation of character, impressing the idea of a goal upon that simple

3. See Rom. 8:31.

bundle. The methods of the natural sciences know nothing of the soul that thus comes to be; it can be known only through personally creative experience.

Hence we shall formulate purely religious statements here as previously. But it would not be correct to say: We will pay no heed whatsoever to science. Our religious convictions should be held quite apart from science, but we should also not force them upon science. What we need is a science that will leave room for our concept of the soul; science need not prove our religious beliefs, but it must leave us room for them. For our part, we must develop our doctrine of the soul in such a way that it does not contest the basic propositions of anthropology, but still insists that purely religious concepts do have a place in the modern world. We must do so, first of all, because the human person indeed is a piece of organized matter. The religious life is always but one moment among many appearances. Science has enabled us to see a far-reaching correspondence between the soul and the body, and we can now see that inheritance does play a role. Naturally, we can no longer draw our anthropology from the Bible. The biblical account of prehistory has only an ethical significance. If the churches could have decided to grant science free license at this point, they would have earned a tremendous confidence. This is something which absolutely must be done. Yet most modern dogmatics are silent upon this point. It should not be this way; we may not force research to adhere to our theories. But the thing that concerns us, the spirit borne of God—*we* know it. And any science that contests this is guilty, we hold, of prejudgment.

We subdivide this topic as follows: (1) the general question of the soul and its infinite value; (2) the question of the image of God in the depths of the soul as it is affirmed by Christianity; (3) the question of the sin which stands in opposition to this image of God; and (4) the question of interpreting human history as salvation history.

§20. The Infinite Value of the Soul

DICTATION

1. Ecclesiastical anthropology consists of a mixture. On the one hand, it includes the biblical account of creation, the view of the human self held in the Old Testament and antiquity, and the Pauline religious analysis of the soul; on the other hand, it embraces Aristotelian anthropology and psychology. Eventually, to be sure, the

contradiction between the soul and the body and the idea of the immortality of the soul came to dominate. The idea of immortality was borrowed from Plato. But now all of this is meaningless. Today our task is simply to work out the *gospel's* idea of the *infinite value of the soul* within the context of modern anthropology and psychology. In the course of this exposition, religious ideas will coincide with speculative and critical doctrines concerning spirit as distinguished from body and soul.

2. *Somatic anthropology* is the first topic for discussion. Here we encounter the idea that all organic life on earth descended from primeval living cells. We do not dispute that the human race has descended from these cells, nor do we deny that humankind has much in common, both physically and psychologically, with the higher levels of life that stand in this line of descent. How the emergence of the human race took place, whether abruptly through heterogeneous reproduction, or gradually through the development of animals' latent hereditary tendencies into specifically human characteristics, we do not know. No matter which, human being is in principle a new being, and faith is right to trace humanity back to divine creation.

The age of the human race is presumably very great, but since it can be figured only in terms of geological epochs, it cannot be precisely fixed. Estimates vary by hundreds of thousands of years. Prehistoric conditions and developments, the various levels of culture (which are largely distinguished by the tools they used), the ice ages, the formation of races, and the question of monophyletic versus polyphyletic origin constitute additional, and, in part, very obscure problems. The genuine historical sources that we do have are, in comparison, very young; they are, at best, no more than about ten thousand years old. And how much longer the human race will remain on the planet depends on the livability of the planet, that is, on how long the warmth of the sun will endure, which absolutely cannot be determined.

Faith sees all this as the *basis* of spiritual, ethical, and religious development. Spiritual development appears for the first time in human beings: natural organisms who constantly triumph over their natural character and differences. This takes place in the realm of spirit—the realm of God. Humankind thereby extends the powers of life that have emerged in this process into the beyond. Faith views spirit's development out of its natural basis as the creative, loving activity of God.

3. That is the physical side of the matter; but in *psychological*

terms, too, the human person is a natural organism, inasmuch as the life of the human soul is, in its psychophysical and inner-psychical processes, a given reality, built upon universal laws—like all nature. All that is necessary is to avoid every materialistic reduction of the soul and its phenomena to mere physical nature; the independence of the psychical must be acknowledged. The question of the relationship between body and soul, which culminates in the question of the relationship between the brain and the soul, is still quite obscure; but at any rate, the question will not be resolved by a psychophysical parallelism, which stands contrary to the manifest facts of experience.

Religious faith need presuppose no more than this relative independence of the life of the soul from physical processes; but it must also reckon with wide-ranging psychophysical and psychological *conditions and limitations* that are imposed on the higher spiritual life. Spiritual life presupposes a basis in the nature of the soul; but this nature also imposes limitations and conditions on the spiritual life by occasional manifestations of ateleology, such as so-called spiritual illnesses, idiotism, hereditary vices and dispositions, etc. Such phenomena are to be viewed only as manifestations of the ateleology present in the world in general. But on the whole, faith understands the naturally endowed, individually constituted, and hereditarily and environmentally conditioned life of the soul to be the indispensable basis and presupposition of the higher, necessary, and unconditional spiritual life.

4. This *spiritual life* grows from the various psychological emissions [*Ablauf*] of the soul by rising above them, even as it continues to presuppose them. The soul's drive to higher development results in independence in thought, morality, and art; and it thereby achieves its own independent character as autonomous spiritual life, rather than merely natural soul-life. The essence of this spiritual life is *freedom,* that is, the task of *self-definition* through ideas of valid truths and unconditional values. Values can be affirmed as valid truths only by a freedom that is free of merely natural psychological determination. The essence of freedom is determination through self-validating truths and values; and freedom, in this sense, constitutes the essence of spirit. Freedom is not produced by natural hereditary factors; it is rather a task that emerges from the growth of spirit. But establishing the existence of the realm of truths and values, and the reality of the freedom that affirms them, is no task for psychology; for psychology is concerned not with freedom, but with the givenness and regularity

of phenomena. This is a task for epistemology and value-theory, which alone can disclose the autonomous essence of spirit.

All that such an epistemology and value-theory can do, however, is to establish the idea that there is a center of these autonomous functions. A *metaphysical theory* would be necessary to describe this center as an independent being, i.e., as a *personality*. But we do not need to busy ourselves with such a metaphysics of the personal spirit, for it is of little consequence whether it is more substantialist or more actualist in its theories. The personal and individual spirit, at any rate, is neither innate nor concurrent, but rather the product of freedom; it comes first through freedom, simultaneously the product of freedom and the divine spirit. This further presupposes that divine reason or divine spirit is latent in the soul, to be aroused only through the freedom of the finite personality. This, in turn, presupposes a thoroughly metaphysical context. This context provides that the individual spirit that has arisen through freedom will also constantly interact with other spirits, being awakened and enhanced by them.

This brings us, in turn, to the idea of a realm of spirits and a community of personalities, something achievable and expressible only in history. If we call this emergent essence of the spirit νοῦς [*nous* or mind], as distinguished from mere ψυχή [*psyche*], we then have a neologism for spirit: the *intelligible "I"* or self.[1] It is this "I" that forms the subject of religious faith and its utterances.[2] The Christian faith ascribes *infinite value* to this "I" because of its freedom and its connection to God. This higher self develops toward complete communion with God and utter superiority over all earthly and sensual values. Sometimes this development takes the form of a pronounced, heroic dualism; but the life of the senses and the psyche is surely not to be rejected, for they are the presupposition of the spirit. They constitute its organ, and, like the rest of world, are to be traced back to divine creation.

1. Literally, the "intelligible I," although it could also be rendered as the "intelligible ego" or "intelligible self."

2. Troeltsch draws once again on Kant, who had applied his distinction between the *appearance* of a thing and the thing *in itself* to the "I" (or ego or self). The appearance of the "I," as it is known empirically, is to be distinguished from the "I" in itself, or the "intelligible I." Hence, according to Kant, "there is no contradiction in supposing that one and the same being is, in the appearance, that is, in its visible acts, necessarily subject to the law of nature, and so far *not free,* while yet, as belonging to a thing in itself, it is not subject to that law, and is therefore *free.*" See Immanuel Kant, *Critique of Pure Reason,* trans. Lewis White Beck (New York: Bobbs-Merrill, 1956), p. 28 (Bxxvii–Bxxviii).

LECTURE

The supra-empirical soul has been a mystery to the human race from the beginning. It was thought of as a small divinity, immolated like incense after death. Hence the practice of exalting the dead through hero-worship, the belief in Hades, and the like. Today Maeterlinck speaks of the mystery of the soul in his book *The Buried Temple*.[3] He knows that something enters and surges through the soul, something that cannot be reduced to the appearances with which we customarily concern ourselves. But otherwise his standpoint is purely contemplative. He does not fully grasp the forward-driving power of a soul that is filled with God; but he does a masterful job of describing what the soul is. Christianity affirms that there is a mysterious depth to the soul, a depth wherein it achieves a supra-human value in communion with God. Hence we speak of "the infinite value of the soul."

The old dogmatics derived the Christian concept of the soul directly from the Bible, beginning with the account of the creation of man on the sixth day and moving on to the story of the Fall, the punishment for sin, death, and destiny after death. All this was further elaborated by reference to the Pauline doctrine of the body and the spirit, distinguishing πνεῦμα [*pneuma* or spirit] from both νοῦς [*nous* or mind] and mere ψυχή [*psyche*]. Greek philosophy provided other elements of church doctrine: The human person was believed to possess a vegetative soul like those of the plants and animals. Above that stood the sensitive soul, and higher still the *anima rationalis* [rational soul], which possessed freedom and was related to the divine *ratio* [reason]. Only the last-named was not thought to be transitory. Platonic thought sharply distinguished the soul that is concerned with sensual matters from the soul that was concerned with God. Hence: the Bible, Paul, Aristotle, and Plato. The poetic side of this view was expressed by Dante and—rather insipidly—by Melanchthon as well.

But these things are no longer credible for us in this form. We cannot describe the central moment of the soul, where it bears God in itself, where it is "of the truth,"[4] without linking it to other contexts. The approach taken to the human person by the *new* sciences is

---

3. Maurice Maeterlinck, *The Buried Temple* (*Le temple enseveli*, 1896), trans. Alfred Sutro (New York: Dodd, Mead, & Co., 1902). See pp. 304–35 for Maeterlinck's discussion of the mystery of "this unconscious life of ours" (p. 304), to which Troeltsch seems to be referring.

4. John 18:37.

not irrelevant for us. We stand before the fundamental fact that all life on our earth must be seen as an unbroken chain. Even though biology cannot eliminate the mysterious character of this impetus, no one can doubt the overall correctness of biology's general viewpoint. Its insight into the cell, which conditions the life of plants, animals, and human beings, is fundamental. The cell is the miracle of the world, and its riddle. The overwhelming magnitude of what the cell has produced leaves an impression of overwhelming greatness. But the problem that this poses remains unresolved. Helmholtz advances the hypothesis that primeval cells came to the earth from distant stars. But neither this hypothesis, should it prove correct, nor others, will be fatal. We lose nothing and gain nothing if two hundred naturalists find themselves contradicting one another.

Here too we must take note of *Darwinian doctrine*. It is essentially an attempt to produce somewhat more teleological [*zweckmässigere*] structures from various combinations. It builds for itself a realm of apparently sequential stages which are in truth conditioned by chance. In the seventies and eighties everyone was caught up in the frenzy of chance generation. But now, for us, variations are no longer determined only by chance and selection. We must presuppose the intentional will of the active individual, and the various great successions of levels are to be treated as new developments whose connections can never be fully explained. It is altogether clear that an animal is not merely a plant that can move around! And it cannot be disputed that there is still something more to a human being than there is to an animal! The clever hound of Mannheim, no matter how intelligent he may be, will never write a *Critique of Pure Reason*. Within the human being there lives a spirit that is unique in principle, no matter how many preparations there may have been for it; human being constitutes a new breakthrough in the midst of this overwhelming realm of cells, and we need not fear that this will be disproved.

Another question associated with anthropology is: How long has the human race been on our planet? Any attempt to answer this question is fraught with great difficulties, for the answer is to be found only in geology—that is, in fossilized bones found in the rocks. But a thousand years more or less makes no difference to the rocks. The most conservative scholarly estimates of the age of the human race now place the figure at about two hundred thousand years. We can be certain that human beings lived in our part of the earth prior to both ice ages. Research has thus extended the duration of the human race so far back into the past that it seems immeasurably distant to us, as we reflect upon the prehistoric exhibits we have seen in our museums. And it is not impossible that this prehistory was itself preceded by a very high level of culture that disappeared without a trace.

Another anthropological question is whether the breakthrough that led to the emergence of the human race came at one or more points. To the question of the age of the human race must be added the question of its dispersion over the planet. One school of research believes in a monophyletic origin, that is, the descent of the human race from a single pair. But this would make it difficult to understand how the human race came to extend over all parts of the earth. Or were there bridges between the continents in primeval times?

Equally difficult is the problem of the races. The external markings of color have a deep psychological impact. For our purposes, this raises the following question: How, in light of the differences and antipathies between the races, can we believe that this contradiction will be overcome? In America the racial hatred between the blacks and the whites [*Schwarzen und Weissen*] is so great that each must have its own separate railway accommodations.[5] In light of such conditions it is very difficult to speak of achieving the ethical and religious unification of the human race.

The question of the future of the human race itself also arises here. Wave after wave of human history has come and gone—we cannot reduce the future as a whole to our own future. But what will the end be like? Presumably a diminution of the sun's energy, accompanied by increasing difficulty in obtaining food, until finally the last human being roasts the last potato over the last glowing ember—and that only if all three of them somehow manage to get together. This is now a customary picture of the end. It has been suggested that the canals on Mars[6] were dug in order to counter the effects of a prolonged drought—a drought that could also be the fate of our planet as its mountains gradually wear down. We would then have to pay millions for our water supply. There are other similar, purely material matters with which we must reckon. In light of such future possibili-

---

5. Literally, "Each must have its own electric railway." Troeltsch almost certainly did not say this, since he had gained a firsthand knowledge of American railroads, which, in many areas, forced black people to accept separate *accommodations,* not separate railroads, during his visit in 1904.

6. Several telescopic observations of Mars at the turn of the century suggested that the planet was crisscrossed with a network of canals. No evidence of these canals, of course, has been observed by any of the interplanetary probes which have visited the planet.

ties, there can be little hope for a thousand-year *Reich*,[7] to say
nothing of how little comfort such a *Reich* would really offer. The
sufferings of the past will not be mitigated by the hope that things
will get better after the passage of a few centuries. The main point
here is only that there must be something more to all this than
somatic-anthropological science recognizes, that this science cannot
uproot us, that its subject must be viewed as extending beyond
nature.

We have already gone into the matter of scientific psychology and
its viewpoint. Scientific psychology does not lead us to the soul, but
only its appearances, its causal regularities, and its connections with
the body; for modern psychology is psychology without a soul. That
does not mean that there is no soul; it only means that the soul
cannot be the subject of a scientific investigation. Our interest in this
has to do with the realization of an antimaterialistic theory; for if the
very possibility of the soul's breaking through the limitations of
nature were eliminated, it would close every path available to us. If
that happened, it would make no difference whether the mechanism
were physical or psychical in nature; we would be imprisoned in
either case, by little bits and pieces of matter or by the tiniest emotions of the soul, respectively.

Now there are psychiatrists who break out of this mechanistic
view by appealing to the human capacity or destiny for ideas
[*Ideebestimmten*]. According to them, there may well be a psychological mechanism in the unconscious, but it is not a closed mechanism.
Correct thinking is not correct because it is the result of psychologically necessary connections. There may be circumstances under which
it is very difficult to mobilize the *idea* against psychological connections, but it is possible, and this is what is decisive. Of course, it must
be conceded that the spiritual life is very much conditioned by
psychophysical and psychological circumstances; see Ribot's unset-
tling book, *The Diseases of Personality*.[8] The soul's health unquestionably depends on its bodily substrate.

This is not an earth-shaking piece of knowledge. Prisons, insane
asylums, and institutions for idiots all constitute a terrible witness to
the power that the body and mere psyche have over the spirit. But
none of this refutes what we have said about the soul. It does not

7. Troeltsch could not, of course, have known that this would become one of Hitler's
favorite terms for the Third Reich; but the coincidence, and Troeltsch's comments
about the ultimate futility of such a *Reich*, should not be allowed pass without remark.
8. Théodule Ribot (1839–1916), *The Diseases of Personality* (translation of *Les
maladies de la personnalité* [Paris: Alcan, 1885]) (Chicago: Open Court, 1891).

show that the achievements of a Helmholtz are, in a certain sense, simply the play of an idiot, nor that great art is simply an interchange of associations. The existence of unfortunate psychic abnormalities is simply another example of the tremendous number of ateleological manifestations with which we simply have to come to terms. We must also make it clear that the higher powers are present, even if only in an elementary fashion, among all who are thus diseased. We recognize this by permitting worship to be held in insane asylums no matter how terrible they may be. The higher powers are still present, but they are undeveloped or blocked. These issues are so indescribably important because they are so often used as arguments against religious belief. Nevertheless, these offer us no basis for clarifying that which arises from the soul. What emerges from the soul is the self-disclosure of a deeper level, something from behind the natural soul.

It is at this point, where we allow ourselves to be determined by valid ideas of the good and the true and no longer by mere nature, that freedom is first offered to us. The "I" under discussion is by no means simply there to begin with, but rather something to be created, something that comes to be through an act of surrender to that which emerges within the "I" as an idea, as the holy. And as soon as we see that, as soon as we contrast the personal to the simple "I," then we see clearly: This "I" is not the subject of psychology. This "I" is not given, but posed, like a task [*kein Gegebenes, sondern ein Aufgegebenes*]. It is not something that simply is, but something that we can come to know only by creating it. Therein lies the connection between spirit and freedom: freedom is not something that *is*, but something *to be achieved*. It is essentially an act, a becoming, not a finished product; it is a struggle to move forwards, which is all too often driven back.

Act, freedom, and personality are all subjects for a value-theory, a philosophy of religion, and an epistemology. Since these disciplines have now become distinct, it is necessary to reunify them in a doctrine of the spirit, as Fichte did. The development of such a metaphysics of spirit and personality that can overcome mechanistic thinking is the most profound and burning task in all contemporary thought.

This brings us to the point where we need to be. The higher powers break forth from the child only slowly. The human being becomes aware of the need for self-concentration and for self-separation from mere determination by nature. But this self-separation can be truly achieved only in religion. Freedom is the product of both divine movement and human self-sacrifice. And that is what gives the soul its infinite value: that for which the human race has everywhere thirsted, that which has been the deepest longing of every age.

§21. The Image of God

DICTATION

1. Our description of spirit lays particular stress on the connection that exists between freedom and the divine spirit that freedom stirs up; together they constitute a principle within the soul that presses on to the fulfillment of personality. This leads us to conceptualize something which is proper to [human] spirit, and yet actually developed only through communion with the divine spirit. Church doctrine referred to this development of spirit as the *image of God*. But the church saw it as something *already* present in the beginning: the original perfection of Paradise, with complete religious knowledge and moral perfection, free from sin and limitation, not bound to the limitations of sensual nature. But, in light of what we now know about the beginning of the human race, it is absolutely impossible that this could have been the case. Even more important, the idea of original perfection is incompatible with the concept of spirit as neither finished nor innate, becoming and taking form in the interaction between freedom and grace. The image of God does not signify some lost original state, but rather a goal to be attained in historical development. It signifies struggle, becoming, a longing and yearning for completion, and hence, the *principle of historical development*. It is not to be drawn from the myth of the primal man, but from the Christian ideal of personality, which firmly derives its content from the person of Jesus.

2. The concept of the image of God entails an essential determination, but this determination is conceivable only if the human soul is already disposed to it. Yet such a disposition can be affirmed only in light of a basic virtual connection between the human and divine spirits. The image of God presupposes the immanence of the divine spirit in the finite, or the human soul's kinship to God. This immanence of the divine spirit in the finite surges into human consciousness, and determines the relationship of the human race to the creaturely realm as we know it.

But how this immanence can come to be, how it can break out of mere disposition into actuality, and why it manifests such different levels of intensity among various persons—these are all questions that can no longer be answered. The same holds true for questions pertaining to the emergence of the natural individual soul. All that we know about the emergence of individuality is the external process of reproduction and the process by which the parental cells come to unite; we know absolutely nothing about the emergence of the soul and whatever connections it may have with the life of the parental souls. Hence there is little to be said about the *emergence of the soul,* an issue which divided the old dogmatics into creationist and traducianist schools, just as there is little that can be said about the emergence of the spirit. Faith perceives the *creative activity of the living God* in both cases, and we do not need to know *how* this activity occurs in order to be certain that it does take place.

3. Just as the concept of the image of God implies the idea of an origin, it also implies the idea of a *goal.* The spiritual life is a principle of infinite development. That is to say that the spiritual life is always only begun here in this earthly life; it can never be considered fully realized. It strives for complete redemption from all limitations and barriers, for complete unification with God. This means that all the ideals and powers of the spiritual life, including those we receive in Christianity, are but the means and powers of a development that presses forward to a conclusion that can lie only in an unknown Beyond. If the meaning of this development is to become one with God, then perhaps the final goal is to be conceived in terms of an ever greater triumph over mere freedom and an ever fuller surrender to God, leading the creature back to God even to the point of the dissolution of its separate existence. The particulars of this subject will be considered in the eschatology.

4. Between the foundation and the goal come both the growing *freedom* of the *personality consecrated for God* and growing love among spirits in the will of God. These characterize an ethic of struggle and exertion like the ethic found in Christianity. To be holy as God is holy, and to show one's love of God in love of one's brothers[1]—or, in short, a pure heart and brotherly love—this is the principle of the prophetic-Christian ethos, corresponding to Christianity's character as a personalistic religion. It is a dualistic ethic which places the religious values of personality and community high above all others; yet it is not antisensual and ascetic, for it seeks only to subordinate the sensual basis of life and the values of intra-worldly ethics to the highest religious values. But that also means that this

---

1. See Matt. 5:43-48.

ethos will always be involved in a struggle on earth; it will always be in the process of becoming, never fully realized. For in every generation, evil—the next topic for discussion—opposes intra-worldly life and its values and relations to the spirit, which extends beyond them. Evil confronts spirit with its basis in, and with the limitations of, intra-worldly nature. But this is a topic for the study of ethics.

LECTURE

Every age has its central question. The people of declining antiquity sought protection from the transitory world and death above all else. Luther's time needed liberation from legalism. For our age, which treats individuals like cogs in a machine, for which money means everything, and which not only appears to shun the soul, but really does—for this age, the *soul* is the central question of life. "Save your soul!" is the authentic cry of our day. The writer who deals with the problem of the soul understands this. Guilt, on the other hand, is today understood by no one, since we have to be clear about the meaning and destiny of the soul before we can talk about guilt. But as for the pessimism about the soul that today dominates widespread circles, Hauptmann's newest novel[2] can serve as grim testimony.

The Christian worldview responds to this with the doctrine of the image of God, which refers to more than the mere soul. The church's longstanding opinion was as follows: human beings originally sprang guiltless from the hand of the creator, bearing the likeness of the divine perfection. This perfection was subsequently lost through sin, and suffering, pain, and death were the result. The same ideas are to be found among the peoples of antiquity. They believed in the golden age, for they were far removed from any concept of becoming and self-development. These were all mythical images, but that does not render them meaningless. This profound, beautifully childlike sense is simply the projection of ideals onto the past. The Fall into sin was the result of distrust: "Did God say 'you shall not eat?' "[3] It was also the beginning of self-deification: "Shall not I do it?"

But the Fall remains a myth, and not only from the standpoint of scientific research. There are also intrinsically religious reasons that such an innate perfection is inconceivable. Spirit is *produced*. The older dogmatics, already aware of this, reformulated the concept of a

2. Gerhart Hauptmann (1862–1946), *Atlantis* (Berlin: S. Fischer, 1912); English translation by Adele and Thomas Seltzer (New York: B.W. Huebsch, 1912). This title was identified by Gertrud von le Fort.
3. Gen. 3:1.

state of perfection into a state of complete naiveté. We, however, must make the most important change: We must stop looking backwards and start looking forwards. The ideal of perfection is not something we have left behind, but a goal that lies ahead. Just like holiness in God and being in God, it can signify only something ultimate. It is something that the imagination can at most intuit: as the establishment of the personality in God, or, alternately, as submersion in God. But for us, the most important thing is for faith to cling to something attainable.

This brings us to the concept of the *end*, which, if it be grasped in its *full* meaning, signifies, just like the concept of the image of God, that what we here attain and love in others is only a beginning. It is intrinsic to this idea that it not be viewed as a purely this-worldly concern. Despite the contemporary world's tendency to view everything exclusively in this-worldly terms, our deepest conviction looks to the Beyond and a life after death. This is not to cast stones at those who cannot share in this conviction. It is only to say to them, The idea of the infinite value of the soul is inconceivable apart from life after death. Life after death is more like the finishing touch that enables humankind, though it be afflicted by a thousand demons— and that even at its best—to be recognized as the fulfillment of the image of God.

We must therefore decide in favor of life after death if we are fully to affirm the image of God. It alone can make great heroism possible. A good portion of the plaintiveness and resignation of the human race stems from its lack of courage to affirm this belief. Belief in immortality was indispensable for Goethe too, although he thought it applied only to the highest in humanity. But it holds true for this highest, too: The inner voice does not lie.

What is true for the goal has held true from the beginning: the goal is possible only if we have been directed to it from the beginning. This signifies humanity's kinship to God. But how this is to be expressed by the individual, finite, limited spirit, is a question that cannot be answered. It is the fundamental mystery of metaphysics. We must postulate it, for we do not know it. The emergence of the individual is concealed from us in darkness, just like death; we can, finally, ascertain nothing but its symptoms.

What lies between the end and the beginning is the concern of ethics. It deals with the growth of the soul into the kingdom of love and spirit, or the self-sanctification of the soul for God and the binding of souls together in him.

§22. Original Sin

DICTATION

1. This ideal, essential image of God, which is known from the gospel, encounters *resistance* in the human race. This resistance, however, is quite variegated, something church doctrine never took into account when tracing it back to the Fall. It can first of all be traced back to actual natural circumstances and limitations, which, despite the fact that all nature is directed toward spirit, nevertheless inflict a variety of limitations and friction upon various individuals. This has already been discussed, under the topics of theodicy and cosmology. Such resistance can be overcome only by faith, hope, and submission. Further limitations are also to be found in the weakness, convolution, and incalculability of human moral strength and goals.

There are all sorts of limitations, then, that involve neither guilt nor will; they arise from the weakness, ignorance, transient emotion, and unavoidable one-sidedness of the human self. Only the corresponding complement of the community, along with energetic reflection on the ideal, can overcome these limitations.

2. But, over and above these limitations, there is also *conscious* opposition to the ideal: a denial of destiny and of the spiritual world itself. And with it comes a fundamental opposition to the divine, whether in the passive form of simple ignorance, or in the active form of struggle, defiance, and revolt. In Christian speech this contradiction is called *sin*. As early as the age of the prophets, sin was seen as the ethical will's antagonism, both secret and open, to God—the rebellion of the flesh against the divine spirit. In the gospel, sin is seen as a contradiction that lies within every soul, but it is also viewed in terms of the conflict between the Kingdom of God and the kingdom of sin, whose ruler will be defeated in the decisive hour. Paul utterly subjectivized sin, construing it as the universal result of the sin of Adam and the cause of human suffering, to be overcome in the death of Christ and in the redemptive realm of the Christ-community. The church developed his view into the dogma of *original sin* or *inherited sin,*[1] which was linked to sexual lust. Original sin

---

1. *Die Erbsünde.* "Original sin" is the customary translation, since both *"die Erbsünde"* and "original sin" translate the same Latin term, Augustine's *peccatum originale.* A literal translation of *die Erbsünde,* however, would be *"inherited* sin," which corresponds more closely to the sense in which Troeltsch uses the term here. That is why two English expressions are used here for the one German term; henceforth, however, only the customary "original sin" will be employed.

effected a damning guilt that extended to the entire human race and condemned it to hell. This, however, could be overcome by the church and its means of grace.

These various views all share the idea of a universal and substantial sinfulness, or *radical evil,* as Kant formulated it.[2] This idea of radical evil, i.e., a principle of contradiction that is closely bound up with the essence of being human, is something with which contemporary thought is familiar, even if its optimistic monism blissfully ignores evil or, at most, understands it in the purely negative sense of the merely not-yet-good. But this fails to appreciate the full seriousness of the fundamental ideas of Christianity. If the image of God essentially consists in freedom, then evil can be understood only in terms of a genuine opposition. This is thoroughly corroborated by the moral consciousness, which, even outside Christianity, has come to a similar conclusion in light of a more profound knowledge of God and the soul. Platonism, Brahmanism, and Buddhism, and several individual thinkers as well, have all attested to the reality of radical evil. The only difference is that they do not refer back to an act of the will, but to materiality, finiteness, and sensuality.

3. The Christian concept of evil thoroughly corresponds to the personal idea of God and the soul. Hence it is a purely religious concept, conceiving antimorality not in exclusively ethical terms, but also from a religious viewpoint: antimorality is construed as rejection of, or antagonism toward, God. It is this *religious* character of antimorality that constitutes its real roots and true depths. Hence the concept of sin, just like the concept of the image of God, is characteristically Christian; and it stands in the same relationship to the truly universal sense of evil that the concept of the image of God stands to the universal but vague struggle for higher life. The importance of the personal and religious character of both good and evil is particularly stressed. Hence full knowledge of sin comes only with faith, which is why the concept of sin can be affirmed only in the total context of the Christian world of ideas. Therefore, the customary dogmatic distinction between natural and supernatural revelation, which held that awareness of sin is based on a pre-Christian, natural knowledge of God, is utterly false. Such awareness arises only in connection with believing affirmation of the Christian idea of God.

---

2. See Immanuel Kant, "Concerning the Indwelling of the Evil Principle with the Good, or, On the Radical Evil in Human Nature," in *Religion within the Limits of Reason Alone,* trans. Theodore M. Greene and Hoyt M. Hudson (New York: Harper & Row, 1960), Book I, pp. 15–39.

But even within the Christian world of ideas, knowledge of sin is directly tied to the tension within the psychological-Christian concept of God, according to which God demands trust, faith, and surrender to his holy love. Hence those church dogmatics that have divided up God between law and grace and separated the Old Testament from the gospel, attributing knowledge of sin to the former,[3] have been psychologically incorrect. In the pure Christian concept of God the two are truly inseparable, and the knowledge of sin, in connection with the concept of holy love, is initially a truly shattering thing; and while the Christian awareness of sin is surely related to a general knowledge of our moral defects, it is still very much more than that.

4. If the concept of sin is thus specifically Christian, springing from the center of Christian faith in God, then the essence of sin is to be measured against the centerpoint of the concept of God, as the Reformers did. The concept of God demands a faithful and trusting disposition of surrender, a disposition that sin rejects. The absence of faith and trust in God—and the resulting intensification of the finite self's quest for its own power and interests—that is the essence of sin. Sin is a disposition that is opposed to God; it expresses itself first, consciously or unconsciously, in a lack of common and ordinary morality. Sin arrives at this characteristic disposition no matter how great its range or frequency. It is always an erroneous disposition, an overall mistake in principle; and its consequence is the complete overthrow of the good, even if a good will remains. The characteristic disposition of sin leads us to recognize individual sin as both *agent and symptom of a principled disposition* that must be resisted. This is the source of the interiority and rigor of the Christian concept of sin, which is what gives it such shocking earnestness.

5. Alongside the radical nature of all sin in principle, there are nevertheless important distinctions to be made among its various manifestations and developments. The first of these distinctions is between *direct* and *indirect sin*. Direct sin is the self-conscious denial of God, along with its results: a turn to the self and the world, to sensuality and egoism as the only gods that remain—gods which, no matter how refined they may become, are unable to remove sinfulness. Indirect sin, on the other hand, is antimorality in its general and ordinary sense, where the bond between morality and the awareness of God is not clearly defined and hence there is no directly self-conscious denial of God. But since all goodness is, at bottom,

3. The original reads "latter," but "former" seems to make more sense.

connected to the concept of God, this antimorality too is sin in an indirect way. Indeed, closer inspection of the matter will reveal that sin is the real root of everyday evil. A psychological consideration of sin will therefore largely consist in uncovering the interconnectedness of everyday evil and its root in sin; whereas direct sin, on the other hand, constitutes an immediate point of contact.

Another distinction has to do with the *magnitude* of the *energy* involved in the negation. The sins of laziness and indifference are to be distinguished from those of active antagonism and opposition. The former block the emergence of the higher spiritual life, while the latter consciously oppose it and gladly ally themselves with antireligious and antimoral theories.

Finally come the incalculable *individual differences* of sinful opposition and the equally incalculable admixtures of the good. Sin is always fully particular, just like the good. This has been ignored by ecclesiastical doctrine, with its starkly universal concept of sin, more metaphysical than psychological.

6. This is a purely psychological and experiential analysis. But any profound grasp of sin unavoidably leaves the impression that such sinfulness is absolutely universal in its extent, that no one is excluded from it. This too is a *purely* experiential observation, a presupposition made by all who share this estimate of sin. But such a purely experiential judgment must nevertheless be rooted in a general, supra-individual, or metaphysical ground. The fact of *universal sinfulness* raises the question of its origin, thereby bringing us face to face with one of the most obscure of all religious problems.

7. Church dogmatics solved this problem with its metaphysic of a protoplasmic Fall, which caused sin and its results to be inherited by the entire species, along with pain, punishment, and death. This effectively robbed individual actual sins of almost all significance, turning them into mere symptoms of original sin. The entire explanation depended on the myth of a primal human pair and, like that myth, is to be expelled from the realm of history.

But even the idea that all this is to be traced to a first sin—whether of angels or human beings—that brought along all the others in its wake, is likewise impossible. First of all, this would mean that sin came to a totally sinless world from some place outside of it, which would signify a failure of the divine will. The idea is also impossible, second, because the primal sin [*Ursünde*] could not possibly be conceived as a conscious act, for spirit would not yet be capable of complete negation. Third, it is impossible to understand contemporary sinfulness in terms of such a primal sin, since contemporary sinfulness has its visible ground in the enduring circumstances of contemporary life. Therefore, universal sinfulness cannot be traced back to a first deed, but must rather reside in the conditions which everywhere attend becoming as such; sin must constantly be producing itself in the situation in which natural being elevates itself to a determination of spirit. Custom, upbringing, and social diffusion can all have only a secondary significance in comparison with this enduring source.

Hence the solution to the *problem of evil* is identical with the solution to the closely related problem of error. Evil follows from the conditions necessary for spirit's becoming; spirit can spring forth only from a natural being that is capable of self-affirmation—even as spirit must break up, burst open, and renew this natural being. Just as thought's capacity for freedom and becoming results in error, so too evil is the result of the ethical spirit's capacity for freedom and becoming. The primal animalistic-eudaemonistic self-affirmation inherent in every successful natural being must, from the viewpoint of spirit, appear to be a God-rejecting self-affirmation. Every individual entity must first confront the sin and guilt of its own animal-sensual self-affirmation, and, on the basis of its own awakened spirituality, conclude that this egoistic-sensual will to self-affirmation is actually a principled opposition to God that must be overcome. Hence the evil that is to be overcome is actually given with each individual entity itself: the emerging spirit comes to see clearly that the instinctive egoism which constitutes the natural organism is the principle of a potential, and indeed already begun, evil.

Hence *universal sinfulness* resides in the metaphysical constitution of human being, although it achieves consciousness as such only in the emergence of the spirit. This universal sinfulness is therefore not sin in the proper sense, and only a conditional guilt attaches to it. *Proper sinfulness* first begins when the sinful movement that arises from this source turns against the spirit or blocks its emergence. Therefore, actual sin or proper sin is to be distinguished from original sin or potential sin, which is not sin in the proper sense; in reality they are quite distinct. To these two types of sin we must add a third type, social sin, which is the type that can be inherited in the proper sense of the term. We must therefore distinguish three types: *potential sin, actual sin,* and inherited *social sin.*

8. The concept of *guilt* is closely tied to the concept of sin. It follows directly from the religious element of the concept of sin: viewed and sensed in terms of its impact on God. The feeling of guilt consists in a sense of the divine will's reaction to sin, a reaction of judgment

and condemnation. Thus the feeling of guilt is differentiated into three levels according to the three different types of sin. It is psychologically impossible for all three levels to share the same intensity of feeling. In every case, however, guilt comes into view only as the *feeling* of guilt, the effect of which upon the soul is to transmute the soul's relationship to God into feelings of alienation and judgment. These feelings, in turn, can issue in a quite diverse variety of psychological reactions: pain, despair, defiance, rebellion, or indifference. The search for God is easily transformed into flight from God. A complete understanding of sin is impossible if this feeling of flight from God is not taken into account; it is the fulfillment of the concept of sin.

We cannot, however, go beyond this subjective feeling of guilt and the real darkening of the soul's relationship to God that it expresses. The concept of *objective* guilt, i.e., an offense to the divine order for which atonement must be demanded, rests on a highly questionable transfer of the juristic order to God, subjecting him to a superimposed law, a law to which every possible cosmic world-order would be subject.

It is also in this sense that we can understand the concept of *punishment,* which is closely linked to the concept of guilt. Punishment cannot consist in a supposed link between sin and the various forms of suffering—all for the purpose of restoring divinely ordained justice—for suffering results from all the processes of nature, which are indifferent to good and evil. To the extent that suffering is caused by a breakdown of psychological and social health as the result of sin, it is a *result* and not a *punishment,* as already explained above in connection with the discussion of the moral world-order. What is perceived in the context of inner psychology as the divine reaction to sin is therefore simply the feeling of guilt and the pain that goes with it. That is the only form of punishment, and all other theories of punishment are mythical in nature. But this does demonstrate a *positive* role for punishment. For if punishment consists in the pain of feeling guilt, then it also constitutes the sting of the desire to overcome sin, the beginning of the need for forgiveness, and the desire for strength to attain the good.

LECTURE

Over against the ideal stands that which impedes its realization: the dark, secret, mysterious side of the concept of the image of God, or *sin.* Dogmatics speaks of original sin. The expression is all right in itself, but too wrapped up with thousands of years past, too antique-sounding. It is better to speak, with Kant, of "radical evil," the sin that is bound up with the soul in root and essence.

The matter under consideration here is this: the soul, as it struggles upward, encounters restraints that bind it down. For some time now, though, it has been recognized that this description does not apply to all evil, even though ever since Augustine the church has traced all creatures' suffering and death back to original sin. But it is no longer possible for our contemporary sensibility to do that. Countless limitations are simply the result of the burdens of our nature. We grow out of nature, and even though we grow beyond it, its counterthrust remains. Our development cannot be separated from the satisfaction of our most basic needs. Anyone for whom even bare existence is a constant struggle will never have a soul free for the higher things. Such limitations lead either to spiritual weakness or to an early death. No guilt attaches to this—these are simply things that are given with the circumstances of our existence.

But even in the internal sphere of ethics, there are limitations that are not yet sin as such. Suffering is part of life. Human potential varies. Many have but a little strength, which can only be turned slowly into energy. Others are often led down an unlucky path by the pressures of life and events, and find it difficult to find the way back. We must be clear about all this if we are not to approach sin on false premises, transforming it into a form of torture. All too many people have done just that, thinking that they must utterly reduce themselves to nothing first in order to commend themselves to the theologians—who, incidentally, are far less gracious than God. And besides, if all of this is counted as sin, we then utterly fail to comprehend sin in its full extent.

The realm of real sin is the *will*. Sin consists utterly and completely in opposition to the grace that draws us to itself. It consists in the rebellious defiance that refuses to give God the glory, whether by means of putting itself at the top—which is not without its demonic greatness—or simply through misery and insignificance. Sin is self-denial. It is "hardening oneself against grace," as Bismarck says. And the most disturbing thing about this self-denial is that it is constantly sprouting up in our soul.

The word "sin" is found throughout the entire Bible. The Bible's finest description of sin is as mistrust. Sin is the great theme of the prophetic proclamation of repentance. For the prophets, sin does not consist in cultic offenses, as for the heathen. It rather consists in this, that human beings will not let themselves be rebuked by God. The prophets were essentially concerned with the sin of the people, but the psalms speak more of personal sin, often with shattering self-knowledge. The New Testament, like the Old, knows nothing of the idea of original sin, but it does objectivize sin as the Kingdom of Satan. Jesus grasped sin with a consistently fine nuance. Paul utterly subjectivized it. Later, under the influence of Gnosticism, sin became ever more closely tied to the opposition between spirit and sensuality. And ever since the time of Augustine, Christianity has spoken of the depravity that came by original sin. Kant saw radical evil not as a poison that had come through a historical Fall but rather as a principle that is everywhere locked in battle with the principle of radical good.

Recently, the concept of sin has undergone an enormous trivialization. Aestheticism and fantasy have repressed or enervated the secrets of the will, even though that is where, according to our finest thinkers, the greatest tasks lie before us. Schelling's basic problem was that a pantheism capable of harmoniously resolving everything was finally impossible. He located the origin of evil in the idea of a world which had detached itself from God; this very detachment was the primal deed of sin. Therefore, according to Schelling, we owe our very existence—our separate existence, that is—to original sin.

Not only does the contemporary world have a limited comprehension of the problem, it also manifests a correspondingly limited strength for overcoming sin. We dare not let ourselves be drawn into this superficiality; on the contrary, we continue to affirm the lofty goals of the image of God and triumph over the world. But whoever earnestly affirms these goals must not be deluded about the limitations that stand in the way. The limitations pose no obstacle for those people who reject these goals; but most who reject them do so only out of a knowledge of human weakness. But that too is to recognize sin.

The general idea of universal sinfulness is not exclusively Christian. It is found wherever the highest spiritual goals are kept in view: in Plato, Neoplatonism, Stoicism, and Brahmanism. Even Schopenhauer, in his own venomous fashion, came to recognize the miserable state of the human race, as long as he still desired such goals. Evil is thus recognized as evil in general, but only religion seeks the roots of evil in the will that turns against God. On non-Christian soil, evil is sensuality: for Neoplatonism, it is the imprisonment of spirit in matter; for Buddhism, it is desire; for Nietzsche it is the masses and their herd instinct. But if sin is not recognized as sin, however, it all becomes cliché, whether on Christian soil or not. The failure to recognize sin frequently results in religious platitudes, although there is no shortage of platitudinous treatments of sin, either. And there is much to make fun of here: original sin is the theologians' dearest treasure.

How are we to formulate this concept? Like all the ones that have gone before, it is a *purely religious* and *Christian-religious* concept. Furthermore, it is to be understood in terms of faith as a whole. Whoever does not recognize the holiness of God, whoever sees the world as confusion and accident, a mere hoax or a fantastic arcanum of beauty—in him the Christian concept of sin cannot take root. It can take root and grow only in a context thoroughly saturated by the Christian world of ideas. For sin is personal opposition to the God who personally seeks us. The concept of sin is completely and utterly bound to the theistic-personalistic concept of God. It is not a scientific or philosophical concept. Christian knowledge of sin presupposes affirmation of the divine will relative to the creature. This has practical significance, for the attempt is frequently made to reverse the sequence, as though someone could be prepared for Christianity by being brought to a knowledge of sin. This is done in the hope that enough still remains of the general awareness of God for at least the feeling of imperfection to be salvaged. This, in turn, is supposed to evoke an awareness of the need for redemption, so that salvation can then be sought in Christianity. So long as the theistic knowledge of God dominated, this approach might have been justified. But this presupposition is no longer with us, and this pre-Christian awareness of sin is an avenue no longer open. Neither can we make use of the general existence of wretchedness in itself—even though awareness of this still remains.

The old dogmatics knew very well why it sought to intensify the natural feeling of sin through a confrontation with the Christian world. The feeling of sin it had in mind arises first through a believing affirmation of the Christian concept of God. But the old dogmatics erred in all other respects, distinguishing the God of law from the God of grace and thereby introducing a division into the Christian concept of God. What is the sense of a devastating divine law if we can see that God's will also demands trust and love from us—trust and love that must be directed to the God of grace? When failure to trust and refusal to love are understood as sin, it is only because God appears to us as love. And this is the real essence of sin: We cannot love and trust, because part of us holds back! Even though this division within the divine essence may not appear impossible from a psychological point of view, it is vexatious, coarse, and intrinsically tactless. Furthermore, it is a blueprint for abstraction. God used to be thus, and now he is thus. There is something artificial and forced about this. This confirms the proposition that the Christian concept of sin can be sustained only in the context of the complete concept of God, that is, through recognition of God as holy love. We have one God, who loves because he is holy, and is holy because he loves.

This makes it altogether clear that it is not the individual deed that is decisive, but the *disposition*—even where there is no deed. A turn to the disposition implies a turn to the creature. Insofar as the self draws itself away from God, it turns to itself, whether on a large or a small scale. From thence comes egoism. The bond of love ceases to endure. In its intercourse with others the human self is left to the common instinct of sympathy, and in other matters lets people do as they will. Hence the real essence of sin is godlessness—that is, to be free of God. The motivating force behind the *disposition* is also the totality. For sin is no single action, but a state of affairs. Whoever breaks the law of God at a single point, breaks the entire law. Kant put it most sharply: The deed does no more than betray the disposition. The seriousness and depth of the Christian concept of sin are based on this observation.

Naturally, as a practical matter, absolute evil is rarely experienced as a totality. Experience is much more likely to manifest a struggle between the two principles. The reason that the deed nevertheless manifests the whole is that each of these two principles seeks the whole self. The totality of good or evil lies in the principle, not the effect. Hence the deed is not something individual, for the whole lies behind it. It is the devil who grasps the little finger but wants the whole hand. Hence the adage "Once is as good as never" [*Einmal ist keinmal*] does not apply; deeds are representatives of the whole. Hence victory over sin comes not by individual deeds, but by victory over the disposition.

The disposition can express itself in a wide variety of intensities and inclinations toward sin. The equality of sin does not apply here; the church erred in this. Equality of sin pertains only insofar as we all have sinned and fallen short of the glory of God.[4] Apart from that, sin, like the good, is individual, and every attempt to systematize and equalize it is false. The root of evil is present everywhere, to be sure, but the root is differentiated too. We are often not sure ourselves where the true root and essence of radical evil lie. We do not usually feel that vanity, self-justification, repression of others, unfriendliness,

4. See Rom. 3:23.

and the like constitute a conscious denial of God. It is only as the result of self-examination that we come to see the root of radical evil that lurks beneath the cloak of the everyday. Moreover, in addition to acts such as these that we do not immediately perceive as sin, there is a whole range of actions that are performed with a truly evil conscience. In such cases the Russian peasant covers his icon so that it will not see what he is doing, and we too hide from God as long as we wander down these paths.

This, then, is the real act of self-refusal. In its strongest and most direct form it appears as defiance, where the self says to God, Your call means nothing to me: it's my life, and I'll do with it as I please! This conscious opposition, this refusal to be overcome or led by God, can take the form of arrogance: What do you want from me? I do not acknowledge your commands, I dispute your existence! But passive sin is the more frequent and more powerful form. Only few have the desire and the ability to turn away from God actively. An enormous amount of evil takes the form of relative good; but it does not participate in the struggle, and hence has no share in anything noble and great. Neither good nor evil can come of it.

Another problem here is this: If we take evil with such seriousness that no one is excluded from it, then we must ask, How can we understand humankind as having come from God, as bearing the kernel of the divine essence? The answer cannot be: I can prove that we are all implicated in evil, but I have to believe that we come from God. The question of the Whence of sin is always problematic. Jesus felt no need to seek an explanation for sin; but the church, Neoplatonism, and Buddhism all inquired into the matter. The church solved the problem by predicating sin of the protoplasm, coining the term "original sin" or "inherited sin."[5] This "original" sin was not only the first sin, but also the *origin* of the sin of succeeding generations. Sin's persistence was then explained as the result of the continuing effect of evil example, or, with Augustine, Adam was seen as the representative of humankind: all have sinned in and with him. Kant too sought the origin of evil, concluding that sin was an act of freedom.

If sin stems from freedom, it would also seem that sin could be overcome by freedom; and this all the more because self-examination compels us to admit that sin arises in us, not as the result of external influences, but from our inmost essence. Hence the origin of sin is not to be sought in the protoplasm, but in the *individual*. Sin constantly re-creates itself anew from the same original source.

5. See p. 241 n. 1 above.

Its causes must lie in the metaphysical constitution of each individual being.

We are born with a host of natural instincts that are altogether indifferent to ethics. Everyone yields to these instincts at the beginning; it is only in the course of higher development, when personality begins to emerge, that we begin to recognize the prominent role that animality plays in us. It becomes a preoccupation of the higher human self. The spirit awakes to find itself in a circumstance where it is already contaminated [*verfälscht*] by the superior power of the flesh in which it grows. But then, it would seem that sin involves neither freedom nor guilt. And hence we have a problem. There is the characteristic experience of the consciousness of guilt: even though we are not guilty, we still have a feeling that that which is, should not be. We awaken with a captive freedom and the sense that this captivity signifies a weakness of the previously slumbering spirit. This captivity constitutes a certain kind of guilt, even if it is simply one part of our development. This could lead to the conclusion that sin is willed by God—and no objection can be made to that conclusion. Sin is given with nature so that it may shatter our defiance and our self-seeking, loosing us from the obstinacy of our finite "I" so that we may give ourselves over to God, where the human self becomes all it can be through grace.

In Christianity, the concept of sin embraces the concept of *guilt*. If we limit our consideration to immorality, it is difficult to introduce the concept of guilt. Immorality is not guilt, but failure with respect to an impersonal moral law. It is only in relation to the living God that we experience a reaction of judgment and condemnation. The wrath of God turns against the sinner who has set himself against the divine will. In pantheism, the feeling of guilt makes no sense: there the highest form of guilt is to feel guilt toward oneself. A genuine feeling of guilt depends on a personal concept of God.

The varieties of guilt vary widely according to psychological circumstances, depending on whether it is a matter of potential, actual, or social sin. The feeling of guilt is weakest in social sin, since there the impact of others must be taken into account along with the individual; for guilt, as a *feeling* of guilt, must always be something purely subjective. Throughout all its stages, from simple indifference through doubt, defiance, and denial, it is the same subjective reflex of muddied communion with God. It is always something that takes place entirely within the soul.

Dogmatics, however, also recognizes the existence of such a thing as *objective* guilt. According to the dogmatic view, God is the inner essence of the moral world-order, and the presence of sin within this order constitutes an act of destruction. Hence, if the sinner feels no guilt, the violation of the world-order requires expiation. The concept of Christ's substitutionary atonement and punitive suffering rests on this doctrine. But how does this idea relate to the concept of God? Are we able to know what constitutes a necessity for God? What more do we know than what our conscience tells us? Juristic concepts cannot be transferred to God; and even if they could, we could still know nothing about it. We know only that which is inside us, namely, the subjective feeling of guilt as something caused by God: a sense of our separation from him, and an awareness that our relationship with him can be restored only through a voluntary admission of our sin, just as in the story of the prodigal son.[6] But nothing objective can be constructed on this foundation.

The last point to be made is this: the feeling of guilt is never simply a matter of the distance between the soul and God. We find ourselves either trivialized or deeply shattered; and no alternative remains except conversion. Hence the feeling of guilt is the one punishment for which it is necessary to distinguish clearly between the punishment and the consequences. It is self-evident that the latter are simply given with evil. The positive side of the matter is that the feeling of guilt also constitutes the sting of the desire for healing. Hence the seeds of conversion are already present in it. This brings us full circle in our discussion of the concept of original sin.

§23. The Religious Vision of History: The Struggle between the Good and Evil Principles in the History of the Human Race[1]

DICTATION

1. The concept of a *religious vision of history as a whole,* where history takes the form of a struggle between flesh and spirit, follows from the foregoing concepts of the image of God and sin. In this struggle, we recognize spirit not merely as the principle of human will, but also as the principle of a living revelation of God; and we believe that this edifying and redemptive revelation will redeem us

---

6. Luke 15:11-24.
§23. 1. Cf. Immanuel Kant, "Concerning the Conflict of the Good with the Evil Principle for Sovereignty over Man," in *Religion within the Limits of Reason Alone,* trans. Theodore M. Greene and Hoyt M. Hudson (New York: Harper & Row, 1960), Book II, pp. 50–78.

from this struggle. And furthermore, inasmuch as we believe this, our entire religious vision of history is transformed into a belief that redemption will be gradually effected in Christianity—redemption from the struggle between flesh and spirit, a struggle that is bound to the essence of being human. It is a belief that salvation will ultimately fill the soul, and it can therefore be described as a faith in salvation history [*Heilsgeschichte*].

Such an interpretation of human history, like the ethical-religious philosophy of history it implies, was present already in prophetic monotheism. The prophets looked forward to the time when all humankind would recognize and worship the one holy God; and they saw Israel cast in the role of the chosen servant of God, entrusted with his proclamation. In Jewish teaching, this belief about history extended all the way from the protoplasm of the beginning down to the apocalyptic Kingdom of God. Jesus' proclamation was concerned with the Kingdom of God as the goal of history; he saw it as the fulfillment of the dominion of God's will. Pauline teaching had the largest vision of history, beginning with the sinlessness of the protoplasm and extending through the Fall and death to Christ's redemption, his reign at the end of days and beyond, finally culminating in the heavenly kingdom. The church's doctrine was erected on this Pauline foundation; its salvation history consisted in the great myth of the blessed state of original perfection, the Fall into sin that brought suffering and death into the world, Christ's redemption and founding of the church, the identification of the church with the Kingdom of God, Christ's return at the end, the Last Judgment, and finally the consignment of souls to heaven, hell, and purgatory.— Protestant dogmatics corrected this myth only with respect to purgatory and the identification of the church with the Kingdom of God. Today, of course, this is all taken more as mythical and symbolic expression of faith's concept of the divine *cultivation and edification* of humankind; we recognize the Christian knowledge of God as the highest redemptive power, even though we must await its consummation in life after death.

2. This religious interpretation of history is a purely religious concept of faith. Empirical history knows nothing of the beginning or ending of the whole; all that we see is a comparatively small part of it, and that not very well. Only faith can relate to the overall origin, meaning, and end of the whole. Moreover, empirical history—including the history of religions—has no bearing on the inner depths of the soul. These depths shun all specific knowledge and representation, while empirical history remains concerned with individual

representation and cultural creation, which must always cling to that which is expressible. And even when historiography does attempt to combine its several areas of research into a unified history of the development of spirit, it still cannot touch the inner realm of personal life, which is the only place where freedom, evil, a good disposition, guilt-consciousness, and redemption alike are all to be found.

Nevertheless, the real essence and meaning of history lie in these most internal and personal of experiences. Hence history too is accessible only to the religious-ethical depths of the self; and only faith can interpret history. Notwithstanding this, however, religious faith must hold *feeling* and *empirical history* close together; and faith can serve to remind empirical history that the ethical-religious struggle against merely natural existence is history's dominant theme. For its part, empirical historical research shows us the ways in which ethical-religious powers have, at various times, burst forth, grown, and insinuated themselves into the whole of history. This is of particular significance in the interpretation of Christianity, whose historical emergence and diffusion constitute a subject for empirical historical research, and yet whose meaning and significance constitute a subject for faith.

3. An important question concerning religious faith and history is whether the struggle between flesh and spirit in the context of redemption is a matter of *continuous progress,* and whether empirical history must therefore finally issue in a unified and redeemed humankind that believes in Christ. That would be like the millennium: the fulfillment of the Kingdom of God on earth, a unified and relatively complete final conclusion. In fact, this is the vision that hovered before the prophets and Jesus, just as it did in apostolic belief. Later on, the church thought only in terms of its own universal triumph and the ultimate unity of humankind in faith. Today the Christian Socialists have revived the idea, conceiving a sort of Kingdom of God on earth, where the material orders of life will correspond to the demands of morality and religion.

This idea of a continuous progress that will gather everything together is undergirded by our immediate historical knowledge, insofar as the historical development of the Mediterranean peoples constituted a connected unity that flowed into Christianity. On the basis of this knowledge, combined with the boldest expectation for the improvement of the organizational and material foundations of the ethical religious life, it became quite conceivable that European culture and Christianity would spread. But, on the other hand, the sum total of European culture that is dominated by Christianity constitutes only a tiny part of all history. The question whether there will be a final religious and cultural unity cannot yet be answered. Belief in a continuing progress that will unify everything is contradicted by the exhaustion and collapse that can and does overpower entire cultures, as well as by the new struggles and adversities that constantly emerge from every new situation. It is also difficult to envision the final state of the human race as one of consummate unity on earth when there are such great external threats to the continued existence of life on the planet. But also from a purely religious standpoint, such continuous progress cannot be required, since faith is directed toward further becoming in the beyond, and not to any earthly goal.

Under these circumstances, it is difficult to anticipate a universal and continuously advancing progress. We must rather await new outbreaks of the battle on new fronts. Earthly life is, and remains, a struggle. Faith gives assurance only that the battle between flesh and spirit can be overcome at every point in history through the religious powers that are then available; hence history has the capacity to break through to the eternal at every point. Therefore, in the Christian faith and through its certainty of God, we possess the strongest power to break through to the eternal; and, on that basis, we can ethicize the struggles of life whenever possible, with a will capable of making sacrifices.

LECTURE

The ideas we have previously considered now lead to an interpretation of history that differs from the empirical approach. At its deepest level, history now appears in terms of the *spirit's struggle with the flesh*. The power of nature continually casts new streams of history upward like a fountain; except that we do not see it as a merely natural process, but rather as the upward struggle of spirit against matter, enabled by the self-communication of God. For the struggling spirit both comes from God and returns to God. God himself stirs up and sets the battle in motion, and, in so doing, draws spirit upwards.

That is easy to say, but difficult to do. In the face of the thousand-fold sorrows and desires of the multitude, it is no easy thing to affirm that no process of nature is at work in all this confusion, that the real process takes place in the depths of all beings that possess a soul capable of being led upward. And this doubt arises not only in connection with the racial question—no matter how much each race may fancy that it is the finest and most spiritual. No, one need only walk down the street and look at the people's faces!

And yet we must affirm this belief. And if we are overwhelmed by the sheer mass of humanity, then we must go down into our own soul. There, this picture of confusion will change. We will be inclined to believe that just as it is in me, so must it be the same in others. Naturally, our hope remains a belief; and whether and where it will prove true, no one can say. It is also a belief that is frequently at odds with the facts. But it is also a belief shared by the entire Bible, no matter how many changes it may have undergone throughout the history of Christianity.

The Old Testament hoped for a kingdom of messianic glory which would be a kingdom of all peoples. Israel, the servant of Yahweh, purified through suffering, would, as Yahweh's prophet, gather all peoples together for him. For Jesus it was the purely ethical idea of an already standing Kingdom of God. Paul wanted to unify the whole of humankind in the Christian community. The Lord will not return until all are gathered! But when the Lord returns, he will set up the Kingdom of Christ on earth—something different from the Kingdom of God that Jesus had in mind—and reign until the end of time, when the Son will put all things back in the hands of the Father.[2]—For Catholicism, the end of all earthly things consists in the dominion of the church, which *is* the Kingdom of Christ. In order to realize this dominion fully, heaven and hell are added to it. And until that dominion is realized, the souls of the dead remain in purgatory, where a step-by-step process of purification takes place. Protestant dogmatics did not change these things, but only internalized them. Only purgatory and the identification of the church with the Kingdom of Christ were dropped. These teachings were all mythical forms of the grand and bold thought that history constitutes the upward movement of spirit.

Now the question arises: What is the relationship between this purely religious concept and *empirical historical research?* What the latter busies itself with is not the true kernel of history: the liberation and growth of the soul. Empirical historiography remains within its rights in its own field, but the tasks it sets for itself concern only externalities of the real process. The fates of all great peoples are important, all the battles and wars are important, but they do not touch at all upon the ultimate reality of the historical process. Even

2. See 1 Cor. 15:22-24.

the history of culture and of art do not touch upon it. They are concerned with those who write poetry and paint pictures, and perhaps here and there a flash of intuition occurs, but nothing more. No one can write a history of the soul. And in comparison with the soul, the powerful drama of a *Faust* or the work of a Phidias remains quite small. Hence historiography is no competition for our faith—and that includes the history of religions. It discusses cults, amulets, and the growth of doctrines; but it knows nothing of the share that the soul has in them. The only meaning the history of religions holds for us—like all history—is to provide knowledge of the external side of things, the veil beneath which a much deeper life moves.

In this connection, we encounter the practically significant problem of whether we may construe this interpretation of history—as a battle between spirit and flesh—in terms of a *continuous growth*. If we could, then the goal of the human race would be for the religious idea to penetrate everything; the whole of culture would then be only its corresponding infrastructure. This is, to speak in profane terms, the question of progress. It is purely a matter of faith, even though many have completely separated it from all religion, treating it like a law of nature. "Development" is the great incantation of the age, a word that has worked untold mischief. Nature knows nothing but a never-ending struggle; as far as "development" goes, it is just as likely that we will someday climb back up into the trees from which we once came down. But people who religiously shun all Christianity still enthusiastically believe in continuous forward development when it comes to the law of nature. This sort of law of nature, though, is just a masquerade for a faith, or else it must be something like a god! What is the prophetic belief except a hope for great improvement in the world? Jesus' Kingdom of God was conceived as the realization of the ideal here on earth. Today, Christian socialist groups have appropriated the idea of the Kingdom of God as a belief in the victory of the powers of life, to come through the renewal of human beings in Christian love, combined with present-day technology. This is also where the idea of missions belongs. Faith in progress is therefore a *religious* faith, and wherever it is replaced with a nonreligious substitute—often by genuinely self-sacrificing persons—it still constitutes a profane echo of religious faith.

This faith does not appear to be contrary to fact. There have been permanent advances in history, even if there have been retrogressions as well; there have been progressive refinements and elevated powers. And so we may have the right to hope that, in the great events of the present—such as, for example, the movements that seek to liberate the enslaved proletariat for a higher spiritual life—we can see the directives of the future. But there are weighty objections to this. What we see as a succession of advances is but a part of Western civilization; and we know not whether it is ultimately destined to fail. And besides: Will it be possible to build an enduring union of the entire human race within this civilization? It is also difficult to think of the final situation of humankind in terms of a consummated unity on earth, for the likely conclusion of life on earth will be a massive increase in the difficulty of mere self-preservation.

But religious considerations too make it difficult to affirm such a continuous progress, for faith points to a becoming which extends beyond the earthly goal. Hence our interpretation of history must be such that we overcome our situation in every present moment, in a victory of the spirit. We have the divine call every day, and we can surrender ourselves to it every day, with as much love as is possible for each of us. If there is a greater consummation of faith, then it must lie in the beyond. But if we do here in every moment what the moment asks, then we will have eternity in the moment as well. God alone has responsibility for everything else.

4

The Christian Concept of Redemption

§24. The Place of the Concept of Redemption in the System

DICTATION

1. The three preceding concepts [God, the world, and the soul] imply the concept of the *redemption* of spirit from the limitations of life in the world, accomplished through the divine loving will that both begets itself and draws spirit from the world to itself. The concept of redemption ties the three previous concepts together. Wherever the three previous concepts are developed, they result in the idea of redemption. Hence the idea of redemption is universal among the higher religions, which have progressed to the point of distinguishing both God and humankind from the world in some way. Even the lower stages of religion have something like a concept of redemption in their idea that the gods bestow their assistance on life, as well as the idea of some kind of inner elevation. And even the morality religions [*Moralitätsreligionen*], which stand farthest removed from the idea of redemption, have a germ of the idea of redemption in their eschatology and their doctrine of a moral world-order.

2. But these ideas of redemption are all very *different*. They mirror the differences present in the various *experiences* of the possession of redemption. Hence their different ideas of revelation express the various differences in general religious strength. But

these differences among the various ideas of redemption cannot be reduced to the supposed difference between the religions that have a merely imaginary or postulated redemption and the religions with really effective redemption. Hence Christianity cannot claim that it alone realizes the redemption that elsewhere is merely imagined or postulated.

On the contrary, the Christian idea of redemption *must* express its own unique religious possession. Christianity has a higher or even more definitive redemption in comparison with the redemptive powers of other religions. Just as Christianity's ideas of God, the world, and the soul are given a specifically Christian formulation in terms of Christianity's ethical personalism, so too Christianity's idea of redemption constitutes a specific form of the general idea of redemption. Hence the relationship between Christian and non-Christian ideas of redemption is *not* a relationship between historically realized and unrealized ideas. Christian redemption is a higher, stronger, and specific redemptive power, alongside which other redemptive powers are not mere ideas and postulates, but rather powers suitable to their general spiritual situation and level. They yield to a higher idea of redemption when the domain to which they correspond undergoes internal dissolution or collides with higher powers.

The *characteristic strengths* of Christian redemption consist in the following: *(a)* the new view of the completed personal spirit, according to which the goal consists not in redemption of the individual consciousness or life, but in fulfillment of the person as spirit, in unity with the divine spirit; *(b)* the means by which personal life and love participate in the living God, who is grasped and affirmed in faith, so that neither cultic rites nor speculative thought, but rather the living and growing grasp of God's love, which gives us certainty and joy, effects redemption; *(c)* the emphasis on redemption from sin and guilt as the most important moment, in which the certainty of God's love grasps us and becomes, above all else, certainty in God's readiness to forgive sin; *(d)* the closely related certainty in the historical forces that produce this certainty in God, forces which are believed to reveal the highest life and love—excluding self-redemption by contemplation or thought; and *(e)* the ethical impact of redemption, which actively saturates and cultivates the world—the world which comes from God and is going back to God—with the interiority and love of the Christian life, but without making this cultivation of the world its final goal.

3. Following the method we have used thus far, redemption is portrayed as the *present experience of union with God* which occurs

ever anew in the inner experience of each Christian. It is necessary, therefore, to analyze the essence and basic components of this contemporary experience. This experience is an interaction between God and the soul, and it is also an ever new work of God himself. Hence it can only be described on the basis of the experience of this divine work.

These are the main components, then, of the idea of redemption: *(a)* redemption from world-weariness [*Weltleid*][1] through the assurance of God's love and wisdom; *(b)* redemption from the consciousness of guilt, through the assurance of God's grace and the forgiveness of sin; *(c)* redemption from ethical and religious impotence, through the elimination of separation from God, and through the realization of divine strength for living; and *(d)* the objective impetus behind this inner interaction and relation, which proceeds from Jesus and the Christian community and provides both a foundation and assurance. Prior to all this, however, must come a consideration of the general problem of the concept of redemption, namely, its relationship to the concept of *development*—a concept that utterly dominates the modern worldview, just as it has already dominated our entire discussion up to this point.

4. Arranging the issues in this way, of course, *reverses* the old dogmatic order, an order which continued to influence even Schleiermacher's discussion. But this reversal, as demonstrated already in Part One, is necessarily implied by the modern method of *Glaubenslehre,* which is a description of personal religious experience, not an explication of authoritative dogmas and biblically revealed doctrines. Hence the present and yet always new experience of redemption naturally stands at the center of the doctrine, while historical matters come under consideration only insofar as they condition and enter into contemporary life. But to be sure, this changed order is required not only by these merely formal grounds, but also by the material ground of the untenability of the orthodox doctrine of redemption, which was constructed under the protection of biblical authority—i.e., the doctrine of a unique, unrepeatable [*einmalig*] act of redemption accomplished by Jesus' sacrificial suffering, which is in turn appropriated by the individual soul in faith. It is untenable for reasons drawn from contemporary ethical sensibility and historical thinking, which, just like modern metaphysics, insist on the continuity of world-processes.

1. Sarah Coakley plausibly suggests "existential anguish" as a translation for *Weltleid,* mentioning that Troeltsch may be close to Hegel's notion of "alienation." See her *Christ Without Absolutes* (Oxford: Clarendon Press, 1988), p. 88 n.21.

Redemption cannot, therefore, be a simple, unrepeatable interruption of the world-order at a single point, no more than sin can be a ruinous event, unwilled by God, that occurred in the world. Rather, like sin, redemption must be willed within the divine life and must be realized in continuity with the development of the world. It cannot be an unrepeatable miracle that takes place at one and only one place and point in time, needing only to be appropriated by later generations. It must rather be *the upraising of the divine spirit in human history as a whole.* As Christian redemption, it signifies the consummation of redemptive powers. It is the living nexus of exalted and trustworthy religious power that proceeds from Jesus—the new birth that is the mark of Christ and the epitome of the Kingdom of God. All the remaining differences from the old orthodox dogma of redemption are based on these. Redemption cannot be the result of a single human being's impact on God, nor the diversion and reconciliation of the divine wrath through substitutionary suffering, nor an unrepeatable revelation and communication of authoritative knowledge, nor the founding of a redemptive cultic institution. It must rather be the inner nexus of an inner process of interaction that comes from the central exaltation of life in Christ—a process that must constantly be repeated anew.

5. Hence both reasons for dropping the old ordering of the topic are closely related. Since the old approach of concentrating all divine action into a single anthropomorphic, supernatural deed has been replaced by the vision of God's constant, living, creative working of redemption, God's activity must be understood first in terms of its universal and extensive effect, and above all in terms of contemporary inner experience. Theology therefore describes redemption as the present experience of liberation and rebirth; but in this experience it sees the continuing power of Jesus both in the present and in the living nexus that proceeds from him.

6. Throughout the Bible and the history of dogma, the concept of redemption has had a very flexible and malleable development. For the prophets, redemption is the return from the exile, the reestablishment of the Davidic kingdom, and the messianic-apocalyptic kingdom, all of which will justify before the whole world the confidence of the pious in God. For Jesus it is the coming of the complete ethical dominion of the Kingdom of God, and the joyful fulfillment of the present messianic age. For the early community and for Paul, redemption is twofold: in the *past* atoning death of the Messiah, and in the *future* return of Christ. Later on, however, the future form of redemption completely receded into the background, becoming the

doctrine of life after death, which made it no longer a part of redemption. Hence the entire emphasis fell on the redemption that took place in the past—the saving deed of Christ.

Correspondingly, Catholicism views redemption as the founding of the church and its provision with the redemptive sacramental means of grace. In Protestantism, redemption is the establishment of the possibility of justification through the substitutionary suffering of Christ and the soul's appropriation of this reconciliation through faith in Christ's saving deed. In neo-Protestantism, the idea of redemption has receded into the background, and its place has been taken by the idea of the example [of Jesus] as that which strengthens or authorizes Christian morality. Schleiermacher reemphasized the idea of redemption and restored it to its preeminent position.[2] For him, "redemption" meant the elevated powers that proceed from Jesus, and our involvement in a living continuity with Christ. For the Hegelians, redemption signified the triumph over finiteness achieved through the principle of God-human-ness [*Gottmenschheit*] that is represented, embodied, and effected in Christ. The Ritschlian school prefers the terms "justification" and "reconciliation," understanding redemption essentially as the assurance of the forgiveness of sins, received through the personality of Jesus, which attests to the grace of God.

With so many different and changing formulations of the concept of redemption, the possibility and freedom of individually different formulations is beyond question; and given the changes in the entire cultural situation that have taken place since the older dogmas of the church were formulated, different formulations are now a necessity. There are, then, three characteristics that contemporary formulations of the concept will share: *(a)* a distancing from the concept of the church and sacraments, and a corresponding emphasis on the ethical and personal impact of Jesus; *(b)* a distancing from the death of Jesus as a world-transforming event, and a corresponding emphasis on Jesus' life and activity; and *(c)* a move away from mere appropriation of a finished deed of salvation toward the present inner life of faith, so that redemption basically consists in nothing more than the planting and development of faith.

---

2. "Christianity . . . is essentially distinguished . . . by the fact that in it everything is related to the redemption accomplished by Jesus of Nazareth," Friedrich Schleiermacher, *The Christian Faith* (1830), trans. H. R. Mackintosh and J. S. Stewart (Edinburgh: T. & T. Clark, 1928), p. 52.

§25. Development and Redemption

DICTATION

1. The church focused on two key events in the history of the world: the world's ruination in the Fall, and its miraculous restoration in the event of redemption. In opposition to this view, modern thinkers, for a variety of reasons drawn from the natural sciences, the philosophy of history, and metaphysics, have brought everything under the *concept of development*. The life and spirit planted by God in the creature is to be developed, through the creature's struggle and labor, into the creature's own possession in God. This modern view is closer to doctrines that have been influenced by Neoplatonism or Aristotelianism than it is to church doctrine, although there is something similar to it in Paul's teaching. But nowhere in church doctrine has the concept of development been set forth with complete purity and consistency; this took place first under the influence of modern speculation.

2. But now the question is whether the concept of development leaves *any* room for the concept of redemption. Redemption is automatically excluded from any purely deterministic and purely optimistic version of the concept of development, as in the case of Leibniz and his followers, and many other thinkers as well. Where no breaks occur in development, when there is no place where the limitations of merely natural existence are recognized as such and overcome by breaking with them, there will be no room for belief in redemption. But where the original position of the creature in nature also includes the bane of limitation, unfreedom, suffering, and sin, and where higher development out of nature into the kingdom of the divine spirit can come only through an *act of freedom*, there the concept of redemption will necessarily find a place in the concept of development. Hence, redemption *is* development, a development that comes only in breaks and leaps, for its real meaning lies in the struggle and free action that breaks out of bondage to nature. But the potential for sin and evil also lies in this freedom at the same time. Sin and redemption, therefore, do not contradict but *fulfill* the underlying concept of development.

3. If we unite development and redemption in terms of the concept of freedom, we must inquire further into the relationship between freedom and redemption, or between freedom and grace. Freedom seems to contradict the character of redemption; it refers everything back to spontaneous human activity, while redemption

refers everything back to the action of God. This contradiction can be removed by a *proper understanding* of the concept of freedom. Freedom is the *emanation of divine power* in the creature; freedom acknowledges this divine power as that which alone is good and true; freedom is surrender to the truths and living powers that grasp us— powers to which we can only submit, truths which are acknowledged necessities. Freedom is the emanation of divine necessity, but at the same time it is a recognition and surrender that breaks with all merely natural determination. Freedom is thus an ever greater growing-into-God[1] until complete unity with the divine will is attained. The authentic deed of the subject consists merely in this breaking away and surrender, but this too is a truly creative act.

4. This concept of freedom, which alludes to the separation and reunion of natural and spiritual necessity—of that which must be and that which ought to be[2]—points to a *tension* in the world and, ultimately, in God. These two opposing movements must belong to the world's constitution from the very beginning; they do not recognize one another in indifference; they separate and ultimately reunite only through struggle and effort. They unite not in indifference, but in the dominion of spirit over nature. This tension, however, accompanies the fundamental act of creation itself, God's *self-transformation* in both *nature* and *creature*. Correspondingly, the world-process consists in the *transformation* of nature and creature *back into spirit* by means of redemption. Insofar as this process of creation consists in God's own self-subjection to the sufferings of finitude, the redemption of the creature is simultaneously God's own redemption as well.

§26. Redemption from Sin, Guilt, and Moral Impotence

a. Redemption from World-Weariness and Evil

DICTATION

1. Christian redemption, in its first and broadest sense, is—like any redemption—redemption from evil. The deepest root of the awareness of evil is the consciousness of guilt, and the ethical and religious impotence that goes along with it. But it would be incorrect to think of redemption in the broadest sense as redemption from

---

1. "Ein Immer-mehr-Hineinwachsen in Gott."
2. Or, "the separation and reunion of the *is* and the *ought*."

guilt. Jesus' preaching of redemption relates to the coming Kingdom of God, and it is only in this general milieu that redemption from guilt begins to enter the picture. Later, eschatological redemption from suffering as a purely internal anticipation forms the general milieu of the Pauline proclamation, in which redemption from guilt and sin are viewed as already accomplished and fulfilled in the work of Jesus. The *eschatological* concept, with its spiritual and religious anticipation of redemption from evil, is therefore one of the basic and essential concepts of Christianity, and it belongs in the forefront of any discussion of redemption.

2. This means that the relationship between *anticipation* on the one hand, and the future *final redemption* on the other, is determinative for the present experience of redemption. But, in correspondence with the essence of purely spiritual and moral religion, the relationship between anticipation and consummation is not simply external and factual, but rather internal and necessary. The coming consummation is only the fulfillment of that which is now already begun and taking place in the complete surrender of the will to God. In the preaching of Jesus, it takes the form of the relationship between the kingdom which is coming and the kingdom which is already present; in Pauline teaching, it is the meaning of the doctrine of the *pneuma* or spirit: The new creation is already begun in the spirit, and the consummation will but manifest the treasures that we already carry in earthen vessels.[1] The inner continuity of this relationship is also emphasized in modern thought insofar as it takes rebirth and new creation as starting points for the development of spirit. But spirit's development already carries the certainty of its consummation within itself, and thereby anticipates blessedness in principle.

3. Redemption from evil and world-weariness [*Weltleid*][2] is already present in this blessedness: positively, insofar as the individual is incorporated in a higher, invisible world of eternal and necessary values; and negatively, insofar as the individual's *attitude* and judgment about the world's evils are altered. Instead of being viewed pessimistically or skeptically, or as suffering that is anxiously to be feared or defiantly to be scorned, the evils of the world are now seen as conditions of life that have been established by God's unsearchable decree; and, given participation in the higher world, these evils become a blessing, that is, they purify the will and stimulate moral

---

1. See 2 Cor. 4:7.
2. Or, "existential anguish" (see p. 262 n.1).

labor. They become a sign that the meaning of life is hidden and lies in the future; they become an impulse to conversion and to the task of earthly meaning, an object of moral labor.

b. Redemption from Guilt

DICTATION

1. The meaning of redemption is not limited to redemption from world-weariness and evil, for the greatest and most oppressive form of evil is sin and guilt. But the most important thing in this connection is the elimination of *guilt:* liberation from feelings of God-forsaken-ness [*Gottesferne*], anxiety, and defiance. It precedes liberation from sin, and it is one of the chief characteristics of Protestant Christianity to insist on this. The individual's disposition must *first* be freed by certainty in the forgiveness of sins, before the long process of liberation from our sinful propensities and errings can get under way. Indeed, it is the new inner strength bestowed by this certainty that begins the process.

2. This certainty in the forgiveness of sins—or the consciousness of justification—is a certainty in *God;* it is, in turn, intrinsically connected with the *overall certainty* that the concept of God offers. Hence this certainty is inherent in Christian religious thought. From the beginning, God appears, through faith, as the one who is essentially forgiving of sins, in just the same way that the creation of the world includes the power of sin from the very beginning. God must not be portrayed in the light of some supposed reconciliation-transaction, as initially ill-disposed toward grace and the forgiveness of sins; rather, the will to forgive sins, just like the will to create, belongs to the essence of God. Just as the knowledge of God is sensed and affirmed by pure faith, so too is the forgiveness of sins sensed and affirmed by pure faith.

c. Redemption from Moral Impotence

DICTATION

1. The proffering of the Christian spiritual world in the Christian knowledge of God, and the offer of forgiveness of sins as the means to participate in this spiritual world, immediately brings forth an *increase in strength,* intrinsically uniting the human will to the divine will, making new and higher achievements possible; it raises up the will that the consciousness of guilt had oppressed and fragmented. Redemption, therefore, is finally healing [*Heilung*], gathering, and

active triumph over sin. Hence it is known in Christian speech as *sanctification* [*Heiligung*]. In Protestant teaching, sanctification is referred back to the changed disposition toward God that results from the consciousness of justification. This active triumph over sin is, to be sure, only the germ and principle of the higher life, and it constantly struggles against the contradictions of mere nature as well as the contradictions of sin. Nevertheless, the one who is reborn continues, by means of confidence in God, to live a life that is qualitatively new in principle.

2. But redemption is not a general increase in *ordinary* strength; it concerns a strength that is directed toward a quite specific goal. Inasmuch as the forgiveness of sins, conceived in the knowledge of God, simultaneously unites the divine and human wills, it enlists the human will in the service of the divine will and its goals. Redemption, therefore, also imparts direction to the image of God and its essential goal. Hence redemption is the genuine goal and realization of the Christian ethos. Redemption is therefore a completely *positive* idea, not the elimination of an obstacle or the restoration of the normal state of affairs; rather, just as sin itself belongs to the plan of the world, so too does the redemption that overcomes sin: it is the means whereby a communion that unites the soul to God and others is developed.

3. Just as the immediate goal of redemption lies in the sphere of practical morality and hence in the formation of a *moral community,* redemption does not work on isolated individuals, but essentially and directly builds community. The will of God, revealed in redemption, is given and mediated in the personality of Jesus and mediated through it. Redemption therefore produces, of itself, a community that acknowledges Jesus. Herein lie the roots of the doctrine of Christian community, or the church, since the word "church" can mean nothing else than the fully free community of the Spirit of Christ.

4. But over and above all this, we must not forget that this mundane, ethical-communitarian goal—redemption as triumph over moral impotence—is not the final goal, but only the next one. Moral redemption or sanctification always remains unfinished in the midst of the struggle and change of earthly life, constantly drawn back into sin and error. It is not the achievement of the final goal, but the conclusive and decisive beginning of the journey—a triumph in its preliminary stages. Redemption always remains a relative achievement. It reaches its conclusion in the *final redemption.* And at this point, the doctrine of redemption passes over into eschatology.

§27. The Character of Redemption as a Whole:
Grace and Rebirth

DICTATION

1. Only when these four ideas are taken together do we have the concept of redemption *as a whole*. But taken together, they bring us to another important concept. Redemption consists in the knowledge of God and its effects, combined with the certainty that we stand, struggling and becoming, in an unfulfilled world that is going on to meet the final consummation. This knowledge, however, is not the automatic result of an immanent dialectic, spontaneously and uniformly produced in each individual by the idea of redemption as faith reflects on the fundamental data of consciousness. That is what rationalism wanted, and still wants. On the contrary: this knowledge is the *fruit of history;* it comes through history, mediated to the individual by the Christian community. It is grasped as a gift of God, a power that seizes and transforms the individual. But, as a historical power, it is not the result of an immanent and necessary dialectic of thought; rather, like all religion, it is a new revelation that grasps us.

Redemption is a *new and creative divine revelation,* which, as such, is vouched to us in the primal history of Christianity, and perceived anew today in every appropriation of Christian thought. The redemptive knowledge of God is a gift of God, the way for which is surely prepared by previous development. But, just like the various junctures within the development itself, this knowledge is a new, creative divine revelation; and as such it continues to bear witness to its contradiction with the merely natural soul. Hence redemption is described as grace in Christian language, signifying above all its character as a gift and an offer that enters into the merely immanent course of events.

2. But to call redemption grace means still more. It signifies that redemption must always be a *gift,* and that it is utterly free of *any* legal or compensatory connotations. It is no reward, but a gift; it can, according to its essence, only be the gift of a free, solicitous revelation of the divine will. It depends only on receptivity and surrender, seeking precisely the humility that will receive the consummation, not from its own human power, but as a gift of God. It is precisely for this reason that the human self is determined by God to receive the consummation as the result of free divine purposiveness. Hence grace represents the *planting of the higher spiritual life from God.* It demands humility and faith, excludes human self-righteousness and merit, and rules out any anthropomorphic righteousness or vengeance

in God. It is the central concept of God's creative, captivating, and consummate love, a love that leads spirits through struggle and labor, through the failure of their own strength and through awareness of the distance that separates them from the divine goal—to the point where they can receive the divine life.

3. This, finally, explains why it is that divine grace can and must also be *forgiveness* of sins without compromising the divine *holiness*. God has ordained both the possibility and the probability of sin for the human race; he has submitted the human race to struggle, hardship, and temptation, all in order to impel it beyond the limitations of self-satisfied worldliness, and also to learn the limits of its power. God can forgive the sin to which he himself has induced the human self and thereby restrained its arrogance—so that the self can, humbly and like a child, give itself to him. The possibility of sin itself is the means whereby humanity is drawn to the true good, which comes from God and not from humanity. Hence sin can be forgiven where it is known in its unholiness, and where that knowledge prompts the reception of true life from God. Under these circumstances, it is self-evident that the *doctrine of atonement by satisfaction* must fall to the wayside. The fact that this doctrine rested on a God-concept of judgment and retribution is sufficient cause for rejection; but besides that, it cannot be reconciled with the modern picture of the historical Christ.

4. The grace of God, then, appears in both our individual and our common life as a radical divine revelation and as the planting of a higher life. And if this is so, then human surrender to that grace comes from a *reversal* and *re-formation* of the direction of one's life, which is known as rebirth and conversion in the language of Christianity. And a new birth it is indeed: triumph over the purely natural soul and its naturally eudaemonistic and individualistic approach to life, triumph over the opposition to God that stems from both the self and sin as a whole. It is an inner revolution, *transposing* life's task to a higher level of necessity and totality, reversing the tendencies of sin; this constitutes the subjective impact and realization of redemption. And because this transformation can take place only in the context of a confident grasp of the true knowledge of God, it can also be described as *faith*. A firm grasp of knowledge, followed by surrender to the will of God while renouncing self-interest, produces religious and moral renewal of itself. In this surrender, faith is the *highest act of freedom.*

Conversion is a necessity in every higher religion; but in Christianity, conversion—the renewal, higher formation, and transformation of the spirit in principle—has become the center of all religious processes. It can come in many forms, from a lengthy inner development to an immediate and total transformation, all according to individual temperament, historical and personal circumstance, and the energy and extent of sin. Strong-willed natures experience conversion as a turning point, a reformation that breaks loose from old relationships, a total revolution; weak and childlike dispositions experience it as a struggle that goes back and forth; heavy sinners experience it as total deliverance; average people, standing under the influence of the Christian spirit, experience it as character development; and those particularly pure persons who are captivated but little by sin experience it as the living out of their deepest, most essential drives. Nevertheless, the concept of conversion cannot be reduced to a simple law of development. It is a development that takes place in the grasp of a divine-creative life.

This view puts the concept of grace and redemption at the center of Christian piety, free from any sense of retribution and judgment, but still filled with captivating and transforming power. Since redemption as we have described it here is a purely ethical-spiritual-personal matter, freed from any remnant of the manipulative magic that intends to control God's grace, the *concept of redemption* is reduced to the *concept of revelation,* while, at the same time, the concept of revelation is construed as *that which proclaims and unlocks life.* This is to acknowledge the relative correctness of the Socinian, Arminian, rationalist, and philosophical critiques of the ecclesiastical concept of redemption. The idea of redemption must be freed from the heteronomous concept of retribution as well as from any miraculous psychological immediacy; it is a work of God and as such is psychologically mediated. Redemption is neither doctrine nor example nor deepening self-knowledge, but a historical revelation and founding by God; its contents do not consist in morality, but in the disclosure and inauguration of a substantial life which captivates thinking, willing, and feeling with its dynamic-personal effects and transmission of spirit. This is how Schleiermacher forever changed the classical rationalistic and philosophical doctrine of redemption.

5. This redemptive knowledge comes to us through history as grace and gift, eliminating any possibility of its being the result of self-activity. For this reason, and because the providence of redemption is referred back exclusively to God, we are led to affirm the monergy[1]

---

1. The opposite of "synergy." *Monergism* was the traditional doctrine that regeneration is the work of the Holy Spirit alone, as opposed to *synergism,* which held that regeneration was cooperative.

of grace; and where this is firmly maintained, the foundation has been laid for predestination. But this means only that we attribute salvation to God alone and not to humankind. Thus predestination does not involve any universal metaphysical *determinism*. Nor may predestination be transformed into a deterministic God-concept in principle; it has to do only with the safeguarding of the concept of grace, the concept that all true goodness and salvation come from God alone and can be grasped only in surrender. Goodness and salvation are neither produced by human beings nor contained in the essential ground of nature. These concepts have already been discussed in connection with the concept of God: the self-positing of God, contrasted with the creature's capacity for only relative creativity.

Here we are concerned in principle only with the concepts of redemption and grace: to maintain their purely divine character without eliminating human freedom in principle. It is for that reason that the two must be brought together as closely as possible. That happens when we acknowledge the purely personal character of religious experience, freed from all magic and miracle, but nevertheless a real experience of new power and not merely the development of something already present in the soul. Since redemption offers the knowledge of God as living and creative power, it can only be admitted and received, not produced. But to admit it and to receive it is a personal act, one which resists the nature of the soul and opens itself to the influx of new creative powers. Redemption is *a divine gift and a human creative act in a single deed*. The divine life can be assimilated only by means of a creative act, a creative act that can follow only from our subordination to an idea that comes to us as necessary, captivating, and dominating. The quantitative balance of human and divine activity—a remnant of Catholic supernaturalism that the Reformers were never able to eliminate—is now to be fully eliminated along with the rest of this supernaturalism. Hence the question whether all people are called and enabled for this creative act remains open.

6. A final and most obscure question that arises in connection with the character of redemption as a whole is the question of whether there is any process that takes place *within God himself,* and, if so, what it is. We can conceive redemption only as a process of human consciousness, and the only distinction we can make between the objective and subjective sides of the concept is the distinction between our conscious experience of redemption (1) as a work of God that takes place within us, and (2) as our own act of surrender.

But if we pursue the former concept—the work of God—further into God himself, and if we consider that, above all, this work of God on us is always accomplished by means of a foundational, creative disclosure of himself, then we will be unable to avoid the conclusion that the redemption of every individual also creates and shapes a *new reality within the divine life itself* every time it happens. How that can be possible in the unity of the divine life eludes human understanding.

This problem takes us beyond not only the concept of redemption but also beyond the religious worldview as a whole. The latter everywhere shows us the living, newly establishing, creative activity of God in the midst of the unity of the divine life. But this only brings us back to the general problem of the concept of God, to which we have already referred. The only thing we can do here is once again to reject pantheism, this time the pantheistic interpretation of redemption, which holds that there may, at most, be something new in the person, but that for God there is never anything but the knowledge of an always identical, never-changing, selfsame world.

§28. The Connection between Redemption and the Historical Personality of Jesus Christ, and the Accomplishment of Redemption Through the Work of the Holy Spirit

DICTATION

1. The concept of redemption leads us back to the concept of revelation; the concept of revelation leads us back to the concept of Christian community and history; and so too the concept of community leads us back to its root: *the historical personality of Jesus.* The personality of Jesus, along with the history that leads us back to him, is the revelation of God. And Jesus brings this about neither as a teacher nor as an example, but as a *personality:* a personality whose religious power and purity, whose knowledge of God and whose proclamation of redemption and the forgiveness of sins creates faith, or completes a faith that is already begun.

Hence the personality of Jesus has an essential and imperishable dogmatic significance, as already shown in Part One.[1] First, it constitutes the authority by which the Christian faith in God is perceived as truth. Second, it communicates the power that flows out of his life,

---

1. See pp. 73–107, and esp. §8, "The Significance of Jesus for Faith."

a power that gives life in God ascendancy over the human disposition. Third, it is the centerpoint of the community that confesses Christian redemption, a community bound together properly only by its confession and veneration of Jesus, who is also the centerpoint of its cultus. Schleiermacher correctly grouped all these dogmatic meanings of Jesus together under the concept of a productive original image.[2] Insofar as this productive original image provides a unique, creative revelation of God, God is in Christ, and we may speak of *God's being in Christ.*

2. Hence a personal relationship to Jesus and the feeling that redemption is to be found in him are part of Christian belief. But this relationship is *mediated by the Christian community;* hence redemption is always contemporary, proceeding from the faith in God that the community mediates to us. We only perceive redemption as something that proceeds from Christ after we reflect on that faith in God and come to recognize that the truth proffered us by the community comes through the image of Christ. Faith in Christ comes first through the contemporary experience of redemption, which is what leads us to venerate Christ's life as the point of departure for divine revelation. This circle, in which each depends on the other, lies in the nature of the matter. Hence it is incorrect to separate the person from the principle, designating the person alone, in opposition to the principle, as the first point of breakthrough. This is what Biedermann did. On the contrary, just as the principle of religious community refers back to Jesus' person and establishes its majesty, so too the impact of his person—i.e., the overwhelming influence of the image of its religious character—establishes the principle. Schleiermacher, Ritschl, and Herrmann all taught this. Thus Herrmann's and Biedermann's teachings are united in a circle. But this circle is also the concrete expression of religious experience; and, in light of the social-psychological conditions necessary for pure ideas and principles to have an impact, it is impossible that the mere idea alone could have an enduring religious impact.

3. Hence it is never solely the historical manifestation of the personality of Jesus that comes under consideration. As a historical manifestation, Christ is a powerful revelation of God, characterized by extraordinary sublimity, mildness, and strength; but he is also a

---

2. "The individual even to-day receives from the picture of Christ, which exists in the community as at once a corporate act and a corporate possession, the impression of the sinless perfection of Jesus . . . ," Friedrich Schleiermacher, *The Christian Faith* (1830), trans. H. R. Mackintosh and J. S. Stewart (Edinburgh: T. & T. Clark, 1928), p. 364.

historically limited individual who partook of the general limitations of his people and his time, as well as the particular limitations of his prophetic calling, i.e., a will that was altogether one-sidedly focused on religious thoughts and on the impending end. This sharply one-sided de-emphasis of intra-worldly goods has often been deeply influential in the history of the Christian ethos. But these historical limitations were shattered by his death, which at the same time freed the spirit contained in this manifestation and enabled it to continue as a progressive principle, changing with the times and their needs. The *Spirit of Christ*[3] retains the content of its historical manifestation and takes all its basic thoughts from there, but also actively continues to develop in the same basic direction and leads into all truth[4], responding to new problems and new life-situations with new disclosures. The Spirit of Christ has set spirit free, that is the meaning of his death. And since this liberation of the spirit is an act of self-sacrifice and soul-power, it signifies that the Spirit of Christ was set free for love and power by the death of Christ. Hence the Spirit of Christ ensouls the community as its driving force; it is the principle of the continuous extension and deepening of the Christian knowledge of God.

This is the profound meaning of the Pauline-Johannine teaching concerning the Spirit. It overcomes the limitations of history and makes Christ present to us; it presents him as a power for growth and becoming, and the simple basic religious ideas of the gospel are set free to live, to be put into practice in new ways. Dogmatics has failed to plumb the depths of this profound Pauline-Johannine teaching for a long time. Schleiermacher attempted it, but he failed to appreciate its chief point: the difference between the temporal, individually limited historical manifestation on the one hand, and the free Spirit on the other. Once this difference is grasped, it resolves the problem of circularity mentioned above. In the Spirit, Christ is a principle that makes divine redemption into an experience—an experience whose source, foothold, and authority derive from the historical manifestation, which, in turn, sets spirit free.

4. This state of affairs implies that the present experience of redemption is linked to the Spirit of the present Christ, and that the connection between the *concept of redemption* and the *historical person of Jesus* is nothing less than *the remaining central concept* of

---

3. "Spirit" is capitalized only when it refers to the Spirit of Christ, the Spirit of the Pauline and Johannine writings, or the Holy Spirit.
4. See John 16:13.

the Christian faith. The whole of the Christian faith effects redemption, and Christ, by means of the Spirit and the community, is present in this faith in its entirety. Hence, in this part of the system, redemption can be described as a purely contemporary experience; here there is no need for any particular reference to history, nor for developing another doctrine of the religious significance of Christ. The singular estimate of the religious significance of the person of Christ precedes all thought about the Christian faith, while, in turn, all individual concepts of the faith proceed from his Spirit and are firmly based in his historical manifestation.

That is why the dogmatic doctrine of the religious significance of Christ should precede—as it has in our exposition—the discussion of the specific concepts of the Christian faith as a whole; it is their presupposition and foundation. It should not be postponed to the doctrine of redemption, as both Schleiermacher and Ritschl did (even though, in other matters, they represent the approach we have taken). But to set the dogmatic doctrine of Christ prior to everything else does not mean that we seek to arouse a religious disposition toward Christ without first having achieved a religious disposition toward the whole of the Christian spirit. For even Part One and its doctrine of Christ are preceded by the basic recognition and principled conviction that Christianity, compared practically and religiously with other religions, is where the central religious truth of life is to be found. The doctrine of Christ as a divine revelation proceeds from a *total position* which is *already decided,* and which constitutes the substructure of the detailed exposition of the redemptive Christian knowledge of God in all its concepts. Hence all that is necessary to describe redemption as the central concept is to refer back to Part One[5] and its discussion of the dogmatic concept of the significance of Christ, and to illustrate its connection to the concept of redemption.

This approach to linking redemption to the person of Christ is starkly different from the approach taken in the old orthodox dogmatics. But it has been a steady undercurrent and point of view practiced in all ecclesiastical and dogmatic religion; and it is the main viewpoint of Pauline-Johannine teaching. The doctrine of the Spirit, of the community, and of the appropriation of the salvation given in Christ, has always accorded with this point of view. On the other hand, the doctrine of a *change brought about in God* by the work of Christ and of the *propitiation of divine wrath* are based on remnants of Jewish reprisal arrangements or naive anthropomorphism, and

5. The text reads "Chapter One," but Part One, esp. §8, is where this is discussed.

especially on the need to explain and justify the death of Christ. The latter could be accomplished only if his death could be viewed as necessary for specific divine purposes, and if its peculiar impact could be linked to Christ's peculiarly superhuman nature. The early community's concept of substitutionary sacrifice, and Paul's concept of the substitutionary suffering of the innocent one—which supported his doctrine of the end of the Law—are remnants of Jewish-legal-retributional argumentation, and they must be eliminated from future development of the Christian sense of grace and redemption. Modern attempts to transform the idea of substitutionary suffering into reconciliation or into a substitutionary experience of guilt either lapse back into the old doctrine, teaching that redemption is essentially a transformation in God, or else they are a disguised version of the doctrine developed here: that redemption consists in the impact of the life and Spirit of Christ on human beings, and in the knowledge of sin and empowerment of religious life which results, so that the impact of Christ on God consists only in intercession and representation, gathering the community together before God in its God-pleasing head.

Hence Jesus' *suffering* and *death* retain a specific meaning. But it is not Paul's meaning of the end of the Law, nor Catholicism's primal image of all substitutionary merit, and certainly not what the central dogma of Protestantism has been. Protestantism in particular is hindered by the central place it has given to the *dogma of satisfaction*. In connection with the doctrine of justification, this dogma, with its understanding of the absolute forgiveness of all sins consisting in a sacrificial death, is contrary to all real ethics. But Christ's death still retains more than the historical significance of merely being a martyr's death. His death signifies *(a)* the essential conflict between the Christian idea and the meaning of the world, i.e., the conflict with natural finite being, a conflict that always returns in one form or another; *(b)* the meaning of suffering as the highest confirmation of, and the most vital means of knowing, the true values and goals of life; *(c)* the loving character of the Christian community, where self-sacrifice and surrender constitute the true pinnacle of God's revelation in Christ; *(d)* the enduring preaching of repentance, wherein Christ's death illustrates that humankind is still everywhere inclined to aggrieve and to attack the divine and hence to violating holiness itself; and *(e)* the meaning of community and sacrifice, where one suffers for the other and takes the other's place, so that everything individual is referred back to a single living interconnectedness.

LECTURE
(synopsis)[6]

The concept of redemption unites all the preceding concepts into a single whole. If the concept of God signifies holy love, if the world is penetrated by this holy love, and if the immeasurable value of the soul holds true, then this all necessarily issues in the postulate that the God of holy love bestows on souls, imprisoned in the world, the strength to overcome the world and sin, all in communion with God; and this is the essence of redemption. We need therefore only to make explicit what is already implicit in the other concepts.

The first thing about the concept of redemption is that Christian redemption is not the only kind there is. Every religion that is aware of the intrinsic difference between God and the world has a belief in redemption. Buddhism is utterly consumed by it. But even the most legalistic religion of all, Judaism, is a religion of redemption when it comes to belief in its Messiah. Islam locates redemption in the hereafter, where the suffering of the righteous will be overcome with the blessedness of heaven. The church knew that redemption was preached apart from Christianity, but it said: There is illusion, here is truth. That is all very easy to say in dogmatics, but how much longer can it still be affirmed in the face of reality? Here in Christianity redemption is supposed to be real, but over there, for good and pious Buddhists, it is supposed to be a delusion? And do our nation-states, with their armored ships and death machines, constitute good examples of realized Christian redemption? Even thoughtful Mohammedans think us dreadfully greedy and power-hungry. Indians are extraordinarily bewildered when they travel through the lands of Christian love: everywhere they go they find bolted doors, and soldiers and police warn them to beware of swindlers! The exact opposite of the doctrine of redemption that has been preached to them!

Hence it is impossible to differentiate Christian redemption from other forms on the basis of the idea of realized redemption alone. We cannot violate anyone just in order to make it easier to build our dogmatic systems. So it is not redemption as such, but the particular content of the Christian concept of redemption, that concerns us here. When the question is posed in this way it becomes easy to acknowledge that God has also attested to himself outside of Christianity, often quite magnificently. We can say that the Christian religion is superior to other religions: by virtue of the pure, deep power

6. See p. 5 n. 2.

of its interiority that overcomes the world and suffering; by virtue of
its certainty in the divine grace that forgives sins; by virtue of its goal
of fulfilling the personal spirit; and by virtue of the supreme activity
of the mind that it strengthens. But it is not superior by virtue of
reality. Instead: God's nurturing expresses itself in all humankind,
and wherever faith in redemption is pure, there is redemption.

That is, to be sure, a profound departure from the old dogmatics,
which could never find anything positive to say about non-Christian
redemption. The difference rests on the following: The old dogmatics
taught that there had been a universal contamination as the result of
the one-time guilt of the protoplasm; this contamination, in turn, was
eliminated by a one-time act of redemption: the substitutionary
sufferings of Christ. Christ was the Second Adam. Just as the first
Adam brought sin down upon the whole human race, the second
Adam removed it.[7] According to this view, redemption is a metaphysical interaction between God and the Messiah. The individual
soul's redemption consists in its appropriation of the merit of Christ,
either by subjective faith or through participation in the sacraments
that lie ready in the church as a form of capital for the salvation of
the soul. This sacramental infusion of grace was overthrown, in
principle, by the Reformation; where the sacrament was retained, it
was construed as the *verbum visible* [visible word]. Yet the Reformation retained the basic belief that redemption is effected by means
of the substitutionary, atoning death of Christ; hence the church
remained the depository of salvation. The consequence of this doctrine, of course, is to allow no redemption outside Christianity and
the church, since apart from them the necessary prerequisite of
insight into the objective facts of salvation is lacking.

We must, for a moment, suspend all our doubts and objections to
the old dogmatic doctrine of redemption, in order to appreciate its
monumental energy. God did not spare his own Son:[8] therein lie both
the fullness of divine grace and the depths of the consciousness of
sin! This doctrine has its greatness! It finds majestic expression in the
works of a Bach and the hymns of a Luther. The Catholic Mass holds
power for us even today. Poetically and musically, these things remain
with us still; but as soon as we subject them to thought, the bottom
drops out. We are no longer capable of empathizing with the idea of
a substitutionary atoning death. We are too aware of the continuity
and unity of the whole world-process to think in that way any longer.

7. See Rom. 5:12-18.
8. See Rom. 8:32.

And there are also ethical objections to the suffering of an innocent person, and historical-biblical objections related to the content of Jesus' proclamation, which never bound the forgiveness of sins to any sacrificial atonement, and certainly not to a substitutionary atonement. The most serious objection, finally, is the religious one: the whole construction of this doctrine of redemption presupposes a juristic idea of God, which, in addition to being a monstrous anthropomorphism, is also plagued by the internal contradiction of requiring God to make satisfaction to himself in the form of a redeeming death.

But this still does not say it all. The unavoidable consequence of this doctrine of a substitutionary atoning death would really be to require the redemption of all. But church dogmatics has not drawn this conclusion. Instead, the central belief in forgiving grace has been encumbered with the prerequisite of belief in the atoning death; and the result is the problem of the relationship between the human and divine components in the redemption of the individual soul, a question which also relativizes the doctrine of redemption by an atoning death. It was from this question that the endless calculations of both the pre- and post-Reformation eras arose. All such calculations rest on a superficial conception—unacceptable to modern religious sensibility—of the relationship between freedom and grace. Indeed, the inner tension between freedom and grace dissolves in religious experience.

Countless numbers of people, therefore, now can accept little of the Christian concept of redemption. But if the idea of rebirth were discarded, it would mean the end of Christianity. Some echoes of Christianity might still be heard in some voices, but there would be no Christianity as a whole. It must be possible to surrender the old dogma and to formulate a new version.

The Christian concept of redemption has had very different interpretations over time. The Old Testament believed in a this-worldly but future redemption, a "rest that awaits the people of God,"[9] a new Israel. This belief was subsequently extended to include a more distant future, a kingdom of righteousness in which the rights of the poor and oppressed would be recognized. This same form of redemption lives in the preaching of Jesus: the kingdom where the will of the heavenly father is done, where the soul, with a childlike trust in God, can see the kingdom of love. Instead of the prophets' severity, an atmosphere of joy and jubilation surrounds Jesus' procla-

9. See Heb. 4:9.

mation. He lives in anticipation of the coming Kingdom; but it remains a Kingdom that is coming. Jesus did not describe his activity as the completion of redemption. He did not say, I shall gain salvation for you through my death, but only: "The Kingdom of God is at hand." He did not, in his simplicity and naiveté, fill in the details.

With Paul it was different. For him and his generation, the question was: Why did Jesus have to suffer? How can we interpret his death as salvation? It is no longer the Jesus in the flesh that concerns Paul, but the risen Jesus: Jesus' death constitutes redemption. His death signifies atonement and triumph over the kingdom of the demons. Hence redemption becomes an event in the past; but here too it was also coming, now in the return of Christ. The primitive community lived with a twofold orientation: We have been purchased at a high price,[10] and yet everything is just a down payment on what is to come.

The eschatological idea receded into the background as the church continued to develop; Jesus' kingdom did not come. The church took the place of the kingdom, with the result that more and more emphasis fell on the past act of redemption. For Catholicism, it was not the death of Jesus that played the major role, but his founding of the Church.[11] Jesus is the Church's high priest, present in it to this day, ruling it through the Pope and his priests. The Church is the great divine miracle for the redemption of humankind. Protestantism rejected this deification of the Church; hence for Protestantism redemption consisted only in the atoning death of Jesus. This full-scale identification of redemption with an atoning death was shattered by the age of the Enlightenment, which took offense at the idea of any blessedness that had to come through Jesus' death, preferring instead to hold up the life of Jesus as an example. The result was an impoverishment of Christian thought.

The doctrine of redemption through a higher power that flows into us returned only with Schleiermacher. According to him, redemption proceeds from a connection with Jesus, but in the sense of transmitting his life and power: Redemption is gaining certainty in God with reference to the person of Jesus. These ideas persist in the Ritschlian school and Herrmann. Hegel offered still another version. For him, it was the idea of the essential unity of God and the human in Jesus that was the key. This fusion of the divine and the finite that took place in Jesus continues to be effective today, according to

10. See 1 Cor. 6:20.
11. "Church" is capitalized only when it is used in this particular sense.

Hegel, consuming the finite within us. So we see that the idea of redemption has changed throughout the history of Christianity, giving us the right to conceive it for our own time in our own way.

We connect with Schleiermacher here: Redemption is simply faith; it is the gaining of certainty in God through the impact of the image of Christ. It is not a divine intervention that took place once for all time, but always a newly achieved, purely inward interaction between God and the soul.[12] God speaks to the soul what no one else can hear! There is no need for divine metaphysical intervention, no need to appropriate Christ's merit; rather: God is, in principle, in his inmost essence, inclined toward grace. Everything simply depends on this, that we take heart, we take courage from his forgiving love. We must therefore describe the Christian concept of redemption according to the same method that we have applied to all the concepts of our *Glaubenslehre:* interpretation of the pious consciousness, not authoritative dogma.

This results in the following: (1) the concept of redemption becomes disassociated from the church, which now only mediates the influence of Christ; (2) the meaning of Jesus becomes disassociated from an atoning death; (3) the meaning of the appropriation of redemption is transformed, for we now have no capital to draw upon, nothing objectively given, only the need to surrender before the act of God that proves itself anew to each believer.—

Our exposition of the concept of redemption requires only a synopsis of what has already been said at other points. A knowledge of the twofold character of all our reality remains basic. We are simultaneously possessed of the brutality of a violent nature and a developing spiritual life that sets itself against that nature. In contrast to the church's doctrine of a primeval perfection that was subsequently altogether ruined by sin, we recognize suffering, sin, and weakness both as given with the essential conditions of organic life, and as grounded in the creative will of God. We do not have any divine plan that thwarts human freedom; we rather have a human freedom which is in the process of becoming. We do not have any repristination of the original idea of creation, but the fulfillment of the original idea of creation: Redemption is to be understood as the finite soul's elevation from creaturely imprisonment to divine spiritual life.

---

12. "The faith of which we are now speaking . . . [is] a certainty of a faith which is entirely inward. That is to say, it cannot exist in an individual until, through an impression which he has received from Christ, there is found in him a beginning," Schleiermacher, *Christian Faith,* p. 68.

Imprisoned in naturalness, the individual human being who simply lives out his instincts finally comes up against a limit where even this mere naturalness grinds itself down; then it truly becomes a case of

> In the midst of gratification,
> I starve for lust.[13]

Thrown back upon his own inner self, searching for the true meaning of life, he finds a layer of his being deeper than he ever found before. And giving himself over to this new motivation, he consummates the break with mere naturalness. But this does not develop in an unbroken ascent: Instead, in the free act of surrender to this higher life, he collides everywhere with the limitations of his creaturely restrictions and self-righteousness, until he finally achieves consummate self-surrender to God in the radical shattering of his own finite power and achievement, receiving his own self back from God as a new being. And it is this *rebirth from God* that we call *redemption*. It is redemption from the world and world-weariness, but not in the Buddhist sense of leaving the world and suffering behind. We do not acknowledge the meaning of life by breaking with life! We are not redeemed from personal life, but *for* personal life. Our redemption means being filled with a positive content for life, a life that enables us to rise above the narrow, splintered imprisonment of the "I" and to triumph over the nothingness of life.

The Eastern religions make use of submergence and recognition, the means of self-salvation. But for us it is not primarily a matter of coming to awareness; it is rather a matter of winning a share in the divine life that seeks us out in spite of all darkness and pain, indeed often precisely as that darkness and pain. For the Eastern religions, the first thing that redemption removes is suffering. But for us, that which comes between us and God is something deeper than suffering, namely guilt. Hence the central certainty of redemption consists first of all in the assurance of God's forgiving love, so that by looking at him we may cast our guilt away. God demands only self-judgment, which is, in truth, self-surrender. Christian redemption from guilt, just like redemption from suffering, is a purely internal process. It has nothing to do with instructions or observing some ritual formulas; the assurance of divine forgiveness illuminates the human self precisely in the depths of its guilt. Redemption is nothing other than faith.

13. *Faust* I, 14, from a soliloquy by Faust. *Die Faustdichtungen* (Zurich: Artemis Verlag, 1950), p. 245; see Charles W. Eliot, ed., *Harvard Classics*, vol. 19 (New York: P. F. Collier and Sons, 1909), p. 137.

But our confidence does not look backwards only; it looks forward as well. On one side stands the ebb of guilt; on the other, courage for new activity. Christian redemption from guilt is also redemption from moral impotence, that is, the elevation of human power through power from God. This is what ecclesiastical language has in view when it refers to the concept of sanctification. Sanctification does not, as the old dogmatics taught, remove an obstacle or restore an original circumstance, but rather creates a *new* human being—the human being as child of God. Not that this frees our life of problems, but rather that we will be impelled through them and beyond them. Redemption from moral impotence does not signify the complete disappearance of evil, but rather our being placed upon a new basis *in principle*. It is not a matter of overexerting one's own strength, but rather of the unpretentious decision to dare to rely on the strength of God with God, who lets the soul "fly upwards as if with wings."

This also implies a new goal for humankind. Redemption does not consume itself in mere perceptions of blessedness, but rather bursts forth on our brothers and sisters. Being a child of God coincides with the Kingdom of God, a bond between all souls who alike have been called to be children of God: one for all and all for one, all from the activity of God. For as far as our eyes can see, redemption everywhere signifies intensified activity, not freedom from work. At this point the concept of redemption passes over into practical Christian ethics.

To recapitulate: Christian redemption from suffering, guilt, and moral impotence is therefore essentially an inner transformation and elevation of human being; it comes from surrender to the illuminating knowledge of the divine will and essence, i.e., the forgiving divine love that draws the creature upwards to itself. But this knowledge is no rational achievement, nor can the human soul achieve it through concentration or self-improvement. Indeed, this redemption stands in contradiction to all the soul's natural desires and possibilities. It is a free gift of God, a self-communication and revelation of God that can be received only in the deepest humility—it is *grace*. But the way this grace grasps us is by exhausting our own strength and allowing us to come to naught, thereby opening us up to the communication of divine strength; so that through *grace* we may become what we had sought in *freedom*. This dissolves the tension between grace and freedom, which was so disastrous for the old dogmatics. It is identical with the more general tension inherent in the concept of a divine absoluteness that coexists with an independent creaturely world; it cannot be overcome by any dialectic, but *is* overcome every time a finite spirit yields to the divine spirit.

This likewise clarifies the relationship of grace and holiness. If redemption is solely accomplished by the gift of a divine grace that elevates the creature to itself—through struggle, guilt, and self-dividedness—then it excludes human merit as well as all anthropomorphic ideas of divine recompense. Sin is *for*given because its possibility *was* given: this is how it is conceivable that the divine holiness can remain inviolate. Just as the possibility of sin is grounded in the essence of the creation, so too is the grace that forgives sin grounded in the essence of God. We cannot think God apart from the concept of grace; not that one concept implies the other, but that each concept *is* the other. Here too lie the profoundest grounds for the task that the doctrine of satisfaction implied. Of course, every attempt to refer ethical demand back to this doctrine is to be rejected: the concept of grace alone signifies the exclusion of all human merit.

This brings us to the conclusion of this summary. If redemption presents itself to our consciousness as the always newly realized union between God and the finite soul, and if in this process the soul itself feels reborn to a new reality, then what does redemption signify for the divine life itself? The answer has already been given elsewhere. If we are to think of redemption at all, it can be only in this way: this new reality for the soul, whenever it occurs, also constitutes the addition of a new reality for God. This brings us face to face once more with the necessity of the concept of God's own self-redemption.—

We now have the task of connecting up the concept of redemption with its sources in *revelation*. Christian redemption is not the result of religious autonomy: we grasp it from history. We grasp it not only in the historically transmitted image of the person of Jesus, in whose name we take courage before God, but also in terms of the Pauline-Johannine teaching of the Spirit. It is in terms of the latter that the death of Jesus reclaims its significance for redemption. This teaching overcomes the historically conditioned elements in the person of Jesus; it liberates his Spirit through suffering and death; and it enables his Spirit to continue and to overflow and to be present from generation to generation. Hence redemption, which consists in confidence in Jesus, is not backward-looking. It is only in the community—the community through which the Spirit of Christ flows, which mediates redemptive faith to the individual, which originates in the historical form of Jesus, and which again and again orders and strengthens its inner self by that historical form—it is only within this community that redemption first becomes connected to history. But this connection to the Spirit of Christ itself constitutes a living life in the midst of a living community. And so the element of truth in the old dogma of the divinity and unsurpassability of the church continues in the Pauline-Johannine doctrine of the Spirit. If the idea is separated from the individual churches—in other words, if it continues to embrace the individual churches and yet extends far beyond them—then it signifies faith in the supra-individual connection of love and spirit that comes from Jesus. And we are convinced, in turn, that this faith is destined for consummation in God, no matter what course our religious destiny may take over the millennia.

We come to the last things. Christian redemption is redemption in the present, but it is not consummated there. It has eternity in time, but its time reaches into eternity: inasmuch as it signifies a growing surrender to God, it cannot remain simply with this life. The concept of redemption passes over into *eschatology*.

Eschatology, however, is not a concept limited to Christianity. It arises in all religions that recognize the contradiction between the absolute and the relative. There are two possible solutions: an immanent, this-worldly redemption and consummation, and an other-worldly one. The two are intermingled in the proclamation of Jesus. The Kingdom of God is an immanent, this-worldly consummation, after which comes the final destiny. Starting with Paul, however, the emphasis fell completely on other-worldly redemption, while the church increasingly took on the role of the Kingdom of God. Later, in combination with Jewish, Platonic, and other elements of late antiquity, the church developed its eschatology of heaven, hell, and the judgment of the dead, all of which were later appropriated by Protestantism. The modern world has, for the most part, transformed these concepts into a starkly rationalized doctrine of immortality, except in those cases where it has been content with the simple idea of continued existence in nothing more than the works of this world.

On the contrary, when the Christian concept of the consummation is affirmed in depth—even when it excludes all approximation to earthly circumstances—it does not consist in the simple continued existence of the soul, but rather in the soul's continuing development and reaching toward God beyond this life. This particular view renders all objections of modern unbelief untenable: There can be no scientific knowledge concerning the relationship of the ethical and religious personality to the creaturely world. And the personality is the only thing that the Christian doctrine of the consummation is concerned about. Here we follow the line that extends from Leibniz to Goethe. The Beyond can be conceived only as a result of the

Here. Only that which here is already directed toward the consummation can achieve it in the Beyond.

But how are we to think about this consummation? It can be conceived only as a step-by-step purification and elevation of the finite spirit, until complete unification with God is realized. Its final fulfillment must therefore lead to a submergence [*Untergang*] in God. Here, as we have already noted, a certain relative right must be granted to pantheistic piety. Our enormous difference with pantheism is that we envision not a submergence into a dead All or into the identity of all things, but rather into the fullness and blessedness of the divine life. This is also what comprises the unity of all other redeemed souls with one another, as seen by Dante's spirit in his sublime poetry, where everything presses toward ever increasing surrender and purification, until, fully sanctified and transfigured, the souls finally submerge into God and also flow into one another.

Here the problem of grace surfaces yet again. Consummation takes place in the finite soul's surrender to divine love, and not everyone accomplishes this surrender. Hence the number of the redeemed is limited. Church dogmatics have also considered this issue. In Catholicism and Lutheranism, all are called to blessedness in principle, but it remains conditional on earthly conduct; in Calvinism, only the elect are redeemed. At bottom, all three traditions share an awareness of, or inclination to, the concept of the particularity of grace. This issue has already been decided for us in the theodicy of this *Glaubenslehre*. We affirm the particularity of grace, but not in terms of an unconditional predestination, and certainly not in terms of any predestination to damnation. It rather signifies only the recognition that different people unquestionably encounter different degrees of ease or difficulty in attaining the divine goal. This is closer to the idea of refining and purification than it is to the idea of the self-destruction of the wicked. Hence the idea of the so-called "restoration of all"[14] has a final probability; indeed, this restoration may also be extended to subhuman creatures as well, in the sense of the entire creation's becoming spirit through infinite reaches of time, so that God will finally be all in all.[15] The individual finite soul, proceeding on its path of purification by following the divine movement, would then both mirror and codetermine the totality of the world-process. The end would return to its beginning. Emanation would become remanation [return], but not in the Neoplatonic sense of consumma-

14. Acts 3:21.
15. See 1 Cor. 15:28.

tion as a natural termination. Rather, just as the going out is posited by the divine will, so too would the consummation come by the unification of surrender with grace.—

The concept of redemption thus consummates for us in the idea of the final redemption, closing the circle of the Christian faith. In the course of our exposition, we have discovered the possibility that other forms of faith are justified, but at the same time we are convinced of this: although our certainty in God may flow to us from many different sources, for us Christianity remains the deepest of them all. And that is why we wish to be Christians. We have a God, who, despite our weakness and wretchedness, will not cut himself off from us; and whosoever confesses *this* faith will be comforted. Therefore: It is not easy to affirm this faith in the midst of our life; but it is equally certain that it is only in the test of practice that its ultimate truth can be decided.

End of the lectures.

5

The Christian Doctrine
of Religious Community
(Fragment)

§29. Religious Community, or the Kingdom of God

DICTATION
(draft)[1]

Religious thought everywhere intensifies the personality by connecting it to the divine essence; but this elevation of the individual personality also *unites different individuals* under a *religious point of view*. Recognition of the single overarching power of God binds and secures individuals together under that which they have over them in common. Furthermore, religious sanctions consolidate the community's moral and ethical commandments into something more than mere social and ethical ties, something even more than mere religious ties—laws so intense that the divine will itself is expressed in them. In addition, the human need for communication and stimulation also leads to the development of religious communities, communities that seek the impact that mass psychological representations of feeling and disposition can provide. Finally, divinity demands adoration, or a cultus; and this cultus—in all its forms, from the crudest

---

1. As Gertrud von le Fort explains in her "Prefatory Remarks" (see p. 6), Troeltsch's lectures ended with the doctrine of redemption, and he never lectured on the subject of dogmatics again. The dictations which follow in chapters 5 and 6 were not prepared for the lectures of 1912–13, but are earlier drafts found in Troeltsch's papers and included by von le Fort for the sake of completeness (presumably following Troeltsch's outline for the semester).

anthropomorphism to the most spiritual exaltation—must be a common cultus, corresponding to the way in which the divine will encompasses the whole.

Hence the concept of community comes to play a role even in the concept of God itself: the deity appears as the founder of the community, and it is essential to the divine will that the community be strengthened. Tribal, national, and universal religions all agree on this. Only the individually splintered and *philosophically broken* religions have lost the idea of a formative community as a divinely willed goal. Such religions ultimately issue in individualistic, splintered movements that are no more than mere personal reflections. But *unbroken* religions still retain the drive to form community, even in their most subjectivist, independent, and monastic forms. That is why philosophical Brahmanism and Buddhism, just like modern philosophical Christianity, have completely lost all communal energy. Nevertheless, wherever divinity is not a mere product of thought, but rather a living will directed toward human beings, the power of community comes through. Eremetism constitutes no exception; for it only realizes the pessimistic asceticism of a community. The eremite fulfills the community's ascetic tendency by displaying the ideal before it.

Hence the idea of community is *central* to Christianity. And, in correspondence with the religious character of Christianity and its God-concept, the Christian concept of community is absolutely free of all the natural conditions that tribal and national religion impose. It concerns itself purely with human community in God, in common recognition of God and love of God, and in common obedience to the command of God. That is the essence of Jesus' constant proclamation of the *Kingdom of God:* the Kingdom is absolutely universal and human. But it is not a merely natural community of humankind in general, united into a great family by virtue of common species and ancestry. Instead, the community of the Kingdom of God is produced from the natural human race only by means of redemption. Only through conversion, renewal, and increase can one belong to this community. It is not the simple idea of humanity as such, but the idea of a humanity chosen, sanctified, and fulfilled by God. Hence it constitutes a smaller circle, set off from humanity. Many are called, but few are chosen,[2] and the way that leads to salvation is narrow.[3]

Therefore, religious community is the *correlate of redemption.*

2. Matt. 22:14.
3. See Matt. 7:24.

Redemption aims at separating the elevated, spiritual human self from the natural human self, a goal that can be achieved only through the creation of a realm where this can happen. This realm or community bears the name of "Kingdom of God," signifying the full lordship of God, where God's will is done and all are children of the heavenly father.[4] And just as redemption belongs to the essence of God, so too it is God who creates the redemption and elevation that constitute the Kingdom of God. His will seeks to elevate the creature to the Kingdom of God, to create redemption, to transform naturality into pneumatic spirituality. Hence the concept of the Kingdom of God embraces the totality of the Christian world of ideas: It is the divine will's goal for the creature; it is the destiny of the soul, the meaning of the world, the goal of redemption. The human Kingdom of God is in the Kingdom of God in principle; it partakes of the great realm of spirits, in which all creatures shall be elevated above the conditions of creation.

This clarifies the *twofold character* of the Kingdom of God: it is viewed in part as an immanent, human community, and in part as a transcendent state of affairs brought about by God. It is a community set into motion by God's will; and, even as it waits for the coming Kingdom, the community itself constitutes an anticipation of the Kingdom. This basic perspective remains potent even when the future grows increasingly distant and the importance of immanent activity grows correspondingly greater. Hence it is permissible to complement the idea of the Kingdom of God with the ideas of redemption, the elevation of life, and the divinization and regeneration of the human being into a child of God. Moreover, the Kingdom of God is *purely* an object of faith both in its present and future orientations, grounded in confidence in the victory of the divine will. The Kingdom also lacks any organization or outer form of community; it extends through all forms of human life, making its community known above all in personal intercourse and moral action.

§30. The Church

DICTATION
(draft)

The community of the Kingdom of God—a community of attitude, activity, and hope—does not satisfy all of religious life's needs

---

4. See, e.g., Matt. 12:50; 5:45.

for community, even if the gospel speaks of no other community. The community also needs a means of nurture that will communicate the religious power and attitude of the Kingdom of God, and it needs a way to unify diverse stimuli in a cultus. For Jesus, both were already present in the Jewish church [sic] and the synagogue, and hence he saw no need for any additional nurture or cultus in the Kingdom of God. But when belief in Christ grew separate from Judaism, a *specific form of community* concerned with the goals of nurture, cultus, and extension became necessary. In this sense, *Paul is the creator of the church,* although the church was already implicit in Christianity's universalism. To be sure, Paul's immediate concern was for the individual congregation, with emphasis on the enthusiasm and individualism to which such a religious movement is naturally inclined. But for Paul the individual congregations were also, entirely of themselves, a complete organism—the body of Christ, brought into being through Baptism and the Lord's Supper, and through a common life of faith.[1] Thus the germ of the church as a supernatural institution was already present with Paul. The church was based on specifically ordained organs for the communication of the Holy Spirit.

On this basis, the Catholic Church, with the introduction of a priesthood and sacraments that could be administered only by the priests, developed the concept of the supernatural institution of the Church, outside which there is no salvation. Its central ideas are the objectivization of salvation, the organization of the Church, and the hierarchy; the Church becomes an object of faith, and faith comes to believe in the Church's victory and infallibility, that is, its indisputable power of conversion.

Protestantism eliminated the link between salvation and the sacerdotal priesthood with its visible means in the sacraments, but it retained the institutional character of the Church insofar as it continued to hold the office of the proclamation of the word of Christ. And the Church also retained a supernatural greatness in this office of the proclamation of Scripture and the administration of the sacraments, which brought about all faith and conversion. Protestantism described this entity as the Universal or Invisible Church—but it was invisible *only* in terms of its impact on the person, not in its visible, supernaturally efficacious powers of word and sacrament. This Universal Church was present in all the *particular* or visible churches, insofar as they, alongside all manner of human works, managed to preserve the pure word and sacrament.

1. See 1 Cor. 12:12-14, 27.

Protestantism distinguished this Universal Church from the particular church, which was to be extended and organized along the lines of governmental districts and boundaries, and according to human laws. Of course, the more that a particular church was based solely on word and sacrament, the purer it was, so that, of course, one's own church was finally the only true one. Only in the adiaphora of cultic and administrative organization was there room for diversity. It was only in its universal form, then, that the Church could serve as an object of dogmatic belief: belief in the power of the office, the word and sacrament—which would never return empty[2]—to effect salvation. The individual particular churches were human institutions, and they could be an object of faith only insofar as they contained the Universal Church within them.

Modern dogmatics, which now knows that Jesus himself did not found a church, but only a community of faith, hope, and love, has transformed the concept of the church as a universal institution back into the concept of the *Kingdom of God*. The church, in the Protestant sense, is no longer bound to any form of organization; it simply expresses faith in the power of the gospel for renewal. The only thing that modern dogmatics adds to the concept of the Kingdom of God is faith in its means, faith in the power of the gospel to renew itself. We believe, then, in the Kingdom of God and the means to extend it.

The term "church," on the other hand, would be better restricted to the particular church. The dogmatic meaning of the church for faith would then be to signify the *need* for an organization devoted to the *pedagogical, cultic, and missionary* functions of the Christian life. These functions can never be left up to individual occasions; they need a common organization to provide them with strength and totality. This stands in opposition to the *churchlessness and religious individualism* of the present, insisting instead upon the need for a specific setting for religion. The second thing that this concept of the particular church implies is a faith that constantly strives to make the church into an organ of the Kingdom of God, and to draw everything human in the church toward the ideal of a purely religious community—despite the practical demands of expedience and effectiveness. The third implication of this faith is a belief in the efficacy and gripping power of the gospel, which can even be described as a means of grace. For it is with the help of the gospel that the pedagogical and cultic and missionary work is carried out, work which can only be accomplished in the forms the particular church still provides.

2. See Isa. 55:11.

§31. The Word as the Means of Grace

DICTATION
(draft)

According to evangelical doctrine, the Word's proper means of grace is the *Word*[1] or *Bible as revelation,* disclosure of the gracious divine will. A religion that is a matter of both attitude and faith requires only that both be based on the knowledge of God. The means to the knowledge of God is the Word; and, since this knowledge entails redemption, grace, and elevation to the Kingdom of God, the *Word* is therefore the proper and essential means of grace.

The question is what is to be included under the *concept* of the Word. According to the old evangelical doctrine, the Word is primarily the Bible, consisting of the Old and New Testaments. It has always been a religious understanding of the Bible, so that all that ever came under consideration was the religious effect of the Bible. The only thing that led to the development of the old doctrine of the Bible's *universal inspiration* was the need to set the religiously efficacious contents of the Bible apart from everything extrabiblical, to make the Bible an absolutely authoritative source for theology, and to endow it with unique powers for conversion and salvation. This had the effect, then, of transforming the Bible as a whole into a means of grace, so that the Bible became the point around which life, culture, and church all were organized.

In contrast, the modern doctrine of inspiration now finds it necessary to undertake the investigation of the Bible anew, *abandoning* the idea that the entire book is formally inspired. Instead, it now concentrates on the Bible's religiously effective and significant elements: the prophets, the Psalms, the words of Jesus, and the letters of Paul. It is in them that the energizing power of God, illuminating the disposition and personality, is expressed. The inspiration of the Bible is a *personal inspiration,* and as such is nothing other than the fulfillment of the religious power and knowledge that attests to itself in the heart and conscience of the reader and listener; it has no significance apart from religion.

Dogmatics divides the contents of this inspired *Word of God,* as it is given in the great religious personalities of the Bible, into *Law* and *Gospel.* The Old Testament was eagerly designated as Law, and the New Testament as Gospel; and the Word of God was subsumed under the distinction between *contritio* and *fides* [contrition and faith] in the

---

1. "Word" is capitalized only when used in this particular sense.

dogma of justification, so that, owing to the abolition of the Law, there remained no content proper to the new life. At least that was the Lutheran doctrine, while the Reformed doctrine provided a closer relationship between Law and Gospel in the life of the regenerate. In modern dogmatics, with its doctrine of justification as the planting of the redeeming and saving knowledge of God, this distinction is now falling away; both Law and Gospel are closely and inseparably bound to the true and effective knowledge of God. A knowledge of divine holiness, or of the Law, leads to the true remorse of repentance and conversion, but it could not do so unless it were somehow also connected with faith in the gracious will of God; for without knowledge of the goal, repentance would be nothing more than desperation and self-repudiation. Similarly, forgiving grace could never take hold without also being perceived as the holy will of God, implying that self-surrender before God also constitutes surrender before God's will and Law. Law and Gospel are therefore *everywhere united,* and it is only together that they constitute the substance of the redeeming knowledge of God. Both the Old and the New Testaments always proclaim Law and Gospel together; but Law never appears in the form of a *law of works-righteousness,* only as the demand for a *disposition to surrender.* A formulation of the Law as a law of works-righteousness is only the most superficial and external formulation of the matter. The teaching of Jesus expressed the true knowledge of the Law just as positively as it expressed confidence in the grace of God, wherein the strength to fulfill God's will is to be found.

If the Word of God is understood in this way, the Bible can be specifically said to partake in the character of the *Word of God* only insofar as the Bible is the original proclamation and tradition of the basic orientation of the Christian life, and insofar as it exemplifies this incomparably lively power. Everything else that partakes of the character of the Word—that which proceeds from the Christian life or merely exemplifies Christian knowledge in a particular and classical way—is mediate and derived. Hence the Word of God is alive and productive down to the present day, and all great Christian devotional books or proclamations *indirectly belong* to the category of the Word of God, inspiration, and the means of grace.

The concept of the Word of God could be further extended to include all powerful and efficacious manifestations of the knowledge of God apart from the specifically Christian realm as well. But no matter how valuable such proclamations may be, the less they have to do with the idea of Christianity, the less they will serve to initiate and edify the Christian life. In particular, such manifestations can have only a secondary significance for Christian culture and congregational education, even though, to be sure, individual personal religious development and the general religious life of all culture will still have to deal with them. For the essence of the Word as a means of grace is still to gather the Christian community for the Kingdom of God, through a specifically Christian knowledge of God.

§32. The Sacraments and the Cultus

DICTATION
(draft)

Built upon the Word is the *cultus:* the organized preaching and presentation of the Christian knowledge of God, and the self-presentation of the community that is thereby gathered before God. Schleiermacher's doctrine of the cultus as effective and presentational activity, i.e., as preaching and common prayer, flows from the dogmatic concept of the church and the means of grace. Everything beyond this comes under the heading of practical theology.

Within the cultus, Baptism and the Lord's Supper occupy two particular positions; for this reason, they bear the name of *sacraments,* and as such constitute a particular theme of dogmatics. On Protestant soil a sacrament can be considered a means of grace only if it mediates in the same way as the Word, and only insofar as it mediates a particular form of the Word, i.e., the *verbum visibile* [the visible word]—as the principal sacramental doctrines of all the Reformers make clear. Anything in either sacrament that goes beyond the specific presentation of the Word does not share in the sacraments' character as means of grace; rather, as Zwingli and (to a somewhat lesser extent) Calvinism quite rightly taught, anything that goes beyond the Word is simply a matter of the community's own specialized activity and performance.

In addition to being a synopsis and presentation of the Christian idea, Baptism is the community's act of admitting and pledging itself to the infant, at the same time that its parents pledge to give it a Christian upbringing. The Lord's Supper, in addition to presenting the gospel through the image of the self-sacrificing savior, is the gathering and presentation of the community as a brotherhood through the image of a common meal. Admission to this highest cultic act also served as a proof of worthiness, which can eventually be connected to church discipline, as it is in Calvinism to this day.

Otherwise, Protestantism has fully eliminated—or will fully eliminate—the Catholic concept of a sacrament. This is the *essential contradiction* between Protestantism and Catholicism; and it is just as decisive for a historical understanding of the two confessions as it is for their contemporary polemic and dogmatic confrontation. Further discussion of the details and administration of the sacraments belongs to practical theology. Dogmatically, the most important thing about the sacraments is their twofold character as solemn and festive representations of the Word, and as an act of the community's common life and confession.

§33. The Task of Missions

DICTATION
(draft)

The *duty of missions* flows from belief in the definitive and consummate meaning of Christian truth. Since this belief is itself a basic component of dogmatics, and since, in combination with Christian universalism and the duty to love humankind, it constitutes a new faith-concept, then the duty of missions and faith in the *success* of missions becomes a *dogmatic concept,* necessary to any exposition of the Christian faith. The Christian faith is cut off from its root and essence if it loses the drive to extend itself.

This extension is *twofold,* involving: (1) inner extension, i.e., the instruction of the coming generation and the religious cultivation of those groups among the people and the churches who have been neglected, and (2) extension to foreign non-Christians, or missions in the customary sense of the word. The former has been acknowledged as a duty of faith from the earliest times. It is a direct concern of the church and hence a matter for practical theology. In recent times, the increase in the number of religious opinions, the colossal increase in population and the growth of large cities, and the accumulation of large masses of people for the sake of industry have posed the task of advocating for Christianity, a task undertaken mostly by free associations; but it is also something that comes under the purview of the church. This activity goes under the name of *inner missions,* and it includes all nonecclesiastical advocacy for Christianity, both in written and in oral forms.

The *second* task has always been linked by the Catholic Church to the concept of the Church itself. The Protestant confessions, preoccupied with their own concerns, let the task fall to the wayside. Lutheranism taught that one should remain in one's calling, while

Calvinism taught predestination and the particularity of the calling to missionary work. It was only the pietist, religious, individualist, and therefore less predestinarian forms of Calvinism that took up the task.

The *dogmatic* meaning of the concept of missions is the establishment of the religious unity of the human race, an ideal which Christianity demands. However, once this idea is grasped in its full extent, various *objections* and *difficulties* arise. First: The appropriation of Christianity requires the attainment of a certain height of intellectual, moral, and formal culture. Peoples that cannot be elevated to this height must gradually disappear or else be won over by a slow cultural education that interacts with religious instruction—almost a complete guardianship over these peoples. Second: Christian missions are themselves divided into many confessions and will continue to be so for the foreseeable future. Hence the unity that missions are supposed to create will be starkly individualized, embracing a variety of very different levels and heights. Third: Peoples with highly developed cultures already have a highly developed religious life that would strongly influence the Christianity they adopt, resulting in new types of Christianity of very different levels. Further: An absolutely universal advocacy of Christianity for all individuals is not possible, since there will always be some who are not capable of it; and there may also be peoples who are likewise incapable and hence will remain at lower levels. This points to the problem of the universality of grace, which will be discussed in the final chapter.

6

The Consummation
(Fragment)

§34. The Place of Eschatology in the System

DICTATION
(draft)

Wherever religion reaches the stage where it consciously formulates thoughts of ethics and redemption, there will arise religious ideas of the *consummation,* or an *eschatology.* Only unethicized and nonindividualistic religions have no eschatology. The latter have only intra-worldly rewards and punishments that extend no farther than the people or the race as a whole. But wherever the individual as such becomes the bearer and object of religion, and salvation becomes more than a simple matter of intra-worldly relationships, eschatological thinking is implied. Moreover, this eschatology comes in *two* forms: either intra-worldly, where the consummation takes place on earth, or other-worldly, where blessedness or unblessedness is decreed after death. The former applies to the distinctly nationalistic religions, like Parsiism [Zoroastrianism] and Judaism, while the latter applies to the decidedly individualistic religions, including the Hellenistic, Indian, and Christian religions.

Christian eschatology grew out of its Jewish background, and it carries the impulse of Judaism in its imagination. In the proclamation of Jesus, the Kingdom of God—along with the dawning of a new spiritual life in his person and his community—is a *human consummation which is to be expected on earth,* a consummation where the entire world will be fully ruled by God's will, and by a purely inter-nal-pious and ethical humankind that does God's will as it is done in heaven. Only after the establishment of this Kingdom of God will the end come, with the judgment of the dead and the final destiny of the individual. Later, in Paul's teaching, the strictly other-worldly ele-ment was emphasized more strongly; what Paul awaited was the end of the earthly world, its transformation into a pneumatic [spiritual] world, the destruction of death, sin, the devil, Satan, and the godless, and, finally, the blessedness to come for those who have been taken into Christianity.

Subsequent ecclesiastical developments downplayed the chiliastic, intra-worldly aspect even more and laid all emphasis on the other-worldly decision, developing the idea of heaven as the place of bless-edness and hell as the place of punishment, offering the so-called Purgatory alongside them as a place for the purification and further development of those who are in principle reconciled with God but otherwise still impure—in other words, the overwhelming majority. As a result, notions of the migration and purification of souls were not lacking, as exemplified especially in the thought of Origen. Reformation teaching eliminated Purgatory, failed to restore chiliasm, and placed all its emphasis on the Last Judgment, where faith alone could decide the matter of reconciliation. Heaven and hell have per-sisted down to the present. A significant *difference* between the two Protestant confessions is that Lutheranism conceives the final con-summation as involving all, making its attainment conditional on the attitude of the will; while Reformed doctrine knows final salvation only as the goal of the predestined, and sees predestination as prep-aration for it.

Jewish, Hellenistic, Platonic, and free poetic reflections all come together in these various forms of thought. Mysticism also plays a role, with its anticipation of the final consummation with its blessed-ness and dwelling in God. All these colorful images show how this dogma, whose object is completely other-worldly and lies beyond experience, produces the most colorful imagination; and they also show just how great a role the world-pictures dominant at a given time have played in its metamorphosis of the doctrine. But anthropo-morphism, along with the imagination, plays the strongest role, both in its treatment of God as judge and king, as well as in its image of the future, which is never more than a poetic transposition of—and improvement upon—finite human conditions.

The break with dogmatic anthropomorphism—a break which is unavoidable in all modern religious thought despite its continued affirmation of the personality of God—will have a very great impact on these traditional forms of thought. The doctrine of the consummation must come to grips with its metaphorical character and its inadequacy; it must be rebuilt quite differently, upon a new foundation, even though its meaning remains unchanged.

To achieve this goal, it is necessary to emphasize the specific ethical and religious idea of Christian eschatology. This idea lies in the specifically Christian concept of *redemption,* which, in turn, determines the concept of the consummation. The essential thing about the Christian concept of redemption is that redemption comes through the true knowledge of the forgiving and sanctifying will of God, and through elevation to participation in the Kingdom of God and the divine personal life. Hence redemption must remain unconsummated under the conditions of earthly life. This, in turn, gives rise to the *postulate of consummation* in a trans-earthly life. The essence of this consummation and how it is to be achieved can be described only in general, poetic terms; they can express the central ideas of the essence of the consummation, but they do not constitute real knowledge, and it therefore can have very different expressions.

Eschatology, therefore, deals essentially with only two questions: (1) the question of the essence of the consummation, or the question of a definitive redemption; and (2) the question of whether all or only a few will participate in this final salvation, or the question of the universality and particularity of grace.

§35. The Essence of the Consummation

DICTATION
(draft)

The essence of the consummation is ultimate union with God; but this union must be begun in earthly life and completed in a life after death. In the religious-moral process, the created spirit frees itself from its natural conditioning, constantly growing out of mere naturality into the divine spiritual life of reason. This growth must find its consummation in *complete separation* from nature and *complete unification* with God. It is only with this that redemption will be consummated. Redemption is redemption from nature and creatureliness, from the struggle with sin and its power.

The world-process leads the creature back to its beginning. The bondage and imprisonment that belong to creatureliness constitute the starting point for the human creature's spiritual and moral process; and the transformation of this creatureliness through the soul's complete return to God—the soul having become both spirit and person—is the end of the process. This is the process of *emanation and remanation* as it was described by Neoplatonism and, in turn, taken up by Origen and Augustine; the only difference is that here it is not a natural process, but one posited from the beginning by the divine will. It is an act of the creature's will as it surrenders itself to the workings of God, a uniting of the divine and human wills in the final goal. *The Christian understanding of the will of God determines the entire concept of the redemption of the world.*

The question of the *how* of this consummation can only be answered thus: Everything earthly, everything limited in space and time will be excluded. Hence it is impossible to form an image of it. One can only say that it includes the vision of the victory of the good, and a unification with God in which the creaturely personality merges into the divine life. The *mysticism of love,* which allows the individual will to merge into the all-will, is the last word.

A further question concerns the connection between this final consummation and *life after death.* Mysticism, in the religious peaks of human life, anticipates and intuits this consummation; but this anticipation is not a real consummation, for earthly life always reasserts itself after these peaks. Hence the final consummation after death essentially remains a postulate. Life after death absolutely cannot be disproved on anthropological or psychological grounds, for the relationship of the morally and religiously formed person to the creaturely soul is completely opaque. Therefore utterly nothing can be said about the manner of this life after death. Possibly it is a further development and purification like Catholicism's Purgatory or Buddhism's transmigration. Something akin to that is quite likely, though incapable of proof. But the final goal of the life after death itself cannot be eternal being, i.e., a being that is absolutely without end, an endless being alongside of God; rather, it can only signify the *ultimate return* of the *purified and sanctified essence of the creature to the deity.*

§36. The Universality and Particularity of Grace

DICTATION
(draft)

The question is whether all creatures and—in our sphere of creation—all human beings are destined to this salvation. An unconditional yes to this question entails the doctrine of the *restoration of all things* or the απυχατάστασις πάγτων,[1] which permits the purification or conversion of all souls for as long as it takes for all to return to God. This doctrine appears impossible, for the line between human and subhuman creatures is sharply drawn; it is inconceivable that animal spirits and plant spirits can be drawn into this process, and hence they are incapable of losing their sin through a willful surrender to redemption. At any rate, such a teaching could be conceived only if all of nature, by some hidden process, were finally to attain to spirit. Whether that will be its destiny, we do not know.

There further remains the second doctrine of a *universalism of grace* dependent upon acceptance by the human will, as Catholicism and Lutheranism teach, Catholicism with the indispensable condition of a purification and development that take place after death. The will that resists redemption, then, given the untenability of the traditional idea of hell, would have to decay in a hell of annihilation and self-destruction, as Paul taught. But the conditions in which the individual will often finds itself—such as spiritual abnormality or overwhelming amorality—frequently constitute *impediments to salvation.* The conditions for the emergence of the spiritual life of redemption are so unequally distributed that it is impossible to attribute universality to the divine will.

This leaves us with the *particularity* of salvation. It need not be a hard and simple predestination. The Calvinistic idea of a predestination to hell as an illustration of the righteousness of God's punishment, at any rate, is completely eliminated. The goals that God has for the unelect are completely unknown to us, just as we do not know what is the goal of the world as a whole. Nor can the predestination to salvation be understood in the sense of a *decretum absolutum* [absolute decree]; it can only be viewed as the setting of the conditions of the possibility for the spiritual personal life of redemption, the realization of which must always remain an act of the will.

So redemption is only one of God's final goals, the one goal known to us, alongside which there are others that remain unknown. What will happen to those who will not attain it, or to those who do not wish to attain it, we cannot say. We can say only what we know of God's world-goal, which is *the development of the God-filled personality;* and all who acknowledge this should set their lives on this goal.

1. Acts 3:21.

Index